C000234042

Hans Holzer's

Haunted America

Hans Holzer's

Haunted America

BARNES
&NOBLE
BOOKS
NEW YORK

This edition published by Barnes & Noble, Inc.,
by arrangement with Hans Holzer.

1993 Barnes & Noble Books

ISBN 1-56619-193-9

Printed and bound in the United States of America

M 9 8 7 6 5 4 3 2 1

Contents

Introduction   xi

Alabama
   The Arguing Ghosts   3
   A Dead Husband's Greeting   6
   The Visions of a Psychic   8

Arkansas
   Grandmother's Ghost   17

California
   The Bride of Nob Hill   21
   Reaching out from Beyond   28
   The Ghost in the Basement   34
   The Lost Sailor   38

Connecticut
   The Tombstones and the Officer   49
   A Houseful of Ghosts   52

District of Columbia
   The White House Ghosts   67

Florida
    The "Stay-Behind" Ghost   75

Georgia
    The Man in White   81
    Uncle Bill   84

Illinois
    The Ghostly Maid   91
    The Ghost Husband   99
    Lizzy's Ghost   101
    Little Girl Lost   106
    The Seminary Ghost   108
    The Suicide Ghost   110
    The Ghost and the Music Teacher   113

Indiana
    The Girl in the Evening Gown   125

Iowa
    The Phantom Dog   129

Kansas
    The Fraternity Ghost   135

Louisiana
    The Ghost Couple and the New Tenants   139

Maine
    Finding Willie   143
    The Sailor's Wife   164

Contents

Maryland
A Ghost Named Frank   185

Massachusetts
Changes in the House   191
The Victorian House Ghost   194
The Ghostly Brother   201
The Protector   204
The Bat   206
The Cry of the Banshee   208

Michigan
The Ghost and the Puppy   213
Conversation with a Ghost   215

Minnesota
The Electrocuted Ghost   219

Missouri
The Ghost and the Golf Cap   223

New Jersey
The Graves on the Hillock   227
The Yellow Church Ghost   233
Mother's Ghost   236
The Party Ghost   238
The Ghostly Nun   240
The Lady of the Spirits   242

New York
The Haunted Murder Room   247
The Ghost of Brooklyn Heights   250

Gertrude, Who Stayed   253
The Ghost and the Love Letters   267
The Indian's Ghost   270
The Soldier's Wife   273
A Caring Ghost Named John   276
Mabel's Ghost   280
The Ghost and the Earrings   283
The Troubled Ghosts on Route 14   294

North Carolina
The Grave of the Ghostly Girl   305

North Dakota
A Houseful of Ghosts   313

Ohio
A Houseproud Ghost   321
The Girls' School Ghost   327
The Burning Ghost   329

Oklahoma
The Ghost of the Murdered Child   333

Pennsylvania
The Little Sister   339
Mrs. Kennedy, Mrs. McBride   341
The Dispossessed Ghost   356
The Ghost Who Did Not Like Ghosts   359
Terror on the Stairs   364
The Banker and the Ghost   373
The Piano-Playing Ghost   379

Contents

Rhode Island
   Passing Through   383

South Carolina
   Family Visits from Beyond   387

Tennessee
   The Ghost of the Henpecked Husband   393

Texas
   The Bryce Avenue Murders   399
   The Case of the Tyler Poltergeists   402

Virginia
   Evelyn   459

Introduction

One of the most troubling aspects of today's world is the matter of beliefs. The power of one's beliefs is a frightening thing. People often believe in things and events whether they have actually happened or not. Because of beliefs people are murdered, wars are fought, crimes are committed. Disbelief, too, contributes its share of tragedies.

Beliefs—and disbeliefs—are emotional in nature, not rational. The reasoning behind certain beliefs may *sound* rational, but it may be completely untrue, exaggerated, taken out of context, or distorted.

Once belief or disbelief by one person becomes public knowledge and spreads to large numbers of people, some very serious problems arise: love and compassion go out the window, and emotionally tinged beliefs (or disbeliefs) take over, inevitably leading to action, and usually to some kind of violence—physical, material, emotional or moral.

In this world of spiritual uncertainty, an ever-increasing contingent of people of all ages and backgrounds want a better, safer world free of fanaticism, a world where discussion and mutual tolerance takes the place of violent confrontation.

It is sad but true that religion, far from pacifying the destructive emotions, frequently contributes to them, and sometimes is found at the very heart of the problem itself. For religion today has drifted so far from spirituality that it no longer represents the link to the deity that it originally stood for, when the world was young and smaller.

When people kill one another because their alleged path to the deity differs, they may need a signpost indicating where to turn to regain what has patently been lost. I think this signpost is the evidence for man's survival of physical death, as shown in these pages, the eternal link between those who have gone on into the next phase of life and those who have been left behind, at least temporarily.

The evidence for the afterlife is not a matter for speculation and in need of further proofs: those who look for the evidence can easily find it, not only in these pages but also in many other works and in the records of scientific research groups investigating psychic phenomena.

Once we realize how the "system" works, and that we pass on to another stage of existence, our perspective on life is bound to change. I consider it part of my work and mission to contribute knowledge to this end, to clarify the confusion, the doubts, the negativity so common in people today, and to replace these unfortunate attitudes with a wider expectation of an ongoing existence where everything one does in one lifetime counts toward the next phase, and toward the return to another lifetime in the physical world.

Those who fear the proof for the continued existence beyond the dissolution of the physical, outer body and would rather not know about it are short-changing themselves, for surely they will eventually discover the truth about the situation first-hand anyway.

If this book fascinates you, even entertains you, so be it; if it teaches you something you were previously unaware of, and if it explains things you wanted—and needed—to know, so much the better.

* * *

I ought to explain what ghosts are, even if you have read many of my previous books or perhaps have a ghost of your own. In my view, ghosts are the surviving emotional memories of people who have died tragically and are unaware of their own passing. A ghost is a split-off part of personality remaining behind in the atmosphere of its previous existence, whether a home or place of work, but closely tied to the spot where death occurred.

Ghosts do not travel, they do not follow people around, and rarely do they leave the immediate vicinity of their own tragedy. Once in a while, ghosts roam a house from top to bottom, or may be observed in the garden or adjacent field. But they do not get on cars or buses, they do not appear at the other end of town: those are free spirits, able to reason for themselves and to attempt communication with the living.

In the mind of the casual observer, of course, ghosts and spirits are the same thing. Not so to the trained parapsychologist: ghosts are similar to psychotic human beings, incapable of reasoning for themselves or taking much action. Spirits, on the other hand, are the surviving personalities of all of us who pass through the door of death in a reasonably normal fashion. A spirit is capable of continuing a full existence in the next dimension, to think, reason, feel, and act, while his unfortunate colleague, the ghost, can do none of those things. All he can do is repeat the final moments of his passing, the unfinished business, as it were, over and over until it becomes an obsession. In this benighted state ghosts are incapable of much action and therefore nearly always harmless. In the handful of cases where ghosts seem to have caused people to suffer, there was a relationship between the person and the ghost. In one case, someone slept in a bed in which someone else had been murdered and was mistaken by the murderer for the same individual. In another case, the murderer returned to the scene of his crime and was attacked by the person he had killed. But by and large ghosts do not attack people, and there is no danger in observing them or having contact with them, *if* one is able to.

The majority of ghostly manifestations draw upon energy from the living to be able to penetrate our three-dimensional world. Other manifestations are subjective, especially where the receiver is psychic. In that case, the psychic person hears or sees the departed individual in his mind's eye only, while others cannot so observe it.

Where an objective manifestation takes place, and everyone present is capable of hearing or seeing it, energy drawn from the living is used by the entity to cause certain phenomena, such as an apparition, a voice phenomenon, or perhaps the movement of objects, the recreation of footsteps or doors opening by themselves, and other signs of a presence. When the manifestations become physical in nature and are capable of being observed by several individuals or recorded by machines, they are called Poltergeist phenomena, or noisy phenomena. Not every ghostly manifestation leads to that stage, but many do. Frequently, the presence in the household of young children or of mentally handicapped older people lends itself to physical manifestations

of this kind, since the unused or untapped sexual energies are free
to be used for that purpose.

It should be kept in mind that the sexual energies and the
glands producing the sexual fluids are identical with the psychic
centers, and when physical energies are not used in one fashion,
they are available for other uses. The so-called ectoplasm that has
been observed under test conditions, especially in seances with
physical mediums, is nothing more than a temporary emanation
from the glandular system of the medium, which must be returned to the body—otherwise serious harm will result.

Ghosts—that is, individuals unaware of their own passing or
incapable of accepting the transition because of unfinished business—will make themselves known to living people at infrequent
intervals. There is no sure way of knowing when or why some
individuals make a post-mortem appearance and others do not. It
seems to depend on the intensity of feeling, the residue of un-
resolved problems, that they have within their system at the time
of death. Consequently, not everyone dying a violent death becomes a ghost; far from it. If this were so, our battlefields and such
horror-laden places as concentration camps or prisons would indeed be swarming with ghosts, but they do not. It depends on the
individual attitude of the person at the time of death, whether he
or she accepts the passing and proceeds to the next stage of existence, or whether he or she is incapable of realizing that a change
is taking place and consequently clings to the familiar physical
environment, the earth sphere.

A common misconception concerning ghosts is that they appear only at midnight, or, at any rate, only at night; or that they
eventually fade away as time goes on. To begin with, ghosts are
split-off parts of personality incapable of realizing the difference
between day and night. They are always in residence, so to speak,
and can be contacted by properly equipped mediums at all times.
They may put in an appearance only at certain hours of the day or
night, depending upon the atmosphere; for the fewer physical
disturbances there are, the easier it is for them to communicate
themselves to the outer world. They are dimly aware that there is
something out there different from themselves, but their dimin-
ished reality does not permit them to grasp the situation fully.
Consequently, a quiet moment, such as is more likely to be found

at night than in the daytime, is the period when the majority of sightings are reported.

Some manifestations occur on the exact moment of the anniversary, because at that time the memory of the unhappy event is strongest. But that does not mean that the presence is absent at other times—merely less capable of manifestations. Since ghosts are not only expressions of human personality left behind in the physical atmosphere but are, in terms of physical science, electromagnetic fields uniquely impressed by the personality and memories of the departed one, they represent a certain energy imprint in the atmosphere and, as such, cannot simply fade into nothingness. Albert Einstein demonstrated that energy can never dissipate, only transmute into other forms. Thus ghosts do not fade away over the centuries; they are, in effect, present for all eternity unless someone makes contact with them through a trance medium and brings reality to them, allowing them to understand their predicament and thus free themselves from their self-imposed prison. The moment the mirror of truth is held up to a ghost, and he or she realizes that the problems that seem insoluble are no longer important, he or she will be able to leave.

Frequently, rescuers have to explain that the only way the ghosts can leave is by calling out to someone close to them in life —a loved one or a friend who will then come and take them away with them into the next stage of existence, where they should have gone long before. This is called the rescue circle and is a rather delicate operation requiring the services of a trained psychical researcher and a good trance medium. Amateurs are warned not to attempt it, especially not alone.

The cases in this book are from my files, which bulge with the interesting experiences of ordinary people in all walks of life, and from all corners of the globe. The majority of the witnesses knew nothing about ghosts, nor did they seek out such phenomena. When they experienced the happenings described in these pages, they were taken by surprise; sometimes shocked, sometimes worried. They came to me for advice because they could not obtain satisfactory counsel from ordinary sources such as psychologists, psychiatrists, or ministers.

Small wonder, for such professionals are rarely equipped to deal with phenomena involving parapsychology. Perhaps in years to come they will be able to do so, but not now. In all cases, I advised the individuals not to be afraid of what might transpire in their presence, to take the phenomenon as part of human existence and to deal with it in a friendly, quiet way. The worst reaction is to become panicky in the presence of ghosts, since it will not help the ghost and will cause the observer unnecessary anxiety. Never forget that those who are "hung up" between two phases of existence are in trouble, and not troublemakers, and a compassionate gesture toward them may very well relieve their anxieties.

The people whose cases I tell of in these pages seek no publicity or notoriety; they have come to terms with the hauntings to which they were witness. In some cases, it has changed their outlook on life by showing them the reality of another world next door. In other cases what was once fear has turned into a better understanding of the nature of man; still other instances permitted the witnesses to the phenomena a better understanding of the current status of loved ones, and the reassuring feeling that they would meet again in a short time on the other side of the curtain.

Remember that any of the phenomena described here could have happened to *you*, that there is nothing *supernatural* about any of this, and that in years to come we will deal with them as ordinary events, part and parcel of human experience.

The average person thinks that there is just one kind of ghost, and that spirits and ghosts are all one and the same. Nothing could be further from the truth; ghosts are not spirits, and psychic impressions are not the same as ghosts. Basically, there are three phenomena involved when a person dies under traumatic, tragic circumstances and is unable to adjust to the passing from one state of existence to the next. The most common form of passing is of course the transition from physical human being to spirit being, without difficulty and without the need to stay in the denser physical atmosphere of the Earth. The majority of tragic passings do not present any problems, because the individual accepts the change and becomes a free spirit, capable of communicating freely with those on the Earth plane, and advancing according to abilities, likes and dislikes, and the help he or she may receive from others already on the other side of life. But a small fraction of those who die tragically are unable to recognize the change in their status and become so-called ghosts: that is, parts of human personality hung up in the physical world, but no longer part of it or able to function in it. These are the only *true* ghosts in the literal sense of the term.

However, a large number of sightings of so-called ghosts are not of this nature, but represent imprints left behind in the atmosphere by the individual's actual passing. Anyone possessed of psychic ability will sense the event from the past and, in his or her mind's eye, reconstruct it. The difficulty is that one frequently does not know the difference between a psychic imprint having no life of its own and a true ghost. Both seem very real, subjectively speaking. The only way one can differentiate between the two phenomena is when several sightings are compared for minute details. True ghosts move about somewhat, although not outside the immediate area of their passing. Imprints are always identical, regardless of the observers involved, and the details do not alter at any time. Psychic imprints, then, are very much like photographs or films of an actual event, while true ghosts are events themselves, capable of some measure of reaction to the environment. Whenever there are slight differences in detail concerning an apparition, we are dealing with a true ghost-personality; but whenever the description of an apparition or scene from the past appears to be identical from source to source, we are most likely dealing only with a lifeless imprint reflecting the event but in no way suggesting an actual presence at the time of the observation.

However, there is a subdivision of true ghosts that I have called the "Stay-Behinds." The need for such a subdivision came to me years ago when I looked through numerous cases of reported hauntings that did not fall into the category of tragic, traumatic passings, nor cases of death involving violence or great suffering—the earmarks of true ghosts. To the contrary, many of these sightings involved the peaceful passings of people who had lived in their respective homes for many years and had grown to love them. I realized, by comparing these cases one with the other, that they had certain things in common, the most outstanding of which was this: they were greatly attached to their homes, had lived in them for considerable periods prior to their death, and were strong-willed individuals who had managed to develop a life routine of their own. It appears, therefore, that the Stay-Behinds are spirits who are more or less aware of passing into the next dimension, but are unwilling to go on. To them, their earthly home is preferable, and the fact that they no longer possess a physical body is no deterrent to their continuing to live in this home.

Some of these Stay-Behinds adjust to their limitations with marvelous ingenuity. They are still capable of causing physical phenomena, especially if they can draw on people living in the house. At times, however, they become annoyed at changes undertaken by the residents in their house, and when these changes evoke anger in them they are capable of some mischievous activities, like Poltergeist phenomena, although of a somewhat different nature. Sometimes they are quite satisfied to continue living their former lives, staying out of the way of flesh-and-blood inhabitants of the house, and remaining undiscovered until someone with psychic ability accidently notices them. Sometimes, however, they *want* the flesh-and-blood people to know they are still very much in residence and, in asserting their continuing rights, may come into conflict with the living beings in the house. Some of these manifestations seem frightening or even threatening to people living in houses of this kind, but they should not be, since the Stay-Behinds are, after all, human beings, who have developed a continuing and very strong attachment to their former homes. Of course, not everyone can come to terms with them.

Not all ghostly sightings are "ghosts": even experienced professional psychics sometimes cannot distinguish between a "living" entity—spirit or ghost—and the psychic impression left behind where an emotional event once took place.

Either way, such experiences prove that there is indeed more to life than sixty-four cents of chemicals, as one psychic researcher put it many years ago. No doubt, with the price of drugs these days, we may be worth as much as sixty-four dollars.

But that, of course, is not the point: the reality of continued existence beyond "death" as we know it stands firmly established scientifically, based not on "belief" but on the evidence readily available to those who truly seek it.

Hans Holzer Ph.D.
New York, 1993

Alabama

The
Arguing
Ghosts

Warren F. Godfrey is an educated man who works for the NASA Center in Houston. He and his wife, Gwen, had no particular interest in the occult and were always careful not to let their imagination run away with them. They lived in a house in Huntsville, Alabama, that was, at the time they moved into it, only three years old. At first they had only a feeling that *the house didn't want them*. There was nothing definite about this, but as time went on they would look over their shoulders to see if they were being followed, and felt silly doing so. Then, gradually, peculiar noises started. Ordinarily such noises would not disturb them, and they tried very hard to blame the settling of the house. There were cracks in the ceiling, the popping and cracking of corners, then the walls would join in, and after a while there would be silence again. Faucets would start to drip for no apparent reason. Doors would swing open and/or shut by themselves, and a dish would shift in the cupboard. All these things could perhaps have been caused by a house's settling, but the noises seemed to become organized. Warren noticed that the house had a definite atmosphere. There seemed to be a feeling that the house objected to the young couple's happiness. It seemed to want to disturb their togetherness in whatever way it could, and it managed to depress them.

Then there were knockings. At first these were regularly spaced, single sharp raps proceeding from one part of the house to another. Warren ran out and checked the outside of the house, under it, and everywhere and could discover no reason for the knocks. As all this continued, they became even more depressed and neither liked to stay alone in the house. About Thanksgiving of

1968 they went to visit Warren's mother in Illinois for a few days. After they returned to the empty house it seemed quieter, even happier. Shortly before Christmas, Warren had to go to Houston on business. While he was gone Gwen took a photograph of their daughter Leah. When the picture was developed there was an additional head on the film, with the face in profile and wearing some sort of hat. Warren, a scientist, made sure that there was no natural reason for this extra face on the film. Using a Kodak Instamatic camera with a mechanism that excludes any double exposure, he duplicated the picture and also made sure that a reflection could not have caused the second image. Satisfied that he had obtained sufficient proof to preclude a natural origin for the second face on the film, he accepted the psychic origin of the picture.

About that time they began hearing voices. One night Warren woke up to hear two men arguing in a nearby room. At first he dismissed it as a bad dream and went back to sleep, but several nights later the same thing happened. After listening to them for a while he shrugged his shoulders and went back to sleep. He could not understand a word they were saying but was sure that there were two men arguing. After several weeks of this his wife also heard the voices. To Warren this was gratifying, since he was no longer alone in hearing them. Both of them generally heard the voices around 1 A.M. and the phenomena occurred only in the master bedroom. In addition to the two men arguing, Gwen also heard a woman crying and Warren heard people laughing. The noises were not particularly directed toward them, nor did they feel that there was anything evil about them. Gradually they learned to ignore them. As a trained scientist, Warren tried a rational approach to explain the phenomena but could not find any cause. Turning on the lights did not help either. There were no television stations on the air at that time of the morning, and there was no house close enough for human voices to carry that far.

In trying to reach for a natural explanation, Warren considered the fact that caves extended underneath the area, but what they were hearing was not the noise of rushing waters. Those were human voices and they were right there in the room with them. They decided to learn to live with their unseen boarders in the hopes that the ghosts might eventually let them in on their "problem." Not that Warren and Gwen could do much about them, but it is always nice to know what your friends are talking about, especially when you share your bedroom with them.

A
Dead Husband's
Greeting

Mrs. H. L. Stevens of Foley, Alabama, is a retired schoolteacher and a careful observer of facts. She has had an interest in ESP since childhood and has had various minor experiences with psychic occurrences herself, so many who could not cope with their own psychic experiences sought her advice as an unofficial counselor.

A fellow teacher, Mrs. B., had just lost her husband. Reluctantly she sold her house and most of the furnishings. The following night, very tired and unhappy, she went to bed early. As a mathematics instructor, she was not given to hallucinations or idle dreams. As she lay in bed unable to fall asleep, she thought over the plans for the delivery of the furniture that had been sold and the disposition of some of the articles that no one had purchased. At the foot of her bed was a dresser on which stood a musical powder box, a special gift from her late husband. Suddenly as she lay there the music box began to play of its own volition. Mrs. B. was terrified, believing that someone had gotten into the room and knocked the lid of the music box aside. That was the only way the box could be activated. The music box played the entire turn and Mrs. B. lay there stiff with fear, expecting someone at any moment to approach the bed. Then there was an interval, perhaps a minute or two, and the music box began again, playing the entire tune as if it had been rewound, although no one approached the bed.

After what seemed like an eternity, she arose and turned on the light. There was no one in the room. The lid was in its proper place on the box. All the doors in the house were locked. There was no way in which the music box could have played of its own accord. Mrs. B. knew then that her late husband wanted her to know he still cared. Somehow this last greeting made things a lot easier for her the next morning.

The
Visions
of a Psychic

rs. Nancy Anglin originally contacted me when I collected material on reincarnation cases for a previous book called *Born Again*. Although she now lives in California, she was then and had been for a long time a resident of Alabama. In her late twenties, she is married to a professional musician and is herself a licensed practical nurse. The Anglins have one son and are a happy, well-adjusted couple. What led me to include Mrs. Anglin's amazing experiences in *Born Again* was the way in which she described her very first memories of coming back into this physical world. These descriptions were not only precise and detailed but matched pretty closely similar descriptions obtained by me from widely scattered sources. It is a scientific axiom that parallel reports from people who have no contact with each other and who cannot draw upon a joint source of information should be accepted at face value. Her reincarnation memories go back to the very moment of her most recent birth. She recounted her earliest experiences in this lifetime to her mother at a time when the little girl could not possibly have had this knowledge. We have her mother's testimony of the validity of this statement. As Nancy Anglin grew up, her talents in the field of extrasensory perception grew with her. All through the years she had visions, clairvoyance, and other forms of extrasensory perception.

Soon after she moved to Montgomery in September 1965 she noticed a vacant house standing on South Court Street. Every time she passed the house she felt herself mysteriously drawn to it but she did not give in to this urge until the summer of 1968. Finally she mustered enough courage to enter the dilapidated old house. It was on a Friday afternoon in May 1968. She and her

husband were with a group of friends at the Maxwell Air Force
Base Noncommissioned Officers Club. The conversation turned to
haunted houses, and no sooner had Mrs. Anglin mentioned the
one she knew on Court Street than the little group decided they all
wanted to visit a haunted house. Mr. Anglin decided to stay behind, but the rest of the group piled into the convertible and drove
to the house. The group consisted of Sergeant and Mrs. Eugene
Sylvester, both in their late thirties; Sergeant and Mrs. Bob Dannly, in their mid-thirties; and Mrs. Harvey Ethridge, thirty-five,
wife of another member of the 604th Band Squadron. The whole
thing seemed like a lark. When they arrived at the house Mrs.
Dannly changed her mind and decided to wait in the car. The rest
of them walked up the shaded back drive around the left side of
the house and entered it through the front door. Since the house
was long vacant it was unlocked. They walked through the hall
into the sitting room to their right. As soon as the group had
entered that particular room Nancy Anglin became extremely
alert and the hair on her arms stood up. Sergeant Dannly noticed
her strange state and immediately asked her if there was anything
wrong. While the others went on, she and Sergeant Dannly remained behind in this room for a few minutes. Both noticed that
the temperature suddenly dropped and that there was an undefinable feeling of another presence about. They knew at once that
they were not alone.

Since the others had gone on to other rooms they decided to
join them in the rear of the house. Near the back stairs by the
kitchen door they discovered, scattered on the floor, old Veterans
of Foreign Wars records that seemed to have been there for a long
time. Eagerly they picked up some of the papers and started to
read them aloud to each other. As they did so they clearly heard
the sound of a small bell. They perked their ears and the sound
was heard once again. Immediately they started to look all over
the first floor of the house. Nowhere was there a bell. Since both of
them had clearly heard the bell they knew that they had not hallu-
cinated it. But as their search for the bell had proven fruitless,
they decided to leave by the front door. They had gone only a few
steps when Sergeant Sylvester cried out in excitement. At his feet
lay an old magazine illustrated with a figure pointing a finger and
a caption reading "Saved by the Bell." This seemed too much of a
coincidence, so they picked up the magazine and went back into

the house. Both sergeants and Nancy Anglin went back into the area where they had heard the mysterious bell. After a moment of quiet they heard it again. As they questioned the origin of the bell and spoke about it the sound became louder and louder. Needless to say, they could not find any source for the ringing and eventually they left the house.

Now Nancy Anglin's curiosity about the house was aroused. The following Sunday she returned to the vacant house, this time armed with a camera and flash bulbs. Again she searched the house from top to bottom for any possible source for the sound of a small bell. Again there was nothing that could have made such a sound. At that point she felt a psychic urge to photograph the staircase where the bell had first been heard. Using a good camera and a setting of infinity and exposing 1/60 of a second at 5.6 on Ektachrome-X color film rated at ASA 64, she managed to produce a number of slides. It was late evening, so she used blue flash bulbs to support the natural light. However, there were no reflective surfaces or odd markings on the wall. Nevertheless, upon examining the developed slides she found that two faces appeared on one of the slides. One seems to be the outline of the head and shoulders of a man and the second one seems to be the face of a woman with her hair piled high on her head and a scarf loosely tied around her shoulders. Nancy Anglin went back to the haunted house many times and heard the bell on several occasions. Others had heard it too. Marion Foster, at the time the Montgomery County Job Corps Director, and Charles Ford, a graduate student in psychology at Auburn University, are among those who heard the bell.

The house in question was known as the Ray-Branch Home. According to Milo Howard, Director of the Alabama State Archives, the house was built in 1856 by a Scottish gentleman by the name of Ray. After the turn of the century the house was sold to the Branch family, who altered the appearance by adding six stately Corinthian columns in front. A member of the Branch family confirmed that their family had lived there for twenty years, after which time the home had been sold to the Veterans of Foreign Wars to be used as state headquarters. Despite diligent search by Nancy Anglin and her librarian friends, nothing unusual could be turned up pertaining to any tragic event in the house. But the records of the mid-nineteenth century are not complete and it is entirely possible that some tragic event did take place of which we have no knowledge. Unfortunately the house has been demolished and replaced by a motel on Interstate Highway 65.

But Nancy had other psychic experiences in Alabama. Prior to her marriage she lived at 710 Cloverdale Road in Montgomery in an old house divided into four apartments, two downstairs and two upstairs. She occupied the upstairs east apartment alone for six months prior to her marriage. When she first moved in, she became immediately aware of an extraordinary presence. After her new husband moved in with her this became even stronger. Her first definite experience took place in August 1966 around three o'clock in the morning. At the time, she was sitting alone in her living room when she heard the sound of a flute playing a wandering mystical pattern of notes. Surprised, she looked up and saw a pink mist approaching from the bedroom where her husband was then sleeping. The mist crossed the living room and entered the den. As the cloud floated out, the music died off. Since her husband is a professional musician and she herself is very interested in singing, this manifestation was of particular importance to her, although she could not understand its meaning.

Soon enough she had another experience. This time she was entirely alone in the big old house when the living-room door began to vibrate with the sound of footsteps. Quivering with fear, she sat while the feet walked up and down in an almost impatient manner. Finally mustering up enough courage she commanded the noise to stop. Whatever was causing the footsteps obeyed her command, and for a few minutes all was quiet. Then it started up again. Paralyzed with fear, she sat there for what seemed an eternity until she heard her downstairs neighbor return home. Quickly she ran downstairs, rang his bell, and asked him to come up to see what he could discover about the mysterious footsteps. The neighbor's arrival apparently did not interfere with the ghost's determination to walk up and down. "Someone's walking around in here," explained the perplexed neighbor. As if to demonstrate her earlier success, Nancy commanded the unseen walker to stop. Sure enough, the footsteps stopped. Shaking his head, the neighbor left, and the footsteps resumed. Finally coming to terms with the unseen visitor, Nancy tried to keep occupied until her husband returned at two o'clock in the morning. As soon as her husband returned they ceased abruptly. Evidently the ghost didn't mind the neighbor but did not want any trouble with a husband. The Anglins never did find out who the ghostly visitor was, but since both of them were so involved with music, it seemed strange to live in an old house where a musician had lived before them. Quite possibly the unseen gentleman himself had manipulated things so that they could get the apartment.

For some unknown reason a certain spot in Alabama has become a psychic focal point for Nancy Anglin, the spot where the O'Neil Bridge crosses from the city of Sheffield to Florence, Alabama. Many years ago she had astral journeys that took her in flight across that bridge during its construction, which occurred before her birth. She remembers the sensational feeling and recalls wondering whether she would make it across or fall to her death. In that dream she clearly saw planks in a crosswalk high above the water and had the feeling of being pursued by some menacing individual. In the dream she looked down upon the water, became dizzy, and then saw nothing further. Every time she has had to cross it in reality, Nancy Anglin has had to suppress a great fear about it. In her childhood she had a firm belief that the bridge would eventually collapse and pull her to her death, despite the fact that it is a sturdy bridge constructed of concrete and steel.

In the fall of 1968 she began having a recurrent dream in which she drove across the O'Neil Bridge from Sheffield to Florence, then took a left turn, traveled down along the river, and rode a long distance until she reached a massive stone house that stood four stories tall. In her vision she spent the night on the third floor of that house. She was visited by a rather fierce female spirit possessed of a resounding voice. With that she awoke.

On December 27, 1968, Nancy Anglin visited some friends on the far side of Florence, Alabama. The conversation turned to haunted houses, stately mansions, and such, and the friends offered to show her an old house they had recently discovered. The group traveled over a series of back roads until they reached a large gray sandstone house standing four stories tall and overlooking the Tennessee River. The house was vacant and the interior had been destroyed long ago by treasure seekers. The stairs leading up to the third floor were torn down. Nancy was fascinated by the house and decided to visit it again on New Year's

Day. This time, however, she traveled in the same direction as she had done in her dream, but she had not yet realized that it was the same house. Somehow the house seemed familiar, but she did not connect this particular house with the one in her recurrent dream. Finally in another dream on March 21, 1969, she realized that the house was the same as the one in her dream vision. Now she found herself on the third floor of the house in a large room containing a chaise longue of an earlier period. She had lain down to rest when she heard a booming angry voice on the floor above her. Then, as if blown by a strong wind, came an apparition from the fourth floor. She could see a face, that of a white woman with narrow features, angry as she said something in a vibrating, commanding voice that awoke Nancy.

A few weeks later the dream repeated itself. By now she knew the name of the house, Smithsonia. Then in early March 1969 she dreamed a variation in which she saw herself on the third floor. Again the forceful female spirit appeared and screamed at her. This time she could make out the words, "Get out, get out!" Subsequently Nancy found herself standing on the grounds with a group of people watching the house go up in flames while a deafening voice raged from within the burning structure. At that she awoke suddenly. Only later in the day did she realize that the house in her dream had been the Smithsonia. On the night of March 29 she awoke to hear a ringing in her ears. Her body was tingling all over as if her circulation had stopped. She felt herself weighted down by some tremendous force and could neither move nor breathe. While her conscious mind seemed to be ascending above herself all she could do was think how to get back into her body and a state of normalcy. After what seemed like an eternity she felt herself catch a deep gulping breath and her senses returned.

In late April she returned home for a visit and was informed that Smithsonia had burned down about three weeks before. The day of the fire matched her last terrifying experience. Was there any connection between the fierce spirit in the burning house and herself and was Nancy Anglin reliving something from her own past, or was she merely acting as the medium for some other tortured soul? At any rate, Smithsonia stands no more.

Arkansas

Grandmother's Ghost

Hollygrove is only a small town in rural eastern Arkansas, but to Sharon Inebnit it is the center of her world. She lives there with her husband, far from metropolitan centers. Her mother lives in Helena, close to the Mississippi state line. Traveling east on Highway 86 and then on 49 Sharon has gone back and forth a few times in her young life. She knows the area well. It is not an area of particular merit but it has one advantage: it's very quiet. About halfway between Hollygrove and Helena stands an old house that for some reason attracted Sharon. Whenever she passed it she wondered about the house's secret.

Sharon has lived with an extraordinary gift of ESP since infancy. That is a subject one doesn't discuss freely in her part of the world. People either ridicule you or, worse, think you're in league with the devil. So Sharon managed to keep her powers to herself even though at times she couldn't help surprising people. She would often hear voices of people who weren't within sight. If she wanted someone to call her, all she had to do was visualize the person and, presto, the person would ring her. Whenever the telephone rings she knows exactly who is calling. Frequently she has heard her neighbors talking 500 yards from her house, and she is so sensitive she cannot stand the television when it is turned on too loud.

Her husband, a farmer of Swiss extraction, is somewhat skeptical of her powers, though less so now than when he first met her. Back in the summer of 1963, when they first kept company, she was already somewhat of a puzzle to him. One day, the fifteen-year-old girl insisted they drive into Helena, which was about five miles from where they were then. He asked why; she insisted that there was a baseball game going on and that a private swimming party was in progress at the municipal pool. She had no particular reason to make this statement, nor any proof that it was correct, but they were both very much interested in baseball games, so they decided to drive on to Helena. When they arrived at Helena they found that a baseball game was indeed going on and that a private swimming party was in progress at the municipal pool, just as Sharon had said. Helena has a population of over 10,000 people. Sharon lives 25 miles away. How could she have known this?

In March 1964 her maternal grandmother passed away. She had been close to her but was unable to see her in her last moments. Thus the death hit her especially hard and she felt great remorse at not having seen her grandmother prior to her passing. On the day of the funeral she was compelled to look up, and there before her appeared her late grandmother. Smiling at her, she nodded and then vanished. But in the brief moment when she had become visible to Sharon the girl understood what her grandmother wanted her to know. The message was brief. Her grandmother understood why she had not been able to see her in her last hours and wanted to forgive her.

California

The
Bride
of Nob Hill

G wen Hinzie is a California woman with unusual psychic gifts. We worked together on a number of investigations, but her "run-ins" with ghosts go back a long, long time, long before she moved to sunny California. We were having coffee one afternoon in San Francisco, when she opened up to me about those early years, and experiences.

"I was born in Los Angeles in 1920 and am of Irish-English descent. I was raised in that city and Beverly Hills, where I attended both public and Catholic schools. I attended the University of Los Angeles and graduated in 1943 with a Bachelor of Arts degree. I have three sisters and our life was fairly ordinary, I think. We were never poor but not rich. After I graduated from the university I worked for several years and married in 1952. I have three children, one of whom is also sensitive.

"When I was twenty-one years old my father passed away from a heart attack. I was in the room at the time of his death. He had been in great pain and was lying on the bed. Hospital attendants were giving oxygen but he lay with his hands clenched. When he stopped breathing, his hand relaxed, and within seconds a white vapor ascended from his opening hand and disappeared. This I have been given to understand as being the release of the soul from the body and have heard of it before.

"When I was about eighteen, our dog Rowdy, then thirteen years old, died. He simply disappeared from our home and I did not at first believe he was dead, although a body looking like his had been found, and I continued for a few days to put his food out by the back door for him. Then one evening *I saw him come up* toward the food. He would not let me touch him and would not touch the food. He then walked away toward the side of the house. In a few minutes I followed him but he had disappeared. Later I saw him on a few occasions on the front lawn, where he had been accustomed to sit, and once heard him barking out there. I told my parents about it but I don't believe they ever saw him.

"This clairvoyance can be less than a blessing. When I was about eight or nine there was a child in our neighborhood who had died of an illness, and one day about a month after his death (I knew him but he was not a friend of mine) I was with some children near his home when I saw him standing on the driveway and I said so. I was called a liar and lost at least one friend as a result of it. After that, I stopped mentioning things I saw. At the time I did not know I saw a ghost. I thought they were not telling me the truth about the boy being dead!

"I saw a ghost in San Francisco in 1947. Until about 1961 or 1962 I did not know whom I had seen. It was *not until then* that I read about her. It was while my roommate and I, vacationing in San Francisco, were riding on a cable car up to Nob Hill. We both saw her. The cable car had stopped at a cross street. There were other people on the street and she caught my attention because of her filmy white dress. It seemed inappropriate. She was a young girl, not pretty, but smiling and apparently nodding to people on the street. She seemed substantial enough until she started to pass a couple of girls on the sidewalk, when her full skirt and part of her body *passed part way through one of the girls*. Just before she passed these girls the side of her gown suddenly appeared spangled with water drops or brilliants, but it seemed as if water had suddenly been sprayed on her gown. Knowing then that she was a ghost, and having caught her eye, I tried to tell her in my mind to go to heaven, but she looked frightened and disappeared. My roommate and others saw her and she has been seen many times walking along the street on Nob Hill."

I decided to go after the story immediately, as it seemed so unusual by ghostly standards: after all, a ghost in the middle of the street seen by several people is out of the ordinary. I requested the testimony of the friend Mrs. Hinzie claimed was with her at the time she had the experience in San Francisco. The friend, Peggy O'Conner, was Gwen Hinzie's roommate for about a year and a

half. Since Miss O'Conner's marriage in 1948 they had not kept
up the contact, however, except for an occasional Christmas card.

"She saw the ghost and was very upset about it," Mrs. Hinzie
explained. "Other people on the cable car I was in also saw the
ghost, as I heard a couple of women comment on it." Imagine
riding up a hill in a cable car, looking out the window, and seeing
a ghost!

I suggested Mrs. Hinzie meet me in San Francisco so we
could locate the exact spot where the incident took place. She
readily agreed, and offered to come with her close friend Sharon
Bettin, with whom she shared many interests; also, Mrs. Bettin's
parents had a house at Santa Cruz, and the two ladies could stay
there.

At the time of the incident, Mrs. Hinzie recalled, she was
staying at the Fairmount Hotel, atop the hill, and the ride was no
more than three or four blocks up the hill. She was reasonably
sure she could find the spot again. Naturally, I was going to bring
Sybil Leek with me, not telling her the reasons.

The story, as reported by James Reynolds in *Ghosts in American Houses*, is quite a shocker, considering the period it occurred
in. It was, of course, unknown to Mrs. Hinzie at the time she saw
the ghost.

The disappearance of Flora Sommerton a few hours before
her debut was a great mystery for many years. Flora was the only
child of Charles Benfow Sommerton, originally from Kansas City,
Kansas. Sommerton, who had built a mansion on Nob Hill, San
Francisco, was rich, his wife was ambitious, and the debut of their
daughter on her eighteenth birthday in 1876 was to be an affair of
splendor. Moreover, Flora's parents had wedding plans for Flora.
They insisted that she should marry in due course a young disso-
lute snob named Hugh Partridge, whom she despised.

On the afternoon of the day of the debut, Mrs. Sommerton
urged Flora to take a long nap in order to be fresh for the party at
ten that evening. Instead, Flora insisted on going out, and she
disappeared. She was last seen by a grocer's delivery boy, to
whom she gave a written message for her mother. The boy deliv-
ered the note to the Sommerton residence, which was in a great
flurry of preparation for the party; in the excitement the maid who
received it promptly mislaid it.

Came early evening and no debutante. Also missing was the

beautiful white gown covered with crystal beads that had been ordered from Paris for the occasion. A family conference was called. A maid finally found the misplaced note. The family decided to carry off the party anyway. The domineering Mrs. Sommerton would not permit her husband to notify the police. Guests were told that Flora had had a sudden illness and had been sent to the country. In spite of all this, the ball was a great success.

In the morning Mr. Sommerton called in the police and put up a huge reward—$250,000—for the return of his daughter. That money was to lie unclaimed in a San Francisco bank for many years, even after Sommerton's death, which occurred shortly after the fire in 1906 that destroyed the Sommerton mansion.

Throughout the decades many tips and clues were offered, but Flora was elusive. Mrs. Sommerton finally called off the search, although there was a little evidence that Flora was still alive. Mrs. Carrie Sommerton died in 1916.

The evidence was an undated letter written to the police by an Adele LaBlanche in Los Angeles. Miss LaBlanche was the prima donna of a touring company that was presenting *The Prince of Pilsen* in Los Angeles. But her letter referred to an incident in Chicago. Miss LaBlanche had sprained her ankle and had been obliged to call upon her understudy, Miss Jarvis. Her costume, however, did not fit the smaller Miss Jarvis. Whereupon the wardrobe mistress, described by Miss LaBlanche as "a quiet, faded, middle-aged woman," fished out a dress she said might do in this emergency. It was out of fashion but beautiful, a creation of white tulle "sprinkled like the heavens on a starry night with crystal beads." Miss Jarvis wore it and then tried to buy it. Said the wardrobe mistress: "No, I cannot sell it. It is my only link with the past. It is Nob Hill and what I might have been." Then, Miss LaBlanche wrote, "a startled look came into her eyes, and she took her dress and fled, again leaving no trace."

The mystery was finally solved in 1926. Flora Sommerton was at last located, dead, in Butte, Montana. Here she had been known as Mrs. Butler, housekeeper for ten years in the Butte Central Hotel. Coroner's verdict: death from heart disease. But the police were skeptical about the name Butler.

In her valise was found a nest of clippings, from all over the United States, dating from 1876 to 1891 and referring to the search for Flora Sommerton, daughter of a multimillionaire nabob. When Mrs. Butler died, she was dressed in a white ball gown conjectured to be of the 1880s and entirely covered with crystal beads. Her age was given as about 57, but she must have been 68 when she was found dead in a hotel room by a housemaid.

The Reynolds account ends with a rumor.

"Now people report seeing a girl in a shimmering dress strolling in streets and gardens in the Nob Hill section of the city. She seems to be returning from a late party. The figure smiles at passersby and moves in a leisurely manner. As in her life, Flora is still walking alone."

The time had come for me to fly to California to follow up on the story so vividly told by Reynolds, and, of course, to check up on Mrs. Hinzie's experiences. It was a warm day in May 1966 when I met Mrs. Hinzie and her friend Mrs. Bettin at the Hilton Hotel in San Francisco.

I had decided to discuss the case once more with the ladies prior to proceeding to the spot. Present during our conversation was my good friend Lori Clerf, a social worker living in the city. Sybil Leek was to join us downstairs about an hour later, just in time for the ride. She could not overhear any of our earlier conversation.

We established once again that the cable car was the California Street line, and that the girl in the party dress had walked down one of the streets crossing California Street.

"You were looking out the window of the cable car when this happened?" I asked.

"No, there was no glass—just the open side of the cable car, where you step up."

No reflection then, on glass. That alternative explanation was out.

"When she walked through two other people, did you think it was unusual?"

"Well, she was also improperly dressed for the street—that's how I noticed her in the first place. Coming home from a party in the middle of the afternoon." Even in San Francisco that might be considered unusual. "As I was looking at her, the dress seemed diaphanous, but you could not see through it. All white, no other colors. And as I was watching her it looked as if there were water suddenly sprayed on her side; it clung there, shining as water does in the sun."

It was time to meet Sybil and go to California Avenue where the ghost of the girl in the party dress might be waiting—if we were lucky.

The important point of the incident was Mrs. Hinzie's total ignorance, at the time she saw her, of the story or tradition about this ghostly girl. It was fifteen years later that she accidentally came across the account in James Reynolds's book in the public library. Thus we must rule out unconscious hallucination of a known event.

When we arrived atop Nob Hill, it was about four in the afternoon, and traffic was heavy. Lori parked her shining white car carefully—that's the only way you can park a car in San Francisco if you don't want it to roll downhill—and we walked a few steps to the street intersection of California where Mrs. Hinzie remembered the incident. What did Sybil feel at this spot? Did the noises of the onrushing traffic blot out all psychic impressions, or did she feel something other than flesh-and-blood and gasoline?

"Yes, I do," Sybil intoned immediately. "I feel fear . . . someone is afraid . . . more than one person involved . . . fear . . . someone wants to run away. . . ."

How right she was!

"What sort of person is it wants to run away?" I prodded.

"A young person," she replied, while trying hard to get an impression above the din of the traffic. No medium ever worked under more trying conditions, but then the experiment was unique.

"Man or woman?"

"Young . . . feeling of panic . . . I feel cold . . . despite this hot day . . . look at the goosepimples on my arms. . . ."

"Why is this person running away?"

"I think there is a link with the house I just pointed out to you."

The house, though old, was not the house belonging to the girl's family, though the spot might have been the same site.

"It's someone who runs away from a house," Sybil continued, "she ran this way."

"She?"

"I don't know . . . but suddenly I felt 'she.' I have 1830 in

my mind—'30 is very clear. Several people are involved in this
. . . this chase. A hounding."

"Any unhappiness involved?"

"The girl . . . she is panic-stricken."

"Why?"

"I have a feeling of terrible disease, horror."

Later I realized that Sybil might have picked up the girl's
death. She had died of heart disease.

Reaching out
from Beyond

In life as in afterlife, communication is a driving force. We want to be acknowledged, even loved and respected. We shudder at isolation and a lack of attention.

Sometimes, when one of us passes over, the change comes so suddenly there isn't time to adjust or to let one's loved ones know that life continues on the other side of the curtain—that the one who has died here is all right over there.

Coronado Beach is a pleasant seaside resort in southern California not far from San Diego. You get there by ferry from the mainland and the ride itself is worth the trip. It takes about fifteen minutes, then you continue by car or on foot into a town of small homes, none grand, none ugly—pleasantly bathed by the warm California sunshine, vigorously battered on the oceanside by the Pacific, and becalmed on the inside of the lagoon by a narrow body of water.

The big thing in Coronado Beach is the U.S. Navy; either you're in it and are stationed here, or you work for them in one way or another: directly, as a civilian, or indirectly by making a living through the people who are in the Navy and who make their homes here.

Gloria Jones is the wife of an advertising manager for a Sidney, Ohio, newspaper, who had returned to Coronado after many years in the Midwest. She is a young woman with a college background and above-average intelligence, and has mixed Anglo-Saxon and Austrian background. Her father died a Navy hero while testing a dive bomber, making her mother an early widow.

Gloria married fairly young, and when her husband took a job as advertising manager in Sidney, Ohio, she went right along with him. After some years, the job became less attractive, and the Joneses moved back to Coronado, where Francis Jones took up work for the Navy.

They have a thirteen-year-old daughter, Vicki, and live a happy, well-adjusted life; Mr. Jones collects coins and Mrs. Jones likes to decorate their brick house surrounded by a garden filled with colorful flowers.

One January, Mrs. Jones sought me out to help her understand a series of most unusual events that had taken place in her otherwise placid life. Except for an occasional true dream, she had not had any contact with the psychic and evinced no interest whatever in it until the events that so disturbed her tranquility had come to pass. Even the time she saw her late father in a white misty cloud might have been a dream. She was only ten years old at the time, and preferred later to think it was a dream. But the experiences she came to see me about were not in that category. Moreover, her husband and a friend were present when some of the extraordinary happenings took place.

Kathleen Duffy was the daughter of a man working for the Convair company. He was a widower and Kathleen was the apple of his eye, but unfortunately Kathleen was a troubled child. Her father had sent her away to a Catholic school for girls in Oceanside, but she ran away twice; after the second time she had to be sent to a home for "difficult" children.

Gloria Jones met Kathleen when both were in their teens. Her mother was a widow and Mr. Duffy was a widower, so the parents had certain things in common. The two girls struck up a close friendship and they both hoped they might become sisters through the marriage of their parents, but it did not happen.

When Kathleen was sent away to the Anthony Home, a reform school in San Diego, Gloria was genuinely sorry. That was when Kathleen was about sixteen years of age. Although they never met again, Kathleen phoned Gloria a few times. She wasn't happy in her new environment, of course, but there was little that either girl could do about it.

In mounting despair, Kathleen tried to get away again but did not succeed. Then one day, she and her roommate, June Robeson, decided to do something drastic to call attention to their dissatisfied state. They set fire to their room in the hope that they might escape in the confusion of the fire. As the smoke of the burning beds started to billow heavier and heavier, they became frightened. Their room was kept locked at all times, and now they started to bang at the door, demanding to be let out.

The matron came and surveyed the scene. The girls had been trouble for her all along. She decided to teach them what she thought would be an unforgettable "lesson." It was. When Kathleen collapsed from smoke inhalation, the matron finally opened the door. The Robeson girl was saved, but Kathleen Duffy died the next day in the hospital.

When the matter became public, the local newspapers demanded an investigation of the Anthony Home. The matron and the manager of the Home didn't wait for it. They fled to Mexico and were never heard from again.

Gradually, Gloria began to forget the tragedy. Two years went by and the image of her friend receded into her memory.

One day she and another friend, a girl named Jackie Sudduth, were standing near the waterfront at Coronado, a sunny, windswept road overlooking the Pacific and the orderly rows of houses that make up Coronado Beach.

The cars were whizzing by as the two girls stood idly gazing across the road. One of the cars coming into view was driven by a young man with a young woman next to him who seemed familiar to Gloria. She only saw her from the shoulders up, but as the car passed close by she knew it was Kathleen. Flabbergasted, she watched the car disappear.

"Did you know that girl?" Jackie inquired.

"No, why?"

"She said your name," her friend reported.

Gloria nodded in silence. She had seen it too. Without uttering a sound, the girl in the passing car had mouthed the syllables "Glo-ri-a."

For weeks afterward, Gloria could not get the incident out of her mind. There wasn't any rational explanation, and yet how could it be? Kathleen had been dead for two years.

The years went by, then a strange incident brought the whole matter back into her consciousness. It was New Year's Eve, twelve years later. She was now a married woman with a daughter. As she entered her kitchen, she froze in her tracks: a bowl was spinning counterclockwise while moving through the kitchen of its own volition.

She called out to her husband and daughter to come quickly. Her daughter's friend Sheryl Konz, age thirteen, was first to arrive in the kitchen. She also saw the bowl spinning. By the time Mr. Jones arrived, it had stopped its unusual behavior.

Over dinner, topic A was the self-propelled bowl. More to tease her family than out of conviction, Mrs. Jones found herself saying, "If there is anyone here, let the candle go out." Promptly the candle went out. There was silence after that, for no current of air was present that could have accounted for the sudden extinguishing of the candle.

The following summer, Mrs. Jones was making chocolate pudding in her kitchen. When she poured it into one of three bowls, the bowl began to turn—by itself. This time her husband saw it too. He explained it as vibrations from a train or a washing machine next door. But why did the other two bowls not move also?

Finally wondering if her late friend Kathleen, who had always been a prankster, might not be the cause of this, she waited for the next blow.

On New Year's Day that following year, she took a Coke bottle out of her refrigerator and set it down on the counter. Then she turned her back on it and went back to the refrigerator for some ice. This took only a few moments. When she got back to the counter, the Coke bottle had disappeared.

Chiding herself for being absentminded, she assumed she had taken the bottle with her to the refrigerator and had left it inside. She checked and there was no Coke.

"Am I going out of my mind?" she wondered, and picked up the Coke carton. It contained five bottles. The sixth bottle was never found.

Since these latter incidents took place during the three years when they lived in Sidney, Ohio, it was evident that the frisky spirit of Kathleen Duffy—if that is who it was—could visit them anywhere they went.

In late May of that year, back again in Coronado, both Mr. and Mrs. Jones witnessed another unusual occurrence. They had locked the breadbox after placing a loaf of bread inside. A moment later, they returned to the breadbox and found it open. While they were still wondering how this could be, the bread jumped out. A practical man, Mr. Jones immediately wondered if they were having an earthquake. They weren't. Moreover, it appeared that their neighbors' breadboxes behaved normally. They shook their heads once more. But this time Mrs. Jones dropped me a letter.

On June 3, I went to San Diego to see the Joneses. Sybil Leek and I braved the bus ride from Santa Ana on a hot day, but the Joneses picked us up at the bus terminal and drove us to the Anthony Home where Kathleen had died so tragically.

Naturally Sybil was mystified about all this, unless her ESP told her why we had come. Consciously, she knew nothing.

When we stopped at the home, we found it boarded up and not a soul in sight. The day was sunny and warm, and the peaceful atmosphere belied the past that was probably filled with unhappy memories. After the unpleasant events that had occurred earlier, the place had been turned into a school for retarded children and run as such for a number of years. At present, however, it stood abandoned.

Sybil walked around the grounds quietly and soaked up the mood of the place.

"I heard something, maybe a name," she suddenly said. "It sounds like Low Mass."

Beyond that, she felt nothing on the spot of Kathleen's unhappy memories. Was it Kathleen who asked for a Low Mass to be said for her? Raised a strict Catholic, such a thought would not be alien to her.

"The place we just left," Sybil said as we drove off, "has a feeling of sickness to it—like a place for sick people, but not a hospital."

Finally we arrived at the corner of Ocean Avenue and Lomar Drive in Coronado, where Gloria Jones had seen the car with Kathleen in it. All through the trip, on the ferry, and down again into Coronado Island, we avoided the subject at hand.

But now we had arrived and it was time to find out if Sybil felt anything still hanging on in this spot.

"I feel a sense of death," she said slowly, uncertainly. "Despite the sunshine, this is a place of death." It wasn't that there was a presence here, she explained, but rather that someone had come here to wait for another person. The noise around us—it was Sunday—did not help her concentration.

"It's a foreign face I see," Sybil continued. "Someone—a

man, with very little hair—who is alien to this place. I see an iris next to his face."

Was the man using the symbol to convey the word Irish perhaps? Was he an ancestor of Kathleen's from over there?

I turned to Mrs. Jones.

"I think what you witnessed here was the superimposition on a pair of motorists of the spirit image of your late friend. These things are called transfigurations. I am sure if the car had stopped, you would have found a stranger in it. Kathleen used her so that you could see her familiar face, I think."

Perhaps Kathleen Duffy wanted to take one more ride, a joy ride in freedom, and, proud of her accomplishment, had wanted her best friend to see her taking it.

There have been no further disturbances or prankish happenings at the Jones house since.

The
Ghost
in the Basement

Mrs. Edith F. is the wife of a law enforcement officer in the West. Her husband puts very little credence in anything "supernatural," but Mrs. F. knows otherwise. The house she and her family live in is only about twelve years old, and fifteen years before, the area was still "in the country," although people may have lived there in a previous house. In fact, rumor has it that some old houses were torn down on the land where her house now stands. The series of odd incidents that convinced Mrs. F. of the reality of another dimension began in the summer of 1972.

At that time her nine-year-old son was in the basement family room, watching television. On the north wall of this large room there was a door leading to a storeroom. A rollaway bed had been put there for possible summer company, and the boy was in this particular bed, propped up with a large pillow. He had just finished a snack, and leaned up to brush the crumbs from under him, when he happened to look up and saw an old woman standing beside the bed, staring at him. He looked away from her for a moment, then returned his eyes onto her; she was still there. Frightened, he began to yell for his mother, at which the woman moved back towards the door. The door opened about two inches, and she quickly slid through it, as if she were two-dimensional.

By that time Mrs. F. arrived downstairs and found her son so frightened he could hardly talk. He described the visitor as very old, with black and gray hair parted in the middle, wearing a long black dress and a single pair of colored beads. Mrs. F. decided not to discuss it with her husband, who would only scoff at it, but decided to return to the basement with her twenty-year-old daughter to see whether anything would occur in her presence.

The two women stood on the spot where the boy had seen the ghost and asked her what she wanted of them. For a moment, nothing happened. Then, suddenly, Mrs. F. felt as though someone were lifting her right arm, which turned tingly and raised up in front of her by its own volition! She broke out in goose pimples and quickly whirled around, running back upstairs.

For several days, she did not dare go back to the basement out of fear that the phenomenon might repeat itself. Still upset by it all, she telephoned the Reverend L. B., a Methodist minister, whom, she hoped, would have an open mind concerning occult phenomena. But on the fourth day, Mrs. F. could not hold back any longer; she had to know what the ghost wanted. Somehow she felt she would get it by writing. Again she went to the basement with her twenty-year-old daughter, said a prayer for protection from evil, and stood upright with a pen in her right hand—why, she didn't really know, for she is *left*-handed. She asked aloud if there was anyone present, and the pen wrote, "Yes. You must watch out to woman," and then it drew an arrow toward the northern part of the room. Mrs. F. demanded to know what the ghost wanted, and in reply, the pencil in her hand wrote, "Priest. Hear my confession." Mrs. F. demanded to know what her name was, and the ghost identified herself as Mary Arthur.

With this information Mrs. F. went to her minister friend, who decided to accompany the two women back to the house. He, too, stood in the basement and asked the ghost to give him a sign that she was present. A lamp, which they knew to be in good order, blinked on and off several times in response to their questions. Then, through automatic writing, the ghost informed them that she had died at age eighty-nine, had had nine children, and knew she had passed on in 1959. But the Methodist minister could not help her, she explained; it had to be a Catholic priest. The Reverend B. offered to talk to his Catholic colleague, but Mrs. F. suggested the ghost might find peace in nearby St. Agnes Church. On this note, the presence disappeared and was gone until the following Monday.

On that day, Mrs. F. was in the basement room, working on an ironing board. It was a very warm day, but suddenly she was startled by walking into a blast of icy air on the spot where the ghost had originally been observed by her son. Quickly she called for her daughter to join her and watch. After a moment, her daughter complained that her arm was being lifted the way her mother's had been before. She felt as if someone held it, and the arm felt tingly. Mrs. F. grabbed a pencil and paper from a nearby desk and gave it to her daughter. Her daughter then wrote "Mary" in exactly the same handwriting as Mrs. F. had originally. Then she handed the pencil and paper back to her mother, afraid to continue. So the mother continued the communication and the ghost wrote "Mary Arthur." Gradually, the reasons for her presence became clear. "Father, forgive me, for I have sinned," the ghost wrote, and demanded that the note be taken to a Roman Catholic priest. But Mrs. F. instead suggested that Mary call out to her loved ones to take her away from the place so she could find peace. "No, because of my sins," the ghost replied, and when Mrs. F. wanted to know what the sins consisted of, she simply said, "the marriage."

It was then that Mrs. F. learned that Mary had been born Catholic, had left the church and married a Lutheran and had had the nine children with him. To her, this marriage was illegal, sinful. Eventually, the Roman Catholic clergy got into the act. But a special priest would have to be sent to exorcise Mary's sins. This did not sit well with Mrs. F., nor with her Methodist friend, neither of whom thought that Mary was evil.

Time passed, and things seemed to quiet down in the basement. Then, on Labor Day of the same year, with her husband and son fast asleep in bed, Mrs. F. was in the kitchen canning tomatoes from their garden. Again she felt Mary's presence upstairs, a strange feeling that was hard to describe. Again, her right arm was tingling and her fingers felt as they did when Mary first wanted to write something through her. However, since the Roman Catholic clergy had been reluctant to enter the case, Mrs. F. determined to ignore her promptings. Here she was, washing tomatoes at her kitchen sink, when all of a sudden she heard a *plop!* behind her, turned around, and saw one of the tomatoes lying split open in the middle of the floor. Since she was the only person in the kitchen, there was no rational explanation for the fall of the tomato. Had it merely fallen off the counter, it would have gone straight down instead of jumping four feet away!

Quietly, Mrs. F. turned in the direction where she assumed her ghost lady was and reprimanded her for throwing the tomato.

"They are saying special prayers at the church for you," she said, and asked Mary to go there and wait for her delivery.

Everything was quiet after that. About ten days later, a lamp in Mrs. F.'s living room blinked on and off four times as if the ghost were trying to tell her she was leaving. This time Mrs. F. did not feel the tingling sensation in her arm, and somehow felt that this was a farewell message. And since that time there has been no sign of Mary's presence. With the help of her minister friend, Mrs. F. was able to check the records of various funeral homes in the area. A black woman named Mary Arthur was buried in 1959.

The
Lost
Sailor

One night in the early spring, the telephone rang and a pleasant voice said, "I think I've got a case for you, Mr. Holzer. I'm calling from Alameda, California."

Before the young lady could run up an impressive telephone bill, I stopped her and asked her to jot down the main points of her story for my records. She promised this, but it took her several months to comply. Evidently the ghost was not so unpleasant as she thought it was the night she had to call me long distance, or perhaps she had learned to live with the unseen visitor.

It had all started four years before when Gertrude Frost's grandmother bought a house in Alameda, an island in San Francisco Bay connected with the mainland by a causeway and mainly covered by small homes—many of which belong to people connected with the nearby naval installations. The house itself was built around 1917.

After the old lady died, Miss Frost's mother had the house. Noises in the night when no one was about kept Miss Frost and her mother and aunt, who shared the house with her, from ever getting a good night's sleep. It did not sound like a very exciting case and I was frankly skeptical since there are many instances where people *think* they hear unnatural noises when in fact they merely ascribe supernormal character to what is actually natural in origin. But I was going to be in the area, and decided to drop in.

I asked Claude Mann, a news reporter from Oakland's Channel 2, to accompany me, my wife, Catherine, and my good friend Sybil Leek, who did not have the faintest idea where Alameda was or that we were going there. Not that Sybil cared—it was merely another assignment and she was willing. The date was July 1,

1965, and it was pleasantly warm—in fact, a most unghostly type of day.

As soon as we approached the little house, we quickly unloaded the camera equipment and went inside, where two of the ladies were already expecting us. I promptly put Sybil into one of the easy chairs and began my work—or rather Sybil began hers.

Although the house was in the middle of the island and no indication of the ocean could be seen anywhere near it, Sybil at once remarked that she felt the sea was connected with the house in some way; she felt a presence in the house but not associated with it directly.

As soon as Sybil was in deep trance, someone took over her vocal chords.

"What is your name?" I asked.

"Dominic."

"Do you live in this house?"

"No house . . . water . . . fort . . . tower . . ."

"What are you doing here?"

"Have to wait . . . Tiana . . ."

"What does Tiana mean?"

"*Tiana* . . . boat . . ."

"Where does the boat go?"

"Hokeite . . . Hokeite . . ."

"What year is this?"

"1902."

"What is your rank?"

"Midshipman." He had difficulty in enunciating. The voice had a strangely unreal quality, not at all like Sybil's normal speaking voice but more like the thin voice of a young man.

I continued to question the ghostly visitor.

"Are you serving on this boat?"

"Left here," he replied. "I'm going to break . . . everything up."

"Why do you want to do that?"

"Those things . . . got to go . . . because they're untidy . . . I shall break them up . . . they say I'm mad . . . I'm not mad. . . ."

"How old are you?"

"Thirty-one."

"Where were you born?"

"I was born . . . Hakeipe."

I was not sure whether he said "Hakeipe" or "Hakeite," but it sounded something like that.

"What state?" I had never heard of such a place.

"No state," the ghost said, somewhat indignant because I did not know better.

"Then where is it?" I demanded.

"In Japan," the ghost informed me. I began to wonder if he didn't mean Hakodate, a harbor of some importance. It had a fair number of foreign people at all times, being one of the principal seaports for the trade with America and Europe. It would be pronounced "Hak-o-deit," not too different from what I had heard through Sybil's mediumship.

"Break them up, break them up," the ghost continued to mumble menacingly, "throw those little things . . . into . . . faces . . . I don't like faces . . . people . . ."

"Do you realize time has gone on?"

"Time goes on," the voice said sadly.

"What are you doing here?" I asked.

"What are *they* doing here?" the ghost shot back angrily.

It was his land, he asserted. I asked if he had built anything on it.

"The tower is here," he said cryptically, "to watch the ships. I stay here."

"Are you American?"

"No, I'm Italian."

"Are you a merchant sailor or Navy?"

"Navy . . . why don't you go away?"

"What do you want here?"

"Nothing."

I explained about his death and this evoked cold anger.

"Smash everything . . ."

I decided to change the subject before the snarling became completely unintelligible.

Claude Mann's cameras were busily humming meanwhile.

"Did you serve in the American Navy?"

"Yes."

"Give me your serial number!"

"Serial . . . one . . . eight . . . eight . . . four . . . three."

"Where did you enlist?"

"Hakkaite."

It did not make sense to me, so I repeated the question. This time the answer was different. Perhaps he had not understood the first time.

"In 'meda," he said.

Sailors call Alameda by this abbreviation. How could Sybil, newly arrived here, have known this? She could not, and I did not.

"Who's your commanding officer?"

"Oswald Gregory."

"What rank?"

"Captain."

"The name of your ship."

"*Triana.*"

"How large a ship?"

"I don't know. . . ."

I asked about his family. Did he have a wife, was he well? He became more and more reluctant. Finally he said:

"I'm not answering questions. . . ."

"Your father's name?" I continued.

"Giuseppe."

"Mother?"

"Matilone."

"Sister or brothers?"

"Four."

They live in "Hokkaipe," he added.

"Where did you go to school?"

"Hokkeipe Mission."

He came to this place in 1902, he asserted, and was left behind because he was sick.

"I wait for next trip . . . but they never came back. I had bad headache. I was lying here. Not a house. Water."

I then asked what he was doing to let people know about his presence.

"I can walk—as well as anyone," he boasted. "I play with water, I drop things. . . ."

I reasoned with him. His father and mother were waiting for him to join them. Didn't he want to be with them? I received a flat "no." He wasn't interested in a family reunion. I tried to explain about real estate. I explained that the house was fully paid for and he was trespassing. He could not have cared less.

I questioned his honesty and he did not like that. It made him waver in his determination to break everything up.

I spoke to him of the "other side" of life. He asked that I take him there.

He now recalled his sisters' names, Matild' and Alissi, or something that sounded like it.

"We've come to fetch you, Dominic," I said, suggesting he "go across."

"You're late," he snarled.

"Better late than never," I intoned. Who said I didn't have as much of a sense of humor as a ghost?

"I was never late," he complained. "I can walk . . . without you!"

Gratitude was not his forte.

I requested that Sybil return to her own body now, but to remain in trance so as to answer my questions on what she could observe in that state.

Soon Sybil's own voice, feeble at first, was heard again from her lips.

I asked her to describe the scene she saw.

"I see a short, dark man," she replied, "who can't walk very well; he was insane. I think he had fits. Fell down. Violent man."

"Do you see a house?"

"No, I see water, and a gray ship. Big ship, not for people. Not for travelling. Low ship."

"Do you see a name on the ship?"

". . . *ana* . . . can't see it properly."

"What is this man doing here?"

"He had a fit here, and fell down and died, and somebody left him here. Somebody picked the body up . . . into the water . . ."

Sybil showed signs of strain and I decided to take her out of trance to avoid later fatigue. As soon as she was "back" to her own self, not remembering anything, of course, that had come through her the past hour, I turned to Miss Frost to find out what it was exactly that had occurred here of an unusual nature.

"Always this uneasy feeling . . . causing nervousness . . .

more at night . . ." she explained, "and noises like small fire-crackers."

Miss Frost is in her thirties, pleasant and soft-spoken, and she holds a responsible position in San Francisco business life.

"If you pay no attention to it," she added, "then it becomes more intense, louder."

"Doesn't want to be ignored, eh?" I said.

"Occasionally at night you hear footsteps in the living room."

"When it is empty?"

"Of course."

"What does it sound like?"

"As if there were no carpets . . . like walking on boards . . . a man's footsteps."

"How often?"

"Maybe three times . . . last time was about three months ago. We've been here four years, but we only heard it about half a year after we moved in. On one occasion there was a noise inside the buffet as if there were a motor in it, which of course there isn't."

"Has anyone else had any experiences of an unusual nature in this house?"

"A painter who was painting a small room in the rear of the house suddenly asked me for a glass of water because he didn't feel well. Because of the noises."

I turned to Miss Frost's aunt, who had sat by quietly, listening to our conversation.

"Have you heard these footsteps?"

"Yes," she said. "I checked up and there was nobody there who could have caused them. That was around two in the morning. Sometimes around five or six also. They went around the bed. We had the light on, but it continued."

With the help of Miss Frost, I was able to trace the history of the area. Originally Alameda was inhabited by Indians and much of it was used as burial ground. Even today bones are dug up now and again. Before the house was built here, the ground was part of the Cohen estate. The water is not far from the house, although it is not actually visible from the house. Prior to Miss Frost, a Mr. Bequette owned the house, but what interested me far more than Mr. Bequette was the fact that many years ago a hospital occupied the land at this spot. Nothing is left of the old hospital.

In 1941, allegedly, the son of the family who lived at this house was killed in action during the war. A mysterious letter reached Miss Frost in February of 1961 addressed to a B. Biehm at her address, but she could not locate this man.

None of this takes us back to 1902 when Dominic said he lived. A Japanese-born Italian sailor serving in the U.S. Navy is a pretty unusual combination. Was Dominic his family name?

I decided to query the Navy Department in the hope that they might have some records about such a man, although I had learned on previous occasions that Naval records that far back are not always complete.

On December 29, 1966, I received this reply from the office of the Chief of Naval Operations:

> *Dear Mr. Holzer:*
> *In reply to your letter of 8 December, we have been unable to find either DOMINIC or Oswald GREGORY in the lists of U.S. Navy officers during this century. The Navy Registers for the period around 1902 list no U.S. Naval ship named TRIANA.*
> *We have very little information on Alameda Island during the early 1900's. The attached extract from the Naval Air Station history, however, may be of some use.*
> > *Sincerely yours,*
> > *F. KENT LOOMIS*
> > *Captain, USN (Ret.)*
> > *Asst. Director of Naval History*

Captain Loomis enclosed a history of the Alameda installations that seems to confirm the picture painted of the area (prior to that installation) by the ghostly sailor:

> *The real story of the U.S. Naval Air Station, Alameda, is how it has "arisen from the waters." How it was thrown up from the bottom of San Francisco Bay; how it was anchored to the earth with grass roots; how it was, by accident, the scene of some of the earliest flights in America. This is the romance of Alameda.*
> *The Navy Department first began to consider the site now occupied by the air station toward the end of the First World War. The intention was to utilize the site as a destroyer base, but the war was over before the plans could be perfected. The land then lapsed into*

oblivion. It was a rather barren land. *When the tide was out it was odious and disagreeable looking. Since people who boil soap are not fastidious concerning olfactory matters, the Twenty Mule Team Borax Company located the site of their first efforts near the "Mole" which went to San Francisco's ferries.*

The main part of Alameda was very pretty, covered with good rich "bottom land" and shade trees, from which it had derived its name during the Spanish occupation days. "Alameda" means "shade" or "shady lane."

In 1776 the land had been granted to Don Luis Peralta, a grizzled old man who immigrated from Tabac in Sonora. His life as a soldier had been crowded with 40 years of service to His Majesty, the King of Spain, and ten children. It was only a small part of the 43,000 acres granted him by a grateful Spain.

He distributed his lands among his children when he felt his time had come. Although the peninsula of Alameda was in the most part fertile, the western tip of it was nothing but barren sands and tidal flats.

In 1876, engineers cut a channel through the peninsula's tip which linked San Leandro Bay with the main bay, and Alameda became an island. Deep water was on the way and dredging was begun to effect this end.

The inability of the U.S. Navy librarian to identify a ship named the *Triana* did not stop me from looking further, of course. Was there ever such a ship? A Captain Treeana commanded one of the three ships of Christopher Columbus and consequently there are towns named for him in the land he and his shipmates helped discover. Spelled nowadays Triana, one of them is in Alabama, and in the city of Huntsville there is a Triana Boulevard. It seems highly likely that so famous a captain's name should at one time or other have been chosen as the name of a ship.

Meanwhile, back at the house, things remained quiet and peaceful for forty-eight hours. Miss Frost was happy for the first time in years.

And then the footsteps and other noises resumed. Dominic wasn't going to ship out, after all.

That was in July 1965. I made certain suggestions. Close the door mentally; gently tell the ghost he must go, over and over again. He was free now to do so—proof of which was the fact that his footsteps, once confined to the living room area, were now heard all over the house.

A year later I still had no news from Alameda. Perhaps no news is good news and the ghostly sailor roams no more.

Connecticut

The Tombstones and the Officer

Betty Ann Tylaska lives in a seaport in Connecticut. Her family is a prominent one going back to Colonial days, and they still occupy a house built by her great-great-great-grandfather for his daughter and her husband back in 1807.

Mrs. Tylaska and her husband, a Navy officer, were in the process of restoring the venerable old house to its former glory. Neither of them had the slightest interest in the supernatural, and to them such things as ghosts simply did not exist except in children's tales.

The first time Mrs. Tylaska noticed anything unusual was one night when she was washing dishes in the kitchen. Suddenly she had the strong feeling that she was being watched. She turned around and caught a glimpse of a man standing in the doorway between the kitchen and the living room of the downstairs part of the house. She saw him only for a moment, but long enough to notice his dark blue suit and silver buttons. Her first impression was that it must be her husband, who of course sometimes wore a Navy uniform. But on checking she found him upstairs, wearing entirely different clothes.

She shrugged the matter off as probably a hallucination due to her tiredness, but the man in blue kept returning. On several occasions, the same uncanny feeling of being watched came over her, and when she turned around, there was the man in the dark blue suit.

It came as a relief to her when her mother confessed that she too had seen the ghostly visitor—always at the same spot, between living room and kitchen. Finally she informed her husband, and to her surprise, he did not laugh at her. But he suggested that if it were a ghost, perhaps one of her ancestors was checking up on them.

Perhaps he wanted to make sure they restored the house properly and did not make any unwanted changes. They were doing a great deal of painting in the process of restoring the house, and whatever paint residue was left they would spill against an old stone wall in the back of the house.

Gradually the old stones were covered with paint of various hues.

One day Mr. Tylaska found himself in front of these stones. For want of anything better to do at the moment, he started to study them. To his amazement, he discovered that one of the stones was different from the others: it was long and flat. He called his wife and they investigated the strange stone; upon freeing it from the wall, they saw to their horror that it was a gravestone—her great-great-great-grandfather's tombstone, to be exact.

Inquiry at the local church cleared up the mystery of how the tombstone had gotten out of the cemetery. It seems that all the family members had been buried in a small cemetery nearby. But it filled up, and one day a larger cemetery was started. The bodies were removed to it and a larger monument had been erected over great-great-great-grandfather's tomb. Since the original stone was of no use any longer, it was left behind. Somehow the stone got used when the old wall was being built. But evidently great-great-great-grandfather did not like the idea. Was that the reason for his visits? After all, who likes having paint splashed on one's tombstone?

The Tylaska family held a meeting to decide what to do about it. They could not very well put two tombstones on grandad's grave. What would the other ancestors think? Everybody would want to have two tombstones then; and while it might be good news to the stonecutter, it would not be a thing to do in practical New England.

So they stood the old tombstone upright in their own backyard. It was nice having grandad with them that way, and if he felt like a visit, why, that was all right with them too.

From the moment when they gave the tombstone a place of

honor, the gentleman in the dark blue suit and the silver buttons never came back. But Mrs. Tylaska does not particularly mind. Two Navy men in the house might have been too much of a distraction anyway.

A
Houseful
of Ghosts

Life can be pretty dull in central Connecticut, especially in the winter. It isn't any more fun being a ghost in central Connecticut, so one cannot really hold it against these Stay-Behinds if they amuse themselves as best they can in the afterlife. Today the house shows its age; it isn't in good condition, and needs lots of repairs. The family isn't as large as it was before some of the younger generation moved out to start lives of their own, but it's still a busy house and a friendly one, ghosts or no ghosts. It stands on a quiet country road off the main route, and on a clear day you can see the Massachusetts border in the distance; that is, if you are looking for it. It is hardly noticeable, for in this part of the country, all New England looks the same.

Because of the incredible nature of the many incidents, the family wants no publicity, no curious tourists, no reporters. To defer to their wishes, I changed the family name to help them retain that anonymity, and the peace and quiet of their country house. The house in question was already old when it appeared on a map of the town drawn in 1761. The present owners, the Harveys, have lived in it on and off all their lives. Mrs. Harvey's great-great-grandparents bought it from the original builder, and her great-great-grandfather died at the old homestead in 1858. Likewise, her great-great-grandmother passed on in 1871, at the age of eighty, and again it happened at home. One of their children died in 1921, at age ninety-one, also at home.

This is important, you see, because it accounts for the events that transpired later in the lives of their descendants. A daughter named Julia married an outsider and moved to another state, but considers herself part of the family just the same, so much so that her second home was still the old homestead in central Connecticut. Another daughter, Martha, was Mrs. Harvey's great-grandmother. Great-grandmother Martha died at age ninety-one, also in the house. Then there was an aunt, a sister of her great-great-grandfather's by the name of Nancy, who came to live with them when she was a widow; she lived to be ninety and died in the house. They still have some of her furniture there. Mrs. Harvey's grandparents had only one child, Viola, who became her mother, but they took in boarders, mostly men working in the nearby sawmills. One of these boarders died in the house too, but his name is unknown. Possibly several others died there also.

Of course the house doesn't look today the way it originally did; additions were built onto the main part, stairs were moved, a well in the cellar was filled in because members of the family going down for cider used to fall into it, and many of the rooms that later became bedrooms originally had other purposes. For instance, daughter Marjorie's bedroom was called the harness room because horses' harnesses were once made in it, and the room of one of the sons used to be called the cheese room for obvious reasons. What became a sewing room was originally used as a pantry, with shelves running across the south wall.

The fact that stairs were changed throughout the house is important, because in the mind of those who lived in the past, the original stairs would naturally take precedence over later additions or changes. Thus phantoms may appear out of the wall, seemingly without reason, except that they would be walking up staircases that no longer exist.

Mrs. Harvey was born in the house, but at age four her parents moved away from it, and did not return until much later. Mrs. Harvey still recalls an incident even from that early age. When she was only four, she remembers very clearly an old lady she had never seen before appear at her bedside. She cried, but when she told her parents about it, they assured her it was just a dream. But Mrs. Harvey knew she had not dreamed the incident; she remembered every detail of the old lady's dress.

When she was twelve years old, at a time when the family had returned to live in the house, she was in one of the upstairs bedrooms and again the old lady appeared to her. But when she talked about it to their parents, the matter was immediately dropped. As Frances Harvey grew up in the house, she couldn't help but notice some strange goings-on. A lamp moved by itself, without anyone being near it. Many times she could feel a presence walking close behind her in the upstairs part of the house, but when she turned around, she was alone. Nor was she the only one to notice the strange occurrences. Her brothers heard footsteps around their beds, and complained about someone bending over them, yet no one was to be seen. The doors to the bedrooms would open by themselves at night, so much so that the boys tied the door latches together so that they could not open by themselves. Just the same, when morning came, the doors were wide open with the knot still in place.

It was at that time that her father got into the habit of taking an after-dinner walk around the house before retiring. Many times he told the family of seeing a strange light going through the upstairs rooms, a glowing luminosity for which there was no rational explanation. Whenever Frances Harvey had to be alone upstairs she felt uncomfortable, but when she mentioned this to her parents she was told not to mind since all old houses made one feel like that. One evening, Frances was playing a game with her grandfather when both of them clearly heard footsteps coming up the back stairs. But her grandfather didn't budge. When Frances asked him who this could possibly be, he merely shrugged and said there was plenty of room for *everyone*.

As the years passed, the Harveys would come back to the house from time to time to visit. On these occasions, Frances would wake up in the night because someone was bending over her. At other times there was a heavy depression on the bed as if someone were sitting there! Too terrified to tell anyone about it, she kept her experiences to herself for the time being.

Then, in the early 1940s, Frances married, and with her husband and two children, eventually returned to the house to live there permanently with her grandparents. No sooner had they moved in when the awful feeling came back in the night. Finally she told her husband, who of course scoffed at the idea of ghosts.

The most active area in the house seemed to be upstairs, roughly from her son Don's closet through her daughter Lolita's room, and especially the front hall and stairs. It felt as if someone were standing on the landing of the front stairs, just watching.

This goes back a long time. Mrs. Harvey's mother frequently complained, when working in the attic, that all of a sudden she would feel someone standing next to her, someone she could not see.

One day Mrs. Harvey and her youngest daughter went grocery shopping. After putting the groceries away, Mrs. Harvey reclined on the living room couch while the girl sat in the dining room reading. Suddenly they heard a noise like thunder, even though the sky outside was clear. It came again, only this time it sounded closer, as if it were upstairs! When it happened the third time, it was accompanied by a sound as if someone were making up the bed in Mrs. Harvey's son's room upstairs.

They had left the bed in disorder because they had been in a hurry to go shopping. No one else could have gone upstairs, and yet when they entered the son's room, the bed was made up as smoothly as possible. As yet, part of the family still scoffed at the idea of having ghosts in the house, and considered the mother's ideas as dreams or hallucinations. They were soon to change their minds, however, when it happened to them as well.

The oldest daughter felt very brave and called up the stairs, "Little ghosties, where are you?" Her mother told her she had better not challenge them, but the others found it amusing. That night she came downstairs a short time after she had gone to bed, complaining that she felt funny in her room, but thought it was just her imagination. The following night, she awoke to the feeling that someone was bending over her. One side of her pillow was pulled away from her head as though a hand had pushed it down. She called out and heard footsteps receding from her room, followed by heavy rumblings in the attic above. Quickly she ran into her sister's room, where both of them lay awake the rest of the night listening to the rumbling and footsteps walking around overhead. The next day she noticed a dusty black footprint on the light-colored scatter rug next to her bed. It was in the exact location where she had felt someone standing and bending over her. Nobody's footprint in the house matched the black footprint, for it was long and very narrow. At this point the girls purchased special night lights and left them on in the hope of sleeping peacefully.

One day Mrs. Harvey felt brave, and started up the stairs in response to footsteps coming from her mother's bedroom. She stopped, and as the footsteps approached the top of the stairs, a loud ticking noise came with them, like a huge pocket watch.

Quickly she ran down the stairs and outside to get her son to be a witness to it. Sure enough, he too could hear the ticking noise. This was followed by doors opening and closing by themselves. Finally, they dared go upstairs, and when they entered the front bedroom, they noticed a very strong, sweet smell of perfume. When two of the daughters came home from work that evening, the family compared notes and it was discovered that they, too, had smelled the strange perfume and heard the ticking noise upstairs. They concluded that one of their ghosts, at least, was a man.

About that time, the youngest daughter reported seeing an old woman in her room, standing at a bureau with something shiny in her hand. The ghost handed it to her but she was too frightened to receive it. Since her description of the woman had been very detailed, Mrs. Harvey took out the family album and asked her daughter to look through it in the hope that she might identify the ghostly visitor. When they came to one particular picture, the girl let out a small cry: that was the woman she had seen! It turned out to be Mrs. Harvey's great-great-aunt Julia, the same woman whom Mrs. Harvey herself had seen when she was twelve years old. Evidently, the lady was staying around.

Mrs. Harvey's attention was deflected from the phenomena in the house by her mother's illness. Like a dutiful daughter, she attended her to the very last, but in March of that year her mother passed away. Whether there is any connection with her mother's death or not, the phenomena started to increase greatly, both in volume and intensity, beginning on July 20. Mrs. Harvey was hurrying one morning to get ready to take her daughter Lolita to the center of town so she could get a ride to work. Her mind was preoccupied with domestic chores, when a car came down the road, with brakes squealing. Out of habit, she hurried to the living room window to make sure that none of their cats had been hit by the car. This had been a habit of her mother's and hers, whenever there was the sound of sudden brakes outside.

As she did so, for just a fleeting glance, she saw her late mother looking out of her favorite window. It didn't register at first, then Mrs. Harvey realized her mother couldn't possibly have been there. However, since time was of the essence, Mrs. Harvey and Lolita left for town without saying anything to any of the others in the house. When they returned, her daughter Marjorie was standing outside waiting for them. She complained of hearing someone moving around in the living room just after they had left, and it sounded just like Grandma when she straightened out the couch and chair covers.

It frightened her, so she decided to wait in the dining room for her mother's return. But while there, she heard footsteps coming from the living room and going into the den, then the sound of clothes being folded. This was something Mrs. Harvey's mother was also in the habit of doing there. It was enough for Marjorie to run outside the house and wait there. Together with her sister and mother, she returned to the living room, only to find the chair cover straightened. The sight of the straightened chair cover made the blood freeze in Mrs. Harvey's veins; she recalled vividly how she had asked her late mother not to bother straightening the chair covers during her illness, because it hurt her back. In reply, her mother had said, "Too bad I can't come back and do it after I die."

Daughter Jane was married to a Navy man, who used to spend his leaves at the old house. Even during his courtship days, he and Mrs. Harvey's mother got along well, and they used to do crossword puzzles together. He was sleeping at the house some time after the old lady's death, when he awoke to see her standing by his bed with her puzzle book and pencil in hand. It was clear to Mrs. Harvey by now that her late mother had joined the circle of dead relatives to keep a watch on her and the family. Even while she was ill, Mrs. Harvey's mother wanted to help in the house. One day after her death, Mrs. Harvey was baking a custard pie and lay down on the couch for a few minutes while it was baking.

She must have fallen asleep, for she awoke to the voice of her mother saying, "Your pie won't burn, will it?" Mrs. Harvey hurriedly got up and checked; the pie was just right and would have burned if it had been left in any longer. That very evening, something else happened. Mrs. Harvey wanted to watch a certain program that came on television at seven-thirty, but she was tired and fell asleep on the couch in the late afternoon. Suddenly she heard her mother's voice say to her, "It's time for your program, dear." Mrs. Harvey looked at the clock, and it was exactly seven-thirty. Of course, her mother did exactly the same type of thing when she was living, so it wasn't too surprising that she should continue with her concerned habits after she passed on into the next dimension.

But if Mrs. Harvey's mother had joined the ghostly crew in the house, she was by no means furnishing the bulk of the phenomena—not by a long shot. Lolita's room upstairs seemed to be the center of many activities, with her brother Don's room next to hers also very much involved. Someone was walking from her bureau to her closet, and her brother heard the footsteps too. Lolita looked up and saw a man in a uniform with gold buttons, standing in the back of her closet. At other times she smelled perfume and heard the sound of someone dressing near her bureau. All the time she heard people going up the front stairs mumbling, then going into her closet where the sound stopped abruptly. Yet, they could not see anyone on such occasions.

Daughter Jane wasn't left out of any of this either. Many nights she would feel someone standing next to her bed, between the bed and the wall. She saw three different people, and felt hands trying to lift her out of bed. To be sure, she could not see their faces; their shapes were like dark shadows. Marjorie, sleeping in the room next to Jane's, also experienced an attempt by some unseen forces to get her out of bed. She grabbed the headboard to stop herself from falling when she noticed the apparition of the same old woman whom Mrs. Harvey had seen the time she heard several people leave her room for the front hall.

One night she awoke to catch a glimpse of someone in a long black coat hurrying through the hall. Mumbling was heard in that direction, so she put her ear against the door to see if she could hear any words, but she couldn't make out any. Marjorie, too, saw the old woman standing at the foot of her bed—the same old woman whom Mrs. Harvey had seen when she was twelve years old. Of course, that isn't too surprising; the room Marjorie slept in used to be Julia's a long time ago. Lolita also had her share of experiences: sounds coming up from the cellar bothering her, footsteps, voices, even the sound of chains. It seemed to her that they came right out of the wall by her head, where there used to be stairs. Finally, it got so bad that Lolita asked her mother to sleep with her. When Mrs. Harvey complied, the two women clearly saw a glow come in from the living room and go to where the shelves used to be. Then there was the sound of dishes, and even the smell of food.

Obviously, the ghostly presences were still keeping house in their own fashion, reliving some happy or at least busy moments from their own past. By now Mr. Harvey was firmly convinced that he shared the house with a number of dead relatives, if not friends. Several times he woke to the sound of bottles being placed on the bureau. One night he awoke because the bottom of the bed was shaking hard; as soon as he was fully awake, it stopped. This was followed by a night in which Mrs. Harvey could see a glow pass through the room at the bottom of the bed. When "they" got to the hall door, which was shut, she could hear it open, but it actually did not move. Yet the sound was that of a door opening. Next she heard several individuals walk up the stairs, mumbling as they went.

The following night a light stopped by their fireplace, and as she looked closely it resembled a figure bending down. It got so that they compared notes almost every morning to see what had been happening in their very busy home. One moonlit night Mrs. Harvey woke to see the covers of her bed folded in half, down the entire length of the bed. Her husband was fully covered, but she was totally uncovered. At the same time, she saw some dark shadows by the side of the bed. She felt someone's hand holding her own, pulling her gently. Terrified, she couldn't move, and just lay there wondering what would happen next. Then the blankets were replaced as before, she felt something cold touch her forehead, and the ghosts left. But the Stay-Behinds were benign, and meant no harm. Some nights, Mrs. Harvey would wake up because of the cold air, and notice that the blankets were standing up straight from the bed as if held by someone. Even after she pushed them back hard, they would not stay in place.

On the other hand, there were times when she accidentally uncovered herself at night and felt someone putting the covers back on her, as if to protect her from the night chills. This was more important, as the house has no central heating. Of course it wasn't always clear what the ghosts wanted from her. On the one hand, they were clearly concerned with her well-being and that of the family; on the other, they seemed to crave attention for themselves also.

Twice they tried to lift Mrs. Harvey out of her bed. She felt herself raised several inches above it by unseen hands, and tried to call out to her husband but somehow couldn't utter a single word. This was followed by a strange, dreamlike state in which she remembered being taken to the attic and shown something. Unfortunately she could not remember it afterwards, except that she had been to the attic and how the floorboards looked there; she also recalled that the attic was covered with black dust. When morning came, she took a look at her feet: they were dusty, and the bottom of her bed was grayish as if from dust. Just as she was contemplating these undeniable facts, her husband asked her what had been the matter with her during the night. Evidently he had awakened to find her gone from the bed.

One night daughter Marjorie was out on a date. Mrs. Harvey awoke to the sound of a car pulling into the driveway, bringing Marjorie home. From her bed she could clearly see four steps of the back stairs. As she lay there, she saw the shape of a woman coming down without any sound, sort of floating down the stairs. She was dressed in a white chiffon dress. At the same moment, her daughter Marjorie entered the living room. She too saw the girl in the chiffon dress come down the stairs into the living room and disappear through a door to the other bedroom. Even though the door was open wide and there was plenty of room to go through the opening, evidently the ghostly lady preferred to walk through the door.

The miscellaneous Stay-Behinds tried hard to take part in the daily lives of the flesh-and-blood people in the house. Many times the plants in the living room would be rearranged and attended to by unseen hands. The Harveys could clearly see the plants move, yet no one was near them; no one, that is, visible to the human eye. There was a lot of mumbling now, and eventually they could make out some words. One day daughter Marjorie heard her late grandmother say to her that "they" would be back in three weeks. Sure enough, not a single incident of a ghostly nature occurred for three weeks. Three weeks later to the day, the phenomena began again. Where had the ghosts gone in the meantime? On another occasion, Marjorie heard someone say, "That is Jane on that side of the bed, but who is that on the other side? The bed looks so smooth." The remark made sense to Mrs. Harvey. Her late mother sometimes slept with Jane, when she was still in good health. On the other hand, daughter Marjorie likes to sleep perfectly flat, so her bed does look rather smooth.

Average people believe ghosts only walk at night. Nothing

could be further from the truth, as Mrs. Harvey will testify. Frequently, when she was alone in the house during the daytime, she would hear doors upstairs bang shut and open again. One particular day, she heard the sound of someone putting things on Jane's bureau, so she tried to go up and see what it was. Carefully tiptoeing up the stairs to see if she could actually trap a ghost, she found herself halfway along the hall when she heard footsteps coming along the foot of son Don's bed, in her direction. Quickly, she hurried back down the stairs and stopped halfway down. The footsteps sounded like a woman's, and suddenly there was the rustle of a taffeta gown. With a whooshing sound, the ghost passed Mrs. Harvey and went into Jane's room. Mrs. Harvey waited, rooted to the spot on the stairs.

A moment later the woman's footsteps came back, only this time someone walked with her, someone heavier. They went back through Don's room, and ended up in Lolita's closet—the place where Lolita had seen the man in the uniform with the shining gold buttons. Mrs. Harvey did not follow immediately, but that night she decided to go up to Lolita's room and have another look at the closet. As she approached the door to the room it opened, which wasn't unusual since it was in the habit of opening at the slightest vibration. But before Mrs. Harvey could close it, it shut itself tight and the latch moved into place of its own accord. Mrs. Harvey didn't wait around for anything further that night.

For awhile there was peace. But in October the phenomena resumed. One night Mrs. Harvey woke up when she saw a shadow blocking the light coming from the dining room. She looked toward the door and saw a lady dressed all in black come into her bedroom and stand close to her side of the bed. This time she clearly heard her speak.

"Are you ready? It is almost time to go."

With that, the apparition turned and started up the stairs. The stairs looked unusually light, as if moonlight were illuminating them. When the woman in black got to the top step, all was quiet and the stairs were dark again, as before. Mrs. Harvey could see her clothes plainly enough, but not her face. She noticed that the apparition had carried a pouch-style pocketbook, which she had put over her arm so that her hands would be free to lift up her skirts as she went up the stairs. The next morning, Mrs. Harvey told her husband of the visitation. He assured her she must have

dreamed it all. But before she could answer, her daughter
Marjorie came in and said that she had heard someone talking in
the night, something about coming, and it being almost time. She
saw a figure at the foot of her bed, which she described as similar
to what Mrs. Harvey had seen.

The night before that Thanksgiving, Marjorie heard footsteps
come down the stairs. She was in bed and tried to get up to see
who it was, but somehow couldn't move at all, except to open her
eyes to see five people standing at the foot of her bed! Two of them
were women, the others seemed just outlines or shadows. One of
the two women wore an old-fashioned-shaped hat, and she looked
very stern. As Marjorie was watching the group, she managed to
roll over a little in her bed and felt someone next to her. She felt
relieved at the thought that it was her mother, but then whoever it
was got up and left with the others in the group. All the time they
kept talking among themselves, but Marjorie could not understand what was being said. Still talking, the ghostly visitors went
back up the stairs.

Nothing much happened until Christmastime. Again the footsteps running up and down the stairs resumed, yet no one was
seen. Christmas night, Jane and her mother heard walking in the
room above the living room, where Mrs. Harvey's mother used to
sleep. At that time, Mr. Harvey was quite ill and was sleeping in
what used to be the sewing room so as not to awaken when his
wife got up early.

On two different occasions Mrs. Harvey had "visitors." The
first time someone lifted her a few inches off the bed. Evidently
someone else was next to her in bed, for when she extended her
hand that person got up and left. Next she heard footsteps going
up the stairs and someone laughing, then all was quiet again.
About a week later, she woke one night to feel someone pulling
hard on her elbow and ankle. She hung onto the top of her bed
with her other hand. But the unseen entities pushed, forcing her
to brace herself against the wall.

Suddenly it all stopped, yet there were no sounds of anyone
leaving. Mrs. Harvey jumped out of bed and tried to turn the light
on. It wouldn't go on. She went back to bed when she heard a
voice telling her not to worry, that her husband would be all right.
She felt relieved at the thought, when the voice added, "But you
won't be." Then the unseen voice calmly informed her that she

would die in an accident caused by a piece of bark from some sort of tree. That was all the voice chose to tell her, but it was enough to start her worrying. Under the circumstances, and in order not to upset her family, she kept quiet about it, eventually thinking that she had dreamed the whole incident. After all, if it were just a dream, there was no point in telling anyone, and if it were true, there was nothing she could do anyway, so there was no point in worrying her family. She had almost forgotten the incident when she did have an accident about a week later. She hurt her head rather badly in the woodshed, requiring medical attention. While she was still wondering whether that was the incident referred to by the ghostly voice, she had a second accident: a heavy pitchfork fell on her and knocked her unconscious.

But the voice had said that she would die in an accident, so Mrs. Harvey wasn't at all sure that the two incidents, painful though they had been, were what the voice had referred to. Evidently, ghosts get a vicarious thrill out of making people worry, because Mrs. Harvey is alive and well, years after the unseen voice had told her she would die in an accident.

But if it were not enough to cope with ghost people, Mrs. Harvey also had the company of a ghost dog. Their favorite pet, Lucy, passed into eternal dogdom the previous March. Having been treated as a member of the family, she had been permitted to sleep in the master bedroom, but as she became older she started wetting the rug, so eventually she had to be kept out.

After the dog's death, Marjorie offered her mother another dog, but Mrs. Harvey didn't want a substitute for Lucy; no other dog could take her place. Shortly after the offer and its refusal, Lolita heard a familiar scratch at the bathroom door. It sounded exactly as Lucy had always sounded when Lolita came home late at night. At first, Mrs. Harvey thought her daughter had just imagined it, but then the familiar wet spot reappeared on the bedroom rug. They tried to look for a possible leak in the ceiling, but could find no rational cause for the rug to be wet. The wet spot remained for about a month. During that time, several of the girls heard a noise that reminded them of Lucy walking about. Finally the rug dried out and Lucy's ghost stopped walking.

For several years the house has been quiet now. Have the ghosts gone on to their just rewards, been reincarnated, or have they simply tired of living with flesh-and-blood relatives? Stay-Behinds generally stay indefinitely; unless, of course, they feel they are really not wanted. Or perhaps they just got bored with it all.

District
of Columbia

The White House Ghosts

With so many skeletons still in the White House from the previous administration, I doubt that President Clinton will want to worry about the ethereal presences in his new home. But "they" may just be kind of glad he is in there now, and manifest somewhere along the line. Especially that old worrier Abe Lincoln, who might see in Clinton a kindred—ah—spirit.

Investigating the persistent reports of ghosts in the White House is not difficult: getting there is. I don't think anyone has had more trouble getting into the White House for a specific purpose than I, except, perhaps, some presidential aspirants such as Thomas E. Dewey. But Mr. Dewey's purpose was a lot easier to explain than mine. How do you tell an official at the presidential mansion that you would like to go to the Lincoln Bedroom to see whether Lincoln's ghost is still there? How do you make it plain that you're not looking for sensationalism, that you're not bringing along a whole covey of newspaper people, all of which can only lead to unfavorable publicity for the inhabitants of the White House, whoever they may be at the time?

Naturally, this was the very difficult task to which I had put myself several years ago. Originally, when I was collecting material for *Window to the Past*, I had envisioned myself going to the Lincoln Bedroom and possibly the East Room in the White House, hoping to verify and authenticate apparitions that had occurred to a number of people in those areas. But all my repeated requests for permission to visit the White House in the company of a reputable psychic were turned down. Even when I promised to submit my findings and the writings based on those

findings to White House scrutiny prior to publication, I was told
that my request could not be granted.

The first reason given was that it was not convenient because
the president and his family were in. Then it was not convenient
because they would be away. Once I was turned down because my
visit could not be cleared sufficiently with Security, and anyway,
the part of the White House I wanted to visit was private.

I never gave up. Deep down I had the feeling that the White
House belongs to the people and is not a piece of real estate on
which anyone—even the presidential family—may hang out a "No
Trespassers" sign. I still think so. However, I got nowhere as long
as the Johnsons were in the White House.

I tried again when I started work on this book. A colonel
stationed in the White House, whom I met through a mutual
friend, Countess Gertrude d'Amecourt, tried hard to get permission for me to come and investigate. He, too, failed.

Next, I received a letter, quite unexpectedly, from the Reverend Thomas W. Dettman of Niagara, Wisconsin. He knew a number of very prominent men in the federal government and offered
to get me the permission I needed. These men, he explained, had
handled government investigations for him before, and he was
sure they would be happy to be of assistance if he asked them. He
was even sure they would carry a lot of weight with the president.
They knew him well, he asserted. Mr. Dettman had been associated with the Wisconsin Nixon for President Committee, and offered to help in any way he could.

After thanking Mr. Dettman for his offer, I heard nothing
further for a time. Then he wrote me again explaining that he had
as yet not been able to get me into the Lincoln Bedroom, but that
he was still working on it. He had asked the help of Representative
John Byrnes of Wisconsin in the matter, and I would hear further
about it. Then Mr. Dettman informed me that he had managed to
arrange for me to be given "a special tour" of the White House,
and, to the best of his knowledge, that included the East Room. He
then asked that I contact William E. Timmons, assistant to the
president, for details.

I was, of course, elated. Imagine, a special tour of the White
House! What could be better than that?

With his letter, Mr. Dettman had included a letter from Senator William Proxmire of Wisconsin, in which the Senator noted

that I would not be able to do research in the Lincoln Bedroom, but that I would be given the special tour of the White House.

I hurriedly wrote a thank-you note to Mr. Dettman, and started to make plans to bring a medium to Washington with me. A few days later Mr. Dettman wrote me again. He had received a call from the White House concerning the tour. He could, he explained, in no way guarantee what *kind* of tour I would be given, nor what I would see. He had done everything possible to help me and hoped I would not be disappointed.

Whether my own sixth sense was working or not, I suddenly thought I had better look into the nature of that "special tour" myself. I wrote and asked whether I would be permitted to spend half an hour in the East Room, since the Lincoln Bedroom had been denied me. Back came a letter dated May 14, 1970, on White House stationery, and signed by John S. Davies, Special Assistant to the President, Office White House Visitors.

"Senator Proxmire's recent letter to Mr. William Timmons concerning your most recent request to visit the White House has been referred to me, as this office is responsible for White House visitors. Unfortunately, as we have pointed out, we are unable to arrange for you to visit the Lincoln Bedroom, as this room is in the President's personal residence area, which is not open to visitors. If you wish to arrange an early-morning special tour, I suggest you contact Senator Proxmire's office. You are also most welcome to come to the White House any time during the regular visiting hours."

I decided to telephone Mr. Davies, since the day of my planned visit was close at hand. It was only then that I realized what that famous "special tour" really was. It meant that I, along with who else might be present at the time at the White House gates, would be permitted to walk through the part of the White House open to all visitors. I couldn't bring a tape recorder. I could not sit down or tarry along the way. I had to follow along with the group, glance up at whatever might be interesting, and be on my way again like a good little citizen. What, then, was so special about that tour, I inquired? Nothing really, I was told, but that is what it is known as. It is called a special tour because you have to have the request of either a senator or a representative from your home state.

I canceled my visit and dismissed the medium. But my reading public is large, and other offers to help me came my way.

Debbie Fitz is a teenage college student who wanted me to
lecture at her school. In return, she offered to get me into the
White House, or at least try to. I smiled at her courage, but told
her to go right ahead and try. She wrote a letter to Miss Nixon,
whom she thought would be favorable to her request, being of the
same age group. After explaining her own interest in ESP research and the importance this field has in this day and age for the
young, she went on to explain who I was and that I had previously
been denied admittance to the White House areas I wished to do
research in. She wrote:

*All he wants to do is take a psychic medium into the room and
scientifically record any phenomena that may exist. This will not
involve staying overnight; it can be done during the day at your
convenience. All investigations are conducted in a scientific manner and are fully documented. It is well known that Lincoln himself
was psychic and held seances in the White House. Wouldn't you, as
a student of White House history and a member of the young, open-
minded generation, like to find out whether or not this room is really
haunted? This will also provide an opportunity for young people
who are interested in other things besides riots and demonstrations
to benefit intellectually from Mr. Holzer's efforts.*

Debbie Fitz never received a reply or an acknowledgment. I,
of course, never heard about the matter again.

Try as I would, I was rebuffed. Just the same, interest in the
haunted aspects of the nation's Executive Mansion remains at a
high level. Several Washington newspapers carried stories featur-
ing some of the psychic occurrences inside the White House, and
whenever I appeared on Washington television, I was invariably
asked about the ghosts at the White House. Perhaps the best account of the psychic state of affairs at number 1600 Pennsylvania
Avenue was written by the *Washington Post* reporter Jacqueline
Lawrence.

"The most troubled spirit of 1600 Pennsylvania Avenue is
Abraham Lincoln, who during his own lifetime claimed to receive
regular visits from his two dead sons, Pat and Willie." After reporting the well-known premonitory dream in which Lincoln saw

himself dead in a casket in the East Room, Miss Lawrence goes on to report that Mrs. Franklin Delano Roosevelt's servant, Mary Evan, had reported seeing Lincoln on the bed in the northwest bedroom, pulling on his boots. "Other servants said they had seen him lying quietly in his bed, and still others vowed that he periodically stood at the oval window over the main entrance of the White House. Mrs. Roosevelt herself never saw Lincoln, but she did admit that when working late she frequently felt a ghostly sort of presence."

Among the visitors to the White House who had experienced psychic occurrences was the late Queen Wilhelmina of the Netherlands. Asleep in the Queen's Bedroom, she heard someone knock at her door, got up, opened it, and saw the ghost of President Lincoln standing there looking at her. She fainted, and by the time she had come to he was gone.

"According to the legend, the spirit of Lincoln is especially troubled and restless on the eve of national calamities such as war."

But Lincoln is not the only ghost at the White House. Household members of President Taft have observed the ghost of Abigail Adams walking right through the closed doors of the East Room with her arms outstretched. And who knows what other specters reside in these ancient and troubled walls?

That all is not known about the White House may be seen from a dispatch of the *New York Daily News* dated November 25, 1969, concerning two new rooms unearthed at the White House. "Two hitherto unknown rooms, believed to date back to the time of Thomas Jefferson, have been unearthed in the White House a few yards away from the presidential swimming pool. The discovery was made as excavation continued on the larger work area for the White House press corps. The subterranean rooms, which White House curator James Ketchum described as storage or coal bins, were believed among the earliest built at the White House. Filled with dirt, they contained broken artifacts believed to date back to President Lincoln's administration."

When I discussed my difficulties in receiving permission for a White House investigation with prominent people in Washington, it was suggested to me that I turn my attention to Ford's Theater, or the Parker House—both places associated with the death of President Lincoln. I have not done so, for the simple reason that in my estimation the ghost of Lincoln is nowhere else to be found but where it mattered to him: in the White House. If there is a transitory impression left behind at Ford's Theater, where he was shot, or the Parker House, where he eventually died some hours later, it would only be an imprint from the past. I am sure that the surviving personality of President Lincoln is to a degree attached to the White House because of unfinished business. I do not think that this is unfinished business only of his own time; so much of it has never been finished to this very day. If there ever was any reason for Lincoln to be disturbed, it is now. The Emancipation Proclamation, for which he stood and which was in a way the rebirth of our country, is still only in part reality. Lincoln's desire for peace is hardly met in these troubled times. I am sure that the disturbances at the White House have never ceased. Telephone calls have been put through to members of the presidential family, and there has been no one on the other end of the line. Moreover, on investigating, it was found that the White House operators had not rung the particular extension telephones.

It is very difficult to dismiss such occurrences as products of imagination, coincidence, or "settling of an old house." Everyone knows the difference between human footsteps caused by feet encased with boots or shoes, and the normal noises of an old house settling slowly and a little at a time on its foundation.

Florida

The "Stay-Behind" Ghost

Mr. and Mrs. E. live in an average, relatively contemporary home in Florida. They moved into this house in August. Neither of them had any particular interest in the occult, and Mr. E. could be classified as a complete skeptic, if anything. For the first few months of their residence, they were much too busy to notice anything out of the ordinary, even if there were such occurrences.

It was just before Christmas when they got their first inkling that something was not as it should be with their house. Mrs. E. was sitting up late one night, busy with last-minute preparations for the holiday. All of a sudden the front door, which was secured and locked, flew open with a violent force, and immediately shut itself again, with the handle turning by itself and the latch falling into place. Since Mrs. E. didn't expect any visitors, she was naturally surprised. Quickly walking over to the door to find out what had happened, she discovered that the door was locked. It is the kind of lock that can only be unlocked by turning a knob. Shaking her head in disbelief, she returned to her chair, but before she could sit down again and resume her chores, the door to the utility room began to rattle as though a wind were blowing. Yet there were no open windows that could have caused it. Suddenly, as she was staring at it, the knob turned and the door opened. Somehow nonplussed, Mrs. E. thought, rather sarcastically, "While you're at it, why don't you shake the Christmas tree too?" Before she had completed the thought, the tree began to shake. For a moment, Mrs. E. stood still and thought all of this over in her mind. Then she decided that she was just overtired and had contracted a case of the holiday jitters. It was probably all due to imagination. She went to bed and didn't say anything about the incident.

Two weeks later, Mrs. E. and her fourteen-year-old daughter were up late talking, when all of a sudden every cupboard in the kitchen opened by itself, one by one. Mrs. E.'s daughter stared at the phenomenon in disbelief. But Mrs. E. simply said, "Now close them." Sure enough, one by one, they shut with a hard slam by themselves, almost like a little child whose prank had not succeeded. At this point Mrs. E. thought it best to tell her daughter of her first encounter with the unseen, and implored her not to be scared of it, or tell the younger children or anyone outside the house. She didn't want to be known as a weird individual in the neighborhood into which they had just moved. However, she decided to inform her husband about what had happened. He didn't say much, but it was clear that he was not convinced. However, as with so many cases of this kind where the men in the house take a lot longer to be convinced than the women, Mr. E.'s time came about two weeks later.

He was watching television when one of the stereo speakers began to tilt back all of a sudden, rocking back and forth on its own, as if held by unseen hands. Being of a practical bent, Mr. E. got up to find an explanation, but there was no wind that would have been strong enough to tilt a twenty-pound speaker. At this point, Mr. E. agreed that there was something peculiar about the house. This was the more likely as their dog, an otherwise calm and peaceful animal, went absolutely wild at the moment the speakers tilted, and ran about the house for half an hour afterward, barking, sniffing, and generally causing commotion.

However, the ghost was out of the bag, so to speak. The two younger children, then nine and ten years old, noticed him—it was assumed to be a man all along. A house guest remarked how strange it was that the door was opening seemingly by itself. Mrs. E. explained this with a remark that the latch was not working properly. "But how did the knob turn, then?" the house guest wanted to know. Under the circumstances, Mrs. E. owned up to their guest. The ghost doesn't scare Mrs. E., but he makes it somewhat unpleasant for her at times, such as when she is taking a shower and the doors fly open. After all, one doesn't want to be watched by a man while showering, even if he *is* a ghost.

The Stay-Behind isn't noticeable all the time, to be sure, but frequently enough to count as an extra inhabitant of the house. Whenever he is near, there is a chill in the hall and an echo. This

happens at various times of day or night, early or late. To the
children he is a source of some concern, and they will not stay
home alone. But to Mrs. E. he is merely an unfortunate human
being, caught up in the entanglement of his own emotions from
the past, desperately trying to break through the time barrier to
communicate with her, but unable to do so because conditions
aren't just right. Sometimes she wishes she were more psychic,
but in the meantime she has settled down to share her home with
someone she cannot see, but who, it appears, considers himself
part of the family.

Georgia

The Man in White

Mrs. W. is a housewife living in Athens, Georgia. She is also a certified nursery school teacher, the mother of six children, and has had ESP experiences for many years past. She is living proof that ESP messages can be very precise at times in giving the recipient an indication of what the message is all about and to prepare the recipient for any shock that might come his or her way. In 1946 Mrs. W. was living in another city in Georgia. At that time she had one son age two and a half, another six months old, and was pregnant with another child. During that period she had many vivid dreams of a psychic nature. But after the third child was born she was particularly disturbed one night by a dream that became so powerful it awoke her. She found herself crying uncontrollably, so much so that her husband was genuinely concerned. When she became calmer she told her husband she had dreamed she saw her brothers and sisters and her mother looking at her through the glass of their front door, saying, "Call an ambulance." The dream had no meaning for her, so after a while she went back to sleep and didn't think about it again. Three months later the dream became a reality. Her brother appeared at her front door and, standing outside the glass, said, "Call an ambulance." He explained that their father, who lived on the next street and who had no telephone, had suffered a heart attack while preparing for bed. The father died three days later. It was only after her grief ceased that Mrs. W. realized that in her dream she had seen all members of her family except one—her father. Had she understood this properly perhaps she would have been more prepared for the shock that was to come her way shortly.

The relationship with her father had been a close one, so she was not surprised that after his passing there were times when she felt him standing near her. She did not see him, yet she knew of his presence. She hesitated to discuss this with her husband out of fear of being ridiculed, or worse. During that time she awakened her husband five or six separate times and asked him to get up and shut the door since Daddy had come in. Her husband didn't like it, but when she insisted, he did get up in order to please his wife. They didn't discuss it until many years later, when her husband admitted that each time she had asked him to close the door it was indeed open and there had been no reason for it to be open.

Mrs. W's husband is the editor of a county newspaper and a very logical man. He learned to accept his wife's special talent as the years rolled by, but there were times when he wished that she weren't as psychic as she was. One night she dreamed that a plane crash had taken place somewhere in back of their house and she saw some Army men drive up in a jeep and take away the bodies of those killed. In the morning she told her husband of this dream. He didn't say anything. Two weeks later, however, he told his wife to quit having "those crazy dreams." It appeared that Mr. W. had been traveling away from home in the direction one might properly call "back of the house" when he saw that an Army plane had crashed and Army personnel in a jeep had driven up to the site and removed some bodies, just as his wife had told him. Mrs. W. realized that she had a very special talent and perhaps had been chosen by some superior intelligence as a communicator.

A month after her daughter Karen was born in 1952 she happened to be lying down for an afternoon nap. She was facing the wall when she felt compelled to turn over in the opposite direction. There she saw the figure of a man in a white robe standing by her bed. Her first thought was that she still had in her system some of the drug that had been given her during the birth and that she was hallucinating. She thought it best to turn back to the wall. Immediately, however, she felt a strong compulsion to turn back, and this time she saw the man pointing his finger at her with a stern look on his face. She got the impression she was to get up immediately and follow him. She did just that and walked straight into the next room. As if acting in a daze she saw herself dial her husband at his office. As soon as her husband came to the phone she told him not to ask questions but if he ever intended to do something that she had asked him for, this was the time to do it.

She told him to go at once to a place called Curry's Creek to see if their son Joe was there. Her husband objected. He knew, he said, that the five-year-old was not there. Nevertheless Mrs. W. insisted. Her plea was so urgent she impressed her husband sufficiently that he did indeed go down to the creek. Ten minutes later he telephoned her asking her how she knew that the boy was indeed at the creek. It appeared that he had found the little boy at the edge of the water looking down into it. The creek furnished the town's water supply and is next to a busy highway a mile outside of town. The child had never been there before. Had Mr. W. not arrived in time the child might very well have drowned. Mrs. W. then realized that the man in the white robe had come to save their child.

Uncle Bill

Tucker, Georgia, about an hour's ride due north of Atlanta, is a pleasant, almost suburban community populated by pleasant, average people. The Stevens house, a landmark as early as 1854, was originally built of huge, hand-hewn chestnut pine logs. The older part was added to by a Baptist minister around 1910. Finally another addition was made to the house in the late 1940s. When the Stevenses bought the house they were told that it was originally built by Indian settlers in the area around 1800, or even before. This is Cherokee Territory and according to the local tradition the Indians brought their sick to this house. They would stay with them overnight on their way to Decatur. Decatur was the town where the famed Dr. Chapman Powell lived. The Powell cabin has been restored and is now located in Stone Mountain Park, but originally it was in Decatur and was moved to the park to better preserve it as a landmark. The Stevens house stands about a mile off the High Tower Trail, which is the old Cherokee trail, and four miles from Stone Mountain Park. Since Mrs. Stevens is herself about one-thirty-second Cherokee, she has a vivid sympathy for all Indian lore and has always been interested in the Indian background of the house.

When they first bought the house in May 1960 the Stevenses lived in it for only a year. Then, for business reasons, they moved down to Florida and sold their house to their in-laws. However, two years later they returned from Florida and bought the house back. During that first year in the house they do not recall anything strange except for a recurrent dream Mrs. Stevens had right from the start when they took up residence at the house. In that dream she saw herself looking up through an opening in the ceiling into the darkness of a loft. She could clearly make out the rafters, wooden beams, and the chimneys. Somehow this dream seemed all very familiar. As soon as she had moved to the house she realized that her dream visions concerned the attic of their house. It looked exactly like the visions she had seen so many years prior to coming to the house. Evidently it was predestined that the Stevenses should take up residence in Tucker. On recollection Mrs. Stevens remembers that her in-laws had no special experiences in the house out of the ordinary during the two years in which they resided there. But then neither of her in-laws professed any particular interest in the occult or was possessed of psychic sensitivities.

As soon as the Stevenses returned to their original home they noticed a strange feeling, perhaps more of a current all around the house. It affected the children as well. They would not want to take a nap or go to bed because they said someone kept touching them. Soon Mrs. Stevens experienced that too. Their smallest children reported seeing a man on the porch when there was no man about. Both Mr. and Mrs. Stevens have a number of times seen a man going across the porch. Sometimes it is only a kind of quick flash and sometimes they can clearly make out a human form. Whenever they have seen something and their children have not, they try their best to keep it from them so as not to alarm them. Nevertheless the children on their own report similar occurrences.

Gradually it has become clear to the Stevenses that the oldest part of the house, the log part, is the center of the psychic phenomena. In the living room–dining room area they have seen a form when there was certainly no one else but themselves in the house. On another occasion Mrs. Stevens has seen a hand materialize by her bed. In August 1968 Mr. Stevens awoke from sound sleep because he had the feeling that there was someone in the house who should not be there. He sat up and looked into the room where their sons were sleeping across from the parents' bedroom. There he saw a gray form standing by their bunkbeds looking at the oldest boy. Fully awake now, Mr. Stevens looked closely at the form and realized it was female. The woman appeared to be wearing a cowl-type hood. When he made a move the form dissolved into thin air. Stevens discussed the appearance with his wife. She had seen a similar form in the boys' room reclining on the lower bunk beside the youngest boy. Moreover, the apparition was not alone. Mrs. Stevens could make out additional figures in the room. Footsteps up and down the stairs when there was no one around to make them had become a common occurrence in the house. The Stevenses thought that the repair work going on in the house might have offended one or the other of its former inhabitants. They were doing their level best to save the old part of the house, repairing what could be repaired and replacing what could not.

It was soon clear to them that they had more than one unearthly visitor in their house. The woman so concerned with the well-being of the children might have been someone left behind from the Indian days or perhaps the shade of a former owner of the house. None of them ever saw her clearly enough to make sure, but there was someone else. In 1966 Mr. Stevens had a strange dream. The dream was followed by similar dreams, continuing, as it were, the narrative of the first one. In these dreams his brother Bill communicated with him. Bill had been killed in a plane crash in North Carolina during World War II. However, in the dreams Bill explained that he was not dead and that he had returned home. In another dream he wanted his brother to accompany him on a trip. In all of these dreams Bill appeared to have aged. He was balding and wearing a tattered officer's khaki uniform. His overcoat in particular was tattered and faded. While the Stevenses discussed these dreams with each other, they made a special point of never talking about them with their children. So the children had no idea that dreams about Uncle Bill had indeed taken place.

About three weeks after the last of this series of dreams involving Bill, all the boys came into the kitchen very much alarmed and white as sheets. They insisted that they had seen a ghost. When questioned about the apparition they said they had seen a man walk across the front room, which is part of the 1910 addition of the house. Immediately the parents checked to see whether a trespasser had perhaps entered the house. There was no one to be seen. Skeptical, and at the same time alarmed, the parents demanded that the boys recount what they had seen. Without a moment's hesitation they described the ghost as being a thin man, sort of crouched down and bald, with clothes rather torn and sort of a faded khaki. They had, in effect, described exactly what Uncle

Bill looked like in the series of dreams their father had had for so long. Only what they had seen was not in the dream state. Uncle Bill evidently had returned from the grave not as a resident ghost, for ghosts do not travel, but to look after the affairs of his brother's family.

Illinois

The
Ghostly
Maid

I received a curious letter from a Mrs. Stewart of Chicago, Illinois, explaining that she was living with a ghost and didn't mind, except that she had lost two children at birth and this ghost was following not only her but also her little girl. This she didn't like, so could I please come and look into the situation?

I could and did. On July 4, I celebrated Independence Day by trying to free a hung-up lady ghost on Chicago's South Side. The house itself was an old one, built around the late 1800s, and not exactly a monument of architectural beauty. But its functional sturdiness suited its present purpose—to house a number of young couples and their children, people who found the house both convenient and economical.

In its heyday, it had been a wealthy home, complete with servants and backstairs for them to go up and down on. The three stories are even now connected by an elaborate buzzer system, which, however, hasn't worked for years.

I did not wish to discuss the phenomena at the house with Mrs. Stewart until after Sybil Leek, who was with me, had had a chance to explore the situation. My good friend Carl Subak, a stamp dealer, had come along to see how I worked. He and I had known each other thirty years ago when we were both students, and because of that he had overcome his own skepticism and come along. Immediately on arrival, Sybil ascended the stairs to the second floor as if she knew where to go. Of course she didn't; I had not discussed the matter with her at all. But despite this promising beginning, she drew a complete blank when we arrived in the apartment upstairs. "I feel absolutely nothing," she confided and looked at me doubtfully. Had I made a mistake? On a hot July day, had we come all the way to the South Side of Chicago on a wild ghost chase?

We gathered in a bedroom where there was a comfortable chair and windows on both sides that gave onto an old-fashioned garden; there was a porch on one side and a parkway on the other. The furniture, in keeping with the modest economic circumstances of the owners, was old and worn, but it was functional and they did not seem to mind.

In a moment, Sybil Leek had slipped into trance. But instead of a ghost's personality, the next voice we heard was Sybil's own, although it sounded strange. Sybil was "out" of her own body, but able to observe the place and report back to us while still in trance.

The first thing she saw were maps, in a large round building somehow connected with the house we were in.

"Is there anyone around?" I asked.

"Yes," Sybil intoned, "James Dugan."

"What does he do here?"

"Come back to live."

"When was that?"

"1912."

"Is there anyone with him?"

"There is another man. McCloud."

"Anyone else?"

"Lots of people."

"Do they live in this house?"

"Three, four people . . . McCloud . . . maps . . ."

"All men?"

"No . . . girl . . . Judith . . . maidservant . . ."

"Is there an unhappy presence here?"

"Judith . . . she had no one here, no family . . . that man went away . . . Dugan went away . . ."

"How is she connected with this Dugan?"

"Loved him."

"Were they married?"

"No. Lovers."

"Did they have any children?"

There was a momentary silence, then Sybil continued in a drab, monotonous voice.

"The baby's dead."

"Does she know the baby's dead?"

"*She cries . . . baby cries* . . . neglected . . . by Judith . . . guilty . . .*"

"Does Judith know this?"

"Yes."

"How old was the baby when it died?"

"A few weeks old."

Strange, I thought, that Mrs. Stewart had fears for her own child from this source. She, too, had lost children at a tender age.

"What happened to the baby?"

"She put it down the steps."

"What happened to the body then?"

"I don't know."

"Is Judith still here?"

"She's here."

"Where?"

"This room . . . and up and down the steps. She's sorry for her baby."

"Can you talk to her?"

"No. She cannot leave here until she finds—You see if she could get Dugan . . ."

"Where is Dugan?"

"With the maps."

"What is Dugan's work?"

"Has to do with roads."

"Is he dead?"

"Yes. She wants him here, but he is not here."

"How did she die?"

"She ran away to the water . . . died by the water . . . but is here where she lived . . . baby died on the steps . . . downstairs . . ."

"What is she doing here, I mean how does she let people know she is around?"

"She pulls things . . . *she cries* . . ."

"And her Christian name?"

"Judith Vincent, I think. Twenty-one. Darkish, not white. From an island."

"And the man? Is he white?"

"Yes."

"Can you see her?"

"Yes."

"Speak to her?"

"She doesn't want to, but perhaps . . ."

"What year does she think this is?"

"1913."

"Tell her this is the year 1965."

Sybil informed the spirit in a low voice that this was 1965 and she need not stay here any longer. Dugan is dead, too.

"She has to find him," Sybil explained and I directed her to explain that she need only call out for her lover in order to be reunited with him "Over There."

"She's gone . . ." Sybil finally said, and breathed deeply.

A moment later she woke up and looked with astonishment at the strange room, having completely forgotten how we got here, or where we were.

There was no time for explanations now, as I still wanted to check out some of this material. The first one to sit down with me was the owner of the flat, Mrs. Alexandra Stewart. A graduate of the University of Iowa, twenty-five years old, Alexandra Stewart works as a personnel director. She had witnessed the trance session and seemed visibly shaken. There was a good reason for this. Mrs. Stewart, you see, had met the ghost Sybil had described.

The Stewarts had moved into the second floor apartment in the winter of 1964. The room we were now sitting in had been hers. Shortly after they moved in, Mrs. Stewart happened to be glancing up toward the French doors, when she saw a woman looking at her. The figure was about five feet three or four, and wore a blue-gray dress with a shawl, and a hood over her head, for which reason Mrs. Stewart could not make out the woman's features. The head seemed strangely bowed to her, almost as if the woman were doing penance.

I questioned Mrs. Stewart on the woman's color in view of Sybil's description of Judith. But Mrs. Stewart could not be sure; the woman could have been white or black. At the time, Mrs. Stewart had assumed it to be a reflection from the mirror, but when she glanced at the mirror, she did not see the figure in it. When she turned her attention back to the figure, it had disappeared. It was toward evening and Mrs. Stewart was a little tired, yet the figure was very real to her. Her doubts were completely dispelled when the ghost returned about a month later. In the meantime she had had the dresser that formerly stood in the line of sight moved farther down, so that any reflection as explanation would simply not hold water. Again the figure appeared at the French doors. She looked very unhappy to Mrs. Stewart, who felt herself strangely drawn to the woman, almost as if she should help her in some way as yet unknown.

But the visual visitations were not all that disturbed the Stewarts. Soon they were hearing strange noises, too. Above all there was the crying of a baby, which seemed to come from the second-floor rear bedroom. It could also be heard in the kitchen, though less loud, and it seemed to come from the walls. Several people had heard it and there was no natural cause to account for it. Then there were the footsteps. It sounded like someone walking down the backstairs, the servants' stairs, step by step, hesitatingly, and not returning, but just fading away!

They dubbed their ghostly guest "Elizabeth," for want of a better name. Mrs. Stewart did not consider herself psychic, nor did she have any interest in such matters. But occasionally things had happened to her that defied natural explanations, such as the time just after she had lost a baby. She awoke from a heavy sleep with the intangible feeling of a presence in her room. She looked up and there, in the rocking chair across the room, she saw a woman, now dead, who had taken care of her when she herself was a child. Rocking gently in the chair, as if to reassure her, the Nanny held Mrs. Stewart's baby in her arms. In a moment the vision was gone, but it had left Alexandra Stewart with a sense of peace. She knew her little one was well looked after.

The phenomena continued, however, and soon they were no longer restricted to the upstairs. On the first floor in the living room, Mrs. Stewart heard the noise of someone breathing close to her. This had happened only recently, again in the presence of her husband and a friend. She asked them to hold their breath for a moment, and still she heard the strange breathing continue as before. Neither of the men could hear it, or so they said. But the following day the guest came back with another man. He wanted to be sure of his observation before admitting that he too had heard the invisible person breathing close to him.

The corner of the living room where the breathing had been heard was also the focal point for strange knockings that faulty pipes could not explain. On one occasion they heard the breaking of glass, and yet there was no evidence that any glass had been broken. There was a feeling that someone other than the visible people was present at times in their living room, and it made them a little nervous even though they did not fear their "Elizabeth."

Alexandra's young husband grew up in the building trade, and now works as a photographer. He too has heard the footsteps on many occasions, and he knows the difference between them and a house settling or timbers creaking—these were definitely human noises.

Mrs. Martha Vaughn is a bookkeeper who had been living in the building for two years. Hers is the apartment in the rear portion of the second floor, and it includes the back porch. Around Christmas of 1964, she heard a baby crying on the porch. It was a particularly cold night, so she went to investigate immediately. It was a weird, unearthly sound—to her it seemed right near the porch, but there was nobody around. The yard was deserted. The sound to her was the crying of a small child, not a baby, but perhaps a child of from one to three years of age. The various families shared the downstairs living room "like a kibbutz," as Mrs. Stewart put it, so it was not out of the ordinary for several people to be in the downstairs area. On one such occasion Mrs. Vaughn also heard the breaking of the *invisible* glass.

Richard Vaughn is a laboratory technician. He too has heard the baby cry and the invisible glass break; he has heard pounding on the wall, as have the others. A skeptic at first, he tried to blame these noises on the steam pipes that heat the house. But when he listened to the pipes when they were acting up, he realized at once that the noises he had heard before were completely different.

"What about a man named Dugan? Or someone having to do with maps?" I asked.

"Well," Vaughn said, and thought back, "I used to get mail here for people who once lived here, and of course I sent it all back to the post office. But I don't recall the name Dugan. What I do recall was some mail from a Washington Bureau. You see, this house belongs to the University of Chicago and a lot of professors used to live here."

"Professors?" I said with renewed interest.

Was Dugan one of them?

Several other people who lived in the house experienced strange phenomena. Barbara Madonna used to live there too. But in May of that year she moved out. She works three days a week as a secretary and moved into the house in November of the previous year. She and her husband much admired the back porch when they first moved in, and had visions of sitting out there drinking a beer on warm evenings. But soon their hopes were dashed by the uncanny feeling that they were not alone, that another presence was in their apartment, especially around the porch. Soon, instead of using the porch, they studiously avoided it, even if it meant walking downstairs to shake out a mop. Theirs was the third-floor apartment, directly above the Stewart apartment.

A girl by the name of Lolita Krol also had heard the baby crying. She lived in the building for a time and bitterly complained about the strange noises on the porch.

Douglas McConnor is a magazine editor, and he and his wife moved into the building in November of the year Barbara Madonna moved out, first to the second floor and later to the third. From the very first, when McConnor was still alone—his wife joined him in the flat after their marriage a little later—he felt extremely uncomfortable in the place. Doors and windows would fly open by themselves when there wasn't any strong wind.

When he moved upstairs to the next floor, things were much quieter, except for one thing: always on Sunday nights, noisy activities would greatly increase toward midnight. Footsteps, the sounds of people rushing about, and of doors opening and closing would disturb Mr. McConnor's rest. The stairs were particularly noisy. But when he checked, he found that everybody was accounted for, and that no living person had caused the commotion.

It got to be so bad he started to hate Sunday nights.

I recounted Sybil's trance to Mr. McConnor and the fact that a woman named Judith had been the central figure of it.

"Strange," he observed, "but the story also fits my ex-wife, who deserted her children. She is of course very much alive now. Her name is Judith."

Had Sybil intermingled the impression a dead maidservant with the imprint left behind by an unfit mother? Or were there two Judiths? An any rate the Stewarts did not complain further about uncanny noises, and the girl in the blue-gray dress never came back.

On the way to the airport, Carl Subak seemed unusually silent as he drove us out to the field. What he had witnessed seemed to have left an impression on him and his philosophy of life.

"What I find so particularly upsetting," he finally said, "is Sybil's talking about a woman and a dead baby—all of it borne out afterwards by the people in the house. But Sybil did not know this. She couldn't have."

No, she couldn't.

In September, three years later, a group consisting of a local television reporter, a would-be psychic student, and an assortment of clairvoyants descended on the building in search of psychic excitement. All they got out of it were more mechanical difficulties with their cameras. The ghosts were long gone.

The
Ghost
Husband

People all over the world have moved into houses that seemed ordinary and pleasant, and spent years without ever encountering anything out of the ordinary. Then, one day, something happens to disturb their tranquility: a ghost appears, strange noises are heard, and a psychic presence makes itself known.

Why is it that phenomena occur at times long after someone moves into an affected house? Of course, there are just as many cases where the ominous presence is felt the very moment one steps across the threshold. But in cases where ghosts make their presence manifest long after the new tenants have moved in, certain conditions have not been right for such manifestations to take place at the beginning. For instance, it may involve the presence of youngsters in the household who furnish the energy for ghosts to appear. Or it may be that the shadowy entities remaining behind in the house are dimly aware of the new tenants, but wish to find out more about them before manifesting to them. Either way, once manifestations begin, the owner of the house has the choice of either ignoring them, fighting them—or coming to terms with them.

In the majority of cases, unfortunately, people simply think that by ignoring the phenomena or trying hard to explain them by so-called natural causes, the matter can be solved. Ignoring problems never helps, in any area of life. When it comes to psychic phenomena, the phenomena may become worse, because even the most benighted ghost, barely aware of its predicament, will become more powerful, more restless, by being ignored.

Take Mrs. A.M.B., for instance. She lives in central Illinois and is by training and profession a practical nurse, engaged in psychiatric work. If anything, she can distinguish psychosis from psychic activity. She has had ESP abilities ever since she can remember. When she was twelve years old, she was playing in front of her house when she met what to her was an old man, inquiring about a certain widow living in the next block of the village. Mrs. B. knew very well that the lady had become a widow when her husband was killed while working as a crossing guard during a blizzard the previous winter. She remembered the man well, but the stranger did not resemble the deceased at all, so she assumed he was a relative inquiring about the dead man.

The stranger wanted to know where the widow had moved to. Mrs. B. explained that the lady had gone to visit a sister somewhere in Missouri, due to the fact, of course, that her husband had been killed in an accident. At that, the stranger nodded; he knew of the accident, he said. "Come," Mrs. B. said to the stranger, "I'll show you where another sister of the widow lives, not more than two blocks away from here. Perhaps they can tell you what town in Missouri she is visiting." The stranger obliged her, and the two were walking along the front porch, toward the steps leading down into the street, still in conversation. At that moment, her mother appeared at the front door in back of her and demanded to know what she was talking about. The girl was surprised, and explained that the gentleman was merely asking where Mrs. C. had gone, and added, "I told him she went to Missouri." But the mother replied, in a surprised tone of voice, "What are you talking about? I don't see anyone." The little girl immediately pointed at the visitor, who by that time had had enough time to get to the steps, for the front porch was rather large.

But—to her shock—she saw no one there! Immediately the girl and her mother walked into the yard, looking about everywhere without finding any trace of the strange visitor. He had simply vanished the moment the little girl had turned around to answer her mother.

Lizzy's Ghost

Mrs. Carolyn K. lived in Chicago, Illinois, with her husband and four children. She had for years been interested in ESP experiences, unlike her husband, who held no belief of this kind. The family moved into its present home some years ago. Mrs. K. does not recall any unusual experiences for the first six years, but toward the end of April, six years after they moved in, something odd happened. She and her husband had just gone to bed and her husband fell asleep almost immediately. Mrs. K., however, felt ill at ease and was unable to fall asleep, since she felt a presence in the bedroom.

Within a few minutes she saw, in great detail, a female figure standing beside the bed. The woman seemed about thirty years old, had fair skin and hair, a trim figure, and was rather attractive. Her dress indicated good taste and a degree of wealth, and belonged to the 1870s or 1880s. The young woman just stood there and looked at Mrs. K., and vice versa. She seemed animated enough, but made no sound. Despite this, Mrs. K. had the distinct impression that the ghost wanted her to know something specific. The encounter lasted for ten or fifteen minutes, then the figure slowly disintegrated.

The experience left Mrs. K. frightened and worried. Immediately she reported it to her husband, but he brushed the incident aside with a good deal of skepticism. In the following two weeks, Mrs. K. felt an unseen presence all about the house, without, however, seeing her mysterious visitor again. It seemed that the woman was watching her as she did her daily chores. Mrs. K. had no idea who the ghost might be, but she knew that their house was no more than fifty years old and that there had been swamp land on the spot before that. Could the ghost have some connection with the land itself, or perhaps with some of the antiques Mrs. K. treasured?

About two weeks after the initial experience, Mr. K. was studying in the kitchen, which is located at the far eastern end of the house, while Mrs. K. was watching television in the living room at the other end of the house. Twice she felt the need to go into the kitchen and warn her husband that she felt the ghost moving about the living room, but he insisted it was merely her imagination. So she returned to the living room and curled up in an easy chair to continue watching television. Fifteen minutes later, she heard a loud noise reverberating throughout the house. It made her freeze with fright in the chair, when her husband ran into the living room to ask what the noise had been.

Upon investigation, he noticed a broken string on an antique zither hanging on the dining room wall. It was unlikely that the string could have broken by itself, and if it had, how could it have reverberated so strongly? To test such a possibility, they broke several other strings of the same zither in an effort to duplicate the sound, but without success. A few weeks went by, and the ghost's presence persisted. By now Mrs. K. had the distinct impression that the ghost was annoyed at being ignored. Suddenly, a hurricane lamp hanging from a nail on the wall fell to the floor and shattered. It could not have moved of its own volition.

Again some time passed, and the ghost was almost forgotten. Mrs. K.'s older daughter, then six years old, asked her mother early one morning who the company was the previous evening. Informed that there had been no guests at the house, she insisted that a lady had entered her bedroom, sat on her bed and looked at her, and then departed. In order to calm the child, Mrs. K. told her she had probably dreamt the whole thing. But the little girl insisted that she had not, and furthermore, she described the visitor in every detail including the "funny" clothes she had worn. Appalled, Mrs. K. realized that her daughter had seen the same ghostly woman. Apparently, the ghost felt greater urgency to communicate now, for a few days later, after going to bed, the apparition returned to Mrs. K.'s bedroom. This time she wore a different dress than on the first meeting, but it was still from the 1880s. She was wiping her hands on an apron, stayed only for a little while, then slowly disintegrated again. During the following year, her

presence was felt only occasionally, but gradually Mrs. K. managed to snatch a few fleeting impressions about her. From this she
put together the story of her ghost. She was quite unhappy about a
child, and one evening the following winter, when Mrs. K. felt the
ghost wandering about in their basement, she actually heard her
crying pitifully for two hours. Obviously, the distraught ghost
wanted attention, and was determined to get it at all costs.

One day the following summer, when Mrs. K. was alone with
the children after her husband had left for work, one of the children complained that the door to the bathroom was locked. Since
the door can be locked only from the inside, and since all four
children were accounted for, Mrs. K. assumed that her ghost lady
was at it again. When the bathroom door remained locked for half
an hour and the children's needs became more urgent, Mrs. K.
went to the door and demanded in a loud tone of voice that the
ghost open the door. There was anger in her voice and it brought
quick results. Clearly the click of a lock being turned was heard
inside the bathroom and, after a moment, Mrs. K. opened the
bathroom door easily. There was no one inside the bathroom, of
course. Who, then, had turned the lock—the only way the door
could be opened?

For awhile things went smoothly. A few weeks later, Mrs. K.
again felt the ghost near her. One of her daughters was sitting at
the kitchen table with her while she was cutting out a dress pattern on the counter. Mrs. K. stepped back to search for something
in the refrigerator a few feet away, when all of a sudden she and
her daughter saw her box of dressmaking pins rise slightly off the
counter and fall to the floor. Neither one of them had been near it,
and it took them almost an hour to retrieve all the pins scattered
on the floor.

A little later, they clearly heard the basement door connecting
the dining room and kitchen fly open and slam shut by itself, as if
someone in great anger was trying to call attention to her presence. Immediately they closed the door, and made sure there was
no draft from any windows.

An instant later, it flew open again by itself. Now they attached the chain to the latch—but that didn't seem to stop the
ghost from fooling around with the door. With enormous force, it
flew open again as far as the chain allowed, as if someone were
straining at it. Quickly Mrs. K. called a neighbor to come over and

watch the strange behavior of the door but the minute the neighbor arrived, the door behaved normally, just as before. The ghost
was not about to perform for strangers.

One evening in the summer some years later, Mr. K. was
driving some dinner guests home and Mrs. K. was alone in the
house with the children. All of a sudden, she felt her ghost following her as she went through her chores of emptying ashtrays and
taking empty glasses into the kitchen. Mrs. K. tried bravely to
ignore her, although she was frightened and she knew that her
ghost knew it, which made it all the more difficult to carry on.

Not much later, the K. family had guests again. One of the
arriving guests pointed out to Mrs. K. that their basement light
was on. Mrs. K. explained that it was unlikely, since the bulb had
burned out the day before. She even recalled being slightly annoyed with her husband for having neglected to replace the bulb.
But the guest insisted, and so the K.'s opened the basement door
only to find the light off. A moment later another guest arrived. He
wanted to know who was working in the basement at such a late
hour, since he had seen the basement light on. Moreover, he saw a
figure standing at the basement window looking out. Once more,
the entire party went downstairs with a flashlight, only to find the
light off and no one about.

That was the last the K.'s saw or heard of their ghost. Why
had she so suddenly left them? Perhaps it had to do with a Chicago newspaperwoman's call. Having heard of the disturbances,
she had telephoned the K.'s to offer her services and that of celebrated psychic Irene Hughes to investigate the house. Although
the K.'s did not want any attention because of the children, Mrs.
K. told the reporter what had transpired at the house. To her
surprise, the reporter informed her that parallel experiences had
been reported at another house not more than seven miles away.
In the other case, the mother and one of her children had observed a ghostly figure, and an investigation had taken place with
the help of Irene Hughes and various equipment, the result of
which was that a presence named Lizzy was ascertained.

From this Mrs. K. concluded that they were sharing a ghost
with a neighbor seven miles away, and she, too, began to call the
ghostly visitor Lizzy. Now if Lizzy had two homes and was shut-
tling back and forth between them, it might account for the long

stretches of no activity at the K. home. On the other hand, if the ghost at the K.'s was not named Lizzy, she would naturally not want to be confused with some other unknown ghost seven miles away. Be this as it may, Mrs. K. wishes her well, wherever she is.

Little Girl Lost

Mrs. J. P. lived in central Illinois, in an old three-story house with a basement. Prior to her acquiring it, it had stood empty for six months. As soon as she had moved in, she heard some neighborhood gossip that the house was presumed haunted. Although Mrs. P. is not a skeptic, she is level-headed enough not to take rumors at face value.

She looked the house over carefully. It seemed about eighty years old, and was badly in need of repair. Since they had bought it at a bargain price, they did not mind, but as time went on, they wondered how cheap the house had really been. It became obvious to her and her husband that the price had been low for other reasons. Nevertheless, the house was theirs, and together they set out to repaint and remodel it as best they could. For the first two weeks, they were too busy to notice anything out of the ordinary. About three weeks after moving in, however, Mr. and Mrs. P. began hearing things such as doors shutting by themselves, cupboards opening, and particularly, a little girl persistently calling, "Mama, Mama" with a great deal of alarm. As yet, Mr. and Mrs. P. tried to ignore the phenomena.

One evening, however, they were having a family spat over something of little consequence. All of a sudden a frying pan standing on the stove lifted off by itself, hung suspended in midair for a moment, and then was flung back on the stove with full force. Their twelve-year-old son flew into hysterics, Mr. P. turned white, and Mrs. P. was just plain angry. How dare someone invade their privacy? The following week, the ten-year-old daughter was watching television downstairs in what had been turned into Mrs. P.'s office, while Mr. P. and their son were upstairs also watching television. Suddenly, a glass of milk standing on the desk in the office rose up by itself and dashed itself to the floor with full force. The child ran screaming from the room, and it took a long time for her father to calm her down.

As a result of these happenings, the children implored their mother to move from the house, but Mrs. P. would have none of it. She liked the house fine, and was not about to let some unknown ghost displace her. The more she thought about it, the angrier she got. She decided to go from floor to floor, cursing the ghost and telling him or her to get out of the house, even if he or she used to own it.

But that is how it is with Stay-Behinds: they don't care if you paid for the house. After all, they can't use the money where they are, and would rather stay on in a place they are familiar with.

The Seminary Ghost

Maryknoll College of Glen Ellyn, Illinois, a Roman Catholic seminary, closed its doors in June 1972, due to a dwindling interest in what it had to offer. In the fall a few years before, a seminarian named Gary M. was working in the darkroom of the college. This was part of his regular assignments, and photography had been a regular activity for some years, participated in by both faculty and students.

On this particular occasion, Mr. M. felt as though he were being watched while in the darkroom. Chalking it up to an active imagination, he dismissed the matter from his mind. But in the spring a few years later, Mr. M. was going through some old chemicals when he received the strongest impression of a psychic presence. He was loading some film at the time, and as he did so, he had the uncanny feeling that he was not alone in the room. The chemicals he had just handled were once the property of a priest who had died three years before. The following day, while developing film in an open tank, he suddenly felt as though a cold hand had gone down his back. He also realized that the chemicals felt colder than before. After he had turned the lights back on, he took the temperature of the developer. At the start it had been 70°F., while at the end it was down to 64°F. Since the room temperature was 68°F., there was a truly unaccountable decrease in temperature.

The phenomena made him wonder, and he discussed his experiences with other seminarians. It was then learned that a colleague of his had also had experiences in the same place. Someone, a man, had appeared to him, and he had felt the warm touch of a hand at his cheek. Since he was not alone at the time, but in a group of five students, he immediately reported the incident to them. The description of the apparition was detailed and definite. Mr. M. quickly went into past files, and came up with several pictures, so that his fellow student, who had a similar experience, could pick out that of the ghostly apparition he had seen. Without the slightest hesitation, he identified the dead priest as the man he had seen. This was not too surprising; the students were using what was once the priest's own equipment and chemicals, and perhaps he still felt obliged to teach them their proper use.

The Suicide Ghost

I n Springfield, Illinois, lived a couple named Gertrude and Russell Meyers. He worked as a stereotyper on the local newspaper, and she was a high-school teacher. Both of them were in their late twenties and couldn't care less about such things as ghosts.

At the time of their marriage, in 1935, they had rented a five-room cottage that had stood empty for some time. It had no particular distinction but a modest price, and was located in Bloomington where the Meyerses then lived.

Gertrude Meyers came from a farm background and had studied at Illinois Wesleyan as well as the University of Chicago. For a while she worked as a newspaperwoman in Detroit, later taught school, and as a sideline wrote a number of children's books. Her husband Russell, also of farm background, attended Illinois State Normal University at Normal, Illinois, and later took his apprenticeship at the Bloomington Pantograph.

The house they had rented in Bloomington was exactly like the house next to it, and the current owners had converted what was formerly one large house into two separate units, laying a driveway between them.

In the summer, after they had moved into their house, they went about the business of settling down to a routine. Since her husband worked the night shift on the newspaper, Mrs. Meyers was often left alone in the house. At first it did not bother her at all. Sounds from the street penetrated into the house and gave her a feeling of people nearby. But when the chills of autumn set in and the windows had to be closed to keep it out, she became gradually aware that she was not really alone on those lonely nights.

One particular night early in their occupancy of the house,

she had gone to bed leaving her bedroom door ajar. It was ten-thirty and she was just about ready to go to sleep when she heard rapid, firm footsteps starting at the front door, inside the house, and coming through the living room, the dining room, and finally approaching her bedroom door down the hall leading to it.

She leapt out of bed and locked the bedroom door. Then she went back into bed and sat there, wondering with sheer terror what the intruder would do. But nobody came.

More to calm herself than because she really believed it, Mrs. Meyers convinced herself that she must have been mistaken about those footsteps. It was probably someone in the street. With this reassuring thought on her mind, she managed to fall asleep.

The next morning, she did not tell her new husband about the nocturnal event. After all, she did not want him to think he had married a strange woman! But the footsteps returned, night after night, always at the same time and always stopping abruptly at her bedroom door, which, needless to say, she kept locked.

Rather than facing her husband with the allegation that they had rented a haunted house, she bravely decided to face the intruder and find out what this was all about. One night she deliberately waited for the now familiar brisk footfalls. The clock struck ten, then ten-thirty. In the quiet of the night, she could hear her heart pound in her chest.

Then the footsteps came, closer and closer, until they got to her bedroom door. At this moment, Mrs. Meyers jumped out of bed, snapped on the light, and tore the door wide open.

There was nobody there, and no retreating footsteps could be heard.

She tried it again and again, but the invisible intruder never showed himself once the door was opened.

The winter was bitterly cold, and it was Russell's habit of building up a fire in the furnace in the basement when he came home from work at three-thirty A.M. Mrs. Meyers always heard him come in, but did not get up. One night he left the basement, came into the bedroom and said, "Why are you walking around this freezing house in the middle of the night?"

Of course she had not been out of bed all night, and told him as much. Then they discovered that he, too, had heard footsteps, but had thought it was his wife walking restlessly about the house.

Meyers had heard the steps whenever he was fixing the furnace in the basement, and by the time he got upstairs they had ceased.

When Mrs. Meyers had to get up early to go to her classes, her husband would stay in the house sleeping late. On many days he would hear someone walking about the house and investigate, only to find himself quite alone. He would wake up in the middle of the night thinking his wife had gotten up, but immediately reassured himself that she was sleeping peacefully next to him. Yet there was *someone* out there in the empty house!

Since everything was securely locked, and countless attempts to trap the ghost had failed, the Meyerses shrugged and learned to live with their peculiar boarder. Gradually the steps became part of the atmosphere of the old house, and the terror began to fade into the darkness of night.

In May of the following year, they decided to work in the garden and, as they did so, they met their next-door neighbors for the first time. Since they lived in identical houses, they had something in common, and conversation between them and the neighbors—a young man of twenty-five and his grandmother—sprang up.

Eventually the discussion got around to the footsteps. It seemed that they, too, kept hearing them. After they had compared notes on their experiences, the Meyerses asked more questions. They were told that before the house was divided, it belonged to a single owner who had committed suicide in the house. No wonder he liked to walk in both halves of what was once his home!

The Ghost
and the
Music Teacher

Belleville, Illinois, is a sleepy town about an hour's drive from St. Louis with a few charming old houses still standing. The people who live in Belleville are seldom troubled by the industrial strife of nearby East St. Louis.

On Main Street near 17th there is an old brick house that has stood the test of time well: built a century and a half ago by a coal miner named Meyer, it has since been remodeled and also been added to, but the original structure is still sound and no one thinks of tearing it down or replacing it with something more up to date.

The house consists of two stories, with the front parlor well lit by large windows looking onto Main Street. There are four rooms downstairs, a kitchen, and a hallway leading to a second section of the house that in turn leads to a small backyard. The house stands near the corner and is accessible from downtown in a matter of minutes. Eventually, it passed out of the Meyer family into other hands, and its history is obscure until it became the property of a certain Mr. and Mrs. Joseph Stricker. Little is known of them but their names.

After the Strickers passed on, the house was acquired by two music teachers, sisters Dollie and Judy Walta, who bought it not as living quarters but in order to turn the place into studios for their music business. Dollie, born in 1929, and Judy, born in 1939, were two of ten children of Fred and Julia Walta, who had come to America from Czechoslovakia while still young. They gave their family a good education, but Judy rebelled against the strict discipline of school and quit after two years of high school, despite an IQ of 134. At sixteen, she was already an accomplished musician and decided to devote her life to the teaching of music. Dollie taught guitar and jointly they operated a music studio in the house. They were there every day except on weekends, and generally left by 9 P.M. or earlier. Occasionally they came in on Saturday mornings. At other times and at night, the house was deserted and well locked up, and the chance of burglars breaking in was small due to its solid construction and the fact that it is on Main Street, usually well guarded by the local police department.

For the first six years of their tenancy, the sisters noticed nothing out of the ordinary in the old house. True, there were the usual squeaking floorboards and the aching sounds of an old house settling on its foundations. But that was to be expected and no one paid any heed to such things. In 1962 they decided to make some alterations in the house to make the layout more suitable to their needs. Shortly after, Judy Walta had to come in late one night because she had forgotten to leave one of the inner doors unlocked so the cleaning woman could get in there in the morning.

She entered from the rear door, which leads to 17th Street, and did not bother to turn on any lights since the door she wanted to unlock was only a few steps beyond the back door. Swiftly she unlocked it and then turned around to leave again. As she did so, she passed a white, misty figure in the hall. There was no mistaking it for anything else, and the whole incident took her so by surprise, she just backed away from it and out the rear door. The next morning, she discussed the matter with her sister and as nothing further happened out of the ordinary, they dropped the subject.

One of their students, a young man by the name of Jim Bawling, had been unhappy at his home and gotten into the habit of spending a great amount of time in their studio. In fact, it had gotten to be a kind of "home away from home" to him and he became genuinely attached to the place and to the sisters. Almost every afternoon he would come in and chat with them, whenever they were free to do so. Eventually, he joined the Navy, and on his first leave, he returned to Belleville for a visit.

On August 26, 1962, the young man drowned in an accident. On August 30, the day after his funeral, the sisters were in the room used for lessons, when a pencil, which had been his and which he had left on his desk on his very last visit, started to roll off the desk, bounced on the eraser, and dropped—pointing to the chair that had been his last seat! There was no one close to the desk at the time, nor was there any movement or vibration outside the house. Moreover, the room is built on a slant and the pencil rolled *against* the slant.

Shortly after this incident, the sisters and many of their students began hearing the back door open by itself and close again. This was immediately followed by the footsteps of someone walking through the hall. At first, they would get up to see who it was, but there was never anyone to be seen. Gradually they realized that these were not the footsteps of a living person. The visitor would come at various times of the day or evening, and then stay away for several months. Then it would all resume. The sisters became used to these sounds, and hardly looked up when they became audible. One day the steps continued and then they could clearly hear someone sit down in the sailor's old chair!

It was clear to them that Jim was trying to make himself felt and wanted to continue his old friendship with them from where he now was. This did not bother them, but it bothered some of their pupils who held less broadminded views of ghosts.

The sisters were sure it was Jim, for this was his chair, and he always came in through the rear door rather than the front entrance. The footsteps continued and the door would still open and close by itself and Judy would just nod and Dollie would say "Hello, Jim" and go on with her work.

But it soon became apparent to Dollie that the footsteps were not always the same: sometimes they were soft and light, as if made by a young person, while at other times they were the heavy, almost clumsy steps of a big man.

On March 25, 1966, the two women were in different parts of the studio busy with their chores. Judy was in the middle room, while Dollie was in the bathroom, with the door open. The time was 1:20 in the afternoon. Independently of each other, the two girls saw the same figure of a man suddenly appear out of nowhere. Judy saw him first. He was a big man, about 5 feet, 11 inches tall, and heavy-set, dressed in gray, and where his face should have been there was just a gray mass. But this was unmistakably a human figure. Thirty seconds later, he appeared to Dollie. She looked at him, and could see right through him into the other room!

They both had the impression that the man was looking *at*

them. As he disappeared toward the rear of the house, they realized they had not heard a single sound. Naturally, they knew this was not Jim, their erstwhile pupil. But who was it?

Since the appearance of the man in gray, the footsteps were not heard again, but the door kept opening and closing as before. Word of their strange house got around, and though they did not exactly cherish the notion, their pupils began to discuss the phenomena with them.

One young man whose work in the Air police had trained him to be a particularly competent observer of details came forward to tell of a strange encounter on May 26 of that year. He was in the downstairs studio room at about 8 P.M. when he suddenly came face to face with a man in gray. He took him to be about thirty years of age and, just like the sisters, he could not make out any facial characteristics. It was almost as if the man did not want his face to be recognized and was hiding it in a blur.

One Saturday, Judy had come to make sure the building was properly locked. This was August 27, 1966, and between 3:00 and 3:30 P.M. she observed in the empty building the snapping of door locks, and a footstep—just one footstep—near the door leading from the hall into the basement of the house. This was immediately followed by the sound of several objects falling to the floor, although nothing was moving. One sound in particular reminded her of the noise made by dropping a small package to the floor, *or the muffled sound of a silencer on a gun,* she thought, with a shudder. What was she thinking? This seemed like a bad melodrama by now.

All this activity began to get on her nerves. The following Tuesday, August 30, the two women had their friends Rita Schulte and Mike Tolan in the house. It was after teaching hours and the foursome was sitting around relaxing. Rita had been taking piano lessons for the past year and was familiar with the "problems" of the house, but Mike laughed at it all, especially the man in gray. "You and your ghosts," he chortled. "It's all in your minds."

At that moment, the toilet was being flushed violently. They looked at each other. Everybody was accounted for and the toilet could not flush by itself. Mike tried and tried to see whether it might accidentally have done so. But it couldn't have. His face took on a more thoughtful mien as he sat down again.

A drum teacher named Dick P., working out of the studio,

often told of the same noises—the back door opening and closing and the footsteps of an unseen visitor coming up and stopping inside the house. One night in early 1966 he was driving by the house. He knew from the sisters that there had never been anything unusual observed upstairs. He also knew the house was locked up tight and empty. But to his surprise, the upper story was lit up as if someone were up there. No reflection from passing cars could account for this. He drove on.

Jack McCormick was a clerk for the Internal Revenue Service, an outfit with little use for ghosts since they don't pay taxes. His son had been studying with the Walta sisters and it was his custom to wait for him in the downstairs waiting room. He, too, was constantly unnerved by the sound of the door opening and closing and footsteps of someone not appearing.

Joe Bauer, a freight handler for the railroad, heard the heavy footfalls of a man coming in the rear door, only to find no one there. Mrs. Bauer took two lessons a week, and he often stayed with her until about eight or nine in the evening. One night while they—the two sisters and the Bauers—were eating and watching TV, Mrs. Bauer felt an icy hand on her back. She felt every finger, but when she shook herself and turned around, she saw that no one was near her. Needless to say, it did not help her appetite.

A little while after, all four saw the umbrella, which had been standing idly and quietly in its stand, move of its own volition. One of the sisters got up and stopped it. But the umbrella would not obey. A few moments later, it started swinging again. At the same time, the back door opened and closed with a bang. Everyone was out of the house faster than you can say "ghost."

The sisters decided something had to be done about the power frightening them in the house. First, the house itself deserved to be carefully scrutinized. It was then they discovered that it actually consisted of three separate units, with the front section, where the main entrance is, constructed at a later date than the rear. The original entrance had been to the rear, and what was the entrance at the time the house had been built, back in the 1840s, was now situated *inside* the house, in the middle of the hallway. It so happened this was the exact spot where the ghostly footsteps had always stopped dead.

The soft footsteps they took to be the sailor's were never heard again nor was anything happening that they could consciously connect with him. They assumed the phenomena he might have caused were merely his way of saying good-bye and that he had long since found a better place to hang around.

But the heavy footsteps and the man in gray remained. So did the mystery of who he was and why he was disturbing the peace of the house. Judy started to talk to various neighbors and take frequent trips to the local library. Under the guise of doing research into the background of their house for reasons of historical curiosity, the girl managed to dredge up quite a bit of information, not necessarily all of it reliable or even true.

The trouble was that in the nineteenth century, Main Street had not yet been named and the town was quite different. It was difficult to trace individual addresses. There was, for instance, the rumor that eighty years before a grocer named Jack Meyer had been murdered in their house. She tried to get proof of this and found that a certain George Meyer, occupation unknown, had indeed been murdered in 1888 in Belleville, Illinois. But there was nothing to show that he had resided at this address.

She continued to search and finally hit paydirt. The local paper of Tuesday, June 26, 1923, carried a one-column notice that immediately excited her.

"Jacob Meyer, aged 77, shot himself today. Aged west side coal miner was despondent because of ill health. Was found dead in chair by wife, bullet through his brain."

Apparently Meyer had been brooding over his bad health the night before. At 10:15 he had lunch—miners rise early for breakfast—and then took a rest in his usual chair. When his wife called out to him and got no reply, she checked to see what was the matter and found blood trickling down his face. Horrified, she called on her brother Alex White to come and help. The brother, who resided next door, came and found life ebbing from the aged man. An instant later, Meyer was dead. At his feet was the .32 caliber revolver he had used to blow his brains out. The bullet had passed through his head and lay nearby on the floor. What was strange was that *nobody had heard the shot*, even though several members of the family had been within a few feet of the man all that time. How was it possible? Evidently he had held the gun to his temple and fired at close range and the sound had somehow been muffled. There had been no threat of suicide beforehand, but

Meyer had told his wife on arising, "Mary, I am feeling very bad today."

Meyer had retired six months before due to failing health. Prior to that he had still worked at a nearby mine despite his advanced age. A native of Germany, where he had been born in 1845, Meyer had come to America to seek his fortune.

Judy Walta put the clipping down and suddenly many things began to fall in place for her.

Why hadn't the ghost shown his face? Was he ashamed of having committed suicide, considered an act of cowardice in those days? Or was it because the bullet had literally torn his face to shreds?

The footsteps were those of a heavy man. Meyer was a heavy man. But the man in gray did not look 77 years of age. This at first threw the sisters for a loop until they understood, from psychic literature, that the dead usually return in their mental imagines to that which they consider the prime of life—usually around age thirty or thereabouts.

They had noticed that the phenomena occurred toward the end of the month, usually after the twentieth and at no other times. Meyer had killed himself June 26, 1923. The suicide, according to the newspaper, took place at their address, in their house, which was Meyer's at the time.

The sound, heard by Judy, of a package dropping sharply to the floor could very well have been a reenactment of the fatal shot that killed him.

In Jacob Meyer's day, the entrance was to the rear of the house and he would have come home that way, every day, from the mine. Was he simply continuing to go through his daily routine, refusing to accept the reality of his suicide?

Somehow the understanding of the problem changed the atmosphere in the house. Not that the phenomena ceased—far from it—but it appeared that the ghostly resident had finally found a kind of relationship with the flesh-and-blood inhabitants of what was once his home.

Cigar smoke now could be smelled on several occasions, although there was no cigar smoker in the house and all doors and windows were shut airtight. The smoke did not originate outside the house. This smell was soon followed, or rather augmented, by the smell of freshly brewed coffee at times when no one was brewing any coffee. The sound of papers rattling, someone sitting down in the chair as if to read a newspaper over morning coffee and perhaps smoke a cigar, and scraping noises of a chair being half-dragged across the floor in plain view of the sisters, contributed to their conviction that their ghostly visitor, far from being ready to leave upon being recognized, was getting ready for a long and—to him—comfortable stay.

If the girls had any doubts as to the identity of the unbidden guest, these were soon dispelled. On the night of April 27, 1967, Dollie and Judy were about to leave the studio for the night when they both distinctly heard the sound of a shot coming from inside the building. They had just locked the back door and knew the house was quite empty. They debated whether to run or go back in and check. Curiosity won out, they unlocked the door again and went back inside. They checked the studio and nothing was out of place. They had just gotten ready to leave again when they heard another shot. The second shot sounded quite muffled, whereas the first one had been loud and clear. It came from the area of the furnace room in the middle of the house.

In November, Dollie was walking under the doorway between the front and back rooms, an area hitherto free from psychic phenomena. She was stopped cold by something that resisted her advance although she could not see anything unusual. She felt that she was walking through heavy water, halfway up to her knees. This was a physical thing, she realized, and in sudden horror it occurred to her that she was trying to penetrate the etheric body of Mr. Meyer. Hastily retreating she left the house in a hurry.

That same month a hat disappeared without a trace. Judy had bought it for a friend for Christmas and had kept it in a box along with other Christmas gifts. None of the other items were disturbed but the hat was gone. The puzzle was made worse by her discovery, several days later, of three dollar bills in the receipt book. Since neither of the girls, nor anyone else had placed them there, this was strange indeed. On checking their receipts and figures they found they were exactly three dollars over. It so happened that the hat, which was never seen again, had cost three dollars.

The reputation of the house as a haunted abode seeped out despite the sisters' reluctance to discuss it except with their friends and pupils, when necessary. One day a woman walked by the house to see if she could have a look at the "ghost." As she looked at the front windows, she found herself tripped by an unseen force. Neighbors picked her up, but word got back to Judy and she interviewed the lady afterwards. Shaking her head, the woman insisted nothing had happened, she had not fallen. Judy was happy to let it go at that. Who wants to admit being tripped by the ghost of a man dead for forty years?

About that time Judy discovered that the ghostly miner's wedding to Mary White had taken place on September 9, 1867. When a man celebrates his one hundredth wedding anniversary he should not have time for such foolishness as tripping people outside haunted houses. Quite possibly Mrs. Meyer has since taken him in hand and made a better home for him beyond the veil. At any rate, the door in the rear no longer opens and closes as it used to, and perhaps Jacob Meyer is now retired for good.

Indiana

The Girl
in the
Evening Gown

You'd never think of Kokomo, Indiana, as particularly haunted ground, but one of the most touching cases I know of occurred there some time ago. A young woman by the name of Mary Elizabeth Hamilton was in the habit of spending many of her summer vacations there in her grandmother's house. The house dates back to 1834 and is a handsome place, meticulously kept up by the grandmother.

Miss Hamilton had never had the slightest interest in the supernatural, and the events that transpired that summer, when she spent four weeks at the house, came as a complete surprise to her. One evening she was walking down the front staircase when she was met by a lovely young lady coming up the stairs. Miss Hamilton noticed that she wore a particularly beautiful evening gown. There was nothing the least bit ghostly about the woman, and she passed Miss Hamilton closely, in fact so closely that she could have touched her had she wanted to. But she did notice that the gown was of a filmy pink material, and her hair and eyes dark brown, and the latter full of tears. When the two women met, the girl in the evening gown smiled at Miss Hamilton and passed by.

Since she knew that there was no other visitor in the house, and that no one was expected at this time, Miss Hamilton was puzzled as to who the lady might be. She turned her head to follow her up the stairs, when she saw the lady in pink reach the top of the stairs and vanish—into thin air.

As soon as she could, she reported the matter to her grandmother, who shook her head and would not believe her account. She would not even discuss it, so Miss Hamilton let the matter drop out of deference to her grandmother. But the dress design had been so unusual she decided to check it out in a library. She found, to her amazement, that the lady in pink had worn a dress of the late 1840s.

In September of the next year, her grandmother decided to redecorate the house. In this endeavor she used many old pieces of furniture, some of which had come from the attic of the house. When Miss Hamilton arrived and saw the changes, she was suddenly stopped by a portrait hung in the hall. It was a portrait of her lady of the stairs. She was not wearing the pink gown in this picture but otherwise it was the same person.

Miss Hamilton's curiosity about the whole matter was again aroused and, since she could not get any cooperation from her grandmother, she turned to her great aunt for help. This was particularly fortunate since the aunt was a specialist in family genealogy.

Finally the lady of the stairs was identified. She turned out to be a distant cousin of Miss Hamilton's, and had once lived in this very house. She had fallen in love with a ne'er-do-well, and after he died in a brawl she threw herself down the stairs to her death.

Why had the family ghost appeared to her, Miss Hamilton wondered. Then she realized that she bore a strong facial resemblance to the ghost. Moreover, their names were almost identical —Mary Elizabeth was Miss Hamilton's, and Elizabeth Mary the pink lady's. Both women even had the same nickname, Libby.

Perhaps the ghost had looked for a little recognition from her family and, having gotten none from the grandmother, had seized upon the opportunity to manifest for a more amenable relative.

Miss Hamilton is happy that she was able to see the sad smile on the unfortunate girl's face, for to her it is proof that communication, though silent, had taken place between them across the years.

Iowa

The Phantom Dog

There are reports of wild animals appearing after their deaths, but the majority of animal-related psychic incidents concern domestic animals, especially dogs and cats. Perhaps it is because our pets take on part of our human personality and thus rise above the status of "dumb animals," or perhaps because the bond of love is so strong between master and pet.

Mrs. Elwood Kruse is a housewife in Burlington, Iowa. Her husband is an electrical engineer and neither of them is a student of occult matters, although Mrs. Kruse has a history of premonitions and similar ESP experiences. She has learned to live with it and, if anything, it has made her even more cautious in accepting unorthodox happenings than if she had no such abilities. She has always loved animals and, having been raised in the country, has always been surrounded by dogs, cats, birds, or fish. Her husband at first had some reservations about having animals in a home, but eventually he gave in and allowed her to get a puppy for their daughters.

It was Christmas, 1964 when she bought an Irish setter puppy and named him Fiaca. The children were elated, and even Mr. Kruse, not overly fond of dogs, came to like the animal.

On December 18, 1965, her husband had to telephone Mrs. Kruse to tell her the sad news. Their dog had been run over by a car and killed instantly. Mrs. Kruse was terribly upset. The Christmas season was at hand and memories of Fiaca's arrival a year before would sadden the holidays. But they tried to bear up under their loss.

On the day before Christmas, exactly one year to the day after the dog's arrival at the Kruse home, Mrs. Kruse was in the kitchen when suddenly she heard a strange noise at the front door. It sounded like a dog scratching to be let in. At once she thought, oh, Fiaca wants to get into the house—then the chilling thought came to her that this could not very well be since he was dead. So she went to the front door and peeked through the glass, but there was nothing outside that could have made the noise. She returned to her kitchen explaining her experience as due to her missing the dog at this time of year.

The incident slipped her mind until a few days after the holiday. She heard the sound very clearly again and knew it was not her imagination playing tricks. Again she looked out the door and saw nothing special. The house was new; the storm door was made of aluminum, and the noise was that of animal claws raking up and down on the metal, just as Fiaca used to do. There was no tree close enough to have caused the noise with branches scraping against the door. She told her husband about the second experience but he would not believe her.

The sounds kept coming back, usually in the afternoon. Then one night in the second week of January 1966, it happened again. This time she was not alone but was playing bridge in the living room with her husband and their friends Mr. and Mrs. Marvin Turl. Mr. Turl is a psychology student with an interest in parapsychology.

Mr. Kruse and Susan Turl kept playing, evidently not hearing anything. But Marvin Turl looked up. He too had heard the scratching. He knew nothing at that time of Mrs. Kruse's earlier experiences. But he confirmed that the noise sounded to him like a dog scratching on the door to be let in. Mrs. Kruse and Mr. Turl went to the door and flipped the porch light on. There was no dog outside. Nothing.

The next day Mrs. Kruse confided the strange happenings to her mother and found her receptive to the idea of a psychic phenomenon involving their dog. She suggested that Mrs. Kruse acknowledge her dog's presence verbally the next time the scratching occurred, and open the door as if the dog were actually present.

Two days went by with Mrs. Kruse hoping the ghostly scratching would return. On the third day, in the afternoon, she heard the familiar scratching again. Quickly she went to the door, opened it wide, and said, "Come on in, Fiaca." She felt terribly silly doing

this, but after she had done it, the depression over the dog's untimely death seemed somehow to have left her and she felt better
about the whole matter. She returned to the kitchen and continued her work.

A little later she found herself in the living room. Imagine her
surprise when she found the carpet near the front door covered by
a whitish substance, similar to fine dust. The substance trailed
into the dining room, where it disappeared for a stretch, only to
reappear near the door leading from the kitchen to the living
room. She found more of the white substance in the hall, most of it
at the end where Fiaca used to curl up on the carpet and sleep.
From that spot he could observe all three bedrooms, and it was his
favorite spot.

Although Mrs. Kruse had no knowledge of the nature of ectoplasm or materializations, it struck her at once that the white
substance marked exactly the way Fiaca used to go about the
house: from the front door into the dining room, then a mad dash
through the kitchen, and then down the hall to check the bedrooms.

She looked at the white stuff but did not touch it. A little later,
her father passed by it and observed it too. But by nightfall it had
somehow dissolved. The scratching at the front door was never
heard again after that day.

Perhaps, Mrs. Kruse thinks, the dog wanted to come home
one more time to make sure everything was all right. The Kruses
are glad he took the trouble, for they know that Fiaca is all right
too, in his new place.

Kansas

The
Fraternity
Ghost

everal years ago, a tragic event took place at a major university campus in Kansas. A member of one of the smaller fraternities, TKE, was killed in a head-on automobile accident on September 21. His sudden death at so young an age—he was an undergraduate—brought home a sense of tragedy to the other members of the fraternity, and it was decided that they would attend his funeral in New York en masse.

Not quite a year after the tragic accident, several members of the fraternity were at their headquarters. Eventually one of the brothers and his date were left behind alone, studying in the basement of the house. Upon completion of their schoolwork, they left. When they had reached the outside, the girl remembered she had left her purse in the basement and returned to get it. When she entered the basement, she noticed a man sitting at the poker table, playing with chips. She said something to him, explaining herself, then grabbed her purse and returned upstairs. There she asked her date who the man in the basement was, since she hadn't noticed him before. He laughed and said that no one had been down there but the two of them. At that point, one of the other brothers went into the basement and was surprised to see a man get up from his chair and walk away. That man was none other than the young man who had been killed in the automobile crash a year before.

One of the other members of the fraternity had also been in the same accident, but had only been injured, and survived. Several days after the incident in the fraternity house basement, this young man saw the dead boy walking up the steps to the second floor of the house. By now the fraternity realized that their dead brother was still very much with them, drawn back to what was to him his true home—and so they accepted him as one of the crowd, even if he was invisible at times.

Louisiana

The
Ghost Couple
and the New Tenants

Thanks to a local group of psychic researchers, a bizarre case was brought to my attention not long ago. In the small town of Lafayette, Louisiana, there stands an old bungalow that had been the property of an elderly couple for many years. They were both retired people, and of late the wife had become an invalid confined to a wheelchair. One day she suffered a heart attack and died in that chair. Partially because of her demise, or perhaps because of his own fragile state, the husband also died a month later. He was found dead and was declared to have died of a heart attack.

Under the circumstances the house remained vacant for a while, since there were no direct heirs. After about nine months, it was rented to four female students from the nearby university. Strangely, however, they stayed only two months—and again the house was rented out. This time it was taken by two women, one a microbiologist and the other a medical technician. Both were extremely rational individuals and not the least bit interested in anything supernatural. They moved into the bungalow, using it as it was, with the furnishings of the dead couple.

Picture their dismay, however, when they found out that all wasn't as it should be with their house. Shortly after moving in, they were awakened late at night by what appeared to be mumbled conversations and footsteps about the house. At first neither woman wanted to say anything about it to the other, out of fear that they might have dreamed the whole thing or of being ridiculed. When they finally talked to each other about their experiences, they realized that they had shared them, detail for detail. They discovered, for instance, that the phenomena always took place between one A.M. and sunrise. A man and a woman were talking, and the subject of their conversation was the new tenants!

"She has her eyes open—I can see her eyes are open now," the invisible voice said, clearly and distinctly. The voices seemed to emanate from the attic area. The two ladies realized the ghosts were talking about *them;* but what were they to do about it? They didn't see the ghostly couple, but felt themselves being watched at all times by invisible presences. What were they to do with their ghosts, the two ladies wondered.

I advised them to talk to them, plain and simple, for a ghost who can tell whether a living person's eyes are open or not is capable of knowing the difference between living in one's own house and trespassing on someone else's, even if it *was* their former abode.

Maine

Finding Willie

There is something lonely and haunting about the landscape Down East as you go further up into Maine toward Canada. Even today there are areas with few houses and even fewer people, with flat country bordering on the pounding sea. In such restrictive environments emotions sometimes run higher than elsewhere, with so little to occupy one's mind or leisure time. And when tragedy strikes, it is not easily forgotten. Not even in death.

Ken Brigham wanted me to know that he had a resident ghost at his summer home in Maine. He assured me that while the lady ghost he was reporting was not at all frightening to him and his family, he would nevertheless prefer she went elsewhere. This is a sentiment I have found pervasive with most owners of haunted property, and while it shows a certain lack of sentimentality, it is a sound point of view even from the ghost's perspective because being an earthbound spirit really has no future, so to speak.

All this happened in January 1967. I was keenly interested. At the time, I was working closely with the late Ethel Johnson Meyers, one of the finest trance mediums ever, and it occurred to me immediately that, if the case warranted it, I would get her involved in it.

I asked Mr. Brigham, as is my custom, to put his report in writing, so I could get a better idea about the nature of the haunting. He did this with the precision expected from a public relations man representing a major instrument manufacturer. This is his initial report:

As a member of the public relation/advertising profession, I've always been considered a cynical, phlegmatic individual and so considered myself. I'm not superstitious, walk under ladders, have never thought about the "spirit world," am not a deeply religious person, etc., but . . .

Eight years ago, my wife and I purchased, for a summer home, a nonworking farm in South Waterford, Maine. The ten-room farmhouse had been unoccupied for two years prior to our acquisition. Its former owners were an elderly couple who left no direct heirs and who had been virtually recluses in their latter years. The house apparently was built in two stages; the front part about 1840, and the ell sometime around 1800. The ell contains the original kitchen and family bedroom; a loft overhead was used during the nineteenth century for farm help and children. The former owners for many years occupied only a sitting room, the kitchen, and a dining room; all other rooms being closed and shuttered. The so-called sitting room was the daily and nightly abode. We never met the Bells, both of whom died of old age in nursing homes in the area, several years before we purchased the farm. They left it to relatives; all the furniture was auctioned off.

The first summer my wife and I set about restoring the farmhouse. The old kitchen became our living room; the Bell's sitting room became another bedroom; the old dining room, our kitchen. One bright noontime, I was painting in the new living room. All the doors were open in the house. Aware that someone was looking at me, I turned toward the bedroom door and there, standing in bright sunlight, was an elderly woman; she was staring at me. Dressed in a matronly housedress, her arms were folded in the stance common to many housewives. I was startled, thinking she must have entered the house via the open front door and had walked through the front sitting room to the now-bedroom. Behind her eyeglasses, she maintained a passive, inquisitive expression. For a moment or two, we stared at each other. I thought, What do you say to a native who has walked through your house, without sounding unneighborly? and was about to say something like What can I do for you? when she disappeared. She was there and then she wasn't. I hurried through the bedrooms and, of course, there was no one.

Once or twice that summer I was awakened by a sudden, chill draft passing through the second-floor room we used as a master bedroom. One early evening, while I was taking a shower, my wife called me from the living room with near-panic in her voice. I

*hurried downstairs as quickly as possible only to have her ask if I
intended to remain downstairs.*

*Before closing the house up for the winter, I casually described
the apparition to local friends without disclosing my reasons, ex-
cusing the inquiry from a standpoint I was interested in the previous owners. Apparently my description was accurate, for our
friends wanted to know where I'd seen Mrs. Bell; I had difficulty
passing it off.*

*My wife wasn't put off, however, and later that evening we
compared notes for the first time. The night she called me, she
explained, she had felt a cold draft pass behind her and had looked
up toward the door of the former sitting room (which was well
lighted). There, in the door, was the clear and full shadow of a small
woman. My wife then cried out to me. The chill breeze went through
the room and the shadow disappeared. My wife reported, however,
that surprisingly enough she felt a sense of calm. No feeling of
vindictiveness.*

*Over the years, we've both awakened spontaneously to the chill
draft and on more than one occasion have watched a pinpoint light
dance across the room. The house is isolated and on a private road,
discounting any possible headlights, etc. After a moment or so, the
chill vanishes.*

*A couple of times, guests have queried us on hearing the house
creak or on hearing footsteps, but we pass these off.*

*The summer before last, however, our guests' reaction was dif-
ferent.*

*A couple with two small children stayed with us. The couple
occupied the former sitting room, which now is furnished as a
Victorian-style bedroom with a tremendous brass bed. Their daughter occupied another first-floor bedroom, and their son shared our
son's bedroom on the second floor. A night light was left on in the
latter bedroom and in the bathroom, thereby illuminating the upper
hallway, and, dimly, the lower hallway. My wife and I occupied
another bedroom on the second floor that is our custom.*

*During the early hours of the morning, we were awakened by
footsteps coming down the upper hallway. They passed our door,
went into the master bedroom, paused, continued into our room and
after a few minutes, passed on and down the staircase. My wife
called out, thinking it was one of the boys, possibly ill. No answer.*

The chill breeze was present, and my wife again saw the woman's shadow against the bedroom wall. The children were sound asleep.

In the morning, our adult guests were quiet during breakfast, and it wasn't until later that the woman asked if we'd been up during the night and had come downstairs. She'd been awakened by the footsteps and by someone touching her arm and her hair. Thinking it was her husband, she found him soundly sleeping. In the moonlight, she glanced toward a rocking chair in the bedroom and said she was certain someone had moved it and the clothes left on it. She tried to return to sleep, but again was awakened, certain someone was in the room, and felt someone move the blanket and touch her arm.

My wife and I finally acknowledged our "ghost," but our woman guest assured us that she felt no fright, to her own surprise, and ordinarily wouldn't have believed such "nonsense," except that I, her host, was too "worldly" to be a spiritualist.

At least one other guest volunteered a similar experience.

Finally I admitted my story to our local friends, asking them not to divulge the story in case people thought we were "kooks." But I asked them if they would locate a photograph of the Bell family. Needless to say, the photograph they located was identical with my apparition. An enlargement now is given a prominent place in our living room.

Although this experience hasn't frightened us with the house, it has left us puzzled. My wife and I both share the feeling that whatever [it is] is more curious than unpleasant; more interested than destructive.

I was impressed and replied we would indeed venture Down East. It so happened that Catherine (whom I was married to at the time) and I were doing some traveling in upper New Hampshire that August, and Ethel Johnson Meyers was vacationing at Lake Sebago. All that needed to be done was coordinate our travel plans and set the date. We picked August 14, 1967. Ken and Doris Brigham suggested we could stay over at the haunted house, if necessary, and I assured them that I doubted the need for it, being a bit cocksure of getting through to, and rid of, the ghost all in the same day.

Crossing the almost untouched forests from New Hampshire to Maine was quite an experience for us; we rode for a very, very long time without ever seeing a human habitation, or, for that matter, a gas station. Before we left, we had received a brief note from Ken Brigham informing me that some of the witnesses to the phenomena at the house would be there for our visit, and I would have a chance to meet them, including Mrs. Mildred Haynes Noyes, a neighbor who was able to identify the ghostly apparition for the Brighams. Most of the phenomena had occurred in the living room, downstairs in the house, as well as in the long central hall, and in one upper-story front bedroom as well.

At the time I had thought of bringing a television documentary crew along to record the investigations, but it never worked out that way, and in the end I did some filming myself and sound recorded the interviews, and, of course, Ethel Meyers's trance.

When we finally arrived at the house in question in Waterford, Maine, Ethel had no idea exactly where she was or why. She never asked questions when I called on her skills. Directly on arrival she began pacing up and down in the grounds adjacent to the house as if to gather her bearings. She often did that, and I followed her around with my tape recorder like a dog follows its master.

"I see a woman at the window, crying," she suddenly said and pointed to an upstairs window. "She wears a yellow hat and dress. There is a dog with her. Not from this period. Looking out, staring at something."

We then proceeded to enter the house and found ourselves in a very well appointed living room downstairs; a fire in the fireplace gave it warmth, even though this was the middle of August. The house and all its furnishings were kept as much as possible in the Federal style, and one had the feeling of having suddenly stepped back into a living past.

When we entered the adjacent dining room, Ethel pointed at one of the tall windows and informed us that the lady was still standing there.

"Dark brown eyes, high cheekbones, smallish nose, now she has pushed back the bonnet hat, dark reddish-brown hair," Ethel intoned. I kept taking photographs, pointing the camera toward the area where Ethel said the ghost was standing. The pictures did not show anything special, but then Ethel was not a photography medium.

I asked Ethel to assure the woman we had come in friendship

and peace, to help her resolve whatever conflict might still keep her here. I also asked her to try to get the woman's name. Ethel seemed to listen, then said, "I like to call her Isabelle, Isabelle . . ."

"How is she connected to the house?"

"Lived here."

I suggested that Ethel inform the woman we wanted to talk to her. Earnestly Ethel addressed the ghost, assuring her of no harm. Instead of being comforted, Ethel reported, the woman just kept on crying.

We asked the ghost to come with us as we continued the tour of the house; we would try and have her communicate through Ethel in trance somewhere in the house where she could be comfortable. Meanwhile Ethel gathered further psychic impressions as we went from room to room.

"Many layers here . . . three layers . . . men fighting and dying here . . ." she said. "Strong Indian influence also . . . then there is a small child here . . . later period . . . the men have guns, bleeding . . . no shoes . . . pretty far back . . . Adam . . . Joseph . . . Balthazar . . . war victims . . . house looks different . . . they're lying around on the floor, in pain . . . some kind of skirmish has gone on here."

I decided to chase the lady ghost again. We returned to the living room. Ethel picked a comfortable chair and prepared herself for the trance that would follow.

"I get the names Hattie . . . and Martin . . . not the woman at the window . . . early period . . . connected with the men fighting . . . not in house, outside . . . Golay? Go-something . . . it is their house. They are not disturbed but they give their energy to the other woman. Someone by the name of Luther comes around. Someone is called Marygold . . . Mary . . . someone says, the house is all different."

I decided to stop Ethel recounting what may well have been psychic impressions from the past rather than true ghosts, though one cannot always be sure of that distinction. But my experience has taught me that the kind of material she had picked up sounded more diffuse, more fractional than an earthbound spirit would be.

"Abraham . . ." Ethel mumbled and slowly went into deep trance as we watched. The next voice we would hear might be her guide, Albert, who usually introduces other entities to follow, or it might be a stranger—but it certainly would not be Ethel's.

"It's a man. Abram . . . Ibram . . ." she said, breathing heavily. I requested Albert's assistance in calming the atmosphere.

Ethel's normally placid face was now totally distorted as if in great pain and her hands were at her throat, indicating some sort of choking sensation; with this came unintelligible sounds of ahs and ohs. I continued to try and calm the transition.

I kept asking who the communicator was, but the moaning continued, at the same time the entity now controlling Ethel indicated that the neck or throat had been injured as if by hanging or strangulation. Nevertheless, I kept up my request for identification, as I always do in such cases, using a quiet, gentle vocal approach and reassurances that the pain was of the past and only a memory now.

Finally, the entity said his name was Abraham and that he was in much pain.

"Abraham . . . Eben . . . my tongue!" the entity said, and indeed he sounded as if he could not use his tongue properly. Clearly, his tongue had been cut out, and I kept telling him that he was using the medium's now and therefore should be able to speak clearly. But he continued in a way that all I could make out was "my house."

"Is this your house?"

"Yes . . . why do you want to know . . . who are you?"

"I am a friend come to help you. Is this your house?"

"I live here . . ."

"How old are you?"

No answer.

"What year is this?"

"Seventy-eight . . . going on . . . seventy-nine . . ."

"How old are you?"

"Old man . . . fifty-two . . ."

"Where were you born?"

"Massachusetts . . . Lowell . . ."

"Who was it who hurt you?"

Immediately he became agitated again, and the voice became unintelligible, the symptoms of a cut-out tongue returned. Once again, I calmed him down.

"What church did you go to?" I asked, changing the subject.
"Don't go to church much . . ." he replied.
"Where were you baptized?"
"St. Francis . . . Episcopal."
I suggested the entity should rest now, seeing that he was getting agitated again, and I also feared for the medium.
"I want justice . . . justice . . ." he said.
I assured him, in order to calm him down, that those who had done him wrong had been punished. But he would have none of it.
"They fight every night out there . . ."
Again, I began to exorcise him, but he was not quite ready.
"My daughter . . . Lisa . . . Elizabeth . . ."
"How old is she?"
"Thirteen . . . she cries for me, she cries for me, she weeps . . . all the blood . . . they take her, too . . ."
"Where is your wife?"
"She left us in misery. Johanna . . . don't mention her . . . she left us in misery."
"What year was that?"
"This year. NOW . . ."
"Why did she leave you?"
"I don't know."
"Where did she go?"
"I don't know."
And he added, "I will go to find her . . . I never see her . . ."
"What about your father and mother? Are they alive?"
"Oh no . . ."
"When did they die?"
"1776."
The voice showed a definite accent now.
"Where are they buried?"
"Over the water . . . Atlantic Ocean . . . home . . ."
"Where did your people come from?"
"Wales . . . Greenough . . ."
Further questioning brought out he was a captain in the 5th regiment.
"Did you serve the king or the government of the colonies?" I asked. Proudly the answer came.
"The king."

When I asked him for the name of the commanding officer of the regiment he served in, he became agitated and hissed at me . . . "I am an American citizen, I'll have you know!"

"Are you a patriot or a Tory?"

"I will not have you use that word," he replied, meaning he was not a Tory.

I went on to explain that time had passed, but he called me mad; then I suggested I had come as a friend, which elicited a bitter reply.

"What are friends in time of war?"

I explained that the war had long been over.

"The war is not over . . . I am an American . . . don't tempt me again . . ."

Once again I pressed him for the name of his commanding officer and this time we received a clear reply: Broderick. He was not infantry, but horse. We were finally getting some answers. I then asked him for the names of some of his fellow officers in the 5th regiment.

"All dead," he intoned, and when I insisted on some names, he added, "Anthony . . . Murdoch . . . Surgeon . . . my head hurts!"

"Any officers you can remember?"

"Matthew . . ."

I asked what battles was he involved in.

"Champlain . . . Saint Lawrence . . . it's bad, it's bad . . ."

He was showing signs of getting agitated again, and time was fleeting.

I decided to release the poor tortured soul, asking him whether he was ready to join his loved ones now. Once again he relived the wars.

"He won't come home again . . . Hatteras . . . fire . . . I'm weary."

I began to exorcise him, suggesting he leave the house where he had suffered so much.

"My house . . . my tongue . . . Indians," he kept repeating.

But finally with the help of Ethel's spirit guide (and first husband) Albert, I was able to help him across. Albert, in his crisp voice, explained that one of the female presences in the house, a daughter of the spirit we had just released, might be able to communicate now. But what I was wondering was whether a disturbed earthbound spirit was in the house also, not necessarily a relative of this man. Albert understood, and withdrew, and after a while, a faint, definitely female voice began to come from the medium's still entranced lips.

"Ella . . ." the voice said, faintly at first.

Then she added that she was very happy and had a baby with her. The baby's name was Lily. She was Ella, she repeated. When I asked who she was in relation to the house, she said, "He always came . . . every day . . . William . . . my house . . ."

"Where is he? You know where he went?"

There was anxiety in her voice now. She said he left St. Valentine's Day, this year . . . and she had no idea what year that was.

Who was Willie? Was he her husband?

This caused her to panic.

"Don't tell them!" she implored me. The story began to look ominous. Willie, Ella, the baby . . . and not her husband?

She began to cry uncontrollably now. "Willie isn't coming anymore . . . where is he?"

What was she doing in the house?

"Wait for Willie . . . by the window . . . always by the window. I wait for him and take care of Lily, she is so sweet. What I can do to find Willie?"

I began to exorcise her, seeing she could not tell me anything further about herself. Her memory was evidently limited by the ancient grief. As I did so, she began to notice spirits. "There is my Papa . . . he will be very angry . . . don't tell anyone . . . take me now . . . my Papa thinks we are married . . . but we have no marriage . . . Willie must marry me . . ."

She cried even harder now.

"Andrew . . . my husband . . ."

Once again I asked Albert, the guide, to lead her outside, from the house. It wasn't easy. It was noisy. But it worked.

"She is out," Albert reported immediately following this emotional outburst, "but her father did find out."

"What period are we in now?"

"The eighteen-something."

"Is there anything in the way of a disturbance from the more recent past?"

"Yes, that is true. An older lady . . . she does not want to give up the home."

Albert then went on to explain that the woman at the window who had been seen had actually been used in her lifetime by the earlier entities to manifest through, which created confusion in her own mind as to who she was. Albert regretted that he could not have her speak to us directly. Andrew, he explained, was that more recent woman's father. Both women died in this house, and since the earlier woman would not let go, the later woman could not go on either, Albert explained.

"We have them both on our side, but they are closer to you because their thoughts are on the earth plane, you can reach them, as you are doing."

After assuring us and the owners of the house that all was peaceful now and that the disturbed entities had been released, Albert withdrew, and Ethel returned to herself, as usual, blissfully ignorant of what had come through her mediumship.

Two of the ladies mentioned earlier, who had been connected with the house and the phenomena therein, had meanwhile joined us. Mrs. Anthony Brooks, a lady who had been sleeping in one of the bedrooms with her husband two years prior to our visit had this to say.

"I had been asleep when I was awakened by ruffling at the back of my head. I first thought it was my husband and turned over. But next thing I felt was pressure on my stomach, very annoying, and I turned and realized that my husband had been sound asleep. Next, my cover was being pulled from the bed, and there was a light, a very pale light for which there was no source. I was very frightened. I went upstairs to go to the bathroom and as I was on the stairs I felt I was being pushed and held on tightly to the banister."

I next talked to Mrs. Mildred Haynes Noyes, who had been able to identify the ghostly lady at the window as being the former resident, Mrs. Bell. Everything she had told the Brighams was being reiterated. Then Ken Brigham himself spoke, and we went over his experiences once more in greater detail.

"I was standing in front of the fireplace, painting, and at that time there was a door to that bedroom over there which has since been closed up. It was a bright morning, about eleven o'clock, the doors were open, windows were open, my wife, Doris, was upstairs at the time, I was alone, and as I stood there painting, I glanced out and there, standing in the doorway, was a woman. As I was glancing at her I thought it peculiar that the neighbors would simply walk through my house without knocking.

"She stood there simply looking at me, with her arms folded, a woman who was rather short, not too heavy, dressed in a flower-print housedress, cotton, she had on glasses and wore flat-heel Oxford shoes, all of this in plain daylight. I did not know what to say to this woman who had walked into my house. I was about to say to her, What can I do for you? thinking of nothing more to say than that, and with that—she was gone. I raced back to the hall, thinking this little old lady had moved awfully fast, but needless to say, there was no one there. I said nothing to anyone, but several weeks later, during the summer, both my wife and I were awakened several times during the night by a very chilly breeze coming into the bedroom. That was one of the bedrooms upstairs. Neither of us said anything but we both sat up in bed and as we did so, we watched a little light dance across the wall! We are very isolated here, and there is no light from the outside whatsoever. This continued for the next year."

At this point it was decided that Mrs. Brigham would tell her part of the story.

"The first summer that we had the house," Mrs. Doris Brigham began, "I was sitting here, about five in the afternoon, my husband was upstairs, and my son was outside somewhere. I was alone and I was aware that someone was here, and on this white doorway, there was a solid black shadow. It was the profile of a woman from top to bottom, I could see the sharp features, the outline of the glasses, the pug in the back of her head, the long dress and shoes—all of a sudden, the shadow disappeared, and a cold breeze came toward me, and it came around and stood in back of my chair, and all of a sudden I had this feeling of peace and contentment, and all was right with the world. Then, all of a sudden, the cold air around my chair, I could feel it moving off. Then, practically every night in the room upstairs, I was awakened for several years in the middle of the night, by a feeling of someone coming into the room. But many times there would be the dancing lights. We moved into another bedroom, but even there we would be awakened by someone running their fingers up my hair! Someone was pressing against me, and the same night, a neighbor was in the house, and she told us the same story. Footsteps of someone coming up the stairs. A feeling of movement of air. A black shadow on the ceiling, and then it disappeared. Often when the children were sick, we felt her around. It was always strong when there were children in the house."

I wondered whether she ever felt another presence in the house, apart from this woman. Mrs. Brigham replied that one time, when she did not feel the woman around, she came into the house and felt very angry. That was someone else, she felt.

I decided it was time to verify, if possible, some of the material that had come through Mrs. Meyers in trance, and I turned to Ken Brigham for his comments.

"It has been one of the most astounding experiences I have ever had," he began. "There are several points that no one could know but my wife and myself. We did a considerable amount of research back through the deeds of the house. This only transpired a few weeks ago. I had been excavating up out front, preparing some drains, when I came across some foreign bricks, indicating that there had been an extension to the house. This is not the original house, the room we are in; there was a cottage here built for Continental soldiers, at the end of the revolutionary war.

"These cottages were given to Massachusetts soldiers in lieu of pay, and they got some acres up here. This house has been remodeled many times, the most recent around 1870. The town here was formed around 1775; the deeds we have are around 1800. Several things about the house are lost in legend. For example, down there is a brook called Mutiny Brook. There was a mutiny here, and there was bloodshed. There were Indians, yes, this was definitely Indian territory. At one time this was a very well settled area; as recently as 1900 there were houses around here."

I realized, of course, that this was no longer the case: the house we were in was totally isolated within the countryside now.

"The original town was built on this hill, but it has disappeared," Mr. Brigham continued, and then disclosed a strange coincidence (if there be such a thing!) of an actual ancestor of his having lived here generations ago, and then moving on to Canada.

"We only just discovered that at one time two brothers with their families decided to share the house and remodel it," Brig-

ham continued his account. "But one of them died before they
could move in. Much of what Mrs. Meyers spoke of in trance is
known only locally."

"What about the two women Mrs. Meyers described?" I
asked. "She mentioned a short, dark-haired woman."

"She was short, but had gray hair when I saw her," Mr.
Brigham said. "A perfectly solid human being—I did not see her
as something elusive. We only told our son about this recently, and
he told us that he had heard footsteps of a man and a woman on
the third floor."

"Anything else you care to comment on?"

"Well, we have the names of some of the owners over a period
of time. There were many, and some of the names in the record
match those given by Ethel Meyers, like Eben."

"When Mrs. Meyers mentioned the name Isabelle," Mrs.
Brigham interjected, "I thought she meant to say Alice Bell,
which of course was the former owner's name—the woman at the
window."

"One thing I should tell you also, there seems to have been a
link between the haunting and the presence of children. One of
the former owners did have a child, although the neighbors never
knew this," Ken Brigham said. "She had a miscarriage. Also,
Lowell, Massachusetts, is where these Continental soldiers came
from; that was the traditional origin at the time. Maine did not yet
exist as a state; the area was still part of Massachusetts. One more
thing: both Mr. and Mrs. Bell died without having any funerals
performed. She died in a nursing home nearby, he in Florida. But
neither had a funeral service."

"Well, they had one now," I remarked and they laughed. It
was decided that the Brighams would search the records further
regarding some of the other things that Ethel had said in trance,
and then get back to me.

Mr. Brigham was as good as his word. On August 21, 1967, he
sent me an accounting of what he had further discovered about
the house, and the history of the area in which it stands. But it was
not as exhaustive as I had hoped even though it confirmed many
of the names and facts Ethel had given us in trance. I decided to
wait until I myself could follow up on the material, when I had the
chance.

Fortunately, as time passed, the Brighams came to visit my

then-wife, Catherine, and myself in August of the following year at our home in New York, and as a result Ken Brigham went back into the records with renewed vigor. Thus it was that on August 20, 1968, he sent me a lot of confirming material, which is presented here.

Ethel Meyers's mediumship had once again been proved right on target. The names she gave us—Bell, Eben, Murdoch, Blackguard, Willie, Abraham—were there in the historical records! Not ghostly fantasies, not guesswork . . . people from out of the past.

August 20, 1968

Dear Hans,

I presume that just about now you're again on one of your trips, but I promised to forward to you some additional information that we've gathered since last summer. Enclosed is a chronology of the history of the house as far as we've been able to trace back. Early this summer (the only time we made it up to Maine) we spent hours in the York, Maine, Registry of Deeds, but the trail is cold. Deeds are so vague that we can't be certain as to whether or not a particular deed refers to our property. We are, however, convinced by style of building, materials, etc., that the back part of our house is much older than thought originally—we suspect it goes back to the mid-1700s.

Although I haven't included reference to it, our reading of the town history (which is extremely garbled and not too accurate) indicates that one of the Willard boys, whose father had an adjoining farm, went off to the Civil War and never returned, although he is not listed as one of the wounded, dead, or missing. If memory serves me right, he was simply listed as W. Willard ("Willie"?). Now the "ghost" said her name was "Isabel"; unfortunately, we can find no records in the town history on the Bell family, although they owned the house from 1851 to 1959 and Eben Bell lived in the town from 1820–1900! This is peculiar in as much as nearly every other family is recounted in the Town History of 1874. Why? Could "Isabel" be a corruption of the Bell name, or perhaps there was an Isabel Bell. Checking backwards in a perpetual calendar it seems that during the mid-1800s Tuesday, St. Valentine's Day, occurred on February 14, 1865, 1860, and 1854; the first seems most logical *since the others do not occur during the Civil War—which ended on [May] 26, 1865!**

Some of my other notes are self-explanatory.

Another question of course concerns the term "Blackguard" for our particular road and hill. An archaic term that connotes "rude" —note also that the map of 1850 does not show a family name beside our house . . . this could be because the property was between owners, or it could be that the owners were "rude"—which also could account for the lack of reference in Town History to the Bell family. It's an interesting sidelight.

Now, to more interesting pieces of information for you: 1) we've finally decided to sell the house and it's just like losing a child . . . I'm personally heartbroken, but I'm also a realist and it is ridiculous to try to keep it when we can't get up there often enough to maintain it. We have a couple of prospective buyers now but since we're not under pressure we want to make sure that any new owners would love it like we do and care for it.

2) And, then the strangest . . . Doris was going through some old photographs of the place and came across a color print from a slide taken by a guest we had there from Dublin, Ireland. And, it truly looks like an image in the long view up the lane to the house. Three persons have noted this now. Then, on another slide it looks as though there were a house in the distance (also looking up the lane) which is only 1½ stories in height. We're having the company photographer blow them up to see what we will see. I'll certainly keep you posted on this!

Well, it all adds up to the fact that we did a lot more work and learned a lot more about the place . . . nearly all of which correlates with Ethel's comments. But as a Yankee realist, I'm just going to have to cast sentiment aside and let it go.

Drop us a line when you get a chance.

Sincerely yours,
Ken Brigham

*"Willie left on Tuesday, St. Valentine's Day."

Two points should be made here regarding this story. Ethel Johnson Meyers had many phases or forms of mediumship, but despite her fervent belief that she might also possess the ability to produce so-called extras, or supernormal photographs, she never did during my investigations. What she did produce at times on her own were so-called scotographs, similar to Rorschach effects used in psychiatry; they were the result of briefly exposing sensitive photographic paper to light and then interpreting the resulting shapes.

But genuine psychic photography shows clear-cut images, faces, figures that need no special interpretation to be understood, and this, alas, did not occur in this case when I took the photographs with my camera in Mrs. Meyers's presence.

After the Brighams had sold the Maine property, they moved to Hampton, Virginia. Ken and Doris looked forward to many years of enjoying life in this gentler climate.

Unfortunately, exactly two years after our last contact, in August 1970, Ken slipped and injured an ankle, which in turn led to complications and his untimely and sudden death.

As for the restless ones up in Maine, nothing further was heard, and they are presumed to be where they rightfully belong.

The following research material, supplied by the late Mr. Ken Brigham, is presented here to give the reader a better feel for the territory and times in which this took place.

Brigham's documentation:
1. Roberts, Kenneth, *March to Quebec*, Doubleday, 1938, p. 32. Listed in the King's Service: Thomas Murdock.
2. Carpenter, Allan, *Enchantment of America—Maine*, Children's Press, 1966, p. 27—85 years of Indian warfare, more than 1,000 Maine residents killed, hundreds captured; by year 1675, there were about 6,000 European settlers in what is now Maine.
3. Smith, Bradford, *Roger's Rangers and the French and Indian War*, Random House, 1956, p. 5—Indians began to slaughter them when they marched out of Fort William Henry to surrender—women and children and men (1757); p. 6—Robert Rogers of New York raised company of rangers in 1755, by 1758 had five companies. Ebenezer Webster came from his home in New Hampshire; p. 46—mentioned Colonel Bradstreet; p. 176—Ebenezer, 1761, returned east to Albany as Captain and then to New Hampshire where he married a girl named Mehitable Smith . . . pushed northward with men under Colonel Stevens and settled on 225 acres at northern edge of town of Salisbury. Later fought in revolutionary war.

Oxford County Registry of Deeds
(References: Book 14, p. 18; Bk. 25, p. 295; Bk. 49, p. 254; Bk. 67,
    p. 264; Bk. 92, p. 158; Bk. 110, p. 149; Bk. 117, p. 268; Bk.
    187, p. 197; Bk. 102, p. 135; Bk. 240, pp. 477–78; Bk. 260, p.
    381)

1805   Abraham (or Abram) Whitney sold to Nathan Jewell
1809   Nathan Jewell sold to William Monroe (part of land and
       the house) (1/9/09)
1823   Jonathan Stone bankrupt and sold to Peter Gerry (house),
       Thaddeus Brown and Josiah Shaw (5/19/23)
1836   Peter Gerry sold to Moses M. Mason (6/14/36)
1848   John Gerry sold to Daniel Billings (5/27/48)
1895   Semantha Bell sold to Caroline Bell (3/4/95)
1940   Edna Culhan (daughter of Caroline Bell) sold to Irving and
       Alice Bell (11/7/40)
1956   Alice Bell transferred to Archie and Ethel Bell (10/12/56)
1959   Archie and Ethel Bell sold to K. E. and D. M. Brigham (1/
       59)

Bk. 3, p. 484, Feb 7, 1799
Isaac Smith of Waterford for $800 sold to Nathaniel Geary of
    Harvard, Lot 2 in 6th Range (southerly half). Deed written
    February 7, 1799, but not recorded until September 24,
    1808. (m. Unice Smith) (See notes 1 and 2)

Vol. 3, p. 99, Jan 6, 1800 (Fryeburg)
Nathaniel Geary and Betey Geary, his wife, sold to Peter Geary for
    $400 westerly end of southern half of Lot 2 in 6th Range.
    Notarized in York, January 6, 1800. On April 2, 1801 Betey
    Geary appeared and signed document which was regis-
    tered on February 11, 1804.

Peter Gerry (or Geary) b. 1776—d. 6/16/1847
m. Mary (b. 1782—d. 3/16/1830)
m. Elizabeth (b. 1787—d. 5/1/1858)
    c. Mary (b. 1834 or 1804—d. 1844)
    (see note 3) John C. (b. 1808)
    Roland (b. 1810—d. 1842)
    m. Maria Farrar (b. 1811—d. 1842)

Abbie (b. 1812—d. 1817)
Elbridge (b. 1815—m. Anna Jenness)

Bk. 92, p. 158, May 27, 1848
John Gerry sold for $100 (?) to Daniel Billings
Daniel Billings (b. 1780 Temple, Massachusetts)
—m. Sarah Kimball (b. 1786)
—c. Louise (m. William Hamlin)
    Caroline (b. 1810—m. G. F. Wheeler—b. 1810)
    George C. (b. 1837—d. 1919)
    —m. Rebecca Whitcomb, private F. Co., 9th Reg.—3 years
    svc. Civil War
    Maria (m. Calvin Houghton)
    James R. (m. Esther Clark)
    John D. (m. Esther Knowlton)
    Miranda

Bk. 102, p. 135, Oct 14, 1851
Daniel Billings sold to William F. Bell of Boston and Timothy Bell
    for $1,400

Bk. 117, p. 268, Dec 24, 1858
William Bell of Waterford paid his father, William F. Bell, $800 for
    Lot 2 in 6th Range

Bk. 187, p. 197, April 3, 1871
William Bell, "for support of self and wife," transferred to Timo-
    thy C. Bell "homestead farm" and its parts of lots

Bk. 240, p. 24, 1894
Timothy Bell left property to his wife Semantha Bell

Bk. 240, pp. 477–78, Mar 4, 1895
Semantha Hamlin Bell transferred to Caroline Bell of Boston
    Caroline Bell (b. 4/4/1848—d. 9/20/1926)
    —m. T. C. Bell (b. 10/10/1829—d. 7/13/1894)
    —m. J. B. Bennett

1905
Caroline Bell (d. 1905?) left property to her son Irving Bell, "her
    sole heir"

Bk. 442, p. 133, Oct 30, 1940
Edna Bell Culhan (unmarried) of Cambridge, Mass., transferred
    to Irving and Alice Bell
Nov. 7, 1940
Irving Bell transferred to Edna Culhan "premises described in
    deed from Semantha to his mother Caroline Bell and he was
    her sole heir."

Bk. 560, p. 381, Oct 12, 1956
Archie and Ethel Bell inherited Lots 1 and 2 in the 5th Range and
    Lots 1 and 2 in the 6th Range from Alice Bell
Jan 1959
Archie and Ethel Bell sold property to K. E. and D. M. Brigham

Notes
1. According to Bk. 2, pp. 445–46: On December 20, 1802, Nathaniel Gerry (wife Betey) for $800 sold to David Whitcomb of
   Boston, Mass., Lot 2 in 6th Range. Deed mentions road running thru land. Registered 1807 and notarized and signed by
   Justice of the Peace Eber Rice.
2. According to Bk. 9, p. 467–68: On November 13, 1810, David
   Whitcomb for $150 sold to Peter Gerry Lot 2 in the 6th Range,
   including "Gerry Road." Apparently both these transactions
   (notes 1 and 2) were concerned with the westerly end of the
   northern half of Lot 2 in the 6th Range.
3. John C. Gerry (b. 1808): m. Nancy Farrar (b. 1810—d. 1841),
   Nancy Sawin (b. 1819). He had an apothecary store in Fryeburg.

Interesting Notes
1. Local cemetery has gravestone of Hon. Lewis Brigham, b.
   1816, d. 1866 (at Amherst, Mass.).
2. Eben Bell (b. 8/5/1820—d. 6/8/1900)
3. Richard and Samuel Brigham, and David Whitcomb, signed
   petition for incorporation on December 19, 1795.
4. Historical:
   Waterford was in York County when it applied for incorporation (January 27, 1796).
   Fryeburg (Pequawkett) was settled in 1763, Inc. 1777; in 1768
   Fryeburg had population 300 plus.

November 17, 1796—Isaac Smith petitioned, with others, Massachusetts for incorporation. Document stated there were fifty to sixty families in "said plantation."

History of Waterford, p. 25—"and when the Indians attacked the growing settlements on the Androscoggin in 1781, and carried Lt. Segar* and others into Canadian captivity, Lt. Stephen Farrington led twenty-three men over this trail in hot, although vain pursuit of the savages."

(*Lt. Nathaniel Segar had cleared a few acres in 1774. A few townships, as Waterford and New Suncook [Lovell and Sweden] had been surveyed and awaited settlers, p. 22)

Waterford, settled 1775, incorporated 1797; population 1790—150; 1800—535

"Spirit of 76" (Commanger/Morris, p. 605)—General Burgoyne surrenders October 1777 . . . General John Stark agreed to work with Seth Warner because Warner was from New Hampshire or the Hampshire Grants (1777).

November 15, 1745—First Massachusetts Regiment, under Sir William Pepperrell—8th company: Capt. Thomas Perkins, Lt. John Burbank, John Gerry (single).

Civil War: "Fifth Regiment commanded by Mark H. Dunnill of Portland. "Fifth was engaged in eleven pitched battles and eight skirmishes ere it entered on terrible campaign of the Wilderness which was an incessant battle. It captured 6 rebel flags and more prisoners than it had in its ranks."

5. Local Notes:
A) Androscoggin Trail was the main Indian route from the East Coast to Canada. Below our property, in the area of Lot 3 in the 4th Range, it follows a brook called "Mutiny Brook." The origin of the term used here is vague, but the natives say Indians mutinied there during the French and Indian Wars.
B) When the town was first settled, the pioneers built their homes on our hill rather than the flat land and the only road around Bear Lake was at the foot of Sweden and Blackguard roads.
C) Our road is called by the archaic word "Blackguard" which connotes villain. No one knows why.

The Sailor's Wife

One of my favorite cases of haunting, and truly a beautiful story of human faith and patience, took me to Maine as part of my work for the NBC television series "In Search of . . ." It was the kind of true story no novelist could invent.

Port Clyde is a lovely little fishing village on the coast of Maine where a small number of native Yankees, who live there all year round, try to cope with a few summer residents, usually from New York or the Midwest. Their worlds do not really mesh, but the oldtimers realize that a little—not too much—tourism is really quite good for business, especially the few small hotels in and around Port Clyde and St. George, so they don't mind them too much. But the Down Easterners do keep to themselves, and it isn't always easy to get them to open up about their private lives or such things as, let us say, ghosts.

Carol Olivieri Schulte lived in Council Bluffs, Iowa, when she first contacted me in November 1974. The wife of a lawyer, Mrs. Schulte is an inquisitive lady, a college graduate, and the mother of what was then a young son. Carol had been intrigued by my books, especially where ghosts were concerned, because she, too, had had a brush with the uncanny.

"It was the summer of 1972," she explained to me, "and I was sleeping in an upstairs bedroom," in the summer cottage her parents owned in Port Clyde. "My girlfriend Marion and her boyfriend were sleeping in a bedroom across the hall with their animals, a Siamese cat and two dogs."

The cat had been restless and crept into Carol's room, touching her pillow and waking her. Carol sat up in bed, ready to turn on the light, when she saw standing beside her bed a female figure in a very white nightgown. The figure had small shoulders and long, flowing hair . . . and Carol could see right through her!

It became apparent, as she came closer, that she wanted to get Carol's attention, trying to talk with her hands.

"Her whole body suggested she was in desperate need of something. Her fingers were slender, and there was a diamond ring on her fourth finger, on the right hand. Her hands moved more desperately as I ducked under the covers."

Shortly after this, Carol had a dream contact with the same entity. This time she was sleeping in another room in the house when she saw the same young woman. She appeared at first in the air, smaller than life size. Her breasts were large, and there was a maternal feeling about her. With her was a small child, a boy of perhaps three years of age, also dressed in a white gown. While the child was with Carol on her bed, in the dream, the mother hovered at some distance in the corner. Carol, in the dream, had the feeling the mother had turned the child over to her, as if to protect it, and then she vanished. Immediately there followed the appearance of another woman, a black-hooded female, seeming very old, coming toward her and the child. Carol began to realize the dark-hooded woman wanted to take the child from her, and the child was afraid and clung to her. When the woman stood close to Carol's bed, still in the dream, Carol noticed her bright green eyes, large crooked nose, and dark complexion. She decided to fight her off, concentrating her thoughts on the white light she knew was an expression of psychic protection, and the dark-hooded woman disappeared. Carol was left with the impression that she had been connected with a school or institution of some kind. At this, the mother in her white nightgown returned and took the child back, looking at Carol with an expression of gratitude before disappearing again along with her child.

Carol woke up, but the dream was so vivid, it stayed with her for weeks, and even when she contacted me, it was still crystal clear in her mind. One more curious event transpired at the exact time Carol had overcome the evil figure in the dream. Her grandmother, whom she described as "a very reasoning, no-nonsense lively Yankee lady," had a cottage right in back of Carol's parents' house. She was tending her stove, as she had done many times before, when it blew up right into her face, singeing her eyebrows. There was nothing whatever wrong with the stove.

Carol had had psychic experiences before, and even her attorney husband was familiar with the world of spirits, so her contacting me for help with the house in Maine was by no means a family problem.

I was delighted to hear from her, not because a Maine ghost was so very different from the many other ghosts I had dealt with through the years, but because of the timing of Carol's request. It so happened that at that time I was in the middle of writing, producing, and appearing in the NBC series called "In Search of . . ." and the ghost house in Maine would make a fine segment.

An agreement was arranged among all concerned—Carol, her husband, her parents, the broadcasting management, and me. I then set about to arrange a schedule for our visit. In the end we decided on May, when the weather would be acceptable, and the water in the house would be turned back on. I requested that all witnesses of actual phenomena in the house be present to be questioned by me.

Carol then sent along pictures of the house and statements from some of the witnesses. I made arrangements to have her join us at the house for the investigation and filming for the period of May 13–15, 1976. The team—the crew, my psychic, and me—would all stay over at a local hotel. The psychic was a young woman artist named Ingrid Beckman, with whom I had been working and helping develop her gift.

And so it happened that we congregated at Port Clyde from different directions, but with one purpose in mind—to contact the lady ghost at the house. As soon as we had settled in at the local hotel, the New Ocean House, we drove over to the spanking white cottage that was to be the center of our efforts for the next three days. Carol's brother Robert had driven up from Providence, and her close friend Marion Going from her home, also in Rhode Island.

I asked Ingrid to stay at a little distance from the house and wait for me to bring her inside, while I spoke to some of the witnesses out of Ingrid's earshot. Ingrid understood and sat down on the lawn, taking in the beauty of the landscape.

Carol and I walked in the opposite direction, and once again we went over her experiences as she had reported them to me in her earlier statement. I questioned Carol about whether there was anything beyond that.

"Now since that encounter with the ghostly lady have you seen her again? Have you ever heard her again?"

"Well about three weeks ago before I was to come out here, I really wanted to communicate with her. I concentrated on it just before I went to sleep, you know. I was thinking about it, and I dreamed that she appeared to me the way she had in the dream that followed her apparition here in this house. And then I either dreamed that I woke up momentarily and saw her right there as I had actually seen her in this bedroom or I actually did wake up and see her. Now the sphere of consciousness I was in—I am doubtful as to where I was at that point. I mean it was nothing like the experience I experienced right here in this room. I was definitely awake, and I *definitely saw that ghost.* As to this other thing a couple of weeks ago—I wasn't quite sure."

"Was there any kind of message?"

"No, not this last time."

"Do you feel she was satisfied having made contact with you?"

"Yeah, I felt that she wanted to communicate with me in the same sense that I wanted to communicate with her. Like an old friend will want to get in touch with another old friend, and I get the feeling she was just saying, 'Yes, I'm still here.' "

I then turned to Carol's brother, Bob Olivieri, and questioned him about his own encounters with anything unusual in the house. He took me to the room he was occupying at the time of the experiences, years ago, but apparently the scene was still very fresh in his mind.

"Mr. Olivieri, what exactly happened to you in this room?"

"Well, one night I was sleeping on this bed and all of a sudden I woke up and heard footsteps—what I thought were footsteps—it sounded like slippers or baby's feet in pajamas—something like that. Well, I woke up and I came over, and I stepped in this spot, and I looked in the hallway and the sound stopped. I thought maybe I was imagining it. So I came back to the bed, got into bed again, and again I heard footsteps. Well, this time I got up and as soon as I came to the same spot again and looked into the hallway it stopped. I figured it was my nephew who was still awake. So I walked down the hallway and looked into the room where my sister and nephew were sleeping, and they were both sound asleep. I checked my parents' room, and they were also asleep. I just walked back. I didn't know what to do so I got into bed again, and I kept on hearing them. I kept on walking over, and they would still be going until I stepped in this spot where they would stop. As soon as I stepped here. And this happened for an hour. I kept getting up. Heard the footsteps, stepped in this spot and they stopped. So finally I got kind of tired of it and came over to my bed and lay down in bed and as soon as I lay down I heard the steps again, exactly what happened before—and they seemed to stop at the end of the hallway. A few minutes later I felt a pressure on my sheets, starting from my feet, and going up, up, up, going up further, further, slowly but surely . . . and finally something pulled my hair! Naturally I was just scared for the rest of the night. I couldn't get to sleep."

I thought it was time to get back to Ingrid and bring her into the house. This I did, with the camera and sound people following us every step of the way to record for NBC what might transpire in the house now. Just before we entered the house, Ingrid turned to me and said, "You know that window up there? When we first arrived, I noticed someone standing in it."

"What exactly did you see?"

"It was a woman . . . and she was looking out at us."

The house turned out to be a veritable jewel of Yankee authenticity, the kind of house a sea captain might be happy in, or perhaps only a modern antiquarian. The white exterior was matched by a spanking clean, somewhat sparse interior, with every piece of furniture of the right period—the nineteenth and early twentieth centuries—and a feeling of being lived in by many people, for many years.

After we had entered the downstairs part, where there was an ample kitchen and a nice day room, I asked Ingrid, as usual, to tell me whatever psychic impression she was gathering about the house, its people, and its history. Naturally, I had made sure all along that Ingrid knew nothing of the house or the quest we had come on to Maine, and there was absolutely no way she could have had access to specifics about the area, the people in the house—past and present—nor anything at all about the case.

Immediately Ingrid set to work, she seemed agitated.

"There is a story connected here with the 1820s or the

1840s," she began, and I turned on my tape recorder to catch the impressions she received as we went along. At first, they were conscious psychic readings, later Ingrid seemed in a slight state of trance and communication with spirit entities directly. Here is what followed.

"1820s and 1840s. Do you mean both or one or the other?"

"Well, it's in that time period. And I sense a woman with a great sense of remorse."

"Do you feel this is a presence here?"

"Definitely a presence here."

"What part of the house do you feel it's strongest in?"

"Well, I'm being told to go upstairs."

"Is it a force pulling you up?"

"No, I just have a feeling to go upstairs."

"Before you go upstairs, before you came here did you have any feeling that there was something to it?"

"Yes, several weeks ago I saw a house—actually it was a much older house than this one, and it was on this site—and it was a dark house and it was shingled and it was—as I say, could have been an eighteenth-century house, the house that I saw. It looked almost like a salt box, it had that particular look. And I saw that it was right on the water and I sensed a woman in it and a story concerned with a man in the sea with this house."

"A man with the sea?"

"Yes."

"Do you feel that this entity is still in the house?"

"I do, and of course I don't feel this is the *original* house. I feel it was on this property, and this is why I sense that she is throughout the house. That she comes here because this is her reenactment."

I asked her to continue.

"I can see in my mind's eye the house that was on this property before, and in my mind I sense a field back in this direction, and there was land that went with this!"

"Now we are upstairs. I want you to look into every room and give me your impressions of it," I said.

"Well, the upstairs is the most active. I sense a woman who is waiting. This is in the same time period. There are several other periods that go with this house, but I will continue with this one. I also see that she has looked out—not from this very same window, but windows in this direction of the house—*waiting for somebody to come back."*

"What about this room?"

"Well, this room is like the room where she conducted a vigil, waiting for someone. And I just got an impression where she said that, 'She' meaning a schooner, 'was built on the Kennebec River.' . . . It seems to be a double-masted schooner, and it seems to be her husband who is on this. And I have an impression of novelties that he has brought her back. Could be from a foreign country. Perhaps the Orient or something like that."

"Now go to the corridor again and try some of the other rooms. What about this one?"

"I sense a young man in this room, but this is from a different time period. It's a young boy. It seems to be 1920s."

"Is that all you sense in this room?"

"That is basically what I sense in this room. The woman of the double-masted schooner story is throughout the house because as I have said, she doesn't really belong to this house. She is basically on the *property*—mainly she still goes through this whole house looking for the man to come home. And the front of the house is where the major activity is. She is always watching. But I have an impression now of a storm that she is very upset about. A gale of some kind. It seems to be November. I also feel she is saying something about . . . flocking sheep. There are sheep on this property."

"Where would you think is the most active room?"

"The most active room I think is upstairs and to the front, where we just were. I feel it most strongly there."

"Do you think we might be able to make contact with her?"

"Yes, I think so. Definitely I feel that she is watching *and I knew about her before I came.*"

"What does she look like?"

"I see a tall woman, who is rather thin and frail with dark hair and it appears to be a white gown. It could be a nightgown I see her in—it looks like a nightgown to me with a little embroidery on the front. Hand done."

"Let us see if she cares to make contact with us."

"All right."

"If the entity is present, and wishes to talk to us, we have come as friends; she is welcome to use this instrument, Ingrid, to manifest."

"She is very unhappy here, Hans. She says her family hailed from England. I get her name as Margaret."

"Margaret what?"

"Something like Hogen—it begins with an H. I don't think it is Hogan, Hayden, or something like that. I'm not getting the whole name."

"What period are you in now?"

"Now she says 1843. She is very unhappy because she wanted to settle in Kennebunk; she does not like it here. She doesn't like the responsibilities of the house. Her husband liked it in this fishing village. She is very unhappy about his choice."

"Is he from England?"

"Yes, their descendants are from England."

"You mean were they born here or in England?"

"That I'm not clear on. But they have told me that their ancestors are English."

"Now is she here . . . ?"

"She calls Kennebunk the city. That to her is a center."

"What does she want? Why is she still here?"

"She's left with all this responsibility. Her husband went on a ship, to come back in two years."

"Did he?"

"No, she's still waiting for him."

"The name of the ship?"

"I think it's St. Catherine."

"Is it his ship? Is he a captain?"

"He is second in command. It's not a mate, but a second something or other."

"What is she looking for?"

"She's looking to be relieved."

"Of what?"

"Of the duties and the responsibilities."

"For what?"

"This house."

"Is she aware of her passing?"

"No, she's very concerned over the flocks. She says it's now come April, and it's time for shearing. She is very unhappy over this. In this direction, Hans, I can see what appears to be a barn, and it's very old fashioned. She had two cows."

"Is she aware of the people in the house now?"

"She wants to communicate."

"What does she want them to do for her?"

"She wants for them to help her with the farm. She says it's too much, and the soil is all rocky and she can't get labor from the town. She's having a terrible time. It's too sandy here."

"Are there any children? Is she alone?"

"They have gone off, she says."

"And she's alone now?"

"Yes, she is."

"Can you see her?"

"Yes, I do see her."

"Can she see you?"

"Yes."

"Tell her that this is 1976, and that much time has passed. Does she understand this?"

"She just keeps complaining; she has nobody to write letters to."

"Does she understand that her husband has passed on and that she herself is a spirit and that there is no need to stay if she doesn't wish to?"

"She needs to get some women from the town to help with the spinning."

"Tell her that the new people in the house are taking care of everything, and she is relieved and may go on. She's free to go."

"She said, 'to Kennebunk?' "

"Any place she wishes—to the city or to join her husband on the other side of life."

"She said, 'Oh, what I would do for a town house.' "

"Ask her to call out to her husband to take her away. He's waiting for her."

"What does Johnsbury mean? A Johnsbury."

"It's a place."

"She asking about Johnsbury."

"Does she wish to go there?"

"She feels someone may be there who could help her."

"Who?"

"It seems to be an uncle in Johnsbury."

"Then tell her to call out to her uncle in Johnsbury."

"She says he has not answered her letters."

"But if she speaks up now he will come for her. Tell her to do it now. Tell Margaret we are sending her to her uncle, with our love and compassion. That she need not stay here any longer. That she need not wait any longer for someone who cannot return. That she must go on to the greater world that awaits her outside, where she will rejoin her husband and she can see her uncle."

"She is wanting to turn on the lights. She is talking about the oil lamps. She wants them all lit."

"Tell her the people here will take good care of the house, of the lamps, and of the land."

"And she is saying, no tallow for the kitchen."

"Tell her not to worry."

"And the root cellar is empty."

"Tell her not to worry. We will take care of that for her. She is free to go—she is being awaited, she is being expected. Tell her to go on and go on from here in peace and with our love and compassion."

"She is looking for a lighthouse, or something about a lighthouse that disturbs her."

"What is the lighthouse?"

"She is very upset. She doesn't feel that it's been well kept; that this is one of the problems in this area. No one to tend things. I ought to be in Kennebunk, she says, where it is a city."

"Who lives in Kennebunk that she knows?"

"No one she knows. She wants to go there."

"What will she do there?"

"Have a town house."

"Very well, then let her go to Kennebunk."

"And go [to] the grocer," she says.

"Tell her she's free to go to Kennebunk. That we will send her there if she wishes. Does she wish to go to Kennebunk?"

"Yes, she does."

"Then tell her—tell her we are sending her now. With all our love . . ."

"In a carriage?"

"In a carriage."

"A black carriage with two horses."

"Very well. Is she ready to go?"

"Oh, I see her now in a fancy dress with a bonnet. But she's looking younger—she's looking much younger now. And I see a carriage out front with two dark horses and a man with a hat ready to take her."

"Did she get married in Kennebunk?"

"No."

"Where did she get married?"

"I don't get that."

"Is she ready to go?"

"Yes, she is."

"Tell her to get into the carriage and drive off."

"Yes, she's ready."

"Then go, Margaret—go."

"She says, many miles—three-day trip."

"All right. Go with our blessings. Do you see her in the carriage now?"

"Yes, the road goes this way. She is going down a winding road."

"Is she alone in the carriage?"

"Yes, she is, but there is a man driving."

"Who is the man who is driving?"

"A hired man."

"Is she in the carriage now?"

"Yes, she is."

"Is she on her way?"

"Yes."

"All right, then wave at her and tell her we send her away with our love."

"She looks to be about twenty-two now. Much younger."

"She's not to return to this house."

"She doesn't want to. She grew old in this house, she says."

"What was the house called then?"

"It was Point something."

"Did they build the house? She and her husband?"

"No, it was there."

"Who built it?"

"Samuel."

"And who was Samuel?"

"A farmer."

"They bought it from him?"

"Yes, they did. She says the deed is in the town hall."
"Of which town? Is it in this village?"
"Next town. Down the road."
"I understand. And in whose name is the deed?"
"Her husband's."
"First name."
"James."
"James what. Full name."
"It's something like Haydon."
"James Haydon from . . . ? What is Samuel's first name?"
"Samuels was the last name of the people who owned it."
"But the first name of the man who sold it. Does she remember that?"
"She never knew it."
"In what year was that?"
"1821."
"How much did they pay for the house?"
"Barter."
"What did they give them?"
"A sailing ship. A small sailing ship for fishing, and several horses. A year's supply of roots, and some paper—currency. Notes."
"But no money?"
"Just notes. Like promises, she says. Notes of promises."
"What was the full price of the house?"
"All in barter, all in exchange up here."
"But there was no sum mentioned for the house? No value?"
"She says, 'Ask my husband.' "
"Now did she and her husband live here alone?"
"Two children."
"What were their names?"
"Philip. But he went to sea."
"And the other one?"
"Francis."
"Did he go to sea too?"
"No."
"What happened to him?"
"I think Francis died."
"What did he die of?"
"Cholera. He was seventeen."

"Where did they get married? In what church?"

"Lutheran."

"Why Lutheran? Was she Lutheran?"

"She doesn't remember."

"Does she remember the name of the minister?"

"Thorpe."

"Thorpe?"

"Yes. Thorpe."

"What was his first name?"

"Thomas Thorpe."

"And when they were married, was that in this town?"

"No."

"What town was it in?"

"A long way away."

"What was the name of the town?"

"Something like Pickwick . . . a funny name like that . . . it's some kind of a province of a place. A Piccadilly—a province in the country she says."

"And they came right here after that? Or did they go anywhere else to live?"

"Saco. They went into Saco."

"That's the name of a place?"

"Yes."

"How long did they stay there?"

"Six months in Saco."

"And then?"

"Her husband had a commission."

"What kind of commission?"

"On a whaling ship."

"What was the name of the ship?"

"*St. Catherine.* I see *St. Catherine* or *St. Catherines.*"

"And then where did they move to?"

"Port Clyde."

". . . and they stayed here for the rest of their lives?"

"Yes, until he went to sea and didn't come back one time."

"His ship didn't come back?"

"No."

"Does she feel better for having told us this?"

"Oh, yes."

"Tell her that she . . ."

"She says it's a long story."

"Tell her that she need not stay where so much unhappiness has transpired in her life. Tell her her husband is over there . . ."

"Yes."

"Does she understand?"

"Yes, she does."

"Does she want to see him again?"

"Yes."

"Then she must call out to him to come to her. Does she understand that?"

"Yes."

"Then tell her to call out to her husband, James, right now."

"He'll take her to Surrey or something like that, he says."

"Surrey."

"Surrey. Some funny name."

"Is it a place?"

"Yes, it is."

"Does she see him?"

"Yes."

"Are they going off together?"

"Yes, I see her leaving, slowly, but she's looking back."

"Tell her to go and not to return here. Tell her to go with love and happiness and in peace. Are they gone?"

"They are going. It's a reunion."

"We wish them well and we send them from this house, with our blessings, with our love and compassion, and in peace. Go on, go on. What do you see?"

"They are gone."

And with that, we left the house, having done enough for one day, a very full day. The camera crew packed up, so that we could continue shooting in the morning. As for me, the real work was yet to come: corroborating the material Ingrid Beckman had come up with.

I turned to Carol for verification, if possible, of some of the names and data Ingrid had come up with while in the house. Carol showed us a book containing maps of the area, and we started to check it out.

"Look," Carol said and pointed at the passage in the book, "this strip of land was owned by John Barter and it was right next to Samuel Gardner . . . and it says John Barter died in 1820

. . . the date mentioned by Ingrid! Ah, and there is also mention of the same Margaret Barter, and there is a date on the same page, November 23, 1882 . . . I guess that is when she died."

"Great," I said, pleased to get all this verification so relatively easily. "What exactly is this book?"

"It's a copy of the town's early records, the old hypothogue, of the town of St. George."

"Isn't that the town right next door?"

"Yes, it is."

"What about the name Hogden or Hayden or Samuel?"

"Samuel Hatton was a sailor and his wife was named Elmira," Carol said, pointing at the book. Ingrid had joined us now, since I saw no further need to keep her in the dark regarding verifications—her part of the work was done.

"We must verify that," I said. "Also, was there ever a ship named *St. Catherine* and was it built on the Kennebec River as Ingrid claimed?"

But who would be able to do that? Happily, fate was kind; there was a great expert who knew both the area and history of the towns better than anyone around, and he agreed to receive us. He was a colorful ex-sailor by the name of Commander Albert Smalley, and he received us in his house in St. George—a house, I might add, that was superbly furnished to suggest the bridge of a ship. After we had stopped admiring his mementos, and made some chitchat to establish the seriousness of our mission, I turned to the Commander and put the vital questions to him directly.

"Commander Albert Smalley, you've been a resident in this town for how long?"

"I was born in this town seventy-six years ago."

"I understand you know more about the history of Port Clyde than anybody else."

"Well, that's a moot question, but I will say, possibly, yes."

"Now, to the best of your knowledge, do the names Samuel and Hatton mean anything in connection with this area?"

"Yes, I know Hatton lived at Port Clyde prior to 1850. That I'm sure about."

"What profession did he have?"

"Sailor."

"Was there a ship named the *St. Catherine* in these parts?"

"Yes, there was."

"And would it have been built at the Kennebec River? Or connected with it in some way?"

"Well, as I recall it was, and I believe it was built in the Sewell Yard at the Kennebec River."

"Was there any farming in a small way in the Port Clyde area in the nineteenth century?"

"Oh yes, primarily that's what they came here for. But fishing, of course, was a prime industry."

"Now there's a lighthouse not far from Port Clyde that I believe was built in the early part of the nineteenth century. Could it have been there in the 1840s?"

"Yes. It was built in 1833."

"Now if somebody would have been alive in 1840, would they somehow be concerned about this comparatively new lighthouse? Would it have worried them?"

"No, it would not. The residence is comparatively new. The old stone residence was destroyed by lightning. But the tower is the same one."

"Now you know the area of Port Clyde where the Leah Davis house now stands? Prior to this house, were there any houses in the immediate area?"

"I've always been told that there was a house there. The Davis that owned it told me that he built on an old cellar."

"And how far back would that go?"

"That would go back to probably 1870. The new house was built around 1870."

"And was there one before that?"

"Yes, there was one before that."

"Could that have been a farmhouse?"

"Yes, it could have been because there is a little farm in back of it. It's small."

"Now you of course have heard all kinds of stories—some of them true, some of them legendary. Have you ever heard any story of a great tragedy concerning the owners of the farmhouse on that point?"

"Whit Thompson used to tell some weird ghost stories. But everyone called him a damned liar. Whether it's true or not, I don't know, but I've heard them."

"About that area?"

"About that area."

"Was there, sir, any story about a female ghost—a woman?"

"I have heard of a female ghost. Yes, Whit used to tell that story."

"What did he tell you?"

"That was a long time ago, and I cannot recall just what he said about it—he said many things—but she used to appear, especially on foggy nights, and it was hard to distinguish her features —that was one of the things he used to tell about—and there was something about her ringing the bell at the lighthouse, when they used to ring the old fog bell there. I don't recall what it was."

"Now the story we found involved a woman wearing a kind of white gown, looking out to sea from the window as if she were expecting her sailor to return, and she apparently was quite faceless at first."

"I don't think Whitney ever told of her face being seen."

"Do you know of anybody in your recollection who has actually had an unusual experience in that particular area?"

"No, I don't."

"Commander, if you had the choice of spending the night in the house in question, would it worry you?"

"No, why should it?"

"You are not afraid of ghosts?"

"No. Why should I be?"

"They are people after all."

"Huh?"

"They are just people after all."

"Yes."

"Have you ever seen one?"

"No, I was brought up with mediums and spiritualists and as a kid I was frightened half to death, I didn't dare go out after dark, but I got over that."

"Thank you very much."

"The lighthouse and the gale . . . the ship in a gale . . . it all seems to fit." Ingrid murmured as we got back into our cars and left the Commander's house.

And there you have it. A girl from the big city who knows nothing about the case I am investigating, nor where she might be taken, and still comes up with names and data she could not possibly know on her own. Ingrid Beckman was (and is, I sup-

pose) a gifted psychic. Shortly after we finished taping the Port
Clyde story, I left for Europe.

While I was away, Ingrid met a former disc jockey then getting interested in the kind of work she and I had been doing so
successfully for a while. Somehow he persuaded her to give a
newspaper interview about this case, which, of course, upset NBC
—since this segment would not air for six months—not to mention
me. The newspaper story was rather colorful, making it appear
that Ingrid had heard of this ghost and taken care of it . . . but
then newspaper stories sometimes distort things, or perhaps the
verification and research of a ghost story is less interesting to
them than the story itself. But to a professional like myself, the
evidence only becomes evidence when it is carefully verified. I
haven't worked with Ingrid since.

As for the ghostly lady of Port Clyde, nothing further has been
heard about her, either, and since we gently persuaded her not to
hang on any longer, chances are that she has long been joined by
her man, sailing an ocean where neither gales nor nosy television
crews can intrude.

Maryland

A Ghost
Named Frank

Mrs. J. H. is a housewife living in Maryland. At the time of the incidents I am about to report, her son, Richard, was seven and her daughter, Cheryl, six. Hers was a conventional marriage, until the tragic death of her husband, Frank. On September 3, he was locking up a restaurant where he was employed near Washington, D.C. Suddenly, two men entered by the rear door and shot him while attempting a robbery. For more than a year after the murder, no clue to the murderers' identities was found.

Mrs. H. was still grieving over the sudden loss of her husband when something extraordinary took place in her home. Exactly one month to the day after his death, she happened to be in her living room when she saw a "wall of light" and something floated across the living room toward her. From it stepped the person of her late husband. He seemed quite real to her, but somewhat transparent. Frightened, the widow turned on the lights and the apparition faded.

From that moment on, the house seemed to be alive with strange phenomena: knocks at the door that disclosed no one who could have caused them, the dog barking for no good reason in the middle of the night, or the cats staring as if they were looking at a definite person in the room. Then one day the two children went into the bathroom and saw their dead father taking a shower! Needless to say, Mrs. H. was at a loss to explain that to them. The widow had placed all of her late husband's clothes into an unused closet that was kept locked. She was the last one to go to bed at night and the first one to arise in the morning, and one morning she awoke to find Frank's shoes in the hallway; no one else in the house could have placed them there.

One day Mrs. H.'s mother, Mrs. D., who lives nearby, was washing clothes in her daughter's basement. When she approached the washer, she noticed that it was spotted with what appeared to be fresh blood. Immediately she and Mrs. H. searched the basement, looking for a possible leak in the ceiling to account for the blood, but they found nothing. Shortly afterward, a sister of the widow arrived to have lunch at the house. A fresh tablecloth was placed on the table. When the women started to clear the table after lunch, they noticed that under each dish there was a blood spot the size of a fifty-cent piece. Nothing they had eaten at lunch could possibly have accounted for such a stain.

But the widow's home was not the only place where manifestations took place. Her mother's home was close by, and one night a clock radio alarm went off by itself in a room that had not been entered by anyone for months. It was the room belonging to Mrs. H.'s grandmother, who had been in the hospital for some time before.

It became clear to Mrs. H. that her husband was trying to get in touch with her, since the phenomena continued at an unabated pace. Three years after his death, two alarm clocks in the house went off at the same time, although they had not been set, and all the kitchen cabinets flew open by themselves. The late Frank H. appeared to his widow punctually on the third of each month, the day he was murdered, but the widow could not bring herself to address him and ask him what he wanted. Frightened, she turned on the light, which caused him to fade away. In the middle of the night Mrs. H. would feel someone shake her shoulder, as if to wake her up. She recognized this touch as that of her late husband, for it had been his habit to wake her in just that manner.

Meanwhile the murderers were caught. Unfortunately, by one of those strange quirks of justice, they got off easy; one of the murderers received three years in prison, the other ten. It seemed like a very light sentence for having taken a man's life so deliberately.

Time went on, and the children were ten and eleven years of age. Mrs. H. could no longer take the phenomena in the house and moved out. The house was rented to strangers who are still living in it. They have had no experiences of an uncanny nature since, after all, Frank wants nothing from *them*.

As for the new house where Mrs. H. and her children live

now, Frank has not yet put in an appearance. But there are occasional tappings on the wall, as if he still wanted to communicate
with his wife. Mrs. H. wishes she could sleep in peace in the new
home, but then she remembers how her late husband, who had
been a believer in scientology, had assured her that when he died,
he would be back. . . .

Massachusetts

Changes
in the House

Mr. Harold B. is a professional horse trainer who travels a good deal of the time. When he does stay at home, he lives in an old home in a small town in Massachusetts. Prior to moving to New England, he and his wife lived in Ohio, but he was attracted by the old-world atmosphere of New England and decided to settle down in the East. They found a house that was more than two hundred years old, but unfortunately it was in dire need of repair. There was neither electricity nor central heating, and all the rooms were dirty, neglected, and badly in need of renovating. Nevertheless, they liked the general feeling of the house and decided to take it.

The house was in a sad state, mostly because it had been lived in for fifty-five years by a somewhat eccentric couple who had shut themselves off from the world. They would hardly admit anyone to their home, and it was known in town that three of their dogs had died of starvation. Mr. and Mrs. B. moved into the house on Walnut Road in October. Shortly after their arrival, Mrs. B. fractured a leg, which kept her housebound for a considerable amount of time. This was especially unfortunate since the house needed so much work. Nevertheless, they managed. With professional help, they did the house over from top to bottom, putting in a considerable amount of work and money to make it livable, until it became a truly beautiful house.

Although Mrs. B. is not particularly interested in the occult, she has had a number of psychic experiences in the past, especially of a precognitive nature, and has accepted her psychic powers as a matter of course. Shortly after the couple had moved into the house on Walnut Road, they noticed that there *was* something peculiar about their home.

One night, Mrs. B. was sleeping alone in a downstairs front room off the center entrance hall. Suddenly she was awakened by the sensation of a presence in the room, and as she looked up she saw the figure of a small woman before her bed, looking right at her. She could make out all the details of the woman's face and stature, and noticed that she was wearing a veil, as widows some- times did in the past. When the apparition became aware of Mrs. B.'s attention, she lifted the veil and spoke to her, assuring her that she was not there to harm her, but that she came as a friend. Mrs. B. was too overcome by it all to reply, and before she could gather her wits, the apparition drifted away.

Immediately, Mrs. B made inquiries in town, and since she was able to give a detailed description of the apparition, it was not long until she knew who the ghost was. The description fit the former owner of the house, Mrs. C., to a tee. Mrs. C. died at age eighty-six, shortly before the B.'s moved into what was her former home. Armed with this information, Mrs. B. braced herself for the presence of an unwanted inhabitant in the house. A short time afterward, she saw the shadowy outline of what appeared to be a heavy-set person moving along the hall from her bedroom. At first she thought it was her husband so she called out to him, but she soon discovered that her husband was actually upstairs. She then examined her room and discovered that the shades were drawn, so there was no possibility that light from traffic on the road outside could have cast a shadow onto the adjoining hall. The shadowy figure she had seen did not, however, look like the out- line of the ghost she had earlier encountered in the front bed- room.

While she was still wondering about this, she heard the sound of a dog running across the floor. Yet there was no dog to be seen. Evidently her own dog also heard or sensed the ghostly dog's doings, because he reacted with visible terror.

Mrs. B. was still wondering about the second apparition when her small grandson came to stay overnight. He had never been to the house before, and had not been told of the stories connected with it. As he was preparing to go to sleep, but still fully conscious, he saw a heavy-set man wearing a red shirt standing before him in his bedroom. This upset him greatly, especially when the man suddenly disappeared without benefit of a door. He described the apparition to his grandparents, who reassured him by telling him a white lie: namely, that he had been dreaming. To this the boy indignantly replied that he had not been dreaming, but in fact had been fully awake. The description given by the boy not only fitted the shadowy outline of the figure Mrs. B. had seen along the corridor, but was a faithful description of the late Mr. C., the former owner of the house.

Although the ghost of Mrs. C. had originally assured the B.'s that they meant no harm and that she had, in fact, come as a friend, Mrs. B. had her doubts. A number of small items of no particular value disappeared from time to time, and were never found again. This happened at times when intruders were completely out of the question.

Then Mrs. B. heard the pages of a wallpaper sampler lying on the dining room table being turned one day. Thinking her husband was doing it, she called out to him, only to find that the room was empty. When she located him in another part of the house, he reported having heard the pages being turned also, and this reassured Mrs. B. since she now had her husband's support in the matter of ghosts. It was clear to her that the late owners did not appreciate the many changes they had made in the house. But Mrs. B. also decided that she was not about to be put out of her home by a ghost. The changes had been made for the better, she decided, and the C.'s, even in their present ghostly state, should be grateful for what they had done for the house and not resent them. Perhaps these thoughts somehow reached the two ghosts telepathically; at any rate, the atmosphere in the house became quiet after that.

The Victorian House Ghost

rs. Geraldine W. is a graduate of Boston City Hospital and works as a registered nurse; her husband is a teacher, and they have four children. Neither Mr. nor Mrs. W. ever had the slightest interest in the occult; in fact, Mrs. W. remembers hearing some chilling stories about ghosts as a child and considering them just so many fairy tales.

One July, the W.'s decided to acquire a house about twenty miles from Boston, as the conditions in the city seemed inappropriate for bringing up their four children. Their choice fell upon a Victorian home sitting on a large rock that overlooked a golf course in this little town. Actually, there are two houses built next door to each other by two brothers. The one to the left had originally been used as a winter residence, while the other, upon which their choice fell, was used as a summer home. It presented a remarkable sight, high above the other houses in the area. The house so impressed the W.'s that they immediately expressed their interest in buying it. They were told that it had once formed part of the H. estate, and had remained in the same family until nine years prior to their visit. Originally built by a certain Ephraim Hamblin, it had been sold to the H. family and remained a family property until it passed into the hands of a family initialed P. It remained in their possession until the W.'s acquired it that spring.

Prior to obtaining possession of the house, Mrs. W. had a strange dream in which she saw herself standing in the driveway, looking up at the house. In the dream she had a terrible feeling of foreboding, as if something dreadful had happened in the house.

On awakening the next morning, however, she thought no more about it and later put it out of her mind.

Shortly after they moved in on July 15, Mrs. W. awoke in the middle of the night for some reason. Her eyes fell upon the ceiling and she saw what looked to her like a sparkler-type of light. It swirled about in a circular movement, then disappeared. On checking, Mrs. W. found that all the shades were drawn in the room, so it perplexed her how such a light could have occurred on her ceiling. But the matter quickly slipped from her mind.

Several days later, she happened to be sitting in the living room one evening with the television on very low since her husband was asleep on the couch. Everything was very quiet. On the arm of a wide-armed couch there were three packages of cigarettes side by side. As she looked at them, the middle package suddenly flipped over by itself and fell to the floor. Since Mrs. W. had no interest in psychic phenomena, she dismissed this as probably due to some natural cause. A short time thereafter, she happened to be sleeping in her daughter's room, facing directly alongside the front hall staircase. The large hall light was burning since the lamp near the children's rooms had burned out. As she lay in the room, she became aware of heavy, slow, plodding footsteps coming across the hallway.

Terrified, she kept her eyes closed tight because she thought there was a prowler in the house. Since everyone was accounted for, only a stranger could have made the noises. She started to pray over and over in order to calm herself, but the footsteps continued on the stairs, progressing down the staircase and around into the living room where they faded away. Mrs. W. was thankful that her prayers had been answered and that the prowler had left.

Just as she started to doze off again the footsteps returned. Although she was still scared, she decided to brave the intruder, whoever he might be. As she got up and approached the area where she heard the steps, they resounded directly in front of her —yet she could see absolutely no one. The next morning she checked all the doors and windows and found them securely locked, just as she had left them the night before. She mentioned the matter to her husband, who ascribed it to nerves. A few nights later, Mrs. W. was again awakened in the middle of the night, this time in her own bedroom. As she woke and sat up in bed, she heard a woman's voice from somewhere in the room. It tried to form words, but Mrs. W. could not make them out. The voice was of a hollow nature and resembled something from an echo chamber. It seemed to her that the voice had come from an area near the ceiling over her husband's bureau, but the matter did not prevent her from going back to sleep, perplexing though it was.

By now Mrs. W. was convinced that they had a ghost in the house. She was standing in her kitchen, contemplating where she could find a priest to have the house exorcised, when all of a sudden a trash bag, which had been resting quietly on the floor, burst and crashed with its contents spilling all over the floor. The disturbances had become so frequent that Mrs. W. took every opportunity possible to leave the house early in the morning with her children, and not go home until she had to. She did not bring in a priest to exorcise the house, but managed to obtain a bottle of blessed water from Lourdes. She went through each room, sprinkling it and praying for the soul of whoever was haunting the house.

About that time, her husband came home from work one evening around six o'clock and went upstairs to change his clothes while Mrs. W. was busy setting the table for dinner. Suddenly Mr. W. called his wife and asked her to open and close the door to the back hall stairs. Puzzled by his request, she did so five times, each time more strenuously. Finally she asked her husband the purpose of this exercise. He admitted that he wanted to test the effect of the door being opened and closed in this manner, because he had just observed the back gate to the stairs opening and closing by itself!

This was as good a time as any to have a discussion of what was going on in the house, so Mrs. W. went up the stairs to join Mr. W. in the bedroom where he was standing. As she did so, her eye caught a dim, circular light that seemed to skip across the ceiling in two strokes; at the same time, the shade at the other end of the room suddenly snapped up, flipping over vigorously a number of times. Both Mr. and Mrs. W. started to run from the room; then, catching themselves, they returned to the bedroom.

On looking over these strange incidents, Mrs. W. admitted that there had been some occurrences that could not be explained by natural means. Shortly after they had moved to the house, he had started to paint the interior, at the same time thinking about making some structural changes in the house because there were certain things in it he did not like. As he did so, two cans of paint were knocked out of his hands, flipping over and covering a good portion of the living room and hall floors.

Then there was that Saturday afternoon when Mr. W. had helped his wife vacuum the hall stairs. Again he started to talk about what bad shape he thought the house was in, and as he condemned it, the vacuum cleaner suddenly left the upper landing and traveled over the staircase all by itself, finally hitting him on the head with a solid thud!

But their discussion did not solve the matter; they had to brace themselves against further incidents, even though they did not know who caused them and why.

One evening Mrs. W. was feeding her baby in the living room near the fireplace, when she heard footsteps overhead and the movement of something very heavy dragging across the floor. This was followed by a crashing sound on the staircase, as if something very heavy had fallen against the railing. Her husband was asleep, but Mrs. W. woke him up and together they investigated, only to find the children asleep and no stranger in the house.

It was now virtually impossible to spend a quiet evening in the living room without hearing some uncanny noises. There was scratching along the tops of the doors inside the house, a rubbing sound along the door tops, and once in a while the front doorknob would turn by itself, as if an unseen hand were twisting it. No one could have done this physically, because the enclosed porch leading to the door was locked and the locks were intact when Mrs. W. examined them.

The ghost, whoever he or she was, roamed the entire house. One night, Mrs. W. was reading in her bedroom at around midnight, when she heard a knocking sound halfway up the wall of her room. It seemed to move along the wall and then stop dead beside her night table. Needless to say, it did not contribute to a peaceful night. By now the older children were also aware of the disturbances. They, too, heard knocking on doors with no one outside, and twice Mrs. W.'s little girl, then seven years old, was awakened in the middle of the night because she heard someone walking about the house. At the time, both her parents were fast asleep.

That year, coming home on Christmas night to an empty

house, or what they *presumed* to be an empty house, the W.'s noticed that a Christmas light was on in the bedroom window. Under the circumstances, the family stayed outside while Mr. W. went upstairs to check the house. He found everything locked and no one inside. The rest of the family then moved into the lower hall, waiting for Mr. W. to come down from upstairs. As he reached the bottom of the stairs, coming from what he assured his family was an empty upper story, they all heard footsteps overhead from the area he had just examined.

On the eve of St. Valentine's Day, Mrs. W. was readying the house for a party the next evening. She had waxed the floors and spruced up the entire house, and it had gotten late. Just before going to bed, she decided to sit down for a while in her rocking chair. Suddenly she perceived a moaning and groaning sound coming across the living room from left to right. It lasted perhaps ten to fifteen seconds, then ended as abruptly as it had begun.

During the party the next evening, the conversation drifted to ghosts, and somehow Mrs. W. confided in her sister-in-law about what they had been through since moving to the house. It was only then that Mrs. W. found out from her sister-in-law that her husband's mother had had an experience in the house while staying over one night during the summer. She, too, had heard loud footsteps coming up the hall stairs; she had heard voices, and a crackling sound as if there had been a fire someplace. On investigating these strange noises, she had found nothing that could have caused them. However, she had decided not to tell Mrs. W. about it, in order not to frighten her.

Because of her background and position, and since her husband had a respected position as a teacher, the W.'s were reluctant to discuss their experiences with anyone who might construe them as imaginary, or think the family silly. Eventually, however, a sympathetic neighbor gave her one of my books, and Mrs. W. contacted me for advice. She realized, of course, that her letter would not be read immediately, and that in any event, I might not be able to do anything about it for some time. Frightening though the experiences had been, she was reconciled to living with them, hoping only that her children would not be hurt or frightened.

On March 3, she had put her three young boys to bed for a nap, and decided to check if they were properly covered. As she went up over the stairway, she thought she saw movement out of the corner of her eye. Her first thought was that her little boy, then four years old, had gotten up instead of taking his nap. But, on checking, she found him fast asleep. Exactly one week later, Mrs. W. was in bed trying to go to sleep when she heard a progressively louder tapping on the wooden mantle at the foot of the bed. She turned over to see where the noise was coming from or what was causing it when immediately it stopped. She turned back to the side, trying to go back to sleep, when suddenly she felt something or someone shake her foot as though trying to get her attention. She looked down at her foot and saw absolutely nothing.

Finally, on March 26, she received my letter explaining some of the phenomena to her and advising her what to do. As she was reading my letter, she heard the sound of someone moving about upstairs, directly over her head. Since she knew that the children were sleeping soundly, Mrs. W. realized that her unseen visitor was not in the least bit put off by the advice dispensed her by the Ghost Hunter. Even a dog the W.'s had acquired around Christmas had its difficulty with the unseen forces loose in the house.

At first, he had slept upstairs on the rug beside Mrs. W.'s bed. But a short time after, he began to growl and bark at night, especially in the direction of the stairs. Eventually he took to sleeping on the enclosed porch and refused to enter the house, no matter how one would try to entice him. Mrs. W. decided to make some inquiries in the neighborhood, in order to find out who the ghost might be or what he might want.

She discovered that a paperhanger, who had come to do some work in the house just before they had purchased it, had encountered considerable difficulties. He had been hired to do some paperhanging in the house, changing the decor from what it had been. He had papered a room in the house as he had been told to, but on returning the next day found that some of his papers were on upside down, as if moved around by unseen hands. He, too, heard strange noises and would have nothing further to do with the house. Mrs. W. then called upon the people who had preceded them in the house, the P. family, but the daughter of the late owner said that during their stay in the house they had not experienced anything unusual. Perhaps she did not care to discuss such matters; at any rate, Mrs. W. discovered that the former owner, Mr. P., had actually died in the house three years prior to their acquisition of it. Apparently, he had been working on the house, which he loved very much, and had sustained a fracture. He recovered from it, but sustained another fracture in the same area of his leg. During the recovery, he died of a heart attack in the living room.

It is conceivable that Mr. P. did not like the rearrangements made by the new owners, and resented the need for repapering or repainting, having done so much of that himself while in the flesh. But if it is he who is walking up and down the stairs at night, turning doorknobs, and appearing as luminous balls of light— who, then, is the woman whose voice has also been heard?

So it appears that the house overlooking the golf course for the past hundred and fifty years has more than one spectral inhabitant in it. Perhaps Mr. P. is only a johnny-come-lately, joining the earlier shades staying on in what used to be their home. As far as the W.'s are concerned, the house is big enough for all of them; so long as they know their place!

The Ghostly Brother

Peter Q. comes from a devout Catholic family, part Scottish, part Irish. One June, Peter Q. was married, and his brother Tom, with whom he had always maintained a close and cordial relationship, came to the wedding. That was the last time the two brothers were happy together. Two weeks later Tom and a friend spent a weekend on Cape Cod. During that weekend, Tom lost his prize possession, his collection of record albums worth several hundred dollars. Being somewhat superstitious, he feared that his luck had turned against him and, sure enough, his car was struck by a hit-and-run driver shortly afterward.

Then, in August of the same year, Tom and his father caught a very big fish on a fishing trip and won a prize consisting of a free trip during the season. As he was cleaning the fish to present it to the jury, the line broke and Tom lost the prize fish. But his streak of bad luck was to take on ominous proportions soon after. Two weeks later, Tom Q. and the same friend who had been with him when his record collection had been stolen were planning another trip together. Tom was very happy the night before because he was looking forward to the trip. He was joyful, and in the course of conversation said, "When I die, I want a good send-off," meaning a good traditional Irish wake. His friend, David, on the other hand, was quiet and withdrawn, not quite himself that evening.

The following morning, the two young men set out on their trip. Before the day was out, they were involved in an automobile accident. Tom Q. died instantly and David died the next day.

Even before the bad news was brought home to Peter Q. and the family, an extraordinary thing happened at their house. The clock in the bedroom stopped suddenly. When Peter checked it and wound it again, he found nothing wrong with it. By then, word of Tom's death had come, and on checking out the time, Peter found that the clock had stopped at the very instant of his brother's death.

During the following days, drawers in their bedroom would open by themselves when there was no one about. This continued for about four weeks, then it stopped again. On the anniversary of Tom's death, Peter, who was then a junior at the university, was doing some studying and using a fountain pen to highlight certain parts in the books. Just then, his mother called him and asked him to help his father with his car. Peter placed the pen inside the book to mark the page and went to help his father. On returning an hour later, he discovered that a picture of his late brother and their family had been placed where Peter had left the pen, and the pen was lying outside the book next to it. No one had been in the house at the time, since Peter's wife was out working.

Under the influence of Tom's untimely death and the phenomena taking place at his house, Peter Q. became very interested in life after death and read almost everything he could, talking with many of his friends about the subject, and becoming all the time more and more convinced that man does in some mysterious way survive death. But his wife disagreed with him and did not wish to discuss the matter.

One night, while her husband was away from the house, Peter's wife received a telepathic impression concerning continuance of life, and as she did so, a glowing object about the size of a softball appeared next to her in her bed. It was not a dream, for she could see the headlights from passing cars shining on the wall of the room, yet the shining object was still there next to her pillow, stationary and glowing. It eventually disappeared.

Many times since, Peter Q. has felt the presence of his brother, a warm, wonderful feeling; yet it gives him goose bumps all over. As for the real big send-off Tom had wanted from this life, he truly received it. The morning after his accident, a number of friends called the house without realizing that anything had happened to Tom. They had felt a strong urge to call, as if someone had communicated with them telepathically to do so.

Tom Q. was a collector of phonograph records and owned many, even though a large part of his collection had been stolen. The night before his fatal accident, he had played some of these records. When Peter later checked the record player, he discovered that the last song his brother had played was entitled "Just One More Day." Of the many Otis Redding recordings his brother owned, why had he chosen that one?

The
Protector

Mrs. M. R. is a housewife in her late forties, living in a medium-sized New England town. Her husband works for the United States Post Office, and Mrs. R. takes care of two of their three children, the oldest being already married and living away from home. She has lived with the psychic world practically from the beginning. When she was only seven years old, she and her sister, two years her senior, were in bed, playing and whispering to each other in order not to wake up their parents, whose room was next to theirs. Suddenly, there appeared a misty figure at the door connecting the children's room with the living room. It drifted through the children's room and stopped at the door to the parents' room, facing the sleeping couple. The children both saw it: the figure seemed grayish-white and had some sort of cord around its waist. At that moment their father awoke and saw it too. Yelling out to it to go away, he awoke his wife. Even though the figure still stood in the doorway of their room, she could not see it. At that moment, the ghost just disappeared.

Although Mrs. R. has had many dreams that later came true, she did not see a ghost again until she was twenty-three years old. At that time she had already given birth to her first child, and she and her husband were staying for a week at her mother's apartment. The child was still in the hospital, having been a premature baby, and Mrs. R. lay in bed, thinking about her child. At that moment there appeared at the door to the room a very tall, dark, hooded figure. Far from being afraid, she watched the figure glide into the room and come around the foot of the bed and toward her to her side. The room seemed filled with a soft glow, not unlike moonlight, even though the shades were down; the furniture could be seen plainly as if there were lights in the room. By now the visitor stood right next to the bed and Mrs. R. was able to look up into his face; but in the emptiness of the hood, where a face should be, there was nothing, absolutely nothing. Then, very slowly, the figure bent over her from its great height, and it was only when the empty hood was almost touching her face that Mrs. R. gave a muffled cry. Apparently, her outcry had broken the spell, for the phantom disappeared as quickly as it had come. Whether there was any connection between the ghostly visitor she had seen as a child and the monklike phantom who came to her many years later, Mrs. R. does not know. But it may well be that both were one and the same, perhaps sent to protect her or guide her in some way, from out of the distant past.

The Bat

When you're a Psychic Investigator and constantly before the public via television, radio, and books, you're bound to meet a lot of strange people. Now some people are strange only in that they have psychic gifts that defy so-called natural explanations. Others, in addition to such gifts, are also strange in their interpretations and attitudes toward the uncanny.

Take the strange case of the bat and the mirror, for instance.

"I'm aggressive, clever, yet sensitive and understanding," writes Mrs. Sophia K., a Boston Greek lady who heard of me through the Bob Kennedy TV show. "All in all I'm a normal human being."

Quite so. Her grandfather was a philosopher, like any good Greek should be, and her husband builds medical instruments at Harvard. The lady herself has a college education and has been active in real estate. They have two children, aged twenty and seventeen, and are not at all interested in psychic matters despite that philosopher-grandfather.

The incident that shook poor Mrs. K. to her bones happened on an ordinary night in July 1963. She was about to retire for the night and transferred a crucifix she wore in her clothes to her nightgown. Her husband was already asleep, as were their two sons; the hour was close to midnight and their bedroom was reasonably light due to street lighting coming in through the large window.

As she lay down in bed, she suddenly felt very strange. Her whole body seemed paralyzed, although she could think as clearly as before. At that precise moment she heard a loud flapping of wings on the right side of her head, and turning her eyes she noticed a most peculiar bird.

It was a bat, but had a human body, arms, legs, and a head, but no face—like a mythological or heraldic animal. Mrs. K. says she saw this thing over her head and she was petrified, which I believe, for I would be petrified if an ordinary bat were to appear over my head, let alone a human one.

Apparently the creature did not like the position over Mrs. K.'s head, for it flew against the closed window, hit it with a bang, and then returned, a prisoner trying to get out. At that moment Mrs. K. reports she noticed a luminous light in the hallway on her right. The bat gave a deafening flap of its wings and flew into the dresser mirror, where it disappeared.

At that moment, Mrs. K.'s body relaxed and her paralysis was completely gone. She woke her husband but he had not heard or felt anything unusual. He assured his beloved wife that she must have been dreaming.

Mrs. K. went to see two priests, for two holy men are better than one, she thought. Both men of the cloth listened to her earnestly, then assured her it was not a dream.

How they could do this, I don't know. But they also warned her that the dresser mirror now contained something unspeakably evil. Until the mirror is put through a church ritual the bat will be in it, Mrs. K. was told. Naturally the ritual was expensive, but then, how many bats fly into dresser mirrors?

Symbolic visions, often involving birds, are nothing new. Whether thought forms can indeed materialize into the physical to such an extent that they appear material is one of the borderline questions not yet fully explored.

The Cry
of the Banshee

I've been all over Ireland three times and have written a book called *The Lively Ghosts of Ireland*, but I've never met anyone in the Emerald Isle who had a banshee. Now there are things a Psychic Investigator considers legitimate and well-supported phenomena in the realm of the Uncanny, such as ghosts, haunted houses, and precognitive experiences.

Then, too, there are borderline cases involving phenomena of a more offbeat kind, such as the legendary stories about the Irish leprechauns and "little people," the fairies and brownies of Britain, and the dwarfs of Central Europe. To reject out of hand all such material as fantasy is of course no more scientific than to admit all spiritualist phenomena as genuine on the face of it without individual search and evaluation. What little we know of nature and our universe should have made us realize how much more there may be that is as yet unrevealed. A little humility can be most useful in modern science, but unfortunately the average physical scientist is filled with his own self-importance and has little patience with the bizarre.

The banshee is a Celtic spirit specializing in death warnings and they say it runs only in "old" Irish families. But I've heard of similar cases in other Celtic traditions and even outside of Britain. The banshee is usually described by those who actually have seen it as the figure of an ugly old woman, seated on the doorstep of the family about to be bereaved, and crying or screaming loudly. Banshees announce the forthcoming death of a member of the family without, however, telling the family who and when. That's part of the banshee game. Naturally the family is scared stiff when the banshee wails and everybody wonders who is next to go.

Died-in-the-wool Irish traditionalists will swear that ban-shees only run in the very good, ancient families and having one may be frightening, but it is also flattering—sort of a pedigree of death.

Now I have always been doubtful about the nature, though not the existence, of such strange creatures as elementals and banshees, considering them indeed part and parcel of ghostly manifestations, and thus human.

I've also learned that you can take the Irishman out of Ire-land, but you can't take Ireland out of the Irishman. Even genera-tions after, an Irish family transplanted into the New World may have the family banshee on their necks. Such is the case with the Shea family who live a pretty prosaic life in northern Massachu-setts. Joanne Shea's grandmother, and even her mother, came from Ireland, as the song goes, and with them came accounts of strange goings-on whenever death was near for a member of the family.

The grandmother's particular banshee was mild in compari-son to that of others: a strange creaking noise on the stairs, which she always tried to tell herself was natural, knowing full well, however, what it meant.

One day the grandmother was visiting Mrs. Shea and her sister and, upon leaving, startled the two girls by telling them it was her last visit. She would never see them again!

The family joked about this. Then two weeks later their grand-mother fell and fractured her hip, and was hospitalized with the injury.

A few days afterward, Mrs. Shea's sister, who is a nun, was standing by a window in her chapel. Suddenly she heard a terrible scream that she later described as sounding like the scream of a wildcat. Terrified, she looked out the window, but could see noth-ing. Later, the two girls compared notes. At the exact moment when the nun had heard the scream, Grandmother had died.

A year went by. One evening, as Joanne lay in bed, she heard her brother's footsteps come up the stairs outside her room. Just then the clock chimed 11 P.M. To her surprise, Joanne clearly heard the footsteps of *two* people coming up the stairs, and won-dered who the friend was her brother was bringing home at so late an hour. At the top of the stairs, the two pairs of footsteps separated, and one person went into the brother's room. The other footsteps came into Joanne's, and she suddenly felt petrified with fear.

Then all of a sudden, there, in front of her bed, stood her late grandmother. Looking at the girl, the apparition turned her head a little, smiled—and then was gone like a puff of smoke. When Joanne reported the matter to her mother the following morning, her mother brushed it aside as "probably a dream."

But then she stopped herself. What was the day's date? It was November 3—the anniversary of Grandmother's passing. Mother had forgotten to put Grandmother's name on the list of those for whom a prayer was to be said in church, as had been the custom in this Catholic family. The matter was immediately attended to, and when Joanne's brother came in that day, she questioned him about the other footsteps she had heard the night before.

He insisted that he had come in quite alone. He had not heard the ghostly steps either. Only Joanne had, and she never saw her late grandmother again after that.

Joanne's older sister, who was later to become a nun, evidently had also inherited the psychic talents so strong on the female side of the family tree.

One evening only the women were home, while the men— Joanne's father and her two brothers—were away at a ball game. Mother was downstairs, and the two girls were in bed in their room upstairs. Joanne was already beginning to doze off, when her sister suddenly jumped out of bed and ran downstairs to her mother's room.

"Did you hear the terrible scream?" the twenty-year-old girl asked her mother, who could only nod a silent yes. But Joanne had not heard it. It was a scream not unlike the cry of the wildcat, coming in from over the hill in back of the house. There was nothing outside in the yard to account for it.

For several days the women of the family were in a dither, waiting for fate to drop the other shoe. Everybody was told to be extremely careful and to avoid accidents. One could never know whom the banshee meant. On the eighth day after the unearthly scream had been heard, the waiting game was over. Joanne's uncle, her mother's brother, was hit by an automobile and died a few days later.

Michigan

The
Ghost
and the Puppy

lice H. lived in a five-room bungalow flat in the Middle West. She worked part-time as a saleswoman, but lived alone. Throughout her long life she never had any real interest in psychic phenomena. She even went to a spiritualist meeting with a friend and was not impressed one way or another. She was sixty-two when she had her first personal encounter with the unknown.

One night she went to bed and awoke because something was pressing against her back. Since she knew herself to be alone in the apartment, it frightened her. Nevertheless, she turned around to look—and to her horror she saw the upper part of her late husband's body. As she stared at him, he glided over the bed, turned to look at her once more with a mischievous look in his eye, and disappeared on the other side of the bed. Mrs. H. could not figure out why he had appeared to her, because she had not been thinking of him at that time. But evidently he was to instigate her further psychic experiences.

Not much later, she had another manifestation that shook her up a great deal. She had been sound asleep when she was awakened by the whimpering of her puppy. The dog was sleeping on top of the bed covers. Mrs. H. was fully awake now and looked over her shoulder where stood a young girl of about ten years, in the most beautiful blue tailored pajamas. She was looking at the dog. As Mrs. H. looked closer, she noticed that the child had neither face nor hands nor feet showing. Shaken, she jumped out of bed and went toward the spirit. The little girl moved back toward the wall, and Mrs. H. followed her. As the little girl in the blue pajamas neared the wall, it somehow changed into a beautiful flower garden with a wide path! She walked down the path in a mechanical sort of way, with the wide cuffs of her pajamas showing, but still with no feet. Nevertheless, it was a happy walk, then it all disappeared.

The experience bothered Mrs. H. so she moved into another room. But her little dog stayed on in the room where the experience had taken place, sleeping on the floor under the bed. That first experience took place on a Sunday in October, at four A.M. The following Sunday, again at four o'clock, Mrs. H. heard the dog whimper, as if he were conscious of a presence. By the time she reached the other room, however, she could not see anything. These experiences continued for some time, always on Sunday at four in the morning. It then became clear to Mrs. H. that the little girl hadn't come for her in particular—but only to visit her little dog.

Conversation
with a Ghost

David H. lives in Michigan. When he was eight he had his first encounter with a ghost. The house his parents lived in was more than a hundred years old, and rather on the large side. David slept in one of two main rooms on the upper floor of the house; the room next to it was unfurnished. One night he was lying in bed when he had a sudden urge to sit up, and as he did so he looked down the hall. All of a sudden he noticed a small, shadowlike man jump down from the attic and run toward him. But instead of coming into his room, he turned down the stairs. David could see that he wore a small derby hat but what was even more fascinating was the fact that the figure walked about two inches above the floor! After the figure had disappeared, David thought it was all his imagination. A particularly bright eight-year-old, he was not easily taken in by fantasies or daydreams.

But the strange figure reappeared several times more, and eventually David came to the conclusion that it was real. He asked his parents whether he could swap rooms with them and they agreed to let him sleep downstairs. It was about that time that his mother told him that she had heard the old piano playing at night downstairs. She had thought that it was the cat climbing up on the keys, but one night the piano played in plain view of herself and one of her daughters, without even a trace of the cat in the room. There was also the sound of pages in a book being turned in the same area, although nobody had a book or turned any pages.

David settled down in his room on the lower floor and finally forgot all about his ghostly experiences. Shortly after, he heard a crunching noise on the stairs, as if someone were walking on them. He assumed it was his mother coming down the stairs to tell him to turn off his radio, but no one came.

As he grew older, he moved back upstairs, since the room on the ground floor had become too small for him. This proved to be somewhat of a strain for him: many times he would be lying in bed when someone would call his name. But there was never anyone there. Exasperated, the youngster spoke up, challenging the ghost to give some sign of his presence so that there could be communication between them. "If you can hear me, make a noise," David said to his ghost. At that very moment, the door to his room began to rattle without apparent cause. Still unconvinced, since the door had rattled before because of natural causes, David continued his monologue with, "If you are there, show yourself," and at that moment he heard a strange noise behind him. The door to his closet, which had been closed, was slowly opening. This wasn't very reassuring, even though it might represent some kind of dialogue with the ghost.

Shortly thereafter, and in broad daylight, just as he had gotten home from school, David heard a very loud noise in the upper portion of the house: it sounded as if all their cats were tearing each other to pieces, and the sound of a lot of coat hangers falling down augmented the bedlam. Quickly, David ran up the stairs—only to find neither cats nor fallen coat hangers. And to this day, David doesn't know who the strange visitor was.

Minnesota

The Electrocuted Ghost

Mrs. Jane Eidson was a housewife in suburban Minneapolis. She was middle-aged and her five children ranged in age from nine to twenty. Her husband, Bill, traveled four days each week. For eight years they had lived in a cottage-type brick house that was twenty-eight years old.

The first time the Eidsons noticed that there was something odd about their otherwise ordinary-looking home was after they had been in the house for a short time. Mrs. Eidson was in the basement sewing, when all of a sudden she felt that she was not alone and wanted to run upstairs. She suppressed this strong urge but felt very uncomfortable. Another evening, her husband was down there practicing a speech when he had the same feeling of another presence. His self-control was not as strong as hers, and he came upstairs.

In discussing their strange feelings with their next-door neighbor, they discovered that the previous tenant also had complained about the basement. Their daughter Rita had never wanted to go to the basement by herself and, when pressed for a reason, finally admitted that there was a man down there. She described him as dark-haired and wearing a plaid shirt. Sometimes he would stand by her bed at night and she would become frightened, but the moment she thought of calling her mother, the image disappeared. Another spot where she felt his presence was the little playhouse at the other end of their yard.

The following spring, Mrs. Eidson noticed a bouncing light at the top of the stairs as she was about to go to bed in an upstairs room that she occupied while convalescing from surgery. The light followed her to her room as if it had a mind of its own. When she entered her room the light left, but the room felt icy. She was disturbed by this, but nevertheless went to bed and soon had forgotten all about it as sleep came to her. Suddenly, in the middle of the night, she woke and sat up in bed. Something had awakened her. At the head of her bed she saw a man who was "beige-colored," as she put it. As she stared at the apparition it went away, again leaving the room very chilly.

About that same time, the Eidsons noticed that their electric appliances were playing tricks on them. There was the time at five A.M. when their washing machine went on by itself, as did the television set in the basement, which could only be turned on by plugging it into the wall socket. When they had gone to bed, the set was off and there was no one around to plug it in.

Who was so fond of electrical gadgets as to turn them on in the small hours of the morning?

Finally Mrs. Eidson found out. In May 1949, a young man who was just out of the service had occupied the house. His hobby was electrical wiring, it seems, for he had put in a strand of heavy wires from the basement underground through the yard to the other end of the property. When he attempted to hook them up with the utility pole belonging to the electric company, he was killed instantly. It happened near the place where Mrs. Eidson's girl had seen the apparition. Since the wires are still in her garden, Mrs. Eidson is not at all surprised that the dead man likes to hang around.

And what better way for an electronics buff to manifest as a ghost than by appearing as a bright, bouncy light? As of this writing, the dead electrician is still playing tricks in the Eidson home, and Mrs. Eidson is looking for a new home—one a little less unusual than their present one.

Missouri

The Ghost
and the Golf Cap

L ana T., one of seven children from eastern Missouri, has ESP to
a considerable extent. Three of her sisters also have this ability,
so perhaps it runs in the family. She and her husband lived in a
big city in central Missouri. Clairvoyant dreams and other verified
incidents of ESP led to an interest in the much-maligned Ouija
board, and she and her three sisters, Jean, Judy, and Tony, became veritable addicts of this little gadget. A close friend and her
husband moved into a nearby house in the same community,
without realizing that the house had become available due to the
suicide of the previous owner.

Mrs. T.'s friend had come from another state, so the local
facts were not too well known to her. When the new owner discovered that her neighbor, Lana T., had psychic gifts and an interest
in occult matters, she confided freely in her. It appeared that one
of the bathrooms was always cold, regardless of the weather outside or the temperature in the rest of the house; a certain closet
door would simply not stay closed; and the heat register was
bound to rattle of its own volition. Objects would move from one
place to another, without anyone having touched them. Footsteps
were heard going up and down the hall, as if someone were pacing up and down. Once the new owner saw a whitish mist that
dissolved immediately when she spoke to it.

Her husband, publisher of a local newspaper, would not even
discuss the matter, considering it foolish. But one night he woke
up and informed her that he had just been touched by a cold,
clammy hand. This was enough to drive the new owner to consult
with her neighbor. Lana T. offered to try and find out who the
disturbing ghost was. Together with one of her sisters, she sat

herself down with her trusty Ouija board and asked it to identify the disturbing entity in the house. Ouija board communication is slow and sometimes boring, but, in this instance, the instrument rapidly identified the communicator as a certain Ted. A chill went down Mrs. T.'s spine, for Ted was the man who had committed suicide in her friend's house.

From then on, a veritable conversation ensued between Mrs. T. and the ghost, in which he explained that he was angry because the new owner had burned something of his. Mrs. T. asked what the new owner could do to satisfy him, and the angry ghost replied that she should destroy something of her own to make up for his loss—something white.

When Mrs. T. described her conversation with the ghost to the new owner of the house, the lady was mystified. She could not recall having burned anything belonging to the former owner. Back to the Ouija board went Mrs. T. When she demanded that the ghost describe the item in question more fully, he replied, somewhat impatiently, that it had been white with green trim and had the letters SFCC on it. Mrs. T. returned to her neighbor with this additional information. This time she struck paydirt: shortly after the couple from out of state had moved into the house, the lady of the house had discovered an old golf cap in the top drawer of one of her closets, white with green trim and the initials of the country club, SFCC, on it! The cap had somehow bothered her, so she had tossed it into the trash can and the contents of the can were later burned.

The ghost had told the truth. But how could she satisfy his strange whim in return? At that time she and her husband had considered buying a small, expensive white marble statue. They decided to forego this pleasure. Perhaps their sacrifice of this "white" item would make up for the lost golf cap? Evidently it did —for the house has been quiet ever since!

New Jersey

The Graves
on the Hillock

E motional ties, unfinished business, concern about loved ones—living or in spirit—can span the centuries, until someone comes along to make contact and set things right. What seems a small matter to us on this side of the veil can turn into an obsession in the surviving mind of someone who passed on with a grievance or problem left unattended prior to death. And then time and place mean very little, really.

Mrs. Ethel Meyers, who has frequently accompanied me on ghost-hunting expeditions, heard from friends living in Bergen County, New Jersey, about some unusual happenings at their very old house. Eventually the "safari for ghost" was organized, and Mr. B., the master of the house, picked us up in his car and drove us to Bergen County. The house turned out to be a beautifully preserved pre-Revolutionary house set within an enclosure of tall trees and lawns.

The building had been started in 1704, I later learned, and the oldest portion was the right wing; the central portion was added in the latter part of the eighteenth century, and the final, frontal portion was built from old materials about seventy years ago, carefully preserving the original style of the house. The present owners had acquired it about a year before from a family who had been in possession for several generations. The house was then empty, and the B.'s refurbished it completely in excellent taste with antiques of the period.

After they moved into the house, they slept for a few days on a mattress on the enclosed porch, which skirted the west wing of the house. Their furniture had not yet arrived, and they didn't mind roughing it for a short while. It was summer, and not too cool.

In the middle of the night, Mrs. B. suddenly awoke with the uncanny feeling that there was someone else in the house besides her husband and herself. She got up and walked toward the corridorlike extension of the enclosed porch running along the back of the house. There she clearly distinguished the figure of a man, seemingly white, with a beard, wearing what she described as "something ruffly white." She had the odd sensation that this man belonged to a much earlier period than the present. The light was good enough to see the man clearly for about five minutes, in which she was torn between fear of the intruder and curiosity. Finally, she approached him, and saw him literally dissolve before her very eyes! At the same time, she had the odd sensation that the stranger came to look *them* over, wondering what they were doing in *his* house! Mrs. B., a celebrated actress and choreographer, is not a scoffer, nor is she easily susceptible. Ghosts to her are something one can discuss intelligently. Since her husband shared this view, they inquired of the former owner about any possible hauntings.

"I've never heard of any or seen any," Mr. S. told them, "but my daughter-in-law has never been able to sleep in the oldest part of the house. Said there was too much going on there. Also, one of the neighbors claims he saw *something*."

Mr. S. wasn't going to endanger his recent real-estate transaction with too many ghostly tales. The B.'s thanked him and settled down to life in their colonial house. But they soon learned that theirs was a busy place indeed. Both are artistic and very intuitive, and they soon became aware of the presence of unseen forces.

One night Mrs. B. was alone at home, spending the evening in the upper story of the house. There was nobody downstairs. Suddenly she heard the downstairs front door open and shut. There was no mistaking the very characteristic and complex sound of the opening of this ancient lock. Next, she heard footsteps, and sighed with relief. Apparently her husband had returned much earlier than expected. Quickly, she rushed down the stairs to welcome him. There was nobody there. There was no one in front of the door. All she found was the cat in a strangely excited state.

Sometime after, Mr. B. came home. For his wife these were

anxious hours of waiting. He calmed her as best he could, having reservations about the whole incident. Soon these doubts were to be dispelled completely.

This time Mrs. B. was away and Mr. B. was alone in the downstairs part of the house. The maid was asleep in her room, the B.'s child fast asleep upstairs. It was a peaceful evening, and Mr. B. decided to have a snack. He found himself in the kitchen, which is located at the western end of the downstairs part of the house, when he suddenly heard a car drive up. Next, there were the distinct sounds of the front door opening and closing again. As he rushed to the front door, he heard the dog bark furiously. But again, there was no one either inside or outside the house!

Mr. B., a star and director, and as rational a man as could be, wondered if he had imagined these things. But he knew he had not. What he had heard were clearly the noises of an arrival. While he was still trying to sort out the meaning of all this, another strange thing happened.

A few evenings later, he found himself alone in the downstairs living room, when he heard carriage wheels outside grind to a halt. He turned his head toward the door, wondering who it might be at this hour. The light was subdued, but good enough to read by. He didn't have to wait long. A short, husky man walked into the room *through* the closed door; then, without paying attention to Mr. B., turned and walked out into the oldest part of the house, again *through a closed door!*

"What did he look like to you?" I asked.

"He seemed dotted, as if he were made of thick, solid dots, and he wore a long coat, the kind they used to wear around 1800. He probably was the same man my wife encountered."

"You think he is connected with the oldest part of the house?"

"Yes, I think so. About a year ago I played some very old lute music, the kind popular in the eighteenth century, in there—and something happened to the atmosphere in the room. As if someone were listening quietly and peacefully."

But it wasn't always as peaceful in there. A day before our arrival, Mrs. B. had lain down, trying to relax. But she could not stay in the old room. "There was someone there," she said simply.

The B.'s weren't the only ones to hear and see ghosts. Last summer, two friends of the B.'s were visiting them, and everybody was seated in the living room, when in plain view of all, the screen

door to the porch opened and closed again of its own volition!
Needless to add, the friends didn't stay long.

Only a day before our visit, another friend had tried to use the
small washroom in the oldest part of the house. Suddenly, he felt
chills coming on and rushed out of the room, telling Mrs. B. that
"someone was looking at him."

At this point, dinner was ready, and a most delicious repast it
was. Afterward we accompanied the B.'s into the oldest part of
their house, a low-ceilinged room dating back to the year 1704.
Two candles provided the only light. Mrs. Meyers got into a comfortable chair, and gradually drifted into trance.

"Marie . . . Catherine . . . who calls?" she mumbled.

"Who is it?" I inquired.

"Pop . . . live peacefully . . . love. . . ."

"What is your name?" I wanted to know.

"Achabrunn."

I didn't realize it at the time, but a German family named
Achenbach had built the house and owned it for several generations. Much later still, I found out that one of the children of the
builder had been called Marian.

I continued my interrogation.

"Who rules this country?"

"The Anglish. George."

"What year is this?"

"56. 1756."

"When did you stay here?"

"Always. Pop. My house. *You* stay with *me.*"

Then the ghost spoke haltingly of his family, his children, of
which he had nine, three of whom had gone away.

"What can we do for you?" I said, hoping to find the reason
for the many disturbances.

"Yonder over side hill, hillock, three buried . . . flowers
there."

"Do you mean," I said, "that we should put flowers on these
graves?"

The medium seemed excited.

"*Ach Gott, ja, machs gut.*" With this the medium crossed herself.

"What is your name?" I asked again.

"Oterich . . . Oblich. . . ." The medium seemed hesitant as

if the ghost were searching his memory for his own name. Later, I found that the name given was pretty close to that of another family having a homestead next door.

The ghost continued.

"She lady . . . I not good. I very stout heart, I look up to good-blood lady, I make her good . . . Kathrish, holy lady, I worship lady . . . they rest on hill too, with three. . . ."

After the seance, I found a book entitled *Pre-Revolutionary Dutch Houses in Northern New Jersey and New York*. It was here that I discovered the tradition that a poor shepherd from Saxony married a woman above his station, and built this very house. The year 1756 was correct.

But back to my interrogation. "Why don't you rest on the hillock?"

"I take care of . . . four . . . hillock . . . Petrish, Ladian, Annia, Kathrish. . . ."

Then, as if taking cognizance of us, he added—"To care for you, that's all I want."

Mrs. B. nodded and said softly, "You're always welcome here."

Afterward, I found that there were indeed some graves on the hill beyond the house. The medium now pointed toward the rear of the house, and said, "Gate . . . we put intruders there, he won't get up any more. Gray Fox made trouble, Indian man, I keep him right there."

"Are there any passages?"

"Yeah. Go dig through. When Indian come, they no find."

"Where?"

"North hillock, still stone floor there, ends here."

From Mr. B. I learned that underground passages are known to exist between this house and the so-called "Slave House," across the road.

The ghost then revealed that his wife's father, an Englishman, had built the passage, and that stores were kept in it along with Indian bones.

"Where were you born?" I inquired.

"Here. Bergenville."

Bergenville proved to be the old name of the township.

I then delicately told him that this was 1960. He seemed puzzled, to say the least.

"In 1756 I was sixty-five years old. I am not 204 years older?"

At this point, the ghost recognized the women's clothing the medium was wearing, and tore at them. I explained how we were able to "talk" to him. He seemed pacified.

"You'll accept my maize, my wine, my whiskey. . . ."

I discovered that maize and wine staples were the mainstays of the area at that period. I also found that Indian wars on a small scale were still common in this area in the middle 1700s. Moreover, the ghost referred to the "gate" as being in the *rear* of the house. This proved to be correct, for what is now the back of the house was then its front, facing the road.

Suddenly the ghost withdrew and after a moment another person, a woman, took over the medium. She complained bitterly that the Indians had taken one of her children, whose names she kept rattling off. Then she too withdrew, and Mrs. Meyers returned to her own body, none the worse for her experiences, none of which, incidentally, she remembered.

Shortly afterward, we returned to New York. It was as if we had just come from another world. Leaving the poplar-lined road behind us, we gradually reentered the world of gasoline and dirt that is the modern city.

Nothing further has been reported from the house in Bergen County, but I am sure the ghost, whom Mrs. B. had asked to stay as long as he wished, is still there. There is, of course, no further need to bang doors, to call attention to his lonely self. They know he is there with them.

The
Yellow Church
Ghost

Yellow Frame Church is an old country church in Yellow Frame, New Jersey. It stands in one of the most isolated areas of the state and is but little known to people outside the immediate area. Even today there is only the minister's house and a graveyard across the street, but no other dwellings close by. In the early 1800s a new minister came to Yellow Frame and, after his very first sermon, dropped dead. He was duly buried in the church yard across from the church. For unknown reasons, however, his body was taken some years later from the churchyard and moved to another cemetery at Johnsonburg, two miles down the road.

So much for the background of the old building. I wouldn't be writing about it if it weren't for a report from an alert reader, Mrs. Johanna C., who lives in a nearby town. Apparently there had been an incident involving a woman on her way home early in the morning, while it was still dark. When the lady passed the church she heard choir music coming from it and saw that both doors were wide open. Curious as to who might be playing the organ that early in the morning, or, rather, that late at night, she stepped up and peered into the church: the inside of the building was quite dark, and when she stepped inside she noticed that there was no one in the church who could have played the organ. Frightened, she left in a hurry.

In the late 1960s, Mr. C. and a group of friends, who had heard the account of the organ music, decided to see for themselves whether there was anything unusual about the church. As so many others who think that Halloween is the time to look for ghosts, Mr. C. and friends picked the night of October 31 to do their ghost hunt. Of course, there is no connection between Halloween, the solemn holiday of witchcraft, the Old Religion, and ghosts; but popular superstition will always link them, since ghosts and witches *seem* to belong to the same level of reference. At any rate, Mr. C. and his friends arrived at Yellow Frame Church at exactly midnight and bravely walked up the steps of the church. At that hour, the church was of course closed. As they confronted the locked doors, the doors suddenly swung open of their own volition, startling the visitors no end. But this did not stop them; they stepped inside the church and, as they did so, each one of the group noticed a strange pressure on his ears as if the air were pushing against them!

One in the group called out, "Reverend, oh Reverend!" but there was no answer. The eerie stillness of the building was too much for them, and they left in a hurry.

A year later, again on Halloween, Mrs. C. went along with the same group to see whether she could experience anything out of the ordinary. They arrived at the church shortly before midnight, driving by it at first to get a look of it. They noticed that both doors were shut. A few minutes later they returned to see that one of the doors was slightly open. They parked their car and stepped inside the church. At that moment Mrs. C. could also feel the strange pressure on her ears. She also felt as if someone were hiding in the church, watching them. There was a peaceful feeling about it, almost, she explained, as if she were being wrapped in a blanket. Mrs. C. decided to spend some time inside the church to see whether it was truly haunted, but the men would have no part of it and insisted that they all leave again. While they stood around inside, discussing whether or not they should go immediately, they clearly heard what appeared to be footsteps in the leaves. It sounded as if someone were walking around just outside the building. However, they did not stay around long enough to find out whether there was, in fact, someone walking who was not a member of their group.

But the matter did not give Mrs. C. any rest, so she returned to the church once more in the company of a girlfriend, this time during daylight hours. She managed to meet the present minister's wife, telling her of their experiences. To their relief, the minister's wife was not at all shocked: not long ago she had awakened at six in the morning, while it was still quite dark outside, and peering out the window toward the church, she became aware of lights in the church going on and off as if someone were signaling with them. Those are the facts; there is also a tradition in the area that the church is haunted by the restless spirit of the original minister, who doesn't like being buried in the wrong cemetery and comes up the Yellow Frame Road searching for his original resting place.

Mother's Ghost

Mrs. V. works as a law secretary for a prominent attorney in New Jersey. She never had any interest in the occult, but her innate psychic sense broke through eventually whether she wanted it or not. At first, there were just trifling things. Like handing her cleaner a pair of gloves and instantly knowing he would lose them. He did. Or looking for the gravestone of a friend in a cemetery she had never been to and finding it "blindly." Then, the night her mother died, she and her sister saw the lights in the living room go on by themselves. Since these were lights that had to be turned on individually, this was unusual indeed.

But on February 16, 1967, Mrs. V. had the shock of her life. It started as an ordinary working day. Her boss was dictating to her at her desk, which was located in a long hallway leading to his private offices. During a pause in the dictation, she looked up idly and saw, to her left, through a glass separation, a woman standing in the hall. The woman looked at her, and then moved quickly behind the elevator wall and out of her line of vision.

The woman was about twelve feet away and Mrs. V. saw her clearly through the glass. Her boss was part-owner of the building and often interviewed prospective tenants, so she assumed this was someone looking for office space and called his attention to the woman.

"Woman? What woman?" he demanded to know. "I don't see anyone."

"She has stepped behind the elevator wall," the secretary explained, somewhat sheepishly. The elevator is one of those older, noisy installations that one can hear approach quite clearly. Neither of them had heard the elevator coming up to the fourth floor, where they were, so they naturally felt the woman had still to be on the landing. But there was nobody there. Had she decided to walk down four flights—most unlikely in view of the elevator's presence—she could not have gotten far as yet. Also, in order to reach the stairwell, the woman would have had to brush past her employer.

Mrs. V. insisted there had been a visitor. The lawyer pressed the elevator button. The cab stopped at the fourth floor. It was empty. Evidently nobody had been riding it during the time of the incident, since the noise of the elevator's coming up could not have escaped them.

"You must have seen your own reflection in the glass partition," he reasoned. Some lawyers will reason peculiarly.

Mrs. V. shook her head. She knew what she had seen was not her own image. To prove her point, she reenacted the whole thing. From the spot she had seen the woman stand, no reflection could be gleaned from inside the office.

The lawyer shrugged and went back to his work. Mrs. V. sat down quietly and tried to collect her thoughts. What had she seen? A woman of about sixty-five years of age, a little stocky in build, wearing a close-fitting hat and a brown, tweedy coat. Moreover, something about the woman's appearance seemed to be vaguely familiar. Then all at once it hit her who the woman was!

It was none other than her late mother, Mrs. T., who had been dead for thirteen years. She had owned a coat similar to the one Mrs. V. had seen and always favored close-fitting hats. Why had her mother's ghost appeared to her at this moment? she wondered. Was it because her father was in ill health? Was this an omen, a warning of his impending death?

Grimly preparing for the unwanted, Mrs. V. went through her work rather mechanically for the next few days.

The following week, she received a phone call from one of her sisters. Her mother's favorite sister, their aunt, had suffered a stroke. One week to the day of her mother's appearance, Mrs. V.'s aunt was dead.

The Party Ghost

It was a warm weekend in June 1971, and a group of New Jersey college students decided to throw a graduation party at a place known as "The Farmhouse," which had been rented for the occasion. Most of the young people were between nineteen and twenty-two years of age, and as the party progressed, the spirits were high. Sometime that evening, a boy named Arthur D., son of a policeman, crashed the party and a fight ensued. According to local newspapers, the fight was part of the shindig, but according to others, the boy was ejected and lay in wait to get even with those who had turned him down. But as a result of the fighting, Arthur lay dead in the street, due to wounds received from a knife. Glen F., a twenty-two-year-old youth at the party, was arrested for his murder. Another boy was in the local hospital, seriously injured, but expected to survive.

In the summer of 1972 the house was rented out to a certain Mrs. Gloria Brown. Mrs. Brown and three children were sleeping in the hayloft of the barn, which is located a certain distance from the main house. One of the girls saw a light in the house go on downstairs and the figure of a man, which she thought was her father. When she investigated, the man tried to grab her. She screamed and her brothers came to her aid. By that time the "man" had run away.

Later that summer, a friend was staying with the Browns one evening. There was a knock at the door of the main house about two o'clock in the morning. The friend got up and answered it, but there was no one outside. She went back to bed, only to be awakened again. This time she opened the door and looked through the screen door to see whether there might be someone outside. There was a man standing outside all right, and she asked whether he was hurt or needed help. Then she noticed that he had neither face nor hands, only a whitish, swirly substance! Horror-stricken, she stared at him and he disappeared just as suddenly as he had come.

At this writing, the restless boy is still unable to find peace: for him, the unlucky party has never broken up.

The Ghostly Nun

Dorothy Mark-Moore was twelve years old when her Aunt Mary bought a house in Green Brook, New Jersey. The house was on Washington Street and the year was 1933. All the members of the family had retired for the night, and it was rather a warm night at that, so Dorothy thought she'd roll up her pajama legs, and go to sleep like that. She awoke in the early hours of the morning with a start and looked around the room. It so happened that it was a moonlit night so she could make out very clearly if there happened to be an intruder in the room.

As she looked toward the window, she saw a woman walk in, return to the window, look out of it and then turn toward her. Frightened, Dorothy pretended to be asleep for a moment, but then she opened her eyes again and to her amazement saw a nun standing there, looking at her from head to foot. Then the nun came over and moved her hand onto her legs. But when the nun touched Dorothy's legs, it felt like an old dried-out piece of wood.

The ghostly nun was now close enough to the bed for Dorothy to make out a ring on her hand and beads around her waist, with a large cross dangling at the end of it. The woman appeared to be in her thirties, and seemed quite solid. Suddenly Dorothy realized she was looking at a ghost. She shot up and looked straight into the nun's face. For a moment, girl and ghost stared at each other. Then the nun's face softened as she walked away from Dorothy and vanished into the wall.

Four years later the ghostly nun returned. This time Dorothy was asleep in another bedroom of the same house and it was around seven o'clock in the morning. All of a sudden, Dorothy heard loud organ music and sat up in bed to find out where it came from. The music became so loud she could not stand it and fell back onto the pillows. It felt as if an invisible hand were holding her down. At that moment, the nun entered the room, with a gentleman in his forties, with dark hair and brown eyes, wearing a dark blue serge suit. Dorothy was petrified with fear, especially as the organ music increased to an almost ear-splitting level. Looking at the two apparitions, she noticed, from the movement of their lips, that they were reciting the Lord's Prayer. As they did so, the music became less loud, and the two figures slowly walked toward the door. As they left the room, the music stopped abruptly. At that moment, Dorothy seemed to snap out of her trance state, sat up in bed, and quickly grabbed all her clothes, running to the bathroom and locking herself in. When she had regained her composure, she made some inquiries about the house and learned that a gentleman of that description had killed himself in the very bathroom into which she had locked herself, some fifty years before.

The Lady
of the Spirits

Jananne B. had truck with the unseen since she was very small. While she was visiting her aunt in New Jersey, she remembers clearly seeing a figure in the old carriage house. There was no one in the carriage house at the time. At age seventeen, Miss B. was spending a weekend with another aunt, also in New Jersey. Both women were occupying the same bed. In the middle of the night the young girl sat up in bed, waking up her aunt. There was a tall man in a brown suit standing next to the bed, she explained, and went on to describe his brown hair and handlebar moustache in great detail. Without saying a word, her aunt got up and brought out the family album. Leafing through it, Miss B. pointed at one particular picture: it was her great-grandfather. She had never seen pictures of him, nor of course ever met him. He had died in the very room and bed in which the two women were sleeping at the time.

When she was twenty-four years old, Jananne moved into what was formerly her brother's room, her brother having moved to his own apartment. The very first night she stayed in the room, she felt a presence, and couldn't sleep. Somehow the room had always been the stuffiest room in the house, but that night it was particularly cold. This upset her greatly since she had put in a great deal of time and effort to redecorate it to her taste. Somehow she went off to sleep that night, trying to forget or ignore her feelings. A few nights later she woke up in the middle of the night, feeling extremely cold. As she sat up in bed, she saw a woman out of the corner of her eye: the woman seemed middle-aged, with brown hair pulled back in a very plain bun, wearing a long, straight skirt and a white ruffled blouse with long sleeves and high collar.

Jananne did not experience a feeling of fear, for somehow she knew the spirit was friendly. The next morning just as she was about to wake up, she saw the name "Elly" being written on the wall above her shelves. There were other lines around the name, but before she could make them out, the vision faded. Since she keeps a dream log, recording all unusual dreams, she immediately wrote this incident down before she could forget it. She also told her mother about the incidents.

Time passed, and several months later a local psychic came to the house to do a reading for the family, using her bedroom to work in. The psychic described the entity in the room precisely the way Jananne had seen it. By now Jananne B. was not the only one to be aware of the ghost. Various friends also heard footsteps overhead while sitting in a room directly underneath hers, and had seen the lights dim of their own volition. Because of the ghostly presence, Jananne's room is unusually cold, and she frequently complains about it. Not long ago, when she remarked how cold it was, the door to the outdoor widow's walk flew wide open and her bedroom door shut of its own volition.

This has happened a number of times, making the room even colder. On several occasions, Miss B. came home to find her bedroom door tightly shut, and very hard to open. Once inside, she noticed that her bedspread was on the floor, propped up against the door from the inside. No one could have placed it there except from inside the room—and the room had been locked.

Soon enough Miss B. realized that she had to get used to sharing her room with the strange lady. Once her mind was made up to accept her as a companion, the phenomenon became less annoying. She decided to take some random pictures of the room to see whether anything unusual would show up. Only the available room light was used, no flash light or electrical lighting. Two of the pictures came back from the laboratory with a white mist on them, one of them showing the letters Elly indistinctly, but nevertheless apparent beyond the shadow of a doubt. Miss B. showed the photographs to her brother, a professional photographer, and to some of his friends. They agreed that double exposure or light leaks were out; the white mist appears to be blotchy, almost like smoke, whereas light leaks would tend to be uniform.

Jananne realizes that Elly is able to manifest for her only because she is psychic. If she needed any further proof of her ability in this respect, it was furnished to her a month later when a friend took her to a certain lady's trailer home for dinner. Jananne's friend asked her to dress lightly because it was always warm there, he said.

But when they arrived at the trailer, it was unusually cold inside. They were having a quiet conversation after dinner, sitting on the couch, when Miss B. looked up and saw the figure of a very sad young man standing in the entrance to the hallway. His head was bowed, and he seemed very lost. Since the hostess had turned out to be rather on the nervous side, Jananne decided not to tell her about the apparition. But on the way home, she informed her friend what she had seen, describing the man in every detail. Her friend swallowed hard, then informed her that the husband of their hostess had disappeared shortly after returning from Vietnam. Three months later his body was found in the woods; he had committed suicide.

New York

The Haunted
Murder Room

Eileen Courtis is a native of London who now resides on the West Coast but who lived previously in New York City. Although she has never gone to college, she has a good grasp of things, an analytical mind, and is not given to hysterics. When she arrived in New York at age thirty-four, she decided to look for a quiet hotel and then search for a job.

The job turned out to be an average office position, and the hotel she decided upon was the Martha Washington, a hotel for women on Twenty-Ninth Street. Eileen was essentially shy and a loner who only made friends slowly.

She was given a room on the twelfth floor and, immediately on crossing the threshold, she was struck by a foul odor coming from the room. Her first impulse was to ask for another room, but she was in no mood to create a fuss, so she stayed.

"I can stand it a night or two," she thought, but did not unpack. It turned out that she stayed in that room for six long months, and yet she never really unpacked.

All her life, Eileen had been having various experiences of what we now call extrasensory perception, and her first impression of her new "home" was that someone had died in it. She examined the walls inch by inch. There was a spot where a crucifix must have hung for a long time, judging by the color of the surrounding wall. Evidently it had been removed when someone moved out—permanently.

That night, after she had gone to bed, her sleep was interrupted by what sounded like the turning of a newspaper page, as if someone were sitting in the chair at the foot of her bed reading a newspaper. Quickly she switched on the light; she was, of course, quite alone. Were her nerves playing tricks on her? It was a strange city, a strange room. She decided to go back to sleep. Immediately the rustling started up again, and then someone began walking across the floor, starting from the chair and heading toward the door of the room.

Eileen turned on every light in the room and it stopped. Exhausted, she dozed off again. The next morning she looked over the room carefully. Perhaps mice had caused the rustling. The strange odor remained, so she requested that the room be fumigated. The manager smiled wryly, and nobody came to fumigate her room. The rustling noise continued night after night, and Eileen slept with the lights on for the next three weeks.

Somehow her ESP told her this presence was a strong-willed, vicious old woman who resented others occupying what she still considered "her" room. Eileen decided to fight her. Night after night, she braved it out in the dark, only to find herself totally exhausted in the morning. Her appearance at the office gave rise to talk. But she was not going to give in to a ghost. Side by side, the living and the dead women now occupied the same room without sharing it.

Then one night, something prevented her from going off to sleep. She lay in bed quietly, waiting.

Suddenly she became aware of two skinny but very strong arms extended over her head, holding a large downy pillow as though to suffocate her! It took every ounce of her strength to force the pillow off her face.

Next morning, she tried to pass it off to herself as a hallucination. But was it? She was quite sure that she had not been asleep.

Still she did not move out, and one evening when she arrived home from the office, she felt a sudden pain in her back, as if she had been stabbed. During the night, she awoke to find herself in a state of utter paralysis. She could not move her limbs or head. Finally, after a long time, she managed to work her way to the telephone receiver and call for a doctor. Nobody came. But her control seemed to start coming back and she called a friend, who rushed over to find Eileen in a state of shock.

During the next few days she had a thorough examination by the company physician, which included the taking of X-rays to determine if there was anything physically wrong with her that could have caused this condition. She was given a clean bill of health and her strength had by then returned, so she decided to quit while she was ahead.

She went to Florida for an extended rest, but eventually came back to New York and the hotel. This time she was given another room, where she lived very happily and without incident for over a year.

One day a neighbor who knew her from the time she had occupied the room on the twelfth floor saw her in the lobby and insisted on having a visit with her. Reluctantly, for she is not fond of socializing, Eileen agreed. The conversation covered various topics until suddenly the neighbor came out with "the time you were living in that haunted room across the hall."

Since Eileen had never told anyone of her fearsome experiences there, she was puzzled. The neighbor confessed that she had meant to warn her while she was occupying that room, but somehow had never mustered enough courage. "Warn me of what?" Eileen insisted.

"The woman who had the room just before you moved in," the neighbor explained haltingly, "well, she was found dead in the chair, and the woman who had it before her was also found dead, in the bathtub."

Eileen swallowed quickly and left. Suddenly she knew that the pillowcase had not been a hallucination.

The Ghost
of Brooklyn Heights

I t all started when I received a letter from Mrs. Gwen Hinzie of Newbury Park, California. She wished to contribute some material to my research efforts.

"In 1946 I was twenty-six years old," she wrote. "I spent about four months in New York City working as a secretary. I lived in Brooklyn Heights—at different times in two different rooming houses—and there (in both) was conscious of ghosts.

"One of these old brownstone houses was in the next block south of the St. George Hotel in Brooklyn Heights and the other about a half block distant. It has been so long ago I cannot remember the street names now.

"In the first house mentioned I lived on the ground floor. It was an old firetrap really and even had rats. It was a four-story building in poor repair.

"I lived in a room off the furnace room that had a door leading out to the side of the building. My only heat was from the furnace room itself and there was a small opening in the wall (covered with coarse wire screening) through which the heat was supposed to pass. I lived there for about one month (November 1946).

"My experiences took place over about a two-week period. The first thing that happened was hearing a woman crying in the night. Then another woman spoke to her sharply and she stopped crying. This seemed to be on the other side of the wall in the room or apartment occupied by the only other tenant on that floor. When I asked her later about this, she denied that anyone ever stayed with her!

"Later, one evening I came into the furnace room to go to my room and passed through what seemed to be a pall of black smoke. There was no smoke odor but the furnace was burning. When I told my landlady about it she said she was sure there was nothing wrong with the furnace.

"Another evening, through the wall opening I previously mentioned, there appeared a *thick white mist*—but it looked more like smoke than mist. I got out of my chair and went to the bed to pick up something to flap away this 'smoke' (it was only halfway through the opening) and when I turned back again it was gone.

"At another later time during the day I found this *thick white mist materializing before my eyes*. Then it disappeared. There was also a black mist that had materialized while my back was turned another time—but this was one that frightened me. The other had not. I spoke to 'it' and said to go away but it was several seconds before it did.

"After I had been there about a week I found it necessary to buy a small electric heater since it was becoming cold in there, and I found I had to sit before my little stove with my coat on. It did not even warm my feet. The heat seemed to radiate only about two and a half to three inches from the stove. I became ill while living in that room with a respiratory infection and was so cold that I found by the time I had been there about three weeks that I could not warm up until I had been in our (too) warm office about two hours!

"By that time I believed there were ghosts there and upon inquiring of the landlady found that she had nothing to say. She merely suggested I find another place to live.

"About the first of December I moved into another brownstone. (I should explain here that when I had first arrived in Brooklyn Heights I was visiting friends and stayed in their apartment. I had not been there a week before I *occasionally saw strangely dressed people on the street*. I thought this was my imagination as I seemed to get carried away thinking of what the old place must have been like in its heyday. I thought at first there might have been a theatre nearby and that these were actors but later found out this was not the case.)

"I soon was busy going back and forth to work and did not see strange people on the street. One of these people that I did remember was a woman—in her twenties or possibly a little older —who was tall, thin and looked about six months pregnant. She wore a dress that was long and had long sleeves or three-quarter-length sleeves and a bustle. The bodice was very snug and the waist very tight but the bulge below the waist suggested pregnancy. She walked rapidly down the street (across the street) away from me.

"Imagine my shock when I entered my new boarding house and saw *the same woman,* dressed the same, standing in the doorway leading from the foyer to the hallway in the rear of the building! She was standing facing the wall, so was sideways to my view, and when I unlocked the door she distinctly jumped and looked with fear on her face toward the door. *Then she calmly walked into the wall.* I never saw her again there or anywhere else."

Gertrude,
Who Stayed

One of the great romantic dramas of the nineteenth century was played out in what is now a pretty seamy section of New York City. This is a true story, immortalized in novels and motion pictures, but only to a point: the most dramatic and shocking details of the story only emerged as a result of my investigation with the late Ethel Johnson Meyers, the great trance medium.

When New York was still young and growing, a neighborhood that is now given over to derelicts and slums was then an elegant, quiet area of homes and gardens. The world was right and peaceful in the young republic circa 1820. Gradually, however, the in people, as we call them nowadays, moved farther uptown, for such is the nature of a city confined to a small island. It can only move up, never down or out. Greenwich Village was still pretty far uptown, although the city had already spread beyond its limits, and the center of New York was somewhere around the city hall district (now considered way downtown).

Real estate developers envisioned the east side of Fifth Avenue as the place to put up elegant homes for the well-to-do. One of the more fashionable architects of that time was John McComb, who had plans for a kind of terrace of houses extending from Lafayette Street to the Bowery, with the back windows of the houses looking out on John Jacob Astor's property nearby. Now Mr. Astor was considered somewhat uncouth socially by some of his contemporaries (on one occasion he mistook a lady's voluminous sleeve for a dinner napkin), but nobody had any second thoughts about his prosperity or position in the commercial world. Thus, any house looking out upon such a desirable neighborhood would naturally attract a buyer, the builders reasoned, and they proved to be right.

Called brownstones because of the dark brick material of their facades, the houses were well-appointed and solid. Only one of them is still left in that area, while garages, factories, and ugly modern structures have replaced all the others.

The house in question was completed in 1830 and attracted the eagle eye of a merchant named Seabury Tredwell, who was looking for a proper home commensurate with his increasing financial status in the city. He bought it and moved in with his family.

Mr. Tredwell's business was hardware, and he was one of the proud partners in Kissam & Tredwell, with offices on nearby Dey Street. A portly man of fifty, Mr. Tredwell was what we would today call a conservative. One of his direct ancestors had been the first Episcopal bishop of New York, and though a merchant, Tredwell evinced all the outward signs of an emerging mercantile aristocracy. The house he acquired certainly looked the part: seven levels, consisting of three stories, an attic and two cellars, large, Federal-style windows facing Fourth Street, a lovely garden around the house, and an imposing columned entrance door that one reached after ascending a flight of six marble stairs flanked by wrought-iron gate lanterns—altogether the nearest a merchant prince could come to a real nobleman in his choice of domicile.

Inside, too, the appointments are lavish and in keeping with the traditions of the times: a Duncan Phyfe banister ensconces a fine staircase leading to the three upper stories and originates in an elegant hall worthy of any caller.

As one steps into this hall, one first notices a huge, high-ceilinged parlor to the left. At the end of this parlor are mahogany double doors separating the room from the dining room, equally as large and impressive as the front room. The Duncan Phyfe table was at one time set with Haviland china and Waterford crystal, underlining the Tredwell family's European heritage. Each room has a large fireplace and long mirrors adding to the cavernous appearance of the two rooms. Large, floor-to-ceiling windows on each end shed light into the rooms, and when the mahogany doors are opened, the entire area looks like a ballroom in one of those manor houses Mr. Tredwell's forebears lived in in Europe.

The furniture—all of which is still in the house—was carefully chosen. Prominent in a corner of the parlor is a large, rectangular piano. (No Victorian drawing room was complete without a piano.) A music box is on top for the delight of those unable to tinkle the ivories yet desirous of musical charms. The box plays "Home Sweet Home," and a sweet home it is indeed.

Farther back along the corridor one comes upon a small family room and a dark, ugly kitchen, almost L-shaped and utterly without charm or practical arrangements, as these things are nowadays understood. But in Victorian New York, this was a proper place to cook. Maidservants and cooks were not to be made cheerful, after all; theirs was to cook and serve, and not to enjoy.

On the first floor—or second floor, if you prefer, in today's usage—two large bedrooms are separated from each other by a kind of storage area, or perhaps a dressing room, full of drawers and cabinets. Off the front bedroom there is a small bedroom in which a four-poster bed takes up almost all the available space. The bed came over from England with one of Mrs. Tredwell's ancestors.

Leading to the third floor, the stairs narrow, and one is well advised to hold on to the banister. The third floor now serves as the curator's apartment. The Old Merchant's House is kept up as a private museum and is no longer at the mercy of the greedy wrecker. But when Seabury Tredwell lived in the house, the servants' rooms were on the third floor. Beyond that, a low-ceilinged attic provided additional space, and still another apartment fills part of the basement, also suitable for servants' usage.

All in all, it is the kind of house that inspires confidence in its owner. Mr. Tredwell's acquisition of the house helped establish him in New York society as a force to be reckoned with, for that, too, was good for his expanding business. He was eminently aided in this quest by the fact that his wife Eliza, whom he had married while still on his way up, had given him six daughters. Three of the girls made good marriages, left the parental homestead, and apparently made out very well, for not much was heard about them one way or another. Of the remaining three girls, however, plenty is recorded.

The three bachelor girls were named Phoebe, Sarah, and Gertrude. Phoebe's main interest was the Carl Fischer piano in the parlor, and she and her sister Sarah would often play to-

gether. Gertrude (called Gitty when young) was the last of the
Tredwell children, born in 1840, and was different from the rest
and kept herself apart. There were also two boys, but somehow
they did not amount to very much, it is said, for it became necessary later, when of all the children only they and Gertrude were
left, to appoint a cousin, Judge Seabury, to supervise the management of the estate. Brother Horace, in particular, was much more
interested in tending the four magnolia trees that dominated the
view from the tearoom.

To this day, nobody knows the real reason for a secret passage
from a trap door near the bedrooms to the East River, a considerable distance. Recently, it was walled up to prevent rats from
coming through it, but it is still there, holding on to its strange
mystery—that is, to those who do not *know*.

Some of the things that transpired behind the thick walls of
the Old Merchant's House would never have been brought to light
were it not for the sensitive who walked its corridors a century
later and bit by bit helped reconstruct what went on when the
house was young. Only then did the various pieces of the jigsaw
puzzle slowly sink into place, pieces that otherwise might never
have found a common denominator.

When the house finally gave up its murky secrets, a strange
calm settled over it, as if the story had wanted to be told after all
those years to free it from the need of further hiding from the
light.

Seabury Tredwell's stern Victorian ways did not sit well with
all members of his family. The spinster girls in particular were
afraid of but respectful toward their father, and found it difficult
to live up to his rigid standards. They wanted to marry but since
no suitable person came along they were just as happy to wait.
Underneath this resignation, however, a rebellious spirit boiled
up in Sarah. Five years older than Gertrude, she could not or
would not wait to find happiness in an age where the word
scarcely had any personal meaning.

Tredwell ruled the family with an iron hand, demanding and
getting blind submission to his orders. Thus it was with considerable misgivings that Sarah encouraged a budding friendship with
a young man her father did not know, or know of, whom she had
met accidentally at a tearoom. That in itself would have been
sufficient reason for her father to disallow such a friendship. He

was a man who considered indecent anyone who referred to chicken limbs as legs. He ordered the legs of his chairs and tables covered, so they might not incite male visitors to unsavory ideas!

It took a great deal of ingenuity for Sarah to have a liaison with a strange man and not get caught. But her mother, perhaps out of rebellion against Tredwell, perhaps out of compassion for her neglected daughter, looked the other way, if not encouraged the relationship. And ingenious Sarah also found another ally in her quest for love. There was a black servant who had known and cared for her since her birth, and he acted as a go-between for her and the young man. For a few weeks, Sarah managed to sneak down to meet her paramour. She had accidentally discovered the secret passageway to the river and used it well. At the other end it led to what was then pretty rough ground and an even rougher neighborhood, but the young man was always there waiting with a carriage, and she felt far safer with him than in the cold embrace of her father's fanatical stare. Although Tredwell boasted to his friends that his house had "seven hundred locks and seven hundred keys," this was one door he had forgotten about.

Why an architect in 1830 would want to include a secret passageway is a mystery on the surface of it. But there were still riots in New York in those years, and the British invasion of 1812 was perhaps still fresh in some people's memories. A secret escape route was no more a luxury in a patrician American home than a priest hole was in a Catholic house in England. One never knew how things might turn. There had been many instances of slave rebellions, and the underground railroad, bringing the escapees up from the South, was in full swing then in New York.

One meeting with the young man, who shall remain nameless here, led to another, and before long, nature took its course. Sarah was definitely pregnant. Could she tell her father? Certainly not. Should they run off and marry? That seemed the logical thing to do, but Sarah feared the long arm of her family. Judge Seabury, her father's distinguished cousin, might very well stop them. Then too, there was the question of scandal. To bring scandal upon her family was no way to start a happy marriage.

Distraught, Sarah stopped seeing the young man. Nights she would walk the hallways of the house, sleepless from worry, fearful of discovery. Finally, she had to tell someone, and that someone was her sister Gertrude. Surprisingly, Gertrude did understand and comforted her as best she could. Now that they shared her secret, things were a little easier to bear. But unfortunately, things did not improve. It was not long before her father discovered her condition and all hell broke loose.

With the terror of the heavy he was, Tredwell got the story out of his daughter, except for the young man's name. This was especially hard to keep back, but Sarah felt that betraying her lover would not lead to a union with him. Quite rightfully, she felt her father would have him killed or jailed. When the merchant discovered that there had been a go-between, and what was more, a man in his employ, the old servant was hauled over the coals. Only the fact that he had been with them for so many years and that his work was useful to the family prevented Tredwell from firing him immediately. But he abused the poor man and threatened him until the sheer shock of his master's anger changed his character: where he had been a pleasant and helpful servant, there was now only a shiftless, nervous individual, eager to avoid the light and all questions.

This went on for some weeks or months. Then the time came for the baby to be born and the master of the house had another stroke of genius. He summoned the servant and talked with him at length. Nobody could hear what was said behind the heavy doors, but when the servant emerged his face was grim and his eyes glassy. Nevertheless, the old relationship between master and servant seemed to have been restored, for Tredwell no longer abused the man after this meeting.

What happened then we know only from the pieces of memory resurrected by the keen insight of a psychic: no court of law would ever uphold the facts as true in the sense the law requires, unfortunately, even if they are, in fact, true. One night there was a whimpering heard from the trap door between the two bedrooms upstairs, where there is now a chest of drawers and the walled-off passageway down to the river. Before the other servants in the house could investigate the strange noises in the night, it was all over and the house was silent again. Tredwell himself came from his room and calmed them.

"It is nothing," he said in stentorian tones, "just the wind in the chimney." Nobody questioned the words of the master, so the house soon fell silent again. But below stairs, in the dank, dark corridor leading to the river, a dark man carried the limp body of a newborn baby that had just taken its first, and last, breath.

Several days later, there was another confrontation. The evil doer wanted his pay. He had been promised a certain sum for the unspeakable deed. The master shrugged. The man threatened. The master turned his back. Who would believe a former slave, a runaway slave wanted down South? Truly, he didn't have to pay such a person. Evil has its own reward, too, and the man went back to his little room. But the imprint of the crime stuck to the small passage near the trap door and was picked up a century later by a psychic. Nobody saw the crime. Nobody may rightfully claim the arrangement between master and servant ever took place. But the house knows and its silence speaks louder than mere facts that will stand up in court.

When Sarah awoke from a stupor, days later, and found her infant gone, she went stark raving mad. For a time, she had to be restrained. Somehow, word leaked out into the streets of the city below, but no one ever dared say anything publicly. Sarah was simply indisposed to her friends. Weeks went by and her pain subsided. Gradually a certain relief filled the void inside her. She had lost everything, but at least her lover was safe from her father's clutches. Although she never knew for sure, whenever she glanced at the old servant, she shrank back: his eyes avoided her and her heart froze. Somehow, with the intuitive knowledge of a mother, she *knew*. Then too, she avoided the passage near the trap door. Nothing could get her to walk through it. But as her health returned, her determination to leave also received new impetus. She could not go on living in this house where so much had happened. One day, she managed to get out of the door. It was a windy fall night, and she was badly dressed for it. Half-mad with fear of being followed, she roamed the streets for hours. Darkness and her mental condition took their toll. Eventually she found herself by the water. When she was found, she was still alive, but expired before she could be brought back to the house.

Her death—by her own hand—was a blow to the family. Word was given out that Sarah had died in a carriage accident. It sounded much more elegant, and though no one ever found out what carriage, as she had been in bed for so long, and had just begun to walk about the house again, it was accepted because of the unspoken code among the Victorians: one man's tragedy is never another's gossip. Then, too, the question of suicide was a thorny one to resolve in an age that had not yet freed the human personality even in the flesh: it had to be an accident.

Thus Sarah was laid to rest along with the others of her family in the Christ Churchyard in Manhasset, Long Island, properly sanctified as behooves the daughter of an important citizen whose ancestor was a bishop.

What had happened to Sarah did not pass without making a deep and lasting impression on the youngest girl, Gertrude. She tried not to talk about it, of course, but it made her more serious and less frivolous in her daily contacts. She was now of the age where love can so easily come, yet no one had held her hand with the slightest effect on her blood pressure. True, her father had introduced a number of carefully screened young men, and some not so young ones, in the hope that she might choose one from among them. But Gertrude would not marry just to please her father, yet she would not marry against his wishes. There had to be someone she could love and whom her father could also accept, she reasoned, and she was willing to wait for him.

While she was playing a game with time, spring came around again, and the air beckoned her to come out into the garden for a walk. While there, she managed to catch the eye of a young man on his way past the house. Words were exchanged despite Victorian propriety, and she felt giddy.

She decided she would not make the mistake her sister had made in seeing the young man secretly. Instead, she encouraged the shy young man, whose name was Louis, to seek entry into her house openly and with her father's knowledge, if not yet blessings. This he did, not without difficulties, and Seabury Tredwell had him investigated immediately. He learned that the young man was a penniless student of medicine.

"But he'll make a fine doctor someday," Gertrude pleaded with her father.

"Someday," the old man snorted. "And what is he going to live on until then? I tell you what. *My* money."

Tredwell assumed, and perhaps not without reason, that everybody in New York knew that his daughters were heiresses and would have considerable dowries as well. This idea so established itself in his mind, he suspected every gentleman caller of being a fortune hunter. The young man was, he argued, not after his daughter's love, but merely her money and that would never do.

Gertrude, although no great beauty, possessed a certain charm and independence. She was petite, with a tiny waistline, blue eyes, and dark hair, and she greatly resembled Britain's Princess Margaret when the latter was in her late twenties.

Tredwell refused to accept the young medical student as a serious suitor. Not only was the young man financially unacceptable, but worse, he was a Catholic. Tredwell did not believe in encouraging marriages out of the faith and even if Louis had offered to change religions, it is doubtful the father would have changed his mind. In all this he paid absolutely no heed to his daughter's feelings or desires, and with true Victorian rigidity, forbade her to see the young man further.

There was finally a showdown between father and daughter. Tredwell, no longer so young, and afflicted with the pains and aches of advancing age, pleaded with her not to disappoint him in his last remaining years. He wanted a good provider for her, and Louis was not the right man. Despite her feelings, Gertrude finally succumbed to her father's pleading and sent the young man away. When the doors closed on him for the last time, it was as if the gates of Gertrude's heart had also permanently closed on the outside world: hence she lived only for her father and his well-being and no young man ever got to see her again.

Seabury Tredwell proved a difficult and thankless patient as progressive illness forced him to bed permanently. When he finally passed away in 1865, the two remaining sisters, Gertrude and Phoebe, continued to live in the house. But it was Gertrude who ran it. They only went out after dark and only when absolutely necessary to buy food. The windows were always shuttered and even small leaks covered with felt or other material to keep out the light and cold.

As the two sisters cut themselves off from the outside world, all kinds of legends sprang up about them. But after Phoebe died and left Gertrude all alone in the big house, even the legends stopped and gradually the house and its owner sank into the oblivion afforded yesterday's sensation by a relentless, everchanging humanity.

Finally, at age ninety-three, Gertrude passed on. The year was 1933, and America had bigger headaches than what to do about

New York's last authentic brownstone. The two servants who had shared the house with Gertrude to her death, and who had found her peacefully asleep, soon left, leaving the house to either wreckers or new owners, or just neglect. There was neither electricity nor telephone in it, but the original furniture and all the fine works of art Seabury Tredwell had put into the house were still there. The only heat came from fireplaces, with which the house was filled. The garden had long gone, and only the house remained, wedged in between a garage and nondescript modern building. Whatever elegance there had been was now present only inside the house or perhaps in the aura of its former glories.

The neighborhood was no longer safe, and the house itself was in urgent need of repairs. Eventually, responsible city officials realized the place should be made into a museum, for it presented one of the few houses in America with everything—from furniture to personal belongings and clothes—still intact as it was when people lived in it in the middle of the nineteenth century. There were legal problems of clearing title, but eventually this was done and the Old Merchant's House became a museum.

When the first caretaker arrived to live in the house, it was discovered that thieves had already broken in and made off with a pair of Sheffield candelabra, a first edition of Charlotte Bronte, and the Tredwell family Bible. But the remainder was still intact, and a lot of cleaning up had to be done immediately.

One of the women helping in this work found herself alone in the house one afternoon. She had been busy carrying some of Miss Gertrude's clothing downstairs so that it could be properly displayed in special glass cases. When she rested from her work for a moment, she looked up and saw herself being watched intently by a woman on the stairs. At first glance, she looked just like Princess Margaret of England, but then she noticed the strange old-fashioned clothes the woman wore and realized she belonged to another age. The tight-fitting bodice had a row of small buttons and the long, straight skirt reached to the floor. As the volunteer stared in amazement at the stranger, wondering who it could be, the woman on the stairs vanished.

At first the volunteer did not want to talk about her experience, but when it happened several times, and always when she was alone in the house, she began to wonder whether she wasn't taking leave of her senses. But soon another volunteer moved into the picture, a writer who had passed the site on her way to the library to do some research. Intrigued by the home's stately appearance, she looked into it further and before long was in love with the house.

There was a certain restlessness that permeated the building after dark, but she blamed it on her imagination and the strange neighborhood. She did not believe in ghosts nor was she given to fancies, and the noises didn't really disturb her. She decided that there was a lot of work to be done if the museum were to take its proper place among other showplaces, and she decided to give the tourists and other visitors a good run for their money—all fifty cents' worth.

The next few weeks were spent in trying to make sense out of the masses of personal effects—dresses, gowns, shoes, hats. The Tredwells had left everything behind them intact—as if they had intended to return to their earthly possessions one of these days and to resume life as it was.

Nothing had been given away or destroyed and Mrs. R., writer that she was, immediately realized how important it was that the residence be kept intact for future research of that period. She went to work at once and as she applied herself to the job at hand, she began to get the *feel* of the house as if she had herself lived in it for many years.

She started her job by taking an inventory of the late Gertrude Tredwell's wardrobe once again. This time the job had to be done properly, for the visitors to the museum were entitled to see a good display of period costumes. As she picked through Gertrude's vast wardrobe one article at a time, she had the uncanny feeling of being followed step for step. The house was surrounded by slums and the danger of real break-ins very great, but this was different: no flesh-and-blood intruders followed her around on her rounds from the third floor down to the basement and back again for more clothes. Often a chilly feeling touched her as she walked through the halls, but she attributed that to the moist atmosphere in the old house.

One day when she entered the front bedroom that used to be Gertrude's, from the hall bedroom, she had the distinct impression of another presence close to her. Something was brushing by her to reach the other door that opened into the front bedroom before she did!

When this happened again sometime later, she began to wonder if the stories about the house being haunted, which circulated freely in the neighborhood, did not have some basis in fact. Certainly there was a presence, and the sound of another person brushing past her was quite unmistakable.

While she was still deliberating whether or not to discuss this with any of her friends, an event took place that brought home the suspicion that she was never quite alone in the house.

It was on a morning several months after her arrival that she walked into the kitchen carrying some things to be put into the display cases ranged along the wall opposite the fireplace. Out of the corner of her eye she caught sight of what looked like the figure of a small, elegant woman standing in front of a huge fireplace. While Mrs. R. was able to observe the brown taffeta gown she was wearing, her head was turned away, so she could not see her features. But there were masses of brown hair. The whole thing was in very soft focus, rather misty without being insubstantial. Her hands, however, holding a cup and saucer, were very beautiful and quite sharply defined against her dark gown.

Mrs. R. was paralyzed, afraid to turn her head to look directly at her. Suddenly, however, without any conscious volition, she spun around and quickly walked out of the room into the hall. By the time she got to the stairs she was covered with cold perspiration, and her hands were shaking so violently she had to put down the things she was carrying.

Now she knew that Gertrude Tredwell was still around, but not the way she looked when she died. Rather, she had turned back her memory clock to that period of her life when she was happiest and her young man had not yet been sent away by a cruel and unyielding father.

When the realization came to Mrs. R. as to who her ghostly friend was, her fears went away. After all, who would have a better right to be in this house than the one who had sacrificed her love and youth to it and what it stood for in her father's view. This change of her attitude must have somehow gotten through to the ghostly lady as well, by some as yet undefinable telegraph connecting all things, living and dead.

Sometime thereafter, Mrs. R. was arranging flowers for the

table in the front parlor. The door was open to the hallway and she was quite alone in the house. She was so preoccupied with the flower arrangement that she failed to notice that she was no longer alone.

Finally, a strange sound caught her attention, and she looked up from the table. The sound was that of a taffeta gown swishing by in rapid movement. As her eyes followed the sound, she saw a woman going up the stairs. It was the same petite figure she had originally seen at the fireplace sometime before. Again she wore the brown taffeta gown. As she rounded the stairs and disappeared from view, the sound of the gown persisted for a moment or two after the figure herself had gotten out of sight.

This time Mrs. R. did not experience any paralysis or fear. Instead, a warm feeling of friendship between her and the ghost sprang up within her, and contentedly, as if nothing had happened, she continued with her flower arrangement.

During this time, the curator of the Old Merchant's House was a professional antiquarian named Janet Hutchinson, who shared the appointments with her friend Emeline Paige, editor of the *Villager*, a neighborhood newspaper, and Mrs. Hutchinson's son, Jefferson, aged fourteen. In addition, there was a cat named Eloise who turned out to be a real fraidicat, probably for good and valid reasons. Although Mrs. Hutchinson did not encounter anything ghostly during her tenure, Ms. Paige did feel very uneasy in the back bedroom, where much of the tragedy had taken place.

Another person who felt the oppressive atmosphere of the place, without being able to rationalize it away for any good reasons, was the novelist Elizabeth Byrd, and her friend, whom I must call Mrs. B., for she shies away from the uncanny in public. Mrs. B. visited the house one evening in 1964. As she stood in what had once been Gertrude's bedroom, she noticed that the bedspread of Gertrude's bed was indented as if someone had just gotten up from it. Clearly, the rough outline of a body could be made out.

As she stared in disbelief at the bed, she noticed a strange perfume in the air. Those with her remarked on the scent, but before anyone could look for its sources, it had evaporated. None of the ladies with Mrs. B. had on any such perfume, and the house had been sterile and quiet for days.

No further reports of any unusual experiences have come to

mind. On one occasion in 1965, photographs of the fireplace near which Mrs. R. had seen the ghost of Gertrude Tredwell were taken simultaneously by two noted photographers with equipment previously tested for proper functioning. This was done to look into the popular legend that this fireplace could not be photographed and that whenever anyone attempted it, that person would have blank film as a result. Perhaps the legend was started by a bad photographer, or it was just that, a legend, for both gentlemen produced almost identical images of the renowned fireplace with their cameras. However, Gertrude Tredwell was not standing in front of it.

This is as it should be. Mrs. R., the untiring spirit behind the Historical Landmarks Society that keeps the building going and out of the wreckers' hands, feels certain that Gertrude need not make another appearance now that everything is secure. And to a Victorian lady, that matters a great deal.

The Old Merchant's House, forever threatened by the wrecker's ball, still receives visitors. I last saw it in the late 1980s with a psychic named Kathleen Roach. Directly she stepped inside Gertrude's parlor, she turned around and asked me to get her out of the house; the jealousy and anger of the old girl evidently never left the house. So if you happen to run into her, be kind.

The Ghost
and the Love Letters

Adriana Victoria is a spunky, adventurous woman of Mexican ancestry. At one time she worked as a housekeeper in a Hollywood mansion that was once the property of the noted actress Carole Lombard. One night, Adriana awoke to see the blood-stained body of the actress standing by her bed, as if begging for attention. By then Adriana knew that she was psychic, she knew that her mother was psychic also, and that this particular talent ran in the family. She accepted it as something perfectly natural and learned to live with it, although at times she underwent frightening experiences that were not easily forgotten.

Miss Victoria now lived in an apartment in New York City consisting of two-and-a-half rooms. In view of the small size of the apartment, it was something of a problem to put up her mother and her two children, but Adriana managed somehow when they came for a visit to New York in the summer of that year. They were on their way from Florida to Europe, and were staying for only a few days.

Since there was little room for everybody, they put a mattress on the living room floor. One night Miss Victoria, sleeping on the mattress, was awakened by two invisible hands that she saw only in her mind's eye. At the same time, she was shaken strongly by the ankles and opened her eyes wide. She couldn't see any intruder, and didn't dare wake the others in the apartment. But nothing further happened until the end of the summer, when her mother left with her granddaughter, leaving Miss Victoria's nine-year-old son at home.

About two months later, Miss Victoria was cleaning up after dinner, and a girlfriend from an apartment in the same building was watching television while waiting for her to finish with the dishes. Suddenly her son came running in and locked himself into the bathroom next to the kitchen, as if he were frightened by something. Before she could figure out what was happening, Miss Victoria heard heavy footsteps coming from the living room in the direction of the kitchen, and stopping right behind her. Quickly, she turned around, but her friend was still sitting on the living room couch watching TV. Obviously she hadn't heard the footsteps. With her friend in the living room on the couch, and her nine-year-old son in the bathroom, there was no one present who could have caused the footsteps. Besides, they were heavy, like those of a man.

That same night, after Adriana entered her bedroom, she saw the figure of a woman standing next to her bed, moving her hands as if she were trying to get some papers or letters in a hurry. Adriana's bed stood against the wall with a night table on either side of it. As she watched in fascinated horror, the apparition was putting imaginary things down from the night table onto the bed. There were some real books on the night table, but they did not move. Standing at the entrance to the room, Adriana looked at the apparition: she could see right through her, but was able to make out that the woman had brown hair down to her shoulders, stood about five feet two or three, and seemed to be about thirty years old. When Adriana made a move toward the bed, the figure looked up and straight at her—then vanished before her very eyes. A little later, Adriana's son came to sleep with her, and of course she did not tell him about the apparition. Evidently, the child had heard the footsteps too, and there was no need to frighten him further.

The following evening around nine o'clock, the boy complained about being frightened by footsteps again. It was difficult for Adriana to explain them to her son, but she tried to calm his fears. The ghost reappeared from time to time, always in the same spot, always seeming to look for some papers, and not necessarily at night: there were times when Adriana saw her standing by her bed in plain daylight.

In July of the following year, Adriana had to go into the hospital for a minor operation. She asked a Spanish-speaking lady, a neighbor, to stay with her son for the four days Adriana was to be in the hospital. The babysitter left the bedroom to the boy and slept on the couch herself.

When Adriana returned from the hospital on the fifth day, the babysitter grabbed her by the hand and rushed her into the bedroom, for she didn't want to talk in front of the boy. She was absolutely terrified. It seems that the previous night, she was awakened toward three in the morning by heavy footsteps right next to her. She was sure that it was a man, and heard him bump into a chair! Frightened, she screamed and called out, "Who's there?" but there was no answer. Through all this the boy had slept soundly.

She turned on the lights, and noticed that the chair had been moved a little from where it had stood before. That was enough for her! She crawled into bed with the boy—and decided never to stay in the apartment overnight again, unless Adriana was there also.

Adriana decided to make some inquiries about the past occupants of her apartment, but all she could ascertain was that two nurses had lived there for about eight years. The building is very old and has a long history, so it may well be that one or more tragedies had taken place in what is now Adriana's apartment.

Adriana found herself invited to a Christmas party, and somehow the conversation drifted to ghosts. Her host did not believe in such things, and doubted Adriana's experiences. When they brought her back to her apartment, Adriana invited them in. She was just bending down trying to open a bottle of soda when she suddenly heard those heavy footsteps again, coming from the bedroom and stopping right at the entrance to the living room. At the same time, the thought crossed her mind that it was like a husband, waking from sleep to greet his wife returning from a party. Somehow this terrified her, and she let out a loud scream. That night she stayed with friends.

After her son left in July of the following year, things seemed to quiet down a little. One night shortly afterward, around six P.M., Adriana returned home from work. As soon as she opened the door, she could smell burned papers. Immediately she checked the kitchen, where everything seemed in order. Suddenly she realized that she could smell the strange smell better in her mind than with her nose. At the same time a thought crossed her mind, "My lady ghost finally found the papers and burned them." Adriana knew that they were love letters, and that all was right now with her ghost. There were no further disturbances after that.

The Indian's Ghost

Not all ghostly visitors are necessarily frightening or negative influences. Take the case of Mrs. M. N. One October, she signed a lease for a lovely old house on Commerce Street in New York's Greenwich Village. Legend had it that the house had been built by Washington Irving, although nothing was offered to substantiate this claim. It was a charming small white house, with three stories and a basement. It had five steps leading up from the street, and was guarded by wrought iron rails. On the first floor there was a narrow hallway, with stairs to the right; then came the living room, to the left, running the full depth of the house. The second story contained the master bedroom, with a bath and a small room, possibly used as a dressing room originally. On the third floor were three small bedrooms with dormer windows and a bathroom.

Mrs. N. loved the house like a friend; and because she was then going through a personal crisis in her life, a group of friends had gathered around her and moved into the house with her. These were people much younger than she who had decided to share the old house with her. Before actually moving into the house, Mrs. N. made the acquaintance of a neighbor, who was astonished at her having taken this particular house.

"For goodness' sake," the neighbor said, "why are you moving in *there*? Don't you know that place is haunted?"

Mrs. N. and her friends laughed at the thought, having not the slightest belief in the supernatural. Several days before the furniture was to be moved into the house, the little group gathered in the bare living room, lit their first fire in the fireplace, and dedicated the house with prayers. It so happened that they were all followers of the Baha'i faith, and they felt that this was the best way to create a harmonious atmosphere in what was to be their home.

They had been in the empty living room for perhaps an hour, praying and discussing the future, when suddenly there was a knock on the door. Dick, one of the young people who was nearest the door, went to answer the knock. There was no one there. It was a brilliant, moonlit night, and the whole of little Commerce Street was empty. Shaking his head, Dick went back into the room, but fifteen minutes later somebody knocked again. Again, there was no one outside, and the knocking sounded once more that night. Just the same, they moved in and almost immediately heard the footsteps of an unseen person. There were six in the house at the time: Kay sleeping on the couch in the basement dining room, Dick on a huge divan in the living room, Mrs. N. in the master bedroom on the second floor, and her fifteen-year-old daughter Barbara in one of the dormer bedrooms; Evie was in the second room and Bruce in the third. The first time they heard the steps, they were all at dinner in the basement dining room. The front door, which was locked, opened and closed by itself, and footsteps went into the living room where they seemed to circle the room, pausing now and again, and then continuing.

Immediately Dick went upstairs to investigate, and found there was no one about. Despite this, they felt no sense of alarm. Somehow they knew that their ghost was benign. From that moment on, the footsteps of an unseen person became part of their lives. They were heard going upstairs and downstairs, prowling the living room, but somehow they never entered one of the bedrooms. Once in a while they heard the opening and then a loud slamming of the front door. They checked, but there was nobody to be seen, and eventually they realized that whoever it was who was sharing the house with them preferred to remain unseen.

Since there were no other uncanny phenomena, the group accepted the presence of a ghost in their midst without undue alarm. One night, however, they had invited a group of Baha'i Youth to stay with them, and as a result, Mrs. N. had to sleep on the couch in the basement dining room. It turned into a night of sheer terror for her; she didn't see anything, but somehow the terror was all about her like a thick fog. She didn't sleep a moment that night. The following morning, Mrs. N. queried Kay, who ordinarily slept on the basement couch, as to whether she had had a similar experience. She had not. However, a few days later, Kay reported a strange dream she had had while occupying the same couch.

She had been awakened by the opening of the area-way door. Startled, she had sat up in bed and watched fascinated as a band of Indians came through the door, moved along the end of the dining room, went through the kitchen and out the back door again, where she could hear their feet softly scuffing the dead leaves! They paid no attention to her at all, but she was able to observe that they were in full war paint.

Since Kay had a lively imagination, Mrs. N. was inclined to dismiss the story. As there were no further disturbances, the matter of the ghost receded into the back of their minds. About a year after they had moved into the house, some of the little group were leaving town and the household was being broken up. It was a week before they were to part when Mrs. N. had an early morning train to catch and, not having an alarm clock herself, had asked Dick to set his for six A.M. and wake her.

Promptly at six A.M. there was a knock at her door, to which Mrs. N. responded with thanks and just as promptly went back to sleep. A few minutes later, there was a second knock on the door, and this time Mrs. N. replied that she was already getting up. Later she thanked her friend for waking her, and he looked at her somewhat sheepishly, asking her not to rub it in, for he hadn't heard the alarm at all. It appears that he had slept through the appointed hour and not awakened Mrs. N. as promised.

However, the friendly ghost had seen to it that she didn't miss her morning train. Was it the same benign spectre who had shielded them from the hostile Indians during their occupancy? That is, if the "dream" of Indians in war paint belonged to the past of the house, and was not merely an expression of a young girl's fancy.

The Soldier's Wife

Mrs. I. B. was a recently married young wife, expecting a baby some months later. She and her husband were looking for a furnished apartment. They had picked their favorite neighborhood, and decided to just look around until they saw a sign saying "Apartment for Rent." At the time, this was still possible. They stopped into a candy store in the area and asked the owner if he knew of a vacant apartment. As they were speaking to the owner, a young soldier, who had been standing in the rear of the store and had overheard the conversation, came over to them. He informed them that he had an apartment across the street from the store. When they inquired why he offered them the apartment, the soldier very quietly explained that he had come home to bury his wife. In his absence abroad, she had gone on a diet and, because of a weakened condition, had suddenly passed away. It had been the soldier's intention to live with her in the apartment after he returned from service. Under the circumstances, Mr. and Mrs. B. could have it until he returned, for he still wanted to live in it eventually.

This was agreeable to the young couple, especially as the apartment was handsomely furnished. A deal was quickly made, and that very night Mr. and Mrs. B. went to sleep in the bedroom of the apartment, with nothing special on their minds.

At four-thirty A.M., Mr. B. got up to go to work while his wife was still fast asleep. It was around five when she heard someone running around in the room, in what sounded like bare feet. The noise awoke her, and as she looked up, Mrs. B. saw at the foot of her bed the figure of a very pretty young woman wearing a nightgown.

Mrs. B. had no idea who the stranger might be, but thought that the young woman had somehow wandered into the apartment and asked her what she wanted. Instead of answering her, however, the young girl simply disappeared into thin air.

Mrs. B. flew into a panic. Dressing in haste, she left the apartment while it was still dark outside and took refuge in her mother's home. Nobody would believe her story, not her mother, not her husband, and, because Mrs. B. was pregnant at the time, her condition was blamed for the "hallucination." Reluctantly, Mrs. B. went back to the apartment the following evening. Shortly after her husband left for work, again early in the morning, Mrs. B. was awakened by the same apparition. This time Mrs. B. did not run out of the house, but instead closed her eyes; eventually the figure faded.

As soon as she was fully awake the next day, Mrs. B. determined to find out who the ghost might have been. Going through the various drawers in the apartment, she came across some photo albums belonging to the soldier. Leafing through them, she gave out a startled cry when her eyes fell on a photograph of the soldier, wearing plain clothes, with the very woman next to him whom she had seen early in the morning! Now Mrs. B. knew that she hadn't imagined the experiences. She showed the album to her husband, feeling that she had been visited by the soldier's dead wife. This time her husband was somewhat more impressed, and it was decided to obtain the "services" of a dog Mrs. B. had grown up with.

That night, the dog slept at the foot of her bed, as she had done many times before Mrs. B. was married. This made Mrs. B. feel a lot safer, but early in the morning she was awakened by her dog. The animal was standing on the foot of her bed, growling at the same spot where Mrs. B. had seen the apparition. The dog's fur was bristling on her back, and it was obvious that the animal was thoroughly scared.

But Mrs. B. did not see the ghost this time. It occurred to her that the ghost might resent her sleeping in what was once the bride's bed, so she and her husband exchanged beds the following night. From that moment on, the apparition did not return in the early mornings, and gradually, Mrs. B. got over her fear. A few weeks passed; then she noticed that in the kitchen some cups would fall off the shelf of their own volition whenever she tried to cook a meal. Then the clock fell off the wall by itself, and it became clear to her that objects were moved about by unseen hands. Some of this happened in the presence of her husband, who was no longer skeptical about it.

He decided it was time for them to move on. He wrote to the soldier, informing him that he was turning the apartment back to the landlord so that he could have it for himself again upon his return. Undoubtedly, that was exactly what the ghostly woman had wanted in the first place.

A Caring Ghost Named John

A lot of people are particular about the privacy of their home. They like it fine when nobody bothers them, except for their own kinfolk. Some do not even mind if a relative or friend stays over or comes to visit them, because, after all, they will leave again in time. But when a ghost overstays his welcome, and stays on and on and on, the matter can become upsetting, to say the least. This becomes even more of a problem when the guest is not aware of the passage of time, or when he thinks that your home is actually his home. When that happens, the owner of the house or apartment is faced with a difficult choice: fight the intruder and do everything at one's command to get rid of him, or accept the invasion of privacy and consider it a natural component of daily living.

When the ghost comes with the house—that is, if he or she lived there before you did—there is a certain sentimentality involved; after all, the previous owner has earlier rights to the place, even if he is dead and you paid for the house, and an attempt to chase him away may create a sense of guilt in some sensitive souls. However, as often as not, the spectral personality has nothing to do with the house itself. The ghost may have lived in a previous dwelling standing on the spot prior to the building of the present one, or he may have come with the land and thus go back even further. This is entirely possible, because a ghost lives in his own environment, meaning that the past is the only world he knows. In some of these cases, telling the ghost to pack up and leave to join the regular spirits on the Other Side of Life will meet resistance: after all, to the ghost you are the invader, the usurper.

He was there first. But whatever the status of the phantom in the house or place, panic will not help much.

The more the current tenant of a house or apartment becomes frightened, the more the ghost derives benefit from it, because the negative nervous energy generated by the present-day inhabitants of a house can be utilized by the ghost to create physical phenomena—the so-called Poltergeist disturbances, where objects move seemingly of their own volition. The best thing to do is to consider the ghost a fellow human being, albeit in trouble, and perhaps not in his right mind. Ghosts have to be dealt with compassionately and with understanding; they have to be persuaded to leave, not forcefully ejected.

Miss Sally S. lived in what was then a nice section of Brooklyn, half an hour from Manhattan and, at the time of the happenings I am about to report, was semi-retired, working two days a week at her old trade of being a secretary. A year after the first phenomena occurred, she moved away to Long Island, not because of her ghostly experiences, but because the neighborhood had become too noisy for her: ghosts she could stand, human disturbances were too much.

Miss S. moved into her Brooklyn apartment in May of the same year. At first, it seemed nice and quiet. Then, on August 3, she had an unusual experience. It must have been around three A.M. when she awoke with an uncanny feeling that she was not alone. In the semidarkness of her apartment, she looked around and had the distinct impression that there was an intruder in her place. She looked out into the room and in the dim light saw what appeared to be a dark figure. It was a man, and though she could not make out any features, he seemed tall and as lifelike as any human intruder might be.

Thinking that it was best for her to play possum, she lay still and waited for the intruder to leave. Picture her shock and surprise when the figure approached her and started to touch her quilt cover. About fifteen minutes prior to this experience, she had awakened because she was cold, and had pulled the cover over herself. Thus she was very much awake when the "intruder" appeared to her. She lay still, trembling, watching his every move. Suddenly he vanished into thin air, and it was only then that Miss S. realized she wasn't dealing with any flesh-and-blood person, but a ghost.

A month later, again around three A.M., Miss S. awoke to see a white figure gliding back and forth in her room. This time, however, she was somewhat sleepy, so she did not feel like doing much about it. However, when the figure came close to her bed, she stuck out her arm to touch it, and at that moment it dissolved into thin air. Wondering who the ghost might be, Miss S. had had another opportunity to observe it in November, when around six A.M. she went into her kitchen to see the dark outline of a six-foot-tall man standing in the archway between the kitchen and dinette. She looked away for a moment, and then returned her gaze to the spot. The apparition was still there. Once more Miss S. closed her eyes and looked away, and when she returned her eyes to the spot, he was gone.

She decided to speak to her landlady about the incidents. No one had died in the house, nor had there been any tragedy to the best of her knowledge, the owner of the house assured her. As for a previous owner, she wouldn't know. Miss S. realized that it was her peculiar psychic talent that made the phenomena possible. For some time now she had been able to predict the results of horse races with uncanny accuracy, getting somewhat of a reputation in this area. Even during her school days, she came up with answers she had not yet been taught. In April of the next year, Miss S. visited her sister and her husband in New Jersey. They had bought a house the year before, and knew nothing of its history. Sally was assigned a finished room in the attic. Shortly after two A.M., a ghost appeared to her in that room. But before she could make out any details, the figure vanished. By now Miss S. knew that she had a talent for such things, and preferred not to talk about them with her sister, a somewhat nervous individual. But she kept wondering who the ghost at *her* house was.

Fourteen years earlier, a close friend named John had passed away. A year before, he had given her two nice fountain pens as gifts, and Miss S. had kept one at home, and used the other at her office. A year after her friend's death, she was using one of the pens in the office when the point broke. Because she couldn't use it anymore, she put the pen into her desk drawer. Then she left the office for a few minutes. When she returned, she found a lovely, streamlined black pen on top of her desk. She immediately inquired whether any of the girls had left it there, but no one had, nor had anyone been near her desk. The pen was a rather expensive Mont Blanc, just the thing she needed. It made her wonder whether her late friend John had not presented her with it even from the Beyond.

This belief was reinforced by an experience she had had on the first anniversary of his passing, when she heard his voice loud and clear calling her "sweetheart"—the name he had always used to address her.

All this ran through her head fourteen years later, when she tried to come to terms with her ghostly experiences. Was the ghost someone who came with the house, someone who had been there before, or was it someone who somehow linked up with her? Then Sally began to put two and two together. She was in the habit of leaving her feet outside her quilt cover because the room was rather warm with the heat on. However, in the course of the night, the temperature in the room fell, and frequently her feet became almost frostbitten as a result. One Saturday night in March, the same year she visited her sister, she was still awake, lying in bed around eleven P.M. Her feet were sticking out of the quilt, as the temperature was still tolerable. Suddenly she felt a terrific tug on her quilt; it was first raised from above her ankles, and then pulled down to cover her feet. Yet she saw no one actually doing it.

Suddenly she remembered how her late friend John had been in the habit of covering her feet when she had fallen asleep after one of his visits with her. Evidently he was still concerned that Sally should not get cold feet or worse, and had decided to watch over her.

Mabel's Ghost

The house on South Sixth Street in Hudson, New York, is one of the many fine old town houses dotting this old town on the Hudson River. It was built between 1829 and 1849, and a succession of owners lived in it to the present day. In 1904 it passed into the hands of the Parker family, who had a daughter named Mabel, a very happy person with a zest for life. In her sixties, she had contracted a tragic illness and suffered very much, until she finally passed away in a nearby hospital. She had been truly house-proud, and hated to leave for the cold and ominous surroundings of the hospital. After she died, the house passed into the hands of Mr. and Mrs. Jay Dietz, who still owned it when I visited them. Mrs. Dietz had been employed by Mabel Parker's father at one time.

The psychic did not particularly interest Mrs. Dietz, although she had had one notable experience the night her stepgrandfather died, a man she had loved very much. She had been at home taking care of him throughout the daytime and finally returned to her own house to spend the night. Everybody had gone to bed, and as she lay in hers with her face to the wall, she became aware of an unusual glow in the room. She turned over and opened her eyes, and noticed that on the little nightstand at the head of the bed was a large ball of light, glowing with a soft golden color. As she was staring at it the telephone rang, and she was told that her stepgrandfather had passed away.

Eleven years before, the Dietzes moved into the house on South Sixth Street. At first the house seemed peaceful enough. Previous tenants included a German war bride and her mother. The old lady had refused to sleep upstairs in the room that later became Mrs. Dietz's mother's. There was something uncanny about that room, she explained. So she slept down on the ground floor on a couch instead. The Dietzes paid no attention to these stories, until they began to notice some strange things about their house. There were footsteps heard going up and down the stairs and into the hall, where they stopped. The three of them, Mr. and Mrs. Dietz and her mother, all heard them many times.

One year, just before Christmas, Mrs. Dietz was attending to some sewing in the hall downstairs while her husband was in the bathroom. Suddenly she thought he came down the hall, which was odd since she hadn't heard the toilet being flushed. But as she turned around, no one was there. A few nights later she went upstairs and had the distinct impression that she was not alone in the room. Without knowing what she was doing, she called out to the unseen presence, "Mabel?" There was no reply then, but one night not much later, she was awakened by someone yanking at her blanket from the foot of the bed. She broke out into goose pimples, because the pull was very distinct and there was no mistaking it.

She sat up in her upstairs bedroom, very frightened by now, but there was no one to be seen. As she did this, the pulling ceased abruptly. She went back to sleep with some relief, but several nights later the visitor returned. Mrs. Dietz likes to sleep on her left side with her ear covered up by the blanket. Suddenly she felt the covers being pulled off her ear, but being already half-asleep, she simply yanked them back. There was no further movement after that.

The upstairs bedroom occupied by Mrs. Dietz's mother seemed to be the center of activities, however. More than once after the older lady had turned out the lights to go to sleep, she became aware of someone standing beside her bed, and looking down at her.

Sometimes nothing was heard for several weeks or months, only to resume in full force without warning. In February of the year I visited the Dietzes, Mrs. Dietz happened to wake up at five o'clock one morning. It so happened that her mother was awake too, for Mrs. Dietz heard her stir. A moment later, her mother went back to bed. At that moment, Mrs. Dietz heard, starting at the foot of the stairs, the sound of heavy footsteps coming up very slowly, going down the hall and stopping, but they were different from the footsteps she had heard many times before.

It sounded as if a very sick person were dragging herself up the stairs, trying not to fall, but determined to get there nevertheless. It sounded as if someone very tired was coming home. Was her friend finding a measure of rest, after all, by returning to the house where she had been so happy? Mrs. Dietz does not believe in ghosts, however, but only in memories left behind.

The Ghost
and the Earrings

ometimes being a psychic investigator puts a heavy moral burden on one, especially where there may be a possibility of preventing someone's death. Of course, you're never sure that you can. Take the case of Valerie K., for instance. The police won't talk about the case, but her friends are only too sure there is something mysterious about her death, and they *will* talk about it. They speak mainly to me, for that's about all they can do about it—now.

To start at the beginning, one April I got a phone call from Sheila M.—an English girl whom I had met through a mutual friend—inviting my wife and me to a cocktail party at her house on New York's East Side. Now if it's one thing my wife and I hate it's cocktail parties, even on the East Side, but Sheila is a nice person and we thought she was likely to have only nice friends, so I said we'd come. The party was on April 20, and when we arrived everybody was already there, drinking and chatting, while the butler passed between the guests, ever so quietly seeing after their needs.

Since I don't drink, I let my wife talk to Sheila and sauntered over to the hors d'oeuvres, searching hopefully for some cheese bits, for I am a vegetarian and don't touch meat or fish. Next to the buffet table I found not only an empty chair, unusual at a cocktail party, but also a lovely young woman in a shiny silver Oriental-style dress. In fact, the young lady was herself Oriental, a very impressive-looking girl perhaps in her middle twenties, with brown hair, dark eyes, and a very quiet, soigné air about her. It turned out that the girl's name was Valerie K., and I had been briefly introduced to her once before on the telephone when

Sheila had told her of my interest in psychic research, and she had wanted to tell me some of her experiences.

We got to talking about our mutual interest in ESP. She sounded far away, as if something was troubling her, but I had the impression she was determined not to allow it to interfere with her enjoyment of the party. I knew she was Sheila's good friend and would not want to spoil anything for her. But I probed deeper, somehow sensing she needed help. I was right, and she asked me if she could talk to me sometime privately. I gave her my telephone number and asked her to call me whenever she wanted to.

When we got home I suppressed a desire to telephone this girl and see if she was all right. I dismissed my feeling as undue sentimentality, for the girl had seemed radiant, and surely the reason for her wanting to see me would have to be psychic rather than personal in the usual sense. All through the weekend I could not get her out of my mind, but I was busy with other work and decided to call her first thing the following week.

Monday night, as I read the *Daily News*, my eye fell on a brief article tucked away inside the newspaper, an article telling of the death of two women early Monday morning. One of the two women was Valerie K.

With a shudder I put down the paper and closed my eyes.

Could I have prevented her death? I will let you be the judge. But first let me tell you what happened in the final hours of this girl's life on earth.

Valerie K. came from a well-to-do Chinese family residing in Hawaii. She was as American as anyone else in her speech, and yet there was that undefinable quality in the way she put her words together that hinted at Eastern thought. After an unhappy and brief marriage to a Hong Kong businessman, she came to New York City to try living on her own. Never particularly close to her parents, she was now entirely self-supporting and needed a job. She found a job vaguely described as a public relations assistant, but in fact was the secretary to the man who did publicity for the company. Somehow she was not quite right for the job or the job for her, and it came to a parting of the ways.

The new girl hired to take her place was Sheila. Despite the fact that the English girl replaced her, they struck up a friendship that developed into a true attachment to each other, so much so that Valerie would confide in Sheila to a greater extent than she would in anyone else.

When Valerie left the office, there was no job waiting for her; fortunately, however, she had met the manager of a firm owned by the same company, and the manager, whose initial was G., took her on for somewhat selfish reasons. He had a sharp eye for beauty and Valerie was something special. Thus she found herself earning considerably more than she would have been paid in a similar job elsewhere. Soon the manager let her know that he liked her and she got to like him, too. Between August and October of the year before her death, they became close friends.

But in October of that year she called her friend Sheila to complain bitterly of the humiliation she had been put through. G. had found another girl to take her place. Innocently, the new girl, Lynn, became the pawn in the deadly game between the manager and the Chinese beauty. G. found fault with her very appearance and everything she did, criticizing her and causing her to lose face —an important matter not easily forgotten.

Still, she cared for the man and hoped that he would resume his former attentions. He didn't, and after a miserable Christmas, which she partially shared with Sheila, the axe fell. He fired her and gave her two weeks' pay, wishing her the best.

When Sheila heard about this she suggested that Valerie register at the Unemployment Office. Instead, the proud girl took sleeping pills. But she either did not take enough or changed her mind in time, for she was able to telephone Sheila and tell her what she had done. A doctor was called and she was saved. She had a session with a psychiatrist after that and seemed much more cheerful.

But the humiliation and rejection kept boiling within her. Nothing can be as daring as a person whose affections have been rejected, and one day Valerie wrote a personal letter to the owner of the companies she had once worked for, denouncing the manager and his work.

As if nourished by her hatred, her psychic abilities increased and she found she was able to influence people through telepathy, to read others' thoughts and to put herself into a state of excitement through a form of meditation. All this was for the purpose of getting even, not only with the manager but with the world that had so often hurt her.

Nobody knew for sure if she ever got a reply to her letter. But she was a regular at an Oriental restaurant near her apartment and became friendly with the owners. There she talked about her plans and how she would show the world what sort of girl she was.

Meanwhile the manager found himself short of help and asked her back. Despite her deep hatred for the man, she went back, all the time scheming and hoping her fortunes would take a turn for the better. But she did confide in Sheila that she had taken a big gamble, and if it worked she'd be all right in more ways than one. The owner of the restaurant saw her on Friday, April 21—a day after the party at which I had met her—and she seemed unusually happy.

She would marry a prominent European, she told him; she had been asked and would say yes. She was almost obsessed at this point with the desire to tell the whole world she would marry him; her parents in Hawaii received a letter requesting them to have formal Chinese wedding attire made up for her in Paris because she would marry soon. Had the idea of getting even with G. robbed her of her senses? It is difficult to assess this, as the principals involved quite naturally would not talk, and even I prefer that they remain anonymous here.

That weekend—April 22 and 23—the pitch of her "wedding fever" rose higher and higher. A neighbor who had dropped in on her at her apartment found her clad only in a bikini and drinking heavily. She observed her running back and forth from her telephone, trying to reach the man overseas she said she would marry. But she couldn't get through to him. In the meantime, she started giving possessions away, saying she would not need them any longer now that she would marry so rich a man.

She also drew up a list of all those whom she would help once she had become the wife of the millionaire. The neighbor left rather perturbed by all this, and Valerie stayed alone in her apartment—or did she?

It was four A.M. when the police received a call from her telephone. It was a complaint about excessive noise. When an officer arrived on the scene at four-twenty A.M., Valerie herself opened the door in the nude.

"Go away," she said, and asked to be left alone. The officer quickly surveyed the scene. She became rude and explained she was expecting a phone call and did not wish to be disturbed. The officer reported that she had been alone and was drinking, and there the matter stood.

The minutes ticked away. It was early Monday morning, April 24.

At precisely five A.M., the building superintendent looked out his window and saw something heavy fall on his terrace.

Rushing to the scene, he discovered Valerie's broken body. She had been killed instantly. The girl had taken two roses with her—but one somehow remained behind on the window sill of the open window from which she had plunged to her death. The other fluttered sadly to earth even as she did.

The police officers found themselves back at the apartment sooner than they had expected, only this time there was a cause for action. After a routine inspection of the girl's tenth floor apartment, her death was put down to accidental death or suicide by falling or jumping from her window. Since she had been drinking heavily, they were not sure which was the actual cause of death.

Monday night Sheila called me frantically, wondering what she should do. There was no one to claim the girl's body. Neither her sister Ethel nor her parents in Hawaii could be reached. I told her to calm down and keep trying, meanwhile berating myself for not having called Valerie in time to prevent her death.

Eventually the parents were found and a proper funeral arranged. But the puzzle remained. Had she committed suicide or not?

Did that call from Europe finally come and was it so humiliating that Valerie could no longer face the world? Was there not going to be a wedding after all—then at least there must be a funeral?

Valerie had been particularly fond of two things in life—flowers and jewelry. To her, losing a favorite piece of jewelry was bad luck. Lynn, the girl who now worked at Valerie's office, is a rather matter-of-fact person not given to emotional scenes or superstitions. Valerie owned a pair of jade earrings that G. had had made for her in the days when they were close. About a month before her death, Valerie gave those earrings to Lynn as a gift. There was a special stipulation, however. She must not wear them around the office, since people had seen Valerie wear them and presumably knew their history.

Lynn agreed not to wear them around the office, but when she wore them outside a most unusual phenomenon took place. Suddenly the earrings would not stay put. One and then the other would drop off her ears as if pulled by some unseen force. That was on April 13, and Valerie was still alive, though she had seemed very distraught.

Word of Lynn's concern with the falling earrings got back to the former owner, and finally Valerie called to assure her the falling was a "good omen." Then a week later, on Saturday, April 22, she suddenly called Lynn shortly before midnight and asked her to wear "her" earrings at the office. Lynn promised she would wear them to work Monday.

That was the day Valerie died. The following day, Lynn was still wearing the earrings, which now seemed to cling properly to her ears. She found herself in the ladies' room, when she felt her right earring forced off and thrown into the toilet. It felt as if it had been snatched from her ear by an unseen hand.

Returning to her desk, she noticed that an unusual chill pervaded the area where Valerie's desk had stood. It disappeared at 4:30, which was the time Valerie usually left for home.

All this proved too much for Lynn and she went on a week's vacation.

Sheila was still very upset when a male friend dropped in to help her in this sorry matter. The gentleman, a lawyer by profession, had taken off his jacket when he suddenly felt a cufflink leave his shirt. It was a particularly intricate piece of jewelry, and no matter how they searched it was never found.

Was the dead girl trying to show her hand? Too fantastic, and yet . . . There was no rational explanation for the sudden disappearance, in plain light and in the presence of two people, of so definite an object as a cufflink.

On Friday of that week, after the girl had been buried, her sister, Ethel, who had finally arrived in town, went to the apartment to find out what she could about her sister's effects.

As soon as she entered the apartment, she realized that a terrific fight had taken place in it. Nothing had been touched from the moment of death until her arrival, as the apartment had been sealed. Three knives were lying on the floor and the place was a shambles. On the table she noticed two glasses, one partially filled with Scotch and one almost empty. When she called the police to report the strange appearance of the place, she was given the cold shoulder.

Who was the person Valerie had entertained during her last hours on earth?

The superintendent reported to the sister that Valerie had received two letters since her death, but when they looked in the mailbox, it was empty. A friend, the owner of the restaurant Valerie had frequented, notified the telephone company to cut off service and forward the final bill to her. She was told the bill could not be found.

And so it went. Was someone covering up his traces? Sheila heard these things and went to work. To her, something was terribly wrong about her friend's death and she was going to find out what. Questioning both the restaurant owner and the girl's sister again, she came upon another strange fact. The ashtrays Ethel had found in the apartment had two different types of cigarettes in them—L&M and Winston. Valerie always smoked L&M, but who smoked Winston?

The police seem not particularly interested in pursuing the matter. They think it was Valerie herself who called them the first time, and that she just decided to end it all in a drunken stupor. That at least is the impression they gave Sheila.

The following day, Saturday, the window was still open. The rose Valerie had left behind was still on the sill, despite the windy weather of April.

That night when Sheila was putting on her jacket, she felt somebody helping her into it. She was alone, or so she thought.

It occurred to her then that Valerie's spirit was not at rest and that I might be able to help. The very least I could do was talk to her *now*, since fate had prevented me from getting to her in time.

I arranged with Betty Ritter to be ready for me the following weekend, without, of course, telling her where we would be going. The date was May 6, the time three P.M., and Sheila was to meet us at the apartment that once belonged to Valerie, but now was cleaned out and ready for the next occupant. The superintendent agreed to let us in, perhaps sensing why we had come, or not caring. At any rate he opened the tenth-floor apartment and left us alone inside.

As we reached the elevator of the East Sixty-Third Street

building, Betty Ritter suddenly remarked that she felt death around her. I nodded and we went upstairs.

As soon as we had stepped through the door into Valerie's place, Betty became a psychic bloodhound. Making straight for the window—now closed—she touched it and withdrew in horror, then turned around and looked at me.

"There is a man here jumping around like mad," she said, "but there is also someone else here—I am impressed with the initial E." She then took off her coat and started to walk toward the bathroom. There she stopped and looked back at me.

"I hear a woman screaming . . . I saw blood . . . now I see the initial M . . . she was harmed . . . it is like suicide . . . as if she couldn't take it any more."

Betty had difficulty holding back her emotions and was breathing heavily.

"She left *two* behind," she said. "I see the initials L. and S."

Betty Ritter, not a trance medium but essentially a clairvoyant, is very strong on initials, names, letters, and other forms of identification and she would naturally work that way even in this case.

"I heard her say, 'Mama, Mama'—she is very agitated."

"I also get a man's spirit here . . . initial J."

"How did this girl die?" I interjected at this point.

"She couldn't take it any more. She shows the initial R. This is a living person. She gulped something, I think."

I thought that Betty was picking up past impressions now and wanted to get her away from that area into the current layer of imprints.

"How exactly did she die?" I queried the medium. Betty had no idea where she was or why I had brought her here.

"I think she tried . . . pills . . . blood . . . one way or the other . . . in the past. She was a little afraid but she did plan this. She is very disturbed now and she does not know how to get out of this apartment. I get the initial G. with her."

I asked Betty to convey our sympathies to her and ask her if there was something she wished us to do.

While Betty talked to the spirit woman in a low voice, I reflected on her evidence so far. The initials given—E. was the first initial of Valerie's sister's name, Ethel, M. was Mary, her mother, and G. the manager of the company with whom she had had a relationship—it all seemed to make sense. Betty Ritter had also correctly "gotten" the attempted suicide by pills and pointed out the window as a "hot" area.

What was to follow now?

"She is crying," Betty reported. "She wants her loved ones to know that she didn't mean it. She shows me the head of an Indian and it is a symbol of a car—a brand name I think—it's red—the initial H. comes with this and then she shows me writing, something she has left unfinished. She asks her mother to forgive her because she could not help herself."

I decided to ask Valerie some important questions through the medium. Was she alone at the time of her death?

"Not alone. Initial A. A man, I feel him walking out of the door. Agitating her, agitating her."

"Was he with her when she died or did he leave before?"

"She says, 'I slammed the door on him.' And then she says, 'And then I did it.' "

"Why?"

"I had gone completely out of my mind . . . could not think straight . . . he drove me to it . . ."

"This man is a living person?"

"Yes."

"Is he aware of what happened to her?"

"Yes."

"Did she know him well?"

"Yes, definitely."

"What was his connection with her?"

Betty was herself pretty agitated now; in psychic parlance, she was really hot.

"I see a bag of money," she reported, "and the letters M. or W."

I handed her some personal belongings of Valerie's, brought to the scene in a shopping bag by Sheila and now placed on the stove for Betty to touch. She first took up a pendant—costume jewelry—and immediately felt the owner's vibrations.

"How I loved this," she mumbled. "I see D. R., Doctor . . . this was given to her and there is much love here in connection with this . . . this goes way back . . ."

Somehow the personalities of Betty Ritter and Valerie K. melted into one now and Betty, not quite herself, seemed not to listen any more to my queries, but instead kept talking as if she were Valerie, yet with Betty's own voice and intonation.

"There's so much I wanted to say and I couldn't at the time. . . ."

Now returning to herself again, she spoke of a man in spirit, who was very agitated and who had possessed the woman, "not a ghost but someone who had died . . . an older man who had a link with her in the past. J. W. Dark-skinned, but not black—India or that part of the world."

It struck me suddenly that she might be talking of Valerie's late husband, the man she had married long ago in Hong Kong; he was much older than she at the time.

"I have a feeling of falling," Betty suddenly said, "I don't know why. May have something to do with her."

I decided to let her walk around the entire apartment and to try to pick up "hot" areas. She immediately went for the lefthand window.

"Something terrible happened here . . . this is the room . . . right here . . . stronger here . . ."

"Is there another woman involved in this story?" I asked.

"I see the initial M." Betty replied, "and she is with a man who is living, and there is also some jealousy regarding a woman's boyfriend . . . she could not take it."

I decided to start the exorcism immediately.

"It's such a short time ago that she went," Betty remarked. "She wants to greet Mary . . . or Marie . . . and an L. To tell L. she is relieved now. Just carry on as usual."

L. was the initial of Lynn, the girl at the office who had encountered the strange happenings with the earrings.

I decided to test this connection.

"Did she communicate with L. in any way?" I asked.

"Yes," Betty nodded, "I see her by L.'s bed . . . perhaps she frightened her . . . but now she knows . . . didn't mean to frighten her . . . she is leaving now, never wants to get back again. . . ."

We were quiet for a moment.

"She's throwing us kisses now," Betty added.

"She would do that," Sheila confirmed, "that was the way she would do it."

And that was that.

Betty lit a cigarette and relaxed, still visibly shaken by the communications for which she had been the carrier. We put Valerie's pitiful belongings back into the paper bag and left the apartment, which now looked shiny and new, having been given a hasty coat of paint to make it ready for the next occupant.

No further snatching of jewelry from anyone's ears occurred after that, and even my friend Sheila no longer tried to reopen the case despite her belief that there was more to it than met the eyes of the police. We decided to allow Valerie a peaceful transition and not to stir up old wounds that would occur with a reopening of the case.

But somehow I can't quite bring myself to forget a scene, a scene I only "saw" through the eyes of a laconic police detective making a routine report: the tall, lovely Oriental woman, intoxicated and nude, slamming the door on the police . . . and two liquor glasses on her table.

Who was that other glass for . . . and who smoked the second cigarette, the brand Valerie never smoked?

Who, then, was the man who left her to die?

The Troubled Ghosts on Route 14

Parker Keegan is a practical man not much given to day-dreaming or speculation. That is as it should be. For Parker makes his living, if you can call it that, driving a truck with high explosives, tanks containing acetylene, oxygen, nitrogen, and other flammable substances for a welding company in upstate New York.

So you see, he has to have his mind on his work all the time, if he wants to get old.

His wife, Rebecca, is a more emotional type. That, too, is as it should be. She is an artist, free-lancing and now and again making sales. There is some Indian blood in her and she has had an occasional bout with the supernatural. But these were mainly small things, telepathy or dream experiences and nothing that really worried her. Neither she nor her husband had any notions that such things as haunted houses really existed, except, of course, in Victorian novels.

Now the Keegans already had one child and Rebecca was expecting her second, so they decided to look for a larger place. As if by the finger of fate, an opportunity came their way just about then. Her teenage cousin Jane telephoned Rebecca at her parents' home to tell them of a house they might possibly rent. It developed she did this not entirely out of the goodness of her heart, but also because she didn't like being alone nights in the big place she and her husband lived in. He worked most of the night in another city.

"There are two halves to this house," Jane explained, and she made it so enticing that Parker and Rebecca decided then and there to drive over and have a look at it.

Even though they arrived there after dark, they saw immedi-

ately that the house was attractive, at least from the outside. Built
in pre-Civil War days, it had stood the test of time well. As is often
the case with old houses, the servants quarters are in a separate
unit and parallel, but do not intrude upon, the main section of the
house. So it was here, and it was the former servants quarters that
Jane and Harry occupied. As the visitors had not spoken to the
landlord about their interest, they entered the unused portion of
the building from their cousin's apartment. This was once the
main house and contained eight rooms, just what they needed.

The ground floor consisted of a large front room with two
windows facing the road and two facing the other way. Next to it
was an old-fashioned dining room, and branching off from it, a
narrow kitchen and a small laundry room. In the dim light they
could make out a marvelous staircase with a lovely, oiled banister.
It was at this point that the two apartments that made up the
house connected, and one could be entered from the other. Underneath the front stairway was a closet and the door leading to
the other side of the house, but they found another, enclosed,
stairway leading from the bedroom at the top of the front stairs
into the dining room. Exactly below this enclosed staircase were
the cellar stairs leading into the basement. There were three cellars, one under the servants quarters, one underneath the front
room, and one below the dining room.

As Rebecca set foot into the cellar under the dining room,
which had apparently served as a fruit cellar, she grew panicky
for a moment. She immediately dismissed her anxiety with a
proper explanation: they had seen the thriller *Psycho* the night
before and this cellar reminded her of one of the gruesome incidents in that movie. But later she was to learn that the feeling of
panic persisted whenever she came down into this particular part
of the basement, even long after she had forgotten about that
movie.

For the present, they inspected the rest of the house. The
upstairs portion contained two large bedrooms and two smaller
ones. Only the larger rooms were heated. There was an attic but
nobody ever investigated it during their entire stay in the house.

They decided the house was just what they wanted and the
next morning they contacted the owner.

George Jones turned out to be a very proper, somewhat tight-lipped man. He inquired what they did for a living and then added, "Are you religious people?"

Rebecca thought this an odd question, but since she had told him she was an artist, she assumed he considered artists somewhat unreliable and wanted to make sure he had responsible and "God-fearing" tenants. Only much later did it occur to her that Jones might have had other reasons.

It was a cold, miserable day in December 1964 when the Keegans moved into their new home. They were happy to get into a home full of atmosphere, for Rebecca was an avid amateur archaeologist who read everything on antiques she could get her hands on. At the same time they were doing a good deed for her cousin, keeping her company on those long nights when her husband was away at work. It all seemed just right and Rebecca did not even mind the difficulties the moving brought them. For one thing, they could not afford professional moving men, but had turned to friends for help. The friends in turn had borrowed a truck that had to be back in the garage by nightfall, so there was a lot of shoving and pushing and bad tempers all around. On top of that, the stinging cold and snow made things even more uncomfortable, and Rebecca could do little to help matters, being pregnant with their second child at the time.

Late that first night, they finally climbed the stairs to the large bedroom. They were both exhausted from the day's work and as soon as they fell into bed, they drifted off into deep sleep.

But even though they were very tired, Rebecca could not help noticing some strange noises, crackling sounds emanating seemingly from her cousin's side of the house. She put them down to steam pipes and turned to the wall.

When the noises returned night after night, Rebecca began to wonder about them. Parker also worked nights now and she and Jane sat up together until after the late show on television was over, around 1:30 A.M. All that time, night after night, they could hear the steam pipes banging away. Nobody slept well in the house and Jane became jumpier and jumpier as time went on. Her mood would change to a certain sullenness Rebecca had not noticed before, but she dismissed it as being due to the winter weather, and of no particular significance.

Then one night, as she was thinking about some of the events of the recent past while lying awake in bed, Rebecca heard footsteps coming up the stairs. They were the steps of a heavy man, and since she had not heard the characteristic clicking of the front door lock, she knew it could not be her husband.

Alarmed, and thinking of burglars, she got out of bed and called out to her cousin. She then went to the top of the stairs and was joined by Jane coming through the connecting door, and standing at the foot of the stairs. What the two women saw from opposite ends of the staircase was far from ordinary. Someone was walking up the stairs and the stairs were bending with each step as if a heavy person were actually stepping upon them!

Only there was no one to be seen. They did not wait until the footsteps of the invisible man reached the top of the stairs. Rebecca dove back into her bedroom banging the door shut after her. Just before she did, she could still hear her young cousin downstairs screaming, before she, too, ran back into the assumed safety of her bedroom.

The experience on the stairs made Jane even moodier than before and it was not long afterward that she took her little girl and left her husband. There had been no quarrel, no apparent reason for her sudden action. He was a handsome young man who had treated her well, and Jane loved him. Yet, there it was— she could not stand the house any longer and did what her panicky mind told her to do.

Rebecca was now left alone nights with the noisy wraith on the stairs and she scarcely welcomed it. Soon after the incident, Jane's abandoned husband sold his belongings and moved away, leaving the former servants quarters empty once again.

It was then that Rebecca kept hearing, in addition to the heavy footsteps, what seemed to be someone crying in the empty side of the house. She convinced herself that it wasn't just a case of nerves when the noises continued at frequent intervals while she was fully awake. Her time was almost at hand, and as often happens with approaching motherhood, she grew more and more apprehensive. It did not help her condition any when she heard a loud banging of the cupboards in the dining room at a time when she was all alone in the house. Someone was opening and closing the doors to the cupboard in rapid succession soon after she had retired for the night. Of course she did not run downstairs to investigate. Who would?

Fortunately, Parker came home a little earlier that night, because when he arrived he found Rebecca in a state of near hysteria. To calm her fears as much as to find out for himself, he immediately went downstairs to investigate. There was no one there and no noise. Getting into bed with the assurance of a man who does not believe in the supernatural, he was about to tell his wife that she must have dreamed it all, when he, too, clearly heard the cupboard doors open and close downstairs.

He jumped out of bed and raced down the stairs. As he took the steps two at a time, he could clearly hear the doors banging away louder and louder in the dining room. It must be stated to Parker's eternal credit, that not once did he show fear or worry about any possible dangers to himself: he merely wanted to know what this was all about.

The noise reached a crescendo of fury, it seemed to him, when he stood before the dining room door. Quickly he opened the door and stepped into the dark expanse of the chilly dining room.

Instantly, the noise stopped as if cut off with a knife.

Shaking his head and beginning to doubt his own sanity, or at least, powers of observation, Parker got into bed once more and prepared to go to sleep. Rebecca looked at him anxiously, but he did not say anything. Before she could question him, the ominous noise started up again downstairs.

Once more, as if driven by the furies, Parker jumped out of bed and raced down the stairs. Again the noise stopped the moment he opened the dining room door.

He slowly went up the stairs again and crawled into bed. Pulling the covers over his ears, he cursed the ghosts downstairs, but decided that his badly needed sleep was more important than the answer to the puzzle.

Shortly after, their son was born. When they returned from the hospital, they were greeted by a new couple, the Winters, who had meanwhile moved into the other half of the house. Although friendly on the surface, they were actually stern and unbending and as they were also much older than the Keegans, the two families did not mingle much. Mrs. Winters was a tough and somewhat sassy old woman and did not look as if anything could frighten her. Her husband worked as a night watchman, and there were no children. It was not long before Mrs. Winters knocked at Rebecca's door in fear.

"Someone is trying to break in," she whispered, and asked to be let in. Rebecca knew better but did not say anything to frighten the old woman even further.

It seemed as if winter would never yield to spring, and if you have ever lived in the cold valleys of upstate New York, you know how depressing life can be under such circumstances.

To brighten things a little, the Keegans acquired a female German shepherd for the children, and also for use as a watch-dog.

All this time Rebecca was sure she was never alone in the house. There was someone watching her, night and day. Her husband no longer scoffed at her fears, but could do little about them. The strange noises in the walls continued on and off and it got so that Rebecca no longer felt fear even when she saw the doorknob of a perfectly empty room turn slowly of its own volition. By now she knew the house was haunted, but as yet she did not realize the nature of the uncanny inhabitants.

One day she left the baby securely strapped in his seat while she ran to catch her little girl who was climbing the front stairs and was in immediate danger of falling off. Just at that precise moment, the strap broke and the baby fell to the floor, fracturing his skull.

All during their stay at the house, someone was always having accidents or becoming unaccountably ill. Their debts increased as their medical expenses grew higher, so it was decided that Rebecca should go to work and earn some money. In addition, Parker started working extra shifts. But far from helping things, this only served to incite the landlord to raise their rent, on the theory that they were earning more. To make things even more difficult for them, Rebecca could not find a proper babysitter to stay with the children while she was at work. Nobody would stay very long in the house, once they got to know it.

She turned to her mother for help, and her mother, after a short stay, refused to spend any more time in the house, but offered to take the children to her own home. There was no explanation, but to Rebecca it seemed ominous and obvious. Finally, her teenage sister consented to become a babysitter for them. She could use the money for school, but soon her enthusiasm waned. She began to complain of a closed-in feeling she experienced in the old house and of course she, too, heard all the strange noises.

Each day, Mary became more and more depressed and ill, whereas she had been a happy-go-lucky girl before.

"There are prowlers about," she kept saying, and one day she came running to Rebecca in abject fear. On a moonless night she happened to be glancing out of a living room window when she saw what appeared to be a face. Rebecca managed to calm her by suggesting she had seen some sort of shadow, but the incessant barking of the dog, for no apparent reason, made matters worse. Added to this were incidents in which objects would simply fly out of their hands in broad daylight. The end of the rope was reached one day when they were all in the front room. It was afternoon and Mary was holding a cup in her hand, about to fill it with tea. That instant it flew out of her hands and smashed itself at Parker's feet. Without saying another word, the young girl went up the stairs to her room. Shortly after, her things all packed, she came down again to say goodbye.

Once again they were without help, when Rebecca's sister-in-law Susan saved the day for them. A simple and quite unimaginative person, she had put no stock in all the tales of goings-on she had heard and was quite willing to prove her point.

Within a day after her arrival, she changed her tune.

"Someone is watching me," she complained, and refused to stay alone in the house. She, too, complained of things flying off the shelves seemingly of their own volition and of cupboard doors opening and closing as if someone were looking in the drawers for something or other.

The footsteps up the stairs continued and Susan heard them many times. She took the dog into the house with her but that was of little use: the dog was more afraid than all of the people together.

Incredible though it seemed to the Keegans, two years had passed since they had come to the House of Evil. That they still had their sanity was amazing, and that they had not moved out, even more of a miracle. But they simply could not afford to, and things were difficult enough in the physical world to allow the unseen forces to add to their problems. So they stuck it out.

It was the night before Christmas of 1966, and all through the house a feeling of ominous evil poisoned the atmosphere. They were watching television in order to relax a little. Rebecca suddenly saw a presence out of the corner of her eye, a person of some kind standing near the window in back of the sofa where her sister-in-law was sitting. Without raising her voice unduly or taking her eyes off the spot, she said, "Susan, get the rifle!" They had a rifle standing ready in the corner of the room.

Only then did Susan take a sharp look at the face peering into the window. It was a man's face, and so unspeakably evil it took her breath away. Scowling at them with hatred, the face remained there for a moment, while Susan grabbed the gun. But when she pointed it toward the window, the face had disappeared.

Immediately, they rushed outside. The ground was frozen hard, so footprints would not have shown, had there been any. But they could not see anyone nor hear anyone running away.

The dog, chained at a spot where an intruder would be visible to her, evidently did not feel anything. She did not bark. Was she in some strange way hypnotized?

Soon after Christmas, Susan had to leave and the Keegans no longer could afford a babysitter. Rebecca had quit her job, and things were rough financially again.

To help matters, they invited a young couple with a small child to move in with them and help share expenses. The husband did not believe in the supernatural and the wife, on being told of their "problems," showed herself open-minded, even interested, although skeptical.

What had appeared to be a sensible arrangement soon turned out a disaster and additional burden to an already overburdened family. The Farmers weren't going to contribute to the household, but spend what money they earned on liquor and racing. The tension between the Keegans and the Farmers mounted steadily. But the monetary problems were not the sole cause. The Farmers, too, noticed the noises and the unbearable, heavy atmosphere of the house and instinctively blamed the Keegans for these things. Then there was a quilt with an early American eagle and ship motif printed on it. Soon the wife had noticed that someone had turned the quilt around after she had put it away safely for the night. In the morning, the motif would face the opposite way. They could not blame the Keegans for that, since the quilt had been stored out of anyone's reach, and they dimly realized that the house was indeed haunted.

As the tension grew, the two couples would scarcely speak to each other even though they naturally shared the same quarters.

Rebecca began to realize that no matter how cheerful a person might have been on the outside, once such a person moved into the House of Evil, there would be changes of personality and character. Although far from superstitious, she began to believe that the house itself was dangerous and that prolonged life in it could only destroy her and her loved ones.

Early in April Rebecca and Parker were in the bedroom upstairs one night, when they saw a form cross from where their telephone was, over their bed, and then down the stairs. As it crossed past the telephone, the phone rang. An instant later, as the form reached the bottom of the stairs, the downstairs telephone also rang.

This brought the Farmers out screaming and demanding to know what was going on?

For once, there was unison in the house as the four adults gathered together soberly downstairs to discuss what they just witnessed and compare impressions.

They agreed there was a blue-white light around the form, a light so intense it hurt the eyes. They all had felt an icy chill as the form passed them. Only Parker bravely insisted it might have been lightning. But nobody had heard any thunder.

For the Farmers, this was the ghost that broke their patience's back. They moved out immediately.

Left once again to themselves, Rebecca and her husband decided it was time for them to look elsewhere, too. Tired from the long struggle with the Uncanny, they moved soon afterwards.

As soon as they had settled in a new house, life took on a different aspect: where ominous presences had dampened their spirits, there was now gaiety and a zest for life they had not known for four years. Nobody has been sick in the family since and they have no problems getting and keeping babysitters.

The House of Evil still stands on lonely Route 14, and there are people living in it now. But whenever Parker has occasion to pass Route 14 in his car, he steps on the gas and drives just a little bit faster. No sense taking chances!

North Carolina

The Grave
of the Ghostly Girl

orothy B., a young Pennsylvanian woman in her early thirties, spent many years living with a maternal uncle and aunt in North Carolina. The house was a two-hundred-year-old farmhouse, surrounded by a medium-sized farm. Her uncle and aunt were in their late fifties, but continued farming on a reduced scale since they lived alone; their two children had long gone to the city. Dorothy was assigned a pleasant corner room in the upper story of the house, and when she moved into it one April, she thought she had, at last, found a place where she could have peace and quiet.

This was very necessary because she had just been through a nervous breakdown due to an unhappy love affair, and had decided to withdraw from life in the city. Fortunately she had saved up some money so she could afford to live quietly by herself for at least a year. When her uncle heard of her predicament, he had offered the hospitality of the house in return for some light chores she could easily perform for him. The first night after her arrival at the farmhouse, Dorothy slept soundly, probably due to the long journey and the emotional release of entering a new phase of her life. But the following night—she remembers this clearly because there was a full moon that night—Dorothy went to bed around ten P.M. feeling very relaxed and hopeful for the future. The conversation at the dinnertable had been about art and poetry, two subjects very dear to Dorothy's heart. Nothing about the house or its background had been mentioned by her uncle and aunt, nor had there been any discussion of psychic phenomena. The latter subject was not exactly alien to Dorothy, for she had had a number of ESP experiences over the years, mainly precognitive in nature and not particularly startling.

She extinguished the lights and started to drift off to sleep. Suddenly her attention was focused on a low-level noise, seemingly emanating from below the ceiling. It sounded as if someone were tapping on the wall. At first Dorothy assumed that the pipes were acting up, but then she remembered that it was the middle of spring and the heat was not on.

She decided not to pay any attention, assuming it was just one of those noises you hear in old houses when they settle. Again she tried to drift off to sleep and was almost asleep when she felt a presence close to her bed. There was an intense chill accompanying that feeling, and she sat bolt upright in bed, suddenly terrified. As she opened her eyes and looked toward the corner of her room, she saw that she was not alone. Due to the strong moonlight streaming in from the window, she could make out everything in the room. Perhaps a yard or a yard and a half away from her stood the figure of a young girl, motionless, staring at her with very large, sad eyes.

Despite her terror, Dorothy could make out that the girl was dressed in very old-fashioned clothes, unlike the kind that are worn today. She seemed like a farm girl; the clothes were simple but clean, and her long brown hair cascaded down over her shoulders. There was a terrible feeling of guilt in her eyes, as if she were desperately seeking help. "What do you want?" Dorothy said, trembling with fear as she spoke. The apparition did not reply, but continued to stare at her. At this moment, Dorothy had the clear impression that the girl wanted her to know how sorry she was. At this point Dorothy's fear got the better of her, and she turned on the light. As she did so, the apparition vanished immediately.

Still shaken, she went back to sleep and managed a somewhat restless night. The following morning she asked her aunt whether there had ever been any psychic experience in the family, in particular whether anyone had ever seen or heard anything unusual in the house. Her aunt gave her a strange look and shook her head. Either there hadn't been anything, or she didn't care to discuss it. Dorothy, as the newcomer, did not feel like pressing her point, so she changed the subject.

That night she went to bed with anticipatory fears, but nothing happened. Relieved that it might all have been her imagination due to the long trip the day before, Dorothy began to forget the incident. Three days later, however, she was again awakened by the feeling of a presence in her room. The cold was as intense as it had been the first time, and when she opened her eyes, there was the same apparition she had seen before. This time she was pleading for help even more, and since Dorothy did not feel the same gripping fear she had experienced the first time, she was able to communicate with the apparition.

"I want to help you; tell me who you are," she said to the spectre, waiting for some sort of reply. After what seemed to her an eternity, but could have been no more than a few seconds, Dorothy received the impression that the girl was in trouble because of a man she had become involved with. To be sure, the ghost did not speak to her; the thoughts came to Dorothy on a telepathic level, haltingly, in bits, picturing the apparition with a tall, good-looking man, also wearing old-fashioned farm clothes. In her mind's eye, Dorothy saw the two lovers, and then she heard what sounded like a tiny infant. At that point, the apparition vanished, leaving Dorothy very much shaken.

The following morning she broached the subject of ghosts to her aunt. But the reaction she got was so cold, she hesitated to go on, and again she did not relate her experiences. Several weeks passed without incident of any kind. That is, except for some strange noises Dorothy ascribed to a settling of the house, or perhaps a squirrel or two in the rafters above her room. It sounded like furtive, light footsteps if one were so inclined to interpret the sounds. Again there was a full moon, and Dorothy realized that she had been at the house for a full month. That night, Dorothy went to bed earlier than usual, hoping to get a good start toward a night's sleep since she had been particularly active during the day helping her aunt clear out a woodshed in the back of the farmhouse.

It had not been an easy chore. Somehow the atmosphere in the woodshed was very depressing, and Dorothy wanted to leave more than once, but hesitated to do so lest her aunt accuse her of being lazy. But the feeling inside the woodshed was heavy with tragedy and unhappiness, even though Dorothy could not pinpoint the reasons for it.

Now she lay in bed, waiting for sleep to come. She had drawn the blinds, but the moonlight kept streaming in through them, bathing the room in a sort of semidarkness that allowed Dorothy to see everything in the room in good detail. After a few minutes she became aware of an intense chill toward the left side of her bed. She realized she was not about to drift into peaceful sleep after all, and prepared herself for what she knew would be her nocturnal visitor. In a moment, there was the pale-looking girl again, this time standing by the window as if she did not dare come near Dorothy.

"Very well," Dorothy thought, "let's get to the bottom of this. I've had about enough of it, and if this ghost is going to make my life miserable here, I might as well know why." Somehow the ghost seemed to have read her mind, because she came closer to the bed, looking at Dorothy again with her large, tearful eyes. As if someone had told her to, Dorothy now closed her own eyes and allowed the apparition to impress her with further details of her story. Again she saw the husky young man and the ghost girl together, and this time there was an infant with them. Next she saw an old woman entering what appeared to be a very run-down shack or room, and something in Dorothy recognized the shack as the woodshed she had been in during the day!

Then something horrible happened: although she could not see it with her mind's eye, Dorothy knew that the child was being *butchered*, and that the old woman was the instigator. Quickly, Dorothy opened her eyes and looked at the apparition. For a moment the girl looked at Dorothy again as if to say *now you understand why I am still here*—but then the ghost faded into the woodwork. Somehow Dorothy was able to sleep peacefully that night, as if a burden had been lifted from her.

The following morning, she told her aunt everything that had happened from the very first day on. This time her aunt did not interrupt her, but listened in stony silence, as Dorothy recounted her ghostly experiences. Finally, she said, "I wish you had been left in peace; that is why I did not want to tell you anything about this ghost." She explained that a young girl named Anne, who had been working for them for a number of years prior to Dorothy's arrival, had also slept in the same room. She, too, had seen the apparition, although she was unable to understand the reasons for the ghostly encounter.

A few years after taking over the farm, Dorothy's uncle had stumbled across an unmarked grave in back of the woodshed. It

was clear to him that it was a grave, even though the headstone
had been partially destroyed by time and weather. He had assumed that it belonged to a slave, for there were slaves in the area
at the time when the farm was first built. But the grave seemed
unusually small, and Dorothy's aunt wondered whether perhaps
it might not be that of a child. As she said this, Dorothy felt a
distinct chill and received the clear impression that her aunt had
hit on something connected with her ghost. On the spur of the
moment, the two women went to the spot where the grave had
been discovered. It was barely discernible amid the surrounding
rocks and earth, but eventually they located it. Dorothy fetched
some flowers from the house and placed them upon what must
have been the headstone at one time. Then she fashioned a crude
cross from two wooden sticks and placed them in the center. This
done, she said a simple prayer, hoping that the soul of whoever
was underneath the stones would find an easy passage into the
world beyond.

When Dorothy went to bed that night, she had a sense of relief
at having done something constructive about her ghost. She half-
expected the ghostly girl to appear again, but nothing happened
that night, or the following night, or any night thereafter, and
eventually Dorothy left the farmhouse to go back to the city about
a year later.

North Dakota

A Houseful of Ghosts

ome ghostly invasions have a way of snowballing from seemingly quiet beginnings into veritable torrents of terror. Mrs. C. of North Dakota is a housewife with an eight-year-old daughter, and a husband who does not believe in ghosts or anything of that nature. They live in an old house that would be a comfortable, roomy house if it weren't for—*them*. Mrs. C. and her family moved into the house in 1970. Whether it was because both she and her husband worked at different times, thus being absent from the house a great deal of the time, or whether the unseen forces had not yet gathered enough strength to manifest, nothing of an uncanny nature occurred until January 1973.

One day during January, Mrs. C. was working in the basement, washing some clothes. All of a sudden she heard someone whistle; no definite tune, just one long whistle repeated several times. Immediately her dog, Pud, ran around the basement to see where the noise came from, but neither Mrs. C. nor her dog could find the origin of the whistle.

The whistling continued on several occasions during the month, and while it seemed puzzling, it did not upset her greatly. At the time she was working nights, returning home between midnight and one A.M. One night during February, she returned home, and as soon as she had entered the house, had a very strange feeling of being watched by someone. At the same time it became freezing cold, and the hair on her arms stood up. She looked all over the house but found no intruder, nothing human that could account for the strange feeling.

Mrs. C. decided to prepare for bed, and changed clothes in the kitchen, as was her custom, in order not to wake her husband, who was already asleep. She then went toward the bedroom in semidarkness, with the lights off but sufficiently illuminated to make out the details of the room. All of a sudden, about a foot and a half in front of her face and a little over her head, she noticed a smoky, whitish-gray haze. To her horror, she saw that in the middle of it there was a human face without either body or neck. It was the head of a bald man, very white, with distinctive black eyes and a very ugly face. All through it and around it was this strange white fog. Mrs. C. had never seen anything like it and became very frightened. She dashed into the bedroom, not sure whether the whole thing had been her imagination, and eventually fell asleep. The next day, the whistling returned and continued all month long. This was followed by a mumbling human voice, at first one person, then later two people speaking. Both she and her daughter heard it. At first the mumbling was heard only in the daytime; later it switched to nighttime as well.

At the time, Mrs. C.'s husband left for work at four o'clock in the morning, and she was in the habit of sleeping on till about eight. But now she could not; as soon as her husband had left for work the mumbling would start, always in the bedroom and seemingly coming from the foot of the bed. It then moved to the side of the bed opposite where she slept, then back to the foot of the bed again, directly in front of her feet. She tried hard not to pay any attention to it, and after listening to it for a while, managed to fall asleep. Soon it sounded as if several women and one man were speaking, perhaps as many as four individuals. This continued every morning until April of that year. Then something new was added to the torment: something that sounded like a faint growling noise.

The growling was the last straw. Mrs. C. became very frightened and decided to do something to protect herself. She recalled a small cross her husband had given her the previous Christmas. Now she put the cross and chain around her neck, never taking it off again.

Mrs. C. loves animals. At the time of the haunting, the family owned two parakeets, six guinea pigs, two dogs, and two cats. Since the uncanny events had started in her house, she had kept a day-to-day diary of strange happenings, not because she hoped to convince her husband of the reality of the phenomena, but to keep her own sanity and counsel. On May 5, 1973, Mrs. C. awoke and found her blue parakeet dead, horribly disfigured in its cage; the green parakeet next to it acted as if it were insane, running back and forth all day, screaming. The following day, May 6, Mrs. C. awoke to find the green bird dead, destroyed in exactly the same way as the first parakeet had been.

Four days later, as she was washing her hair, Mrs. C. felt the chain with the cross being lifted up from the back of her neck by an unseen hand and unclasped, then dropped to the floor. When she turned around, there was no one in back of her. Still shaken, she left her house at nine-thirty to do some errands. When she returned at eleven o'clock, she found one of her guinea pigs lying on the living room floor, flopping its head in a most pitiful fashion. A short time later the animal died. Its neck had been broken by an unseen force. No one had been in the house at the time, as her daughter and a friend who had slept over had accompanied Mrs. C. on her errands. What made the incident even more grisly was the fact that the guinea pig had been kept in a cage, that the cage was locked, and that the key rested safely in Mrs. C.'s cigarette case that she took when she went out of the house.

Two weeks passed. On May 25, while taking a bath, Mrs. C. felt the necklace with the cross being lifted up into the air from the back of her neck and pulled so hard that it snapped and fell into the tub. This was the beginning of a day of terror. During the night, the two children heard frightening noises down in the basement, which kept them from sleeping. Mrs. C., exhausted from the earlier encounters, had slept so deeply she had not heard them. The children reported that the dogs had growled all night and that they had heard the meowing of the cats as well.

Mrs. C. went downstairs to check on things. The dogs lay asleep as if exhausted; the cats were not there, but were upstairs by now; on the floor, scattered all over the basement, lay two of the remaining guinea pigs. One was alive and well in its cage, but two others lay dead inside their cage, which was still locked and intact. Their bodies were bloody and presented a horrible sight— fur all torn off, eyes gone, and bodies torn apart. At first Mrs. C. thought that the dogs might have attacked them, but soon realized that they could not have done so inside the animals' cages.

For a few days, things quieted down somewhat. One morning, the ominous growling started again while Mrs. C. was still in bed. Gradually, the growling noise became louder and louder, as if it were getting closer. This particular morning the growling had started quietly, but when it reached a deafening crescendo, Mrs. C. heard over it a girl's voice speak quite plainly, "No, don't hurt her! Don't hurt her!" The growling continued, nevertheless. Then, as Mrs. C. looked on in horror, someone unseen sat down in front of her feet on the bed, for the bed sank down appreciably from the weight of the unseen person.

Then the spectral visitor moved up closer and closer in the bed toward her, while the growling became louder. Accompanying it was the girl's voice, "No, no! Don't do it!" That was enough for Mrs. C. Like lightning, she jumped out of bed and ran into the kitchen and sat down trembling. But the growling followed her from the bedroom, started into the living room across from the kitchen, then went back to the bedroom—and suddenly stopped.

That was the last time Mrs. C. slept on in the morning after her husband left for work. From that moment on she got up with him, got dressed, and sat in the kitchen until the children got up, between seven-thirty and nine A.M.

About that time they heard the sound of water running, both at night and in the morning upon arising. Even her husband heard it now and asked her to find out where it was coming from. On checking the bathroom, kitchen, upstairs sink, basement bathroom, and laundry room, Mr. and Mrs. C. concluded that the source of the running water was invisible.

From time to time they heard the sound of dishes being broken and crashing, and furniture being moved with accompanying loud noise. Yet when they looked for the damage, nothing had been touched, nothing broken.

At the beginning of the summer of 1973, Mrs. C. had a sudden cold feeling and suddenly felt a hand on her neck coming around from behind her, and she could actually feel fingers around her throat! She tried to swallow and felt as if she were being choked. The sensation lasted just long enough to cause her great anxiety, then it went away as quickly as it had come.

Some of the phenomena were now accompanied by rapping on the walls, with the knocks taking on an intelligent pattern, as if someone were trying to communicate with them. Doorknobs would rattle by themselves or turn themselves, even though there was no one on the other side of them. All over the house footsteps were heard. One particular day, when Mrs. C. was sitting in the kitchen with her daughter, all the doors in the house began to rattle. This was followed by doors all over the house opening and slamming shut by themselves, and the drapes in the living room opening wide and closing quickly, as if someone were pulling them back and forth. Then the window shades in the kitchen went up and down again, and windows opened by themselves, going up, down, up, down in all the rooms, crashing as they fell down without breaking.

It sounded as if all hell had broken loose in the house. At the height of this nightmare, the growling started up again in the bedroom. Mrs. C. and her little daughter sat on the bed and stared toward where they thought the growling came from. Suddenly Mrs. C. could no longer talk, no matter how she tried; not a word came from her mouth. It was clear to her that something extraordinary was taking place. Just as the phenomena reached the height of fury, everything stopped dead silent, and the house was quiet again.

Thus far only Mrs. C. and her little daughter shared the experiences, for her husband was not only a skeptic but prided himself on being an atheist. No matter how pressing the problem was, Mrs. C. could not unburden herself to him.

One night, when the couple returned from a local stock car race and had gone to bed, the mumbling voices started up again. Mrs. C. said nothing in order not to upset her husband, but the voices became louder. All of a sudden Mr. C. asked, "What is that?" and when she informed him that those were the ghostly voices she had been hearing all along, he chided her for being so silly. But *he* had heard them too. A few days later Mr. C. told his wife he wanted a cross similar to the one she was wearing. Since his birthday was coming up, she bought one for him as a gift. From that moment on, Mr. C. also always wore a necklace with a cross on it.

In despair Mrs. C. turned to her brother, who had an interest in occult matters. Together with him and her young brother-in-law, Mrs. C. went downstairs one night in August to try and lay the ghosts to rest. In a halting voice, her brother spoke to the unseen entities, asking them to speak up or forever hold their peace. There was no immediate response. The request to make their presence felt was repeated several times.

All of a sudden, all hell broke loose again. Rattling and bang-

ing in the walls started up around them, and the sound of walking
on the basement steps was clearly heard by the three of them. Mrs.
C.'s brother started up the stairs and, as he did so, he had the chill
impression of a man standing there.

Perhaps the formula of calling out the ghosts worked, because the house has been quiet since then. Sometimes Mrs. C.
looks back on those terrible days and nights, and wishes it had
happened to someone else, and not her. But the empty cages
where her pet animals had been kept are a grim reminder that it
had all been only too true.

A Houseproud Ghost

Ours is not a very sentimental time, and properties change hands without much ado. Someone owns a house, showers attention and love on it, then the owner dies and the house passes into different hands. Different owners have different ideas regarding what gives them comfort in what is now their home. But sometimes . . . sometimes the previous owner has not quite left.

Reba B. is a sensitive, fragile-looking lady with two grown children. She was born in Kentucky, and hails from an old family in which the name Reba has occurred several times before. She works as a medical secretary and doctor's assistant, and nowadays shares her home with three cats; she is divorced and her children have moved away. Mrs. B. wondered whether perhaps she had a particular affinity for ghosts, seeing that she has encountered denizens of the Other World so many times, in so many houses. It wasn't that it bothered her to any extent, but she had gotten used to living by herself except for her cats, and the idea of having to share her home with individuals who could pop in and out at will, and who might hang around her at times when she could not see them did not contribute to her comfort.

Her psychic ability goes back to age three, when she was living with her grandparents in Kentucky. Even then she had a vivid feeling of presences all around her, not that she actually saw them with her eyes. It was more a sensitivity to unseen forces surrounding her—an awareness that she was never quite alone. As soon as she would go to bed as a child, she would see the figure of a man bending over her, a man she did not know. After a long period of this she wondered if she was dreaming, but in her heart she knew she was not. However, she was much too young to worry about such things, and as she grew up, her ability became part of her character, and she began to accept it as "normal."

This incident begins when she happened to be living in Cincinnati, already divorced. Her mother shared an old house with her, a house that was built around 1900; it had all the earmarks of the post-Victorian era: brass door knobs, little doorbells that were to be turned by hand, and the various trimmings of that age. The house consisted of three floors; the ground floor contained an apartment, and the two ladies took the second and third floor of the house. Reba had her bedroom on the third floor; it was the only bedroom up there, situated in the middle of the floor.

One day she was coming up those stairs and was approaching the window when she saw a man standing by it. He vanished as she came closer, and she gave this no more thought until a few days later.

At that time she happened to be lying in bed, propped up and reading a book. She looked up and saw a man who had apparently come up the stairs. She noticed his features fully: his eyes were brown, and he also had brown hair. Immediately she could sense that he was very unhappy, even angry. It wasn't that she heard his voice, but somehow his thoughts communicated themselves to her, mind to mind.

From her bed she could see him approach, walking out to a small landing and standing in front of her door. Next to her room was a storage room. He looked straight at Reba, and at that moment she received the impression that he was very angry because she and her mother were in the house, because they had moved into *his* house.

Although Reba B. was fully conscious and aware of what was going on, she rejected the notion that she was hearing the thoughts of a ghost. But it did her no good; over and over she heard him say or think, "Out, out, I want you out, I don't want you here." At that moment he raised his arm and pointed outward, as if to emphasize his point. The next moment he was gone. Reba thought for a moment, whether she should tell her mother, whose bedroom was downstairs. She decided against it, since her mother had a heart condition and because she herself wasn't too sure the incident had been quite real. Also, she was a little frightened and did not want to recall the incident any more than she had to. After a while, she went off to sleep.

Not too long after that her daughter, who was then fourteen, and her eleven-year-old son were home with her from school. It was a weekend, and she wanted the children to enjoy it. Consequently, she did not tell them anything about her ghostly experience. She had gone into the front storage room, when she thought she saw someone sitting on the boxes stacked in the storage area.

At first she refused to acknowledge it, and tried to look away, but when her gaze returned to the area, the man was still sitting there, quietly staring at her. Again she turned her head, and when she looked back, he was gone. The following weekend, her children were with her again. They had hardly arrived when her daughter returned from the same storage room and asked, "Mother, is there someone sitting in there?" and all Reba could do was nod, and acknowledge that there was. Her daughter then described the stranger and the description matched what her mother had seen. Under the circumstances, Reba B. freely discussed the matter with her children. But nothing further was done concerning the matter, and no inquiries were made as to the background of the house.

Summer came, and another spring and another summer, and they got into the habit of using the entrance at the side of the house. There were some shrubs in that area, and in order to enter the apartment in which they lived, they had to come up the stairs where they would have a choice of either walking into the living room on the second floor, or continuing on to the third floor where Reba's bedroom was. The tenant who had the ground-floor apartment also had his own entrance.

One warm summer evening, she suddenly felt the stranger come into the downstairs door and walk up the stairs. When she went to check, she saw nothing. Still, she *knew* he was in the house. A few days passed, and again she sensed the ghost nearby. She looked, and as her eyes peered down into the hall, she saw him walking down the hall toward her. While she was thinking, "I am imagining this, there is no such thing as a ghost," she slowly walked toward him. As he kept approaching her, she walked right through him! It was an eerie sensation: for a moment she could not see, and then he was gone. The encounter did not help Reba keep her composure, but there was little she could do about it.

Many times she sensed his presence in the house without seeing him, but early one evening, on a Sunday, just as it got dark, she found herself in the living room on the second floor of the house. She had turned on the television set, which was facing her, and she kept the volume down so as not to disturb her mother, whose room was on the same floor. She had altered the furniture in the room somewhat, in order to be closer to the television set, and there were two lounge chairs, one of which she used, and the other one close by, near the television set, so that another person could sit in it and also view the screen. She was just watching television, when she sensed the stranger come up the stairs again and walk into the living room. Next he sat down in the empty chair close to Reba, but this time the atmosphere was different from that first encounter near the door of her room. He seemed more relaxed and comfortable, and Reba was almost glad that he was there keeping her company. Somehow she felt that he was glad to be in the room with her, and that he was less lonely because of her. He was no longer angry; he just wanted to visit.

Reba looked at the stranger's face and noticed his rather high-bridged nose. She also had a chance to study his clothes; he was wearing a brown suit, rather modern in style. Even though the house was quite old, this man was not from the early years, but his clothes seemed to indicate a comparatively recent period. As she sat there, quietly studying the ghost, she got the feeling that he had owned the house at one time, and that their living room had been the sitting room where the ghost and his wife had received people.

Reba somehow knew that his wife had been very pretty—a fair-complexioned blonde, and she was shown a fireplace in the living room with a small love seat of the French Provincial type next to it, drawn up quite close to the fireplace. She saw this in her mind's eye, as if the man were showing her something from his past. At the same time, Reba knew that some tragedy had occurred between the ghost and his wife.

Suddenly, panic rose in Reba, as she realized she was sharing the evening with a ghost. Somehow her fears communicated themselves to her phantom visitor, for as she looked close, he had vanished.

As much as she had tried to keep these things from her mother, she could not. Her mother owned an antique covered casserole made of silver, which she kept at the head of her bed.

The bed was a bookcase bed, and she used to lift the cover and put in receipts, tickets, and papers whenever she wanted.

One day, Reba and her mother found themselves at the far end of her bedroom on the second floor. Her bed was up against the wall, without any space between it and the wall. As the two ladies were looking in the direction of the bed, they suddenly saw the silver casserole being picked up, put down on the bed, turned upside down, and everything spilled out of it. It didn't fly through the air, but moved rather slowly, as if some unseen force were holding it. Although her mother had seen it, she did not say anything because she felt it would be unwise to alarm her daughter; but later on she admitted having seen the whole thing. It was ironic how the two women were trying to spare each other's feelings—yet both knew that what they had witnessed was real.

The ghost did not put in any further appearances after the dramatic encounter in the living room. About a year later, the two ladies moved away into another old house far from this one. But shortly before they did, Reba's mother was accosted on the street by a strange middle-aged lady, who asked her whether she was living in the house just up the street. When Reba's mother acknowledged it, the lady informed her the house had once belonged to her parents. Were they happy in it, Reba's mother wanted to know. "Very happy," the stranger assured her, "Especially my father." It occurred to Reba that it might have been he who she had encountered in the house; someone so attached to his home that he did not want to share it with anyone else, especially flesh-and-blood people like her mother and herself.

The new home the ladies moved into proved "alive" with unseen vibrations also, but by now they didn't care. Reba realized that she had a special gift. If ghosts wanted her company, there was little she could do about it.

She had a friend who worked as a motorcycle patrolman, by the name of John H. He was a young man and well liked on the force. One day he chased a speeder, and was killed in the process. At the time, Reba was still married, but she had known John for quite a few years before. They were friends, although not really close ones, and she had been out of touch with him for some time. One morning, she suddenly sensed his presence in the room with her; it made no sense, yet she was positive it was John H. After a while, the presence left her. She remarked on this to her mother and got a blank stare in return. The young man had been killed on the previous night, but Reba could not have known this. The news had come on the radio just that morning, but apparently Reba had had advance news of a more direct kind.

Reba B. shared her interest in the occult with an acquaintance, newscaster Bill G. In his position as a journalist, he had to be particularly careful in expressing an opinion on so touchy a subject as extrasensory perception. They had met at a local restaurant one evening, and somehow the conversation had gotten around to ghosts.

When Mr. G. noticed her apprehension at being one of the "selected" ones who could see ghosts, he told her about another friend, a young medium who had an apartment not far away. One evening she walked out onto her patio and saw a man in old-fashioned clothes approach her. The man tried to talk to her, but she could not hear anything. Suddenly he disappeared before her eyes. The young lady thought she was having a nervous breakdown, and consulted a psychiatrist; she even went into a hospital to have herself examined, but there was nothing wrong with her. When she returned to her home and went out onto the patio again, she saw the same ghostly apparition once more. This time she did not panic, but instead studied him closely. When he disappeared she went back into her apartment, and decided to make some inquiries about the place. It was then that she discovered that a long time ago, a man of that description had been hanged from a tree in her garden.

"These things *do* happen," Bill G. assured Reba, and asked her not to be ashamed or afraid of them. After all, ghosts are people too. Since then, Reba had come to terms with her ghostly encounters. She has even had an experience with a ghost cat—but that is another story.

The
Girls' School
Ghost

I n one of the quietest and most elegant sections of old Cincinnati, where ghosts and hauntings are rarely whispered about, stands a lovely Victorian mansion built around 1850 in what was then a wealthy suburb of the city.

The house was brought to my attention some years ago by John Strader of Clifton, a descendant of one of the early Dutch families who settled Cincinnati, and himself a student of the paranormal. The owners at that time were the Stenton family, or rather, of one of the apartments in the mansion, for it had long been subdivided into a number of apartments lived in by various people.

Soon after they had taken up residence in the old house, the Stentons were startled by noises, as if someone were walking in the hall, and when they checked, there was never anyone about who could have caused the walking. Then, two weeks after they had moved in, and always at exactly the same time—2:10 A.M.— they would hear the noise of a heavy object hitting the marble floor; of course there was nothing that could have caused it.

Shortly thereafter, while Mrs. Stenton and her father were doing some research work in the flat, someone softly called out her name, Marilyn. Both heard it. What really upset them was the sound of arguing voices coming from the area of the ceiling in their bedroom: Mrs. Stenton had the impression that there were a group of young girls up there.

But the most dramatic event was to transpire a couple of weeks later. Someone had entered the bedroom, and as she knew she was alone, her family being in other parts of the house, she was frightened, especially when she saw what appeared to be a misty figure. As soon as she had made eye contact with it, the figure shot out of the room, through the French doors leading to a studio, managing to knock the Venetian blinds on the doors, causing them to sway back and forth.

Shortly before I visited Cincinnati to deal with this case, Mrs. Stenton had another eerie experience. It was winter and had been snowing the night before. When Mrs. Stenton stepped out onto their front porch, she immediately noticed a fresh set of foot prints on the porch, heading *away* from the house.

The house was originally built in 1850 as a large private home; later it became a girls' school, and much later an apartment house of sorts. The Stenton's apartment is the largest in the house, encompassing seven rooms.

When I looked into the case I discovered some additional details. In 1880 a young man of the Henry family had committed suicide in the house by shooting himself, and after the family moved the house could not be sold for a long time. It became known as being haunted and was boarded up. Finally a girls' school, the Ealy School, bought it in 1900.

Other tenants had also encountered unusual phenomena ranging from "presences" to noises of objects hitting floors, and footsteps following one around when no one was, in fact, doing so. Even the dog owned by one of the tenants would under no condition enter the area of the disturbances and would put up a fearsome howl.

But the item most likely to have an answer to the goings-on came to me by talking to some of the oldsters in the area: one of the young girls in the school was said to have hanged herself upstairs, above the Stenton's apartment. Was it her ghost or that of young Henry who could not leave well enough alone?

The Burning Ghost

I treat each case reported to me on an individual basis. Some I reject on the face of the report, and others only after I have been through a long and careful investigation. But other reports have the ring of truth about them and are worthy of belief, even though some of them are no longer capable of verification because witnesses have died or sites have been destroyed.

A good example is the case reported to me by Mrs. Edward Needs, Jr., of Canton, Ohio. In a small town by the name of Homeworth, there is a stretch of land near the highway that is today nothing more than a neglected farm with a boarded-up old barn still standing. The spot is actually on a dirt road, and the nearest house is half a mile away, with wooded territory in between. This is important, you see, for the spot is isolated and a man might die before help could arrive. On rainy days, the dirt road is impassable. Mrs. Needs has passed the spot a number of times, and does not particularly care to go there. Somehow it always gives her an uneasy feeling. Once, their car got stuck in the mud on a rainy day, and they had to drive through open fields to get out.

It was on that adventure-filled ride that Mr. Needs confided for the first time what had happened to him at that spot on prior occasions. It was the year when Edward Needs and a friend were on a joy ride after dark. At that time Needs had not yet married his present wife, and the two men had been drinking a little, but were far from drunk. It was then that they discovered the dirt road for the first time.

On the spur of the moment, they followed it. A moment later they came to the old barn. But just as they were approaching it, a man jumped out of nowhere in front of them. What was even more sobering was the condition this man was in: engulfed in flames from head to toe! Quickly Needs put his bright headlights on the scene, to see better. The man then ran into the woods across the road and just disappeared.

Two men never became cold sober more quickly. They turned around and went back to the main highway fast. But the first chance they had, they returned with two carloads full of other fellows. They were equipped with strong lights, guns, and absolutely no whiskey. When the first of the cars was within twenty feet of the spot where Needs had seen the apparition, they all saw the same thing: there before them was the horrible spectacle of a human being blazing from top to bottom, and evidently suffering terribly as he tried to run away from his doom. Needs emptied his gun at the figure: it never moved or acknowledged that it had been hit by the bullets. A few seconds later, the figure ran into the woods—exactly as it had when Needs had first encountered it.

Now the ghost posse went into the barn, which they found abandoned although not in very bad condition. The only strange thing was spots showing evidence of fire: evidently someone or something had burned inside the barn without, however, setting fire to the barn as a whole. Or had the fiery man run outside to save his barn from the fire?

Oklahoma

The Ghost
of the Murdered Child

O n January 7, Mr. and Mrs. S. moved into an older house on South Fourth Street, a rented, fully-furnished two-bedroom house in a medium-sized city in Oklahoma. Mrs. S.'s husband was a career service man in the Army, stationed at a nearby Army camp. They had a small boy, and looked forward to a pleasant stay in which the boy could play with neighborhood kids, while Mrs. S. tried to make friends in what to her was a new environment.

She was not easily frightened off by anything she cannot explain, and the occult was the last thing on her mind. They had lived in the house for about two weeks when she noticed light footsteps walking in the hall at night. When she checked on them, there was no one there. Her ten-year-old son was sleeping across the hall, and she wondered if perhaps he was walking in his sleep. But each time she heard the footsteps and would check on him, she found him sound asleep. The footsteps continued on and off for a period of four months.

Then one Sunday afternoon at about two o'clock, when her husband was at his post and her son in the backyard playing, she found herself in the kitchen. Suddenly she heard a child crying very softly, as if afraid to cry aloud. At once she ran into the backyard to see if her son was hurt. There was nothing wrong with him, and she found him playing happily with a neighborhood boy. It then dawned on her that she could not hear the child crying outside the house, but immediately upon reentering the house, the faint sobs were clearly audible again.

She traced the sound to her bedroom, and when she entered the room, it ceased to be noticeable. This puzzled her to no end, since she had no idea what could cause the sounds. Added to this

were strange thumping sounds, which frequently awakened her in
the middle of the night. It sounded as if someone had fallen out of
bed.

On these occasions, she would get out of bed quickly and rush
into her son's room, only to find him fast asleep. A thorough check
of the entire house revealed no source for the strange noises. But
Mrs. S. noticed that their Siamese cat, who slept at the foot of her
bed when these things happened, also reacted to them: his hair
would bristle, his ears would fly back, and he would growl and
stare into space at something or someone she could not see.

About that time, her mother decided to visit them. Since her
mother was an invalid, Mrs. S. decided not to tell her about the
strange phenomena in order to avoid upsetting her. She stayed at
the house for three days, when one morning she wanted to know
why Mrs. S. was up at two o'clock in the morning making coffee.
Since the house had only two bedrooms, they had put a half-bed
into the kitchen for her mother, especially as the kitchen was very
large and she could see the television from where she was sleeping. Her mother insisted she had heard footsteps coming down
the hall into the kitchen. She called out to what she assumed was
her daughter, and when there was no answer, she assumed that
her daughter and her son-in-law had had some sort of disagree-
ment and she had gotten up to make some coffee.

From her bed she could not reach the light switch, but she
could see the time by the illuminated clock and realized it was two
o'clock in the morning. Someone came down the hall, entered the
kitchen, put water into the coffee pot, plugged it in, and then
walked out of the kitchen and down the hall. She could hear the
sound of coffee perking and could actually smell it. However,
when she didn't hear anyone coming back, she assumed that her
daughter and son-in-law had made up and gone back to sleep.

She did likewise, and decided to question her daughter about
it in the morning. Mrs. S. immediately checked the kitchen, but
there was no trace of the coffee to be found, which did not help
her state of mind. A little later she heard some commotion outside
the house, and on stepping outside noticed that the dogcatcher
was trying to take a neighbor's dog with him. She decided to try
and talk him out of it, and the conversation led to her husband
being in the service, a statement that seemed to provoke a negative reaction on the part of the dogcatcher. He informed Mrs. S.

that the last GI to live in the house was a murderer. When she wanted to know more about it, he clammed up immediately. But Mrs. S. became highly agitated. She called the local newspaper and asked for any and all information concerning her house. It was then that she learned the bitter truth.

In October two years before, a soldier stationed at the same base as her husband had beaten his two-year-old daughter to death. The murder took place in what had now become Mrs. S.'s bedroom. Mrs. S., shocked by the news, sent up a silent prayer, hoping that the restless soul of the child might find peace and not have to haunt a house where she had suffered nothing but unhappiness in her short life.

Pennsylvania

The Little Sister

Mary Carol Henry was in her early thirties, lived in Montgomery, and was married to a medical technician in the USAF. The mother of seven children, she has had psychic experiences from early childhood. When Mary was twelve years old one of her older brothers moved to Pittsburgh. She lent a helping hand with the furniture and other belongings and decided to stay overnight so she could help them finish up the work early in the morning. The house was an old four-story one in the Hazelwood section of Pittsburgh. Mary and the children slept up on the third floor, but she felt very uneasy about staying. Somehow the house bothered her. Since she had promised to stay overnight, however, she went to bed around 10 P.M. and lay in bed for a while thinking about why the house had troubled her. Her brother's baby slept in the same room with her and after a while her brother came up to check on the child. She then heard him go back downstairs.

Mary wasn't sure how much time had elapsed when she thought she heard him come up again. There was the rustling of newspapers or something that sounded like it, and she assumed it was her brother, since he was in the habit of taking a newspaper with him when he went to the bathroom. She turned over, and instead of her brother, to her amazement she saw a young girl come out of a closet. Immediately she recognized her as her little sister Patsy, who had been killed in a gas explosion in August 1945 at the age of five. The ghost wore the same gown she had been buried in and she looked exactly as she had when she was alive but somehow larger in build. Her apparition was enveloped by a green light. As Mary stared in disbelief the ghost came over to the bed and sat on the side of it. Mary saw the bed actually sink in where Patsy sat down. Her sister put her hands on Mary's and kissed her on the cheek. Mary felt the kiss as if it were the kiss of a living person. Then the apparition vanished. Still dazed with fear, Mary sprang out of bed and spent the rest of the night on the stairs. When she told her experience to her mother later, her mother assured her that her late sister had only come back to comfort her in what must have been unfamiliar surroundings, for if Mary was to see a ghost that night it might just as well be someone in the family, not a stranger.

Mrs. Kennedy,
Mrs. McBride

rs. G. threw a hasty look toward the third floor window of the modest wooden house on Mountview Place set back a few paces from the street. Then she shuddered and quickly hurried past, without looking back. Mrs. G. knew that was the best way to pass *that* house.

Everyone in the neighborhood knew the house was haunted and there was no point in seeing things one wasn't supposed to. Still—if the figure at the window was there, perhaps a glance would not hurt. It was a question of curiosity versus fear of the unknown, and fear won out.

The house itself looks like a typical lower-middle-class dwelling built around the turn of the century. White sides are trimmed in green, and a couple of steps lead up to the entrance door. Its three stories—you can call the third floor an attic, if you prefer— look no different than the floors in any of the smaller houses in suburban Pittsburgh. There is an appropriately sized backyard to the rear of the house, with some bushes and flowers. And there are houses to each side of this one. The block is quiet with very little traffic running through it. By car, it is about forty minutes from downtown Pittsburgh, and most people don't go there more than maybe once in a while to shop. Life on Mountview Place is unexciting and drab and if it weren't for people like Mrs. G. worrying about the third-floor window, nobody would even notice the house. But things were a little different when it was new and the neighborhood was a lot more rustic than it is now.

The early history of the house is somewhat shrouded, except that it was already in existence exactly as it looks today at the turn of the century. At that time Mr. Allshouse, the local plumber, was

only a mere child. So he did not know the strange man who came
to live in the house until many years later. But in 1908, a Hollander named Vander bought the house and he and his family
lived in it until his wife died. In 1953 he left the house, and thereby
hangs the first part of this strange tale. Although there were three
children in the Vander family, he evidently had decided not to
remain where his wife had died, but we can't be altogether sure as
to why he left. In later years Mr. Allshouse and Vander had become friends, and even after his wife's passing Vander maintained
contact with the plumber.

One day Allshouse was walking toward the house when he
met Vander's niece en route. They stopped to chat and he mentioned where he was going. "Then you don't know?" the niece
intoned. "My uncle has been dead for a month."

This came as a surprise to the plumber and he wondered how
the otherwise hale and hearty Hollander had died so suddenly. He
remembered well their initial meeting several years before, when
Vander had needed some repairs done in the house. The work
completed, the plumber presented his bill. Mr. Vander asked him
to wait.

"Don't believe much in banks," he explained. "You don't
mind taking cash, do you?"

"Not at all," the plumber assured him. The Dutchman then
walked up the shaky stairs to the attic. Allshouse could clearly
hear him walk about up there as if he were moving some heavy
object around, looking for something. Then he heard the sound of
a drawer closing, and soon after, the Dutchman's heavy footsteps
came down the stairs again.

"Here's your money," he said and smiled. He was a friendly
man who didn't mind a chat with strangers. After a minute or two
of discussing the state of the world and the weather in Pittsburgh
in particular, the two men parted.

And now Vander was dead. It seemed very strange to the
plumber. Why had Vander left the comfortable house just before
his death and what was to happen to the house now?

Two weeks went by and other matters occupied the plumber's
mind. He was walking down Trenton Avenue one afternoon when
he looked up and who should be trotting toward him but Mr.
Vander!

Without thinking, the plumber called out a friendly "Hello!"

The man did not react, so Allshouse shouted, "Mr. Vander! Mr. Vander!"

At this the man, who had meanwhile passed him, turned, smiled rather wanly, and said, "Hello." But he did not stop to chat as he had always done before, and it seemed strange that this time Vander was cool and distant when normally he had been so friendly.

Long after the Dutchman had disappeared in the opposite direction, the plumber wondered why his friend had behaved so strangely. Then it suddenly hit him that the man had been dead and buried for six weeks.

Prior to his death Vander had sold the house to a couple named McBride. Apparently it was a private transaction, for no one knows exactly how it happened, or even why, but the McBrides were installed in the house by the time Mr. Vander passed on, or at least part of the way on.

The McBrides had no children, and Mrs. McBride was crippled, having once fallen in an alley. Consequently she dragged one leg in a rather pronounced manner when walking.

Around 1964, Mrs. McBride died, leaving the house to her husband, Franklin. Soon after, Mr. McBride's usual calm behavior changed rapidly. Where he had hardly been known for any eccentricities in the neighborhood, he seemed now a subject for discussion up and down the street. For one thing, he soon refused to go upstairs under any circumstances, and made his bed in an old Morris chair in the front parlor downstairs.

On more than one occasion, neighbors saw the man run out into the street in a state of abject fear. Not understanding his reasons, gossip blamed it on alcohol, but the fact is Mr. McBride never drank anything at all. Ultimately, the widow's sister, Mrs. Naugle, had him placed in the state mental institution at Torrence.

The power of attorney then passed into her hands, and it was she who rented the house to the Kennedy family. For about a year the house had stood empty after Mr. McBride's forced departure. In that time, dust had gathered and the house looked eerie even in the daytime. But at night people absolutely refused to walk close by it and even sensible people would rather cross the street to the other side than face walking close to its windows.

Mrs. Evelyn Kennedy had not heard anything special about the house one way or the other. It seemed like the kind of house she wanted for her brood and so she and her husband rented it in 1965. For almost a year the Kennedys lived quietly in the house on Mountview Place and kept busy with the ordinary routines of daily living. There was, first of all, Mrs. Evelyn Kennedy herself, a portly lady of mixed Irish-German ancestry, age forty-five and lively and articulate. At one time she had operated a beauty parlor downtown but now she was much too busy for that. Some of her equipment was still in the attic and on occasion she would perform her erstwhile duties for family or friends there.

Mr. Wilbert Kennedy managed a nearby gas station. Five years her senior, he is a wiry, quiet-spoken man who is rarely around the house, the nature of his business being one of long hours.

Of their four children, two are married and live away from home. The other two daughters, Claudia and Penny, live with their parents. Claudia was married, but her husband had disappeared, and at twenty-four, she was kept busy with her two children, Debra, then seven, and Maria, then one. Penny, unmarried, was eighteen at the time they moved into the house. Except for an occasional friend, this was the entire cast of characters in the strange tale that was about to unfold.

On July 7, 1966, the landlady, Mrs. Naugle, decided she wanted to sell the house. Why she suddenly decided to sell, no one but she knows and she is hardly likely to tell us. But the very same real estate dealer, a man named McKnight, who had gotten the Kennedys into the house, was now entrusted with the disposal of the house to a new owner. Where this would leave the tenants no one knew or cared.

Actually, selling the house should not have proved too difficult. It was reasonably well kept, had an attractive exterior and a nice, large backyard, and the block was quiet and treelined. The downstairs parlor was separated from the dining room by a heavy oaken double door that could be pulled back entirely to make the downstairs into one large room if one had many guests. To the right was the staircase that led straight up two flights. The second story contained the bedrooms and the third floor, actually the attic, was occupied by an additional bedroom in front and a large "rear room," which Mrs. Kennedy had filled with the remnants of her beauty parlor days and sundry suitcases, boxes, and the sort of things people have placed into attics ever since houses were built with them. The house was eminently suitable for any family with children.

Although the "For Sale" sign was up outside their home, the Kennedys continued with their daily business. Somehow they felt it would be some time before the house would be sold and then, perhaps, to an owner who did not wish to live in it. Why worry?

Penny, a determined young lady, had decided she preferred the privacy of the attic to the family presence on the second floor and moved her bed to the empty bedroom in the attic. The day after the "For Sale" sign had been installed outside, she came down to use the bathroom.

When she went back up to the attic, she found her way barred by a woman standing at the window. Since it was broad daylight, Penny had ample opportunity to look her over. She was an elderly woman with gray hair, wearing a somewhat unusual amount of rouge on her face. Her blue dress was like a long robe. In her hands she held some beads, and when Penny noticed her, the woman held out her arms toward her, all the while smiling at her. But Penny did not feel friendly at all. She knew there couldn't possibly be anyone of flesh and blood standing there. She let out a scream and rushed down the stairs, almost falling in the process.

Within hours, she was back in her old room on the second floor, and ten horses wouldn't get her up into the attic again.

But her troubles were far from over even on the second floor. The water kept turning itself on day and night. Her alarm clock was unplugged. Jewelry disappeared and could not be found despite careful and exhaustive search. The next day it would be back at the same spot it disappeared from.

Soon the phenomena spread to other members of the family. Mrs. Evelyn Kennedy, suffering from arthritis and a bad heart, would sometimes be unable to bend down because of swollen legs. One day she found herself all alone in the house. Her shoes were always kept under a chest of drawers in the bedroom. That day the shoes had somehow been pushed too far back under the chest and she could not reach them.

"Oh my," she said out loud. "I wish I could get at my shoes. What shall I do?"

With that she entered her bathroom for a shower. Afterwards, as she opened the bathroom door, the door hit something solid. She looked down. Someone had placed her shoes, which a few minutes before had been under the chest of drawers in her room, in front of the bathroom door. Yet she was alone in the house.

Mrs. Kennedy put two and two together. Who was the woman in the blue robe that had frightened her daughter Penny?

Cautiously, she called the landlady, Mrs. Naugle, and explained what had happened.

"Oh my God," the lady sighed, "that sounds just like my sister. She was laid out in a blue robe." But she would not discuss this any further. It upset her, and she wanted no part of it.

Shortly after, Mrs. Kennedy was ironing downstairs in the parlor. All of a sudden a heavy object shot out of the door jamb and narrowly missed her. She stopped working and examined the object. It was a homemade pin of some sort. When she showed it to the landlady, the latter turned away, advising her to destroy the object. It was even harder to talk about the house after that incident.

Sobbing sounds were soon heard in the dining room when it was completely empty. Up in the attic the family would hear the sound of someone dragging legs, someone crippled, and they remembered in terror how the late Mrs. McBride had been thus afflicted. Was this her ghost, they wondered?

They had scarcely enough time to worry about what to do about all this that had suddenly burst upon them, when Mrs. Kennedy got to talking to the mailman, Mr. Packen, who lived nearby. Somehow the talk turned to psychic phenomena and the mailman nodded gravely.

"I seen her, too," he confided, "back in '63, I seen her sweeping the pavement. Right in front of the house. I seen her."

"Who have you seen?" asked Mrs. Kennedy, as if she didn't know.

"Who but that lady, Mrs. McBride?" the mailman answered. "Big as life she was."

He in turn had been no stranger to this sort of thing. In his own house down the street he once saw a little old lady who seemed strangely familiar. As a mailman, he knows most of his "customers" well enough and the little old lady in his house rang a bell.

"What are you doing in my house?" he demanded. "You're supposed to be dead!"

Reproachfully he glanced at her and she nodded sadly and

dissolved into the evening mist. So it wasn't particularly shocking for him to hear about the goings-on at the Kennedy house.

The little old lady who had visited the mailman apparently had some business of her own, and as it is unfinished business that keeps these denizens of the netherworld from going on into the Great Beyond, he wondered what it was she had wanted.

One afternoon, ten-year-old Debra was playing in the downstairs parlor, when she felt herself not alone. In looking up she saw a little old lady standing in the room. Wearing black clothes, she seemed strangely old-fashioned and unreal to her, but there was no doubt in Debra's mind that she had a visitor. While she rose to meet the stranger, the woman disappeared. Having heard of her Aunt Penny's encounter with the lady on the stairs, she knew at once that this was not the same person. Whereas the lady on the stairs had been tall and smiling, this woman was short and bent and quizzical in her expression.

The excitement of this vision had hardly died down when Mrs. Kennedy found her work in the kitchen interrupted by the feeling that she was about to have a visitor. Since she was alone in the house at the moment, she immediately proceeded to the front door to open it. Without thinking anything special, she opened the front door and standing there was a lady. She was short of stature, her dress had big, puffed sleeves, she wore gloves, and carried a big black umbrella. Mrs. Kennedy also noticed a golden pin and the bustle of her dress. In particular, she was astonished to see her large hat, in a style no woman would wear today.

As she still wondered who this strange woman might be, she motioned to her to come in, which the woman did, brushing past her. Only then did it occur to Mrs. Kennedy that she had *not* heard the doorbell ring! Turning around and going after her visitor, she found that no one had come in.

Now she, too, realized that someone other than the late Mrs. McBride, if indeed it was she, kept coming to the house. It was the mailman's friend; strange as it might seem, but from the description she was sure it was the same person.

The mystery deepened even further when Debra reported seeing a man in the kitchen at a time when no man was in the house. The man had worn a blue shirt and brown pants, but they were not the sort of clothes worn by people today. He stood in a corner of the kitchen as if he belonged there and though Debra was frightened, she managed to see enough of the wraith before he faded away again.

It was a Monday night some weeks after this experience that Claudia and Penny were alone on the stairs. Mr. Kennedy and the two grandchildren were already in bed in their rooms. All the lights were out and only the street lights cast a reflection of sorts into the house through the windows. Suddenly the two girls heard the sound of someone running from the kitchen toward the living room. They looked up and what they saw made their blood turn to ice: there in the dim light of the kitchen stood the outline of a very large man. With a huge leap, he came after them. Faster than lightning, they ran up the stairs, with the shadowy man in hot pursuit. As they looked back in sheer terror, they saw him coming, but he stopped at the landing. Then he was gone, like a puff of smoke.

From that moment on, the two young women refused to stay downstairs at night.

The downstairs parlor was as "unsafe" from the incursions of the ghosts as was the attic, and before long even the backyard was no longer free from whatever it was that wanted attention. It was almost as if the unseen forces were engaged in a campaign of mounting terror to drive home the feeling that *the ghosts*—not the Kennedys—were in possession of the house.

Lights would go on and off by themselves. Water started to gush in the bathroom and when they investigated they found someone unseen had turned the tap on. Late at night they often heard someone cry softly in their backyard. Enough light from the windows illuminated that plot of land to assure them that it was no human agent. They huddled together, frightened, desolate, and yet unwilling to give up the house they truly loved. The attic was particularly active during those weeks immediately following the landlady's decision to sell their house. Someone was moving heavy furniture around up there at night—or so it sounded. Nothing ever was changed in the morning. Mrs. Kennedy sought the advice of a good friend, Mrs. Lucille Hags, who had been to the house often.

One evening, when things had been particularly active, Evelyn Kennedy dialed her friend. The soothing voice at the other end of the phone momentarily calmed her. But then she clearly heard someone else dialing her phone.

"Are you dialing?" she asked her friend, but Mrs. Hags had not touched her telephone either. Perhaps there had been some kind of cross-connection. Mrs. Kennedy decided to ignore it and bravely started to tell her friend what had happened that evening at the house.

"I wonder if it has something to do with Mrs. McBride," she ventured. No sooner had she said this, when heavy breathing, the breath of someone very close by, struck her ear.

"Do you hear that?" she asked, somewhat out of breath now herself.

"Yes, I did," said Mrs. Hags. Six times the heavy breathing interfered with their telephone conversation during the following weeks. Each time it started the moment either of them mentioned the phenomena in the house. Was one of their ghostly tenants listening in? So it would seem. The telephone people assured Mrs. Kennedy there was nothing wrong with her line.

Nothing wrong? she asked herself. Everything was wrong; the house was all wrong and what were they to do?

One sunny morning she decided to fight back. After all, this had been their happy home for a while now and no phantoms were going to drive them out of it. She tried to reason it out but no matter how many of the noises she could explain by ordinary causes, so many things remained that simply could not be explained away. There were, as far as she could make out, three ghosts in the house. The two women and the heavy-set man. She wasn't quite sure who the man was, and yet it seemed to her it must be Vander, whose money had always been hidden up there in the attic. Had he returned for it, or was he simply staying on because he didn't like the way he left? Those were the questions racing through Mrs. Kennedy's mind often now.

To be sure, at least one of the Stay-Behinds was friendly.

There was the time Mrs. Kennedy slipped on the stairs and was about to fall headlong down the whole flight of stairs. It was a warm summer day and she was alone at home, so that she would have lain there helpless had she injured herself. But something kept her from falling! Some force stronger than gravity held on to her skirts and pulled her back onto her feet. It wasn't her imagination and it wasn't a supreme effort of her own that did it. She was already halfway into the air, falling, when she was yanked back, upright.

Shortly after, she managed to repair to the attic, where her hair-drying equipment was stored. As she sat there, resting, she suddenly felt something wet and cold across her legs. She reached down only to feel a soft, moist mass that dissolved rapidly at her touch. This was enough to give her the willies, and she began to fear for her life, bad heart and all.

And yet, when the prospective buyers came more frequently to look at the house, and it seemed that the house might be sold after all, she found herself turning to her ghostly protector.

"Please, Mrs. McBride," she prayed silently, "don't let her sell the house!"

As if by a miracle, the most interested buyer, who had been close to a decision in favor of taking the house, went away and was never seen again. The house remained unsold. Coincidence? If there be such things, perhaps. But not to Mrs. Kennedy.

She did not particularly care to have word of their predicament get around. It was bad enough to have ghosts, but to be known as a haunted family was even worse. And yet how could it be avoided? It wasn't just she and her two daughters who experienced these strange things. Even her husband, who wasn't exactly given to belief in ghosts, was impressed when he saw a chair move from under a desk by its own force. He tried it several times afterward, hoping he could duplicate the phenomena by merely stomping his feet or gently touching the chair, but it required full force to move it.

The insurance man who had been servicing them for years was just as doubtful about the whole thing when he heard about it. "No such thing as a ghost," he commented as he stood in the hallway. At this moment the banister started to vibrate to such an extent they thought it would explode. He grabbed his hat and took his doubts to the nearest bar.

Sandra, a friend, had been sitting with Mrs. Kennedy downstairs not long ago, when suddenly she clearly heard someone in the bedroom overhead, the footsteps of someone running across it.

"I didn't know you had other company," she remarked to Mrs. Kennedy.

"I don't," Mrs. Kennedy answered dryly, and the friend left, somewhat faster than she had planned to.

Penny, twenty-one years old and single, turned out to be more psychic than any of them. Hardly had she recovered from her terrible experience on the stairs when something even more unspeakable occurred. One evening, as she was retiring for the night and had the lights turned off in her room, she felt something cold lie down in bed beside her. With a scream she jumped out and switched the lights back on. There was nothing, but a chill still pervaded the entire area.

In the summer of 1967, Penny found herself alone on the stairs on one occasion, when she suddenly heard a voice speak to her. "It's all right . . . she can come out now," a woman said somewhere in back of her. There was no one visible who could have spoken these words and no one nearby. Besides, it was not a voice she recognized. It sounded strangely hollow and yet imperious at the same time. Someone was giving an order, but who, and to whom? Clearly, this someone still considered herself mistress of this house.

Although Penny had no particular interest in psychic matters, she wondered about these phenomena. Who was the man she had seen on the stairs? Who was the woman whose voice she had heard?

Somewhere she read an advertisement for a pendulum as an aide to psychic perception. As soon as it had come in the mail, she retired to her room and tried it out. Holding the pendulum over a piece of board, she intoned, more in jest than for serious research reasons, "Mr. Vander, are you here?"

With a swift move, the pendulum was ripped from her hands and landed clear across the room. She hasn't used it since, nor does she really care if Mr. Vander is the ghost she saw. She just wants to be left alone.

Somehow the summer passed, and it was in September 1967 that Mrs. Kennedy realized there was more to this triangle of ghosts than just their presence. She was standing outside, chatting with a neighbor.

"Are the children having a party?" the neighbor asked.

"Why, no," she replied, knowing full well the children were all out of the house at the moment.

She was wondering why her neighbor had asked such a peculiar question, and was about to say so, when she heard a loud noise coming from the empty house; it sounded indeed as if a group of children were having a party upstairs, running up and down in the house. All she could do was shrug and turn away.

Maria, the three-year-old, was a precocious youngster who spoke better than her years would call for. One day she accompanied her grandmother to the attic. While Mrs. Kennedy was busy with her chores in the front room, the little girl played in the rear of the attic. Suddenly she came running out of the back room and beckoned her grandmother to follow her.

"There is a nice lady back there and she likes me," she explained.

Immediately Mrs. Kennedy went back, but she saw nothing this time.

Whether this visit to the attic had stirred up some sort of psychic contact, or whether her growing years now allowed her to express herself more clearly, the little girl had something more to say about the ghosts before long. Naturally, no one discussed such matters with her. Why frighten the child?

"There is a little boy in the attic," Maria explained earnestly, "and his name is Yackie. He died up there. He plays snowball out the window because he isn't allowed out of the attic."

At first these stories were dismissed as the fantasies of a child. Mrs. Kennedy was even a bit amused about the way Maria said "Yackie" instead of Jackie. They did not wish to stop her from telling this story over and over, out of fear that repressing her might make it seem more interesting. But as the weeks went on the little girl developed a strange affinity for the attic, especially the rear portion.

"Why are you always running up there, Maria?" her grandmother finally asked.

"Because," the little girl said, and became agitated, "because there is a man up there. Yackie told me about him."

"What about this man?"

"He died. He was shot in the head and all of his blood came out and he's buried in the backyard under the bushes."

"Why was he shot in the head, child?" the grandmother asked, almost as if she believed the story.

"Because he was crazy and he cried, that's why," the child replied. Her grandmother was silent for a moment, trying to sort things out.

Could a three-year-old make up such a yarn? she wondered.

"Come," the little girl said, and took her by the hand, "I'll show you." She led Mrs. Kennedy to the dining room window and pointed at the bushes in their backyard.

"It's under the bushes there," Maria repeated and stared out the window.

Mrs. Kennedy shuddered. It was a spot she had wondered about many times. No matter how she tried, no matter what she planted, *nothing would grow on that spot!*

But as it turned colder, the house seemed to settle down and the disturbances faded away. True, no one came to inquire about buying it either. The Kennedys half believed their troubles might just have faded away, both their worldly and their unworldly difficulties.

They thought less and less about them and a spark of hope returned to Mrs. Kennedy about staying on at the house. She tried to make some discreet inquiries about the former owners of the house and even attempted to find the official records and deeds of sale. But her efforts were thwarted on all sides. Neighbors suddenly turned pale and would not discuss the matter. Nobody admitted knowing anything at all about the Mr. Vander. Why, for instance, had she been told he left no children when he died? Only accidentally did she discover that there were three children. Was one of them named Jackie perhaps? She could not be sure.

The winter came, and a bitterly cold winter it was. Late in January, her composure was rudely shattered when a representative of the real estate agent paid them a visit. The house was being offered for sale once again.

That day one of her married daughters was visiting Mrs. Kennedy. She had brought her baby along and needed some toys for it to play with. "Go up into the attic. There's plenty of stuff there," Mrs. Kennedy suggested.

The woman, accompanied by her sister Claudia, went up into the attic. She was barefoot and casually dressed. Suddenly, Claudia pushed her to one side. "Watch out," she said and pointed to the floor boards. There, stuck between two boards, with the cutting edge pointing up, was a single-edged razor blade.

Somewhat shaken by their experience, the two women went back downstairs, after having pulled the blade out of the floor with some difficulty. It had been shoved into the crack between the boards with considerable strength. Nobody in the house used single-edged razor blades. In fact, few people do nowadays. The only man in the house uses an electric shaver.

Suddenly, the activities started all over. The front door would continually open and shut by itself, and there was never anyone there when someone went to check. This happened mainly at night and in each case Mrs. Kennedy found the door securely locked. The door she and the others heard open was not a physical door, apparently, but an echo from the past!

The Kennedys were patient for several days, then they decided that something had to be done. It was a nice house all right, but sooner or later someone would buy it, and unfortunately they couldn't afford to buy it themselves. Since they could neither stop the landlady from trying to sell it, nor the ghostly inhabitants from playing in it, it was perhaps the wisest thing to look for another home.

By April they had finally found a nice house in nearby Penn Hills, and the moment they set foot in it they knew it would do fine. With her deeply developed psychic sense Mrs. Kennedy also knew at once that she would have no problems with unseen visitors in *that* house.

It gave them a degree of pleasure to be moving out on their landlady rather than waiting to be evicted by the new owner. Gradually their belongings were moved to their new home.

On the last day, when almost everything had already been removed, Mrs. Kennedy, her husband, and their son, who had come to help them move, stood in the now almost empty house once more. There were still a few boxes left in the cellar. The two men went back into the cellar to get them out, while Mrs. Kennedy waited for them upstairs.

"Come," Mr. Kennedy said, and shivered in the spring air, "it's late. Let's finish up."

The clock of a nearby church started to strike twelve midnight.

They loaded the boxes into the car, carefully locked the front door of the house and then the garden gate.

At this precise moment, all three clearly heard the front door open and close again, and loud steps reverberate inside the empty house.

"There must be someone in there," Mrs. Kennedy's son murmured. He did not believe in ghosts and had always pooh-poohed the tales told by his mother and sisters.

Quickly he unlocked the gate and front door once more and reentered the dark house.

After a few moments, he returned, relocked house and gate, and, somewhat sheepishly, shook his head.

"Nothing. It's all empty."

Not at all, Mrs. Kennedy thought, as the car pulled out into the night, not at all.

That was only the reception committee for the next tenant.

The Dispossessed Ghost

O nly a small fraction of ghosts are "fortunate" enough to be relieved of their status by an investigation in which they are freed from their surroundings and allowed to go into the greater reaches of the World Beyond. The majority have no choice but to cling to the environment in which their tragedy has occurred. But what about those who are in an environment that suddenly ceases to exist? As far as houses are concerned, tearing down one house and building another on the spot doesn't alter the situation much. Frequently, ghosts continue to exist in the new house, even more confused than they were in the old one. But if the environment is radically changed and no new dwelling is erected on the spot, what is there to occupy the ghost in his search for identity?

Mrs. Robert B., mother of four children, leads a busy life in Pittsburgh. Because of her interest in parapsychology, she was able to assist her parents in a most unusual case. In a small town north of Pittsburgh on the Ohio River, her parents occupied a house built approximately seventy-five years ago. They were the second owners, the house having been planned and partially built by the original owner, a certain Daniel W.

Mr. W. had lived in the house with his brother and sister for many years, and had died a bachelor at the age of ninety-four. His last illness was a long one, and his funeral was held in what later became the living room of Mrs. B.'s parents. Thus, Mr. W. not only "gave birth" to the little house, but he lived in it for such a long period that he must have become very attached to it, and formed one of those rare bonds that frequently lead to Stay-Behinds, people who live and die in their houses and just don't feel like leaving them.

One spring, Mrs. B.'s parents decided to remodel the house somewhat. In particular, they tore through the wall connecting her mother's bedroom with that of her father, which was next to it. Each room had a cupboard in it, but instead they decided to build a new closet with sliding doors. Although they had occupied the house for fourteen years, this was the first change they had made in it.

One week after the alteration had been completed, Mrs. B.'s mother found it difficult to fall asleep. It was toward one o'clock in the morning and she had been tossing for hours. Suddenly, from the direction of the cupboard in the left-hand corner of the room, came the sound of heavy breathing. This startled her, as she could also hear her husband's breathing from the room next to hers. The mysterious breathing was husky, labored, and sounded as though it came from an echo chamber. Frightened, she lay still and listened. To her horror, the breathing sound moved across the room and stopped in front of the bureau against the far wall. Then, as she concentrated on that spot, she saw a mist starting to form above the chest. At this point, she managed to switch on the light and call out, "Who is there?" Immediately, the breathing stopped.

Mrs. B.'s mother then called Mrs. B., knowing of her interest in the occult, and reported the incident to her. Her daughter advised her not to be alarmed, but to watch out for further occurrences, which were bound to happen. Sure enough, a few days later a curtain was pulled back in full view of her mother, as if by an unseen hand, yet no window was open that would have accounted for it. Shortly thereafter, a chair in the living room sagged as if someone were sitting in it, yet no one was visible. That was enough for one day! A few days later, a window was lowered in the hall while Mrs. B.'s mother was talking to her on the telephone and there was no one else in the house. Shadowlike streaks began to appear on the dining room and living room floors; a Japanese print hanging in the living room, two by four feet in size and very heavy, moved of its own volition on the wall. Mrs. B.'s father began to hear the heavy breathing on his side of the dividing wall, but as soon as he had taken notice of it, it moved to the foot of his bed.

By now it was clear to both parents that they had a ghost in the house; they suspected the original owner. Evidently he was displeased with the alterations in the house, and this was his way of letting them know. Mr. W.'s continued presence in the house also shook up their dog. Frequently she would stand in the hall downstairs and bark in the direction of the stairs, with the hair on her back bristled, unable to move up those stairs. At times she would run through the house as if someone were chasing her—someone unseen, that is.

It looked as if Mrs. B.'s parents would have to get used to the continued presence of the original owner of the house, when the authorities decided to run a six-lane state highway through the area, eliminating about half of the little town in which they lived, including their house. This has since been done, and the house exists no more. But what about Mr. W.? If he couldn't stand the idea of minor alterations in his house, what about the six-lane highway eliminating it altogether?

Ghosts, as a rule, do not move around much. They may be seen in one part of the house or another, not necessarily in the room in which they died as people, but there are no cases on record in which ghosts have traveled any kind of distance to manifest.

The Ghost Who Did Not Like Ghosts

Mrs. S. F. works in an assembly plant, putting together electronic parts. She is a middle-aged woman of average educational background, is divorced, and is living in a house in central Pennsylvania. A native of Pittsburgh, she went to public school in that city where her father worked for a steel company, and she has several brothers and sisters.

When she was fourteen years of age, she had her first remembered psychic experience. In the old house her parents then lived in, she saw a column of white smoke in front of her, but since she didn't understand it, it didn't bother her, and she went off to sleep anyway.

Many times she would get impressions of future events and foretell things long before they happened, but she paid little attention to her special gift. It was only when she moved into her present house that the matter took on new dimensions.

The house Mrs. F. moved into is a small house, two stories high, connected to two similar houses by what is locally called a party wall, in which two houses share the same wall. Two rooms are downstairs and two rooms are upstairs. Her house has its bathroom down in the cellar, and when you first enter it, you are in the living room, then the kitchen. Upstairs there are two bedrooms, with the stairs going up from the kitchen. There is no attic; the house is small and compact, and it was just the thing Mrs. F. needed since she was going to live in it alone. The house next door was similar to hers, and it belonged to a woman whose husband had passed away some time previously. Next to that was another similar house in which some of the widowed woman's family lived at the time Mrs. F. moved in. There were four houses in all, all identical and connected by "party walls." The four houses share a common ground, and seemed rather old to her when she first saw them.

When Mrs. F. moved into the house, she decided to sleep in the bedroom in back of the upper story and she put her double bed into it. But after she had moved into the house, she discovered that the back room was too cold in the winter and too hot in the summer, so she decided to sleep in the front room, which had twin beds in it. Depending upon the temperature, she would switch from one bedroom to the other. Nothing much out of the ordinary happened to her at first, or perhaps she was too busy to notice.

Then one spring night, when she was asleep in the back bedroom, she woke from her sound sleep around four o'clock in the morning. Her eyes were open, and as she looked up, she saw a man bending over her, close to her face. She could see that he had a ruddy complexion, a high forehead, and was partly bald with white hair around his ears.

When he noticed that she was looking at him, he gave her a cold stare and then slowly drifted back away from her until he disappeared. She could not see the rest of his body, but had the vague impression of some sort of robe. Immediately Mrs. F. thought she had had a hallucination or had dreamed the whole thing, so she went back to sleep.

Not much later Mrs. F. was in bed, reading. It was around two-thirty in the morning. The reading lamp was on, as was the light in the hall, when she suddenly heard a swishlike sound followed by a thump. At the same time something punched her bed, and then hit her in the head. She clearly felt a human hand in the area of her eye, but could not see anything. Immediately she wondered what could have hit her. There was no one in the room but her. After a while, she dismissed the matter from her mind and went back to reading.

A few days later, when she was reading again in the late hours of the night, she noticed that the bed would go down as if someone had sat on it. It clearly showed the indentation of a human body, yet she could not see anything. This disturbed her, but she decided to pay it no attention—until one night she also heard a man's voice coming to her as if from an echo chamber. It sounded as if someone were trying to talk to her but couldn't get the words out properly, like a muffled "hello."

Mrs. F. never felt comfortable in the back bedroom, so she decided to move into the front room. One night she was in bed in that room when her eyes apparently opened by themselves and rested on a cupboard door across from the bed. This time she clearly saw the figure of a man, but she couldn't make out legs or feet. It was a dark silhouette, but she could clearly see his rather pointed ears. His most outstanding features were his burning eyes and those strangely pointed ears. When he saw her looking at him, he moved back into the door and disappeared.

Again, Mrs. F. refused to acknowledge that she had a ghost, but thought it was all a hallucination since she had been awakened from a deep sleep. Not much later, she happened to be watching television a little after midnight. As she got up to get some potato chips from a cupboard in the corner, she happened to glance at the wall in the hallway as she rounded the bend of the hall. There was the same man again. She could clearly make out his face and the pointed ears, but again he had neither legs nor feet. As soon as the ghost realized that she had discovered him, he quickly moved back into the wall and disappeared. Now Mrs. F.'s composure was gone; clearly, the apparition was not a hallucination, since she was fully awake now and could not blame her dreams for it.

While she was still debating within herself what this all meant, she had another experience. She happened to be in bed reading when she thought she heard something move in the kitchen. It sounded like indistinct movements, so she tried to listen, but after awhile she didn't hear anything further and went back to reading. A little while later she decided to go down to get a fruit drink out of the refrigerator. The hall lights were on, so the kitchen wasn't too dark. Just the same, when she reached the kitchen, Mrs. F. turned on the fluorescent lights. As soon as the lights came on, she saw the same ghostly apparition standing there in the kitchen, only this time there was a whole view of him, with feet, legs, and even shoes with rounded toes. He wore pants and a shirt, and she could see his color; she could see that he had curly hair, a straight nose, and full lips. She particularly noticed the full lips, and, of course, the pointed ears.

At first the apparition must have been startled by her, perhaps because he had thought that it was the cat coming down the stairs into the kitchen. He turned toward her and Mrs. F. could see his profile. As soon as he noticed her, he ran into the wall and disappeared. But she noticed that his legs started to shake when the lights went on, as if he were trying to get going and didn't quite know how. Then he hunched over a little, and shot into the wall.

Mrs. F. was shocked. She shut off the light and went back to bed. For a long time she just lay there, with the eeriest, chilliest feeling. Eventually she drifted off to sleep again. The entire incident puzzled her, for she had no idea who the ghost might be. One day she was leaving her house, and as she passed her neighbor's house, there was a young man sitting on the steps looking out into the street. She saw his profile, and like a flash it went through her mind that it was the same profile as that of the man she had seen in her kitchen! She looked again, and noticed the same full lips and the same pointed ears she had seen in the face of the ghost!

Immediately she decided to discuss the matter with a neighbor, Mrs. J. M. Mrs. M. lived at the end of the street, and she was a good person to talk to because she understood about such matters. In fact, Mrs. F. had spent a night at her house at one time when she was particularly upset by the goings-on in her *own* house. The neighbor assured her that the widow's son, the one she had seen sitting on the steps, was the very image of his father. The reason Mrs. F. had not seen him before was that he was married and lived somewhere else, and had just been visiting on that particular day.

Well, Mrs. F. put two and two together, and realized that the ghost she had seen was her late neighbor. On making further inquiries, she discovered that the man had suffered from rheumatic fever, and had been in the habit of lying on a couch to watch television. One day his family had awakened him so he wouldn't miss his favorite program. At that moment he had a heart attack, and died right there on the couch. He was only middle-aged.

With this information in her hands, Mrs. F. wondered what she could do about ridding herself of the unwelcome visitor from next door. In August a niece was visiting her with some friends and other relatives. One of the people in the group was an amateur medium, who suggested that they try their hand at a seance. There were about seven in the group, and they sat down and tried to make contact with the late neighbor. The seance was held in the upstairs bedroom, and they used a card table borrowed from Mrs. M. from the other end of the street.

They all put their hands on the table, and immediately felt that the table was rising up. Nothing much happened beyond that, however, and eventually the amateur medium had to leave. But Mrs. F. wanted an answer to her problem, so she continued with those who were still visiting with her. They moved the table down into the kitchen, turned out all the lights but one, and waited. Mrs. F. asked the ghost questions: who he was, what he wanted, and so on. Sure enough, her questions were answered by knocks. Everybody could hear them, and after awhile they managed to get a conversation going. From this communication, Mrs. F. learned that her neighbor had been forty-three years old when he died, that his name was Bill, and that he wasn't very happy being dead! But apparently he appreciated the fact that they had tried to get through to him because he never appeared to Mrs. F. again after that.

Terror
on the Stairs

$\mathbb{S}$ omerset is one of those nondescript small towns that abound in rural Pennsylvania and that boast nothing more exciting than a few thousand homes, a few churches, a club or two, and a lot of hardworking people whose lives pass under pretty ordinary and often drab circumstances. Those who leave may go on to better things in the big cities of the East, and those who stay have the comparative security of being among their own and living out their lives peacefully. But then there are those who leave not because they want to but because they are driven by irresistible forces greater than themselves.

The Manners are middle-aged people with two children, a fourteen-year-old son and a six-year-old daughter. The husband ran a television and radio shop, which gave them an average income, neither below middle-class standards for a small town, nor much above it. Although Catholic, they did not consider themselves particularly religious. Mrs. Manner's people originally came from Austria, so there was enough European background in the family to give their lives a slight continental tinge, but other than that, they were and are typical Pennsylvania people without the slightest interest in, or knowledge of, such matters as psychic research.

Of course, the occult was never unknown to Mrs. Manner. She was born with a veil over her eyes, which to many means the Second Sight. Her ability to see things before they happened was not "precognition" to her, but merely a special talent she took in her stride. One night she had a vivid dream about her son, then miles away in the army. She vividly saw him walking down a hall in a bathrobe, with blood running down his leg. Shortly after she awakened the next day, she was notified that her son had been attacked by a rattlesnake and, when found, was near death. One night she awoke to see an image of her sister standing beside her bed. There was nothing fearful about the apparition, but she was dressed all in black.

The next day that sister died.

But these instances did not frighten Mrs. Manner; they were glimpses into eternity and nothing more.

As the years went by, the Manners accumulated enough funds to look for a more comfortable home than the one they were occupying, and as luck—or fate—would have it, one day in 1966 they were offered a fine, old house in one of the better parts of town. The house seemed in excellent condition; it had the appearance of a Victorian home with all the lovely touches of that bygone era about it. It had stood empty for two years, and since it belonged to an estate, the executors seemed anxious to finally sell the house. The Manners made no special inquiries about their projected new home simply because everything seemed so right and pleasant. The former owners had been wealthy people, they were informed, and had lavished much money and love on the house.

When the price was quoted to them, the Manners looked at each other in disbelief. It was far below what they had expected for such a splendid house. "We'll take it," they said, almost in unison, and soon the house was theirs.

"Why do you suppose we got it for such a ridiculously low price?" Mr. Manner mused, but his wife could only shrug. To her, that was not at all important. She believed one should never look a gift horse in the mouth.

It was late summer when they finally moved into their newly acquired home. Hardly had they been installed when Mrs. Manner knew there was something not right with the place. From the very first, she felt uncomfortable in it, but being a sensible person, she had put it down to being in a new and unaccustomed place. But as this feeling persisted she realized that she was being *watched* by some unseen force all the time, day and night, and her nerves began to tense under the strain.

The very first night she spent in the house, she was aroused at exactly two o'clock in the morning, seemingly for no reason. Her hair stood up on her arms and chills shook her body. Again, she put this down to having worked so hard getting the new home into shape.

But the "witching hour" of two A.M. kept awakening her with the same uncanny feeling that something was wrong, and instinctively she knew it was not her or someone in her family, who was in trouble, but the new house.

With doubled vigor, she put all her energies into polishing furniture and getting the rooms into proper condition. That way, she was very tired and hoped to sleep through the night. But no matter how physically exhausted she was, at two o'clock the uncanny feeling awoke her.

The first week somehow passed despite this eerie feeling, and Monday rolled around again. In the bright light of the late-summer day, the house somehow seemed friendlier and her fears of the night had vanished.

She was preparing breakfast in the kitchen for her children that Monday morning. As she was buttering a piece of toast for her little girl, she happened to glance up toward the doorway. There, immaculately dressed, stood a man. The stranger, she noticed, wore shiny black shoes, navy blue pants, and a white shirt. She even made out his striped tie, and then went on to observe the man's face. The picture was so clear she could make out the way the man's snowy white hair was parted.

Her immediate reaction was that he had somehow entered the house, and she was about to say hello when it occurred to her that she had not heard the opening of a door or any other sound—no footfalls, no steps.

"Look," she said to her son, whose back was turned to the apparition, but by the time her children turned around, the man was gone like a puff of smoke.

Mrs. Manner was not too frightened by what she had witnessed, although she realized her visitor had not been of the flesh-and-blood variety. When she told her husband about it that evening, he laughed.

Ghosts, indeed!

The matter would have rested there had it not been for the fact that the very next day something else happened. Mrs. Manner was on her way into the kitchen from the backyard of the house, when she suddenly saw a woman go past her refrigerator. This time the materialization was not as perfect. Only half of the body was visible, but she noticed her shoes, dress up to the knees, and that the figure seemed in a hurry.

This still did not frighten her, but she began to wonder. All those eerie feelings seemed to add up now. What had they gotten themselves into by buying this house? No wonder it was so cheap. It was haunted!

Mrs. Manner was a practical person, the uncanny experiences notwithstanding, or perhaps because of them. They had paid good money for the house and no specters were going to dislodge them!

But the fight had just begun. A strange kind of web began to envelop her frequently, as if some unseen force were trying to wrap her in a wet, cold blanket. When she touched the "web," there was nothing to be seen or felt, and yet the clammy, cold force was still with her. A strange scent of flowers manifested itself out of nowhere and followed her from room to room. Soon her husband smelled it too, and his laughing stopped. He, too, became concerned: their children must not be frightened by whatever it was that was present in the house.

It soon was impossible to keep doors locked. No matter how often they would lock a door in the house, it was found wide open soon afterward, the locks turned by unseen hands. One particular center of activities was the old china closet, and the scent of flowers was especially strong in its vicinity.

"What are we going to do about this?" Mrs. Manner asked her husband one night. They decided to find out more about the house, as a starter. They had hesitated to mention anything about their plight out of fear of being ridiculed or thought unbalanced. In a small town, people don't like to talk about ghosts.

The first person Mrs. Manner turned to was a neighbor who had lived down the street for many years. When she noticed that the neighbor did not pull back at the mention of weird goings-on in the house, but, to the contrary, seemed genuinely interested, Mrs. Manner poured out her heart and described what she had seen. In particular, she took great pains to describe the two apparitions. The neighbor nodded gravely.

"It's them, all right," she said, and started to fill Mrs. Manner in on the history of their house. This was the first time Mrs. Manner had heard of it and the description of the man she had seen tallied completely with the appearance of the man who had owned the house before.

"He died here," the neighbor explained. "They really loved their home, he and his wife. The old lady never wanted to leave or sell it."

"But what do you make of the strange scent of flowers?" Mrs. Manner asked.

"The old lady loved flowers, had fresh ones in the house every day."

Relieved to know what it was all about, but hardly happy at the prospect of sharing her house with ghosts, Mrs. Manner then went to see the chief of police in the hope of finding some way of getting rid of her unwanted "guests."

The chief scratched his head.

"Ghosts?" he said, not at all jokingly. "You've got me there. That's not my territory."

But he promised to send an extra patrol around in case it was just old-fashioned burglars.

Mrs. Manner thanked him and left. She knew otherwise and realized the police would not be able to help her.

She decided they had to learn to live with their ghosts, especially as the latter had been in the house before them. Perhaps it wouldn't be so bad after all, she mused, now that they knew who it was that would not leave.

Perhaps one could even become friendly, sort of one big, happy family, half people, half ghosts? But she immediately rejected the notion. What about the children? So far, they had not *seen* them, but they knew of the doors that wouldn't stay shut and the other uncanny phenomena.

Fortunately, Mrs. Manner did not understand the nature of Poltergeists. Had she realized that the very presence of her teenage son was in part responsible for the physical nature of the happenings, she would no doubt have sent him away. But the phenomena continued unabated, day and night.

One night at dinner, with everyone accounted for, an enormous crash shook the house. It felt as if a ton of glass had fallen on the kitchen floor. When they rushed into the kitchen, they found everything in order, nothing misplaced.

At this point, Mrs. Manner fell back on her early religious world.

"Maybe we should call the minister?" she suggested, and no sooner said than done. The following day, the minister came to their house. When he had heard their story, he nodded quietly and said a silent prayer for the souls of the disturbed ones.

He had a special reason to do so, it developed. They had been among his parishioners when alive. In fact, he had been to their home for dinner many times, and the house was familiar to him despite the changes the present owners had made.

If anyone could, surely their own minister should be able to send those ghosts away.

Not by a long shot.

Either the couple did not put much stock into their minister's powers, or the pull of the house was stronger, but the phenomena continued. In fact, after the minister had tried to exorcise the ghosts, things got worse.

Many a night, the Manners ran out into the street when lights kept going on and off by themselves. Fortunately, the children slept through all this, but how long would they remain unaffected?

At times, the atmosphere was so thick Mrs. Manner could not get near the breakfast nook in the kitchen to clear the table. Enveloped by the strong vibrations, she felt herself tremble and on two occasions fainted and was thus found by her family.

They were seriously considering moving now, to let the original "owners" have the house again. They realized now that the house had never been truly "empty" for those two years the real estate man had said it was not in use.

It was 2 A.M. when they finally went up to bed. Things felt worse than ever before. Mrs. Manner clearly sensed *three* presences with her now and started to cry.

"I'm leaving this house," she exclaimed. "You can have it back!" Her husband had gone ahead of her up the stairs to get the bedding from the linen closet. She began to follow him and slowly went up the stairs. After she had climbed about halfway up, something forced her to turn around and look back.

What she saw has remained with her ever since, deeply impressed in her mind with the acid of stark fear.

Down below her on the stairway was a big, burly man, trying to pull himself up the stairs. His eyes were red with torture as he tried to talk to her. Evidently he had been hurt, for his trousers and shirt were covered with mud. Or was it dried blood? He was trying to hang on to the banister and held his hands out toward her.

"Oh, God, it can't be true," she thought and went up a few more steps. Then she dared look down again.

The man was still holding out his hand in a desperate move to get her attention. When she failed to respond, he threw it down in a gesture of impatience and frustration. With a piercing scream, she ran up the stairs to her husband, weeping out of control.

The house had been firmly locked and no one could have gained entrance. Not that they thought the apparitions were flesh-and-blood people. The next morning, no trace of the nocturnal phenomenon could be found on the stairs. It was as if it had never happened.

But that morning, the Manners decided to pack and get out fast. "I want no more houses," Mrs. Manner said firmly, and so they bought a trailer. Meanwhile, they lived in an apartment.

But their furniture and all their belongings were still in the house, and it was necessary to go back a few more times to get them. They thought that since they had signed over the deed, it would be all right for them to go back. After all, it was no longer *their* house.

As Mrs. Manner cautiously ascended the stairs, she was still trembling with fear. Any moment now, the specter might confront her again. But all seemed calm. Suddenly, the scent of flowers was with her again and she knew the ghosts were still in residence. As if to answer her doubts, the doors to the china closet flew open at that moment.

Although she wanted nothing further to do with the old house, Mrs. Manner made some more inquiries. The terrible picture of the tortured man on the stairs did not leave her mind. Who was he, and what could she have done for him?

Then she heard that the estate wasn't really settled, the children were still fighting over it. Was that the reason the parents could not leave the house in peace? Was the man on the stairs someone who needed help, someone who had been hurt in the house?

"Forget it," the husband said, and they stored most of their furniture. The new house trailer would have no bad vibrations and they could travel wherever they wanted.

After they had moved into the trailer, they heard rumors that the new owners of their house had encountered problems also. But they did not care to hear about them and studiously stayed away from the house. That way, they felt, the ghosts would avoid them also, now that they were back in what used to be their beloved home!

But a few days later, Mrs. Manner noticed a strange scent of flowers wafting through her brand-new trailer. Since she had not bought any flowers, nor opened a perfume bottle, it puzzled her. Then, with a sudden impact that was almost crushing, she knew where and when she had smelled this scent before. It was the personal scent of the ghostly woman in the old house! Had she followed her here into the trailer?

When she discussed this new development with her husband that night, they decided to fumigate the trailer and get rid of the scent, if they could. Somehow they thought they might be mistaken and it was just coincidence. But the scent remained, clear and strong, and the feeling of a presence that came with it soon convinced them that they had not yet seen the last of the Somerset ghosts.

They sold the new trailer and bought another house, a fifty-seven-year-old rambling home in a nearby Pennsylvania town called Stoystown, far enough from Somerset to give them the hope that the Unseen Ones would not be able to follow them there.

Everything was fine after they had moved their furniture in and for the first time in many a month, the Manners could relax. But about two months after they had moved to Stoystown, the scent of flowers returned. Now it was accompanied by another smell, resembling burned matches.

The Manners were terrified. Was there no escape from the Uncanny? A few days later, Mrs. Manner observed a smokey form rise up in the house. Nobody had been smoking. The form roughly resembled the vague outlines of a human being.

Her husband, fortunately, experienced the smells also, so she was not alone in her plight. But the children, who had barely shaken off their terror, were now faced with renewed fears. They could not keep running, and running away from what?

They tried every means at their command. Holy water, incense, a minister's prayer, their own prayers, curses and commands to the Unseen, but the scent remained.

Gradually, they learned to live with their psychic problems. A mother possessed of definite mediumistic powers from youth and a young adult in the household are easy prey to those among the restless dead who desire a continued life of earthly activities. With the physical powers drawn from these living people, they play and continue to exist in a world of which they are no longer a part.

As the young man grew older, the available power dwindled and the scent was noticed less frequently. But the tortured man on the stairs of the house in Somerset will have to wait for a more willing medium to be set free.

The Banker
and the Ghost

I f there is anything more staid than a North Philadelphia banker I
wouldn't know it. But even bankers are human and sometimes
psychic. In William Davy's case there had been little or no occasion to consider such a matter except for one long-forgotten incident when he was eight years of age. At that time he lived with his
parents in Manchester, England. On one particular morning, little
William insisted that he saw a white shadow in the shape of a man
passing in front of the clock. The clock, it so happened, was just
striking the hour of 8:30 A.M. His mother, reminded by the sound
of the clock, hurriedly sent the boy off to school, telling him to
stop his foolishness about white shadows. By the time the boy
returned home, word had reached the house that his favorite
grandfather, who lived halfway across England in Devon, had
passed away. The time of his death was 8:30 A.M.

Eventually, Mr. Davy moved to Philadelphia, where he is an
officer in a local bank, much respected in the community and not
the least bit interested in psychic matters. His aged father, William Sr., came to live with him and his family in the home they
bought in 1955. The house is a splendid example of Victorian
architecture, built on three levels on a plot surrounded by tall
trees in what is now part of North Philadelphia, but what was at
the time the house was built a separate community, and originally
just farmland.

The ground floor has a large kitchen to one side, a large living
room, with fireplace, separated from a dining room by a sliding
double door. Upstairs are bedrooms on two floors, with the third
floor the one-time servants quarters, as was customary in Victorian houses. The Davy family did some remodeling downstairs,

but essentially the house is as it was when first built, sometime in the late 1880s, according to a local lawyer named Huston, who is an expert on such things. At any rate, in 1890 it already stood on the spot where it is today.

William Sr. was a true English gentleman given to historical research, and a lover of ghost stories, with which he liked to regale his family on many occasions. But what started as a purely literary exercise soon turned into grim reality. Shortly after his arrival, William Sr. complained of hearing unusual noises in the house. He had a room on the third floor and was constantly hearing strange noises and floorboards creaking as if someone were walking on them.

His son laughed at this and ascribed it to his father's vivid imagination, especially after his many fictional ghost stories had set the mood for that sort of thing. But the older Davy insisted to his last day that he was being troubled by an unseen entity. After he passed away in February 1963, Mr. and Mrs. Davy thought no more of the matter. The house was a peaceful home to them and they enjoyed life.

Several months later, Mr. Davy was sitting by himself in the living room, reading. The time was 10 P.M. and he was tired. He decided to call it a day, and got up to go to bed. As he walked toward the hallway between the living room and the staircase, he literally stepped into a cloud of pungent perfume, which he instantly identified as a very strong bayberry scent. For a moment he stood in utter amazement, then slowly continued into the hall and up the stairs. The perfume still surrounded him, as if someone invisible, wearing this heavy perfume, were walking alongside him!

Upon reaching the first landing he went into the bedroom. At that point, the perfume suddenly left him, just as suddenly as it had come.

"Mary," he asked his wife, "did you by any chance spill some perfume?" She shook her head emphatically. She did not even own any such scent, and there had been no one else in the house that day or evening.

Puzzled but not particularly upset, Mr. Davy let the matter drop and he would have forgotten it entirely had not another event taken him by surprise.

Several months later he was again sitting in the living room, the time being around 10 P.M. He put down his book, and went toward the hallway. Again, he walked into a heavy cloud of the same perfume. Again it followed him up the stairs. As he climbed he felt something—or someone—brush against his right leg. It made a swishing sound but he could not see anything that could have caused it. When he got to the landing, he stopped and asked Mary to come out to him.

His wife had suffered a fractured skull when she was young and as a consequence had lost about seventy percent of her sense of smell.

When Mary joined him at the landing, he asked her if she smelled anything peculiar. "Oh my word," she said, immediately, "what a heavy perfume!" They were standing there looking at each other in a puzzled state. "What on earth is it?" Mary finally asked. He could only shrug his shoulders.

At that precise moment, they clearly heard footsteps going up the stairs from where they were standing, to the third floor!

Since neither of them saw any person causing the footsteps, they were completely unnerved, and refused to investigate. They did not follow the footsteps up to the third floor. They knew only too well that there wasn't any living soul up there at the moment.

One evening Mary was reading in bed, on the second floor, when she found herself surrounded by the same bayberry perfume. It stayed for several seconds, then died away. Since she was quite alone in the house and had been all evening, this was not very reassuring. But the Davys are not the kind of people that panic easily, so she shrugged it off as something she simply could not explain. On another occasion, Mr. Davy saw a patch of dull, white light move through the living room. From the size of the small cloud it resembled in height either a large child or a small adult, more likely a woman than a man. This was at 3 A.M. when he had come downstairs because he could not sleep that night.

In April the Davys had gone to Williamsburg, Virginia for a visit. On their return, Mr. Davy decided to take the luggage directly upstairs to their bedroom. That instant he ran smack into the cloud of bayberry perfume. It was as if some unseen presence wanted to welcome them back!

One of Mary's favorite rings, which she had left in her room, disappeared only to be discovered later in the garden. How it got there was as much of a mystery then as it is now, but no one of flesh and blood moved that ring. Naturally the Davys did not discuss their unseen visitor with anyone. When you're a Philadelphia banker you don't talk about ghosts.

In September of the same year, they had a visit from their niece and her husband, Mr. and Mrs. Clarence Nowak. Mr. Nowak is a U.S. government employee, by profession a chemical engineer. Their own house was being readied, and while they were waiting to move in they spent two weeks with their uncle and aunt. The niece was staying on the second floor, while Mr. Nowak had been assigned the room on the third floor that had been the center of the ghostly activities in the past. After they had retired, Mr. Nowak started to read a book. When he got tired of this, he put the book down, put the lights out and got ready to doze off.

At that precise moment, he clearly heard footsteps coming up and he was so sure it was Mary coming up to say goodnight that he sat up and waited. But nobody came into his room and the footsteps continued!

Since he is a man of practical outlook, this puzzled him and he got out of bed and looked around. The corridor was quite empty, yet the footsteps continued right in front of him. Moreover, they seemed to enter the room itself and the sound of steps filled the atmosphere of the room as if someone were indeed walking in it. Unable to resolve the problem, he went to sleep.

The next night, the same thing happened. For two weeks, Mr. Nowak went to sleep with the footsteps resounding promptly at 10 P.M. But he had decided to ignore the whole thing and went to sleep, steps or no steps.

"It seemed, when I was in bed," he explained to his aunt, somewhat sheepishly, "the footsteps were coming up the stairs, and when I was lying there it seemed as if they were actually in the room, but I could not distinguish the actual location. When I first heard them I thought they were Mary's, so I guess they must have been the footsteps of a woman."

Mr. Nowak is not given to any interest in psychic phenomena, but on several occasions his wife, also named Mary, as is her aunt, did have a rapport bordering on telepathic communication with him—far beyond the possibilities of mere chance. Thus it is very likely that the chemist's natural tendency toward extrasensory perception played a role in his ability to hear the steps, as it certainly did in the case of Mr. Davy, whose own childhood had shown at least one marked incident of this sort.

But if the ghostly presence favored anyone with her manifestations, it would seem that she preferred men. Mary Nowak slept soundly through the two weeks, with nary a disturbance or incident.

Clifford Richardson, another nephew of the Davys, came from Oklahoma to visit the Nowaks one time, and in the course of the visit he decided to stay a night at the Davys. Mr. Richardson is the owner of an insurance agency and not the least bit interested in the occult. On his return to the Nowaks the following day, he seemed unusually pensive and withdrawn. Finally, over coffee, he opened up.

"Look, Mary," he said, "your husband Bucky has stayed over at Uncle Ned's house for a while. Did he sleep well?"

"What do you mean?" Mary asked, pretending not to know.

"Did he ever hear any sounds?"

Mary knew what he meant and admitted that her husband had indeed "heard sounds."

"Thank God," the insurance man sighed. "I thought I was going out of my mind when I heard those footsteps."

He, too, had slept in the third-floor bedroom.

What was the terrible secret the little bedroom held for all these years?

The room itself is now plainly but adequately furnished as a guest room. It is small and narrow and undoubtedly was originally a maid's room. There is a small window leading to the tree-studded street below. It must have been a somewhat remote room originally where a person might not be heard, should he cry for help for any reason.

The Davys began to look into the background of their house. The surrounding area had been known as Wright's Farm, and a certain Mrs. Wright had built houses on the property toward the late 1880s. The house was owned by four sets of occupants prior to their buying it and despite attempts to contact some of those who were still alive, they failed to do so. They did not discuss their "problem" with anyone, not even Mary's aged mother, who was now staying with them—no sense frightening the frail old lady. Then again the Davys weren't really frightened, just curious. Mary was a student of group dynamics and education at nearby Temple

University, and the phenomena interested her mildly from a researcher's point of view. As for William Davy, it was all more of a lark than something to be taken seriously, and certainly not the sort of thing one worries about.

When their inquiries about the history of the house failed to turn up startling or sensational details, they accepted the presence as something left over from the Victorian age and the mystique of it all added an extra dimension, as it were, to their fine old home.

Then one day, in carefully looking over the little room on the third floor, Mr. Davy made an interesting discovery. At waist height, the door to the room showed heavy dents, as if someone had tried to batter it down. No doubt about it, the damage showed clear evidence of attempted forcing of the door.

Had someone violated a servant up there against her wishes? Was the door to the bedroom battered down by one of the people in the house, the son, perhaps, who in that age was sacrosanct from ordinary prosecution for such a "minor" misdeed as having an affair with the maid?

The strong smell of bayberry seemed to indicate a member of the servant class, for even then, as now, an overabundance of strong perfume is not a sign of good breeding.

There have been no incidents lately but this does not mean the ghost is gone. For a Victorian servant girl to be able to roam a house at will is indeed a pleasure not easily abandoned—not even for the promised freedom of the Other Side!

The Piano-Playing Ghost

Margaret C., who lived in New York state, decided to spend Christmas with her sister and brother-in-law in Pennsylvania. The husband's mother had recently passed away, so it was going to be a sad Christmas holiday for them.

Mrs. C. was given a room on the second floor of the old house, close to a passage that led to the downstairs part of the house. Being tired from her long journey, she went to bed around eleven, but found it difficult to fall asleep. Suddenly she clearly heard the sound of a piano being played in the house. It sound like a very old piano, and the music on it reminded her of music played in church. At first Mrs. C. thought someone had left a radio on, so she checked but found that this was not the case. Somehow she managed to fall asleep despite the tinkling sound of the piano downstairs. At breakfast, Mrs. C. mentioned her experience to her sister. Her sister gave her an odd look, then took her by the hand and led her down the stairs and pointed to an old piano. It had been the property of the dead mother who had recently passed away, but it had not been played in many years, since no one else in the house knew how to play it. With mounting excitement, the two women pried the rusty lid open. This took some effort, but eventually they succeeded in opening the keyboard.

Picture their surprise when they found that thick dust had settled on the keys, but etched in the dust were unmistakable human fingerprints. They were thin, bony fingers, like the fingers of a very old woman. Prior to her passing, the deceased had been very thin indeed, and church music had been her favorite. Was the lady of the house still around, playing her beloved piano?

Rhode Island

Passing Through

Just as the Germans have a peculiar name—Poltergeist—for the noisy ghost phenomena associated with disturbances of a physical nature, so they have a special term for the terrifying experience of a warning of impending death. These announcements of disaster or doom are called *Gaenger* in Central Europe, a word meaning literally, "he who will go" (offstage), the stage being our physical world.

In a memorable but now very rare book called *Gaenger, Geister und Gesichter* ("Death Announcements, Ghosts and Visions"), Friedrich von Gaggern reported some of these occurrences that were peculiarly tied in with the Germanic mood and landscape.

I was thinking of the Gaggern work when I first heard about Jane Marquardt of Rhode Island. Not so much because of her Germanic name—after all, it is her husband's—but because of the nature of the incidents that both enlivened and beclouded her life.

The most terrifying of these incidents took place when she was eighteen, at the time of World War II. Her boyfriend was a bombardier overseas, while she lived with her family in Chicago. One night she awoke from deep sleep with the sudden realization that someone was pounding on her bedroom door. There was no rational explanation for the loud knocks. She got up and checked the time. It was just 3 A.M. With a vague feeling of uneasiness, she returned to bed. Somehow she connected the uncanny knocks with her boyfriend. He was due to return home soon, and they would be married.

Was it fear or the natural worry about a boy overseas in the war, or was it something more?

For two days Jane lived in a state of suspended animation. Then a telegram arrived with the tragic news that her boyfriend had been killed. He and his buddies had safely completed their seventy-fourth mission and were returning home to their quarters in a bus. The bus went out of control and plunged over a cliff, killing the entire crew. Everyone on that bus was due for a furlough and return to the United States. The time of the accident was exactly 3 A.M., allowing for the difference in time zones.

South Carolina

Family Visits from Beyond

Susan D. of Columbia, South Carolina, was born in Texas. Her father was in the service at first and after the war her parents moved to South Carolina, where her father's family had lived for generations. Susan is the eldest of three sisters. They grew up in a small town in the upper section of the state and then moved to Columbia, where her father became the superintendent of a state boarding school for unusual students. At that point Susan was seventeen. Later she entered a local college and stayed for two years. She is presently living with her husband, who is also in education, and they have a little boy. Because of a background of premonitions she had some interest in studying psychic phenomena, but this interest was rather on the vague side.

The first complete incident Susan can remember happened when she was just twelve years old. At that time she had spent the night with her grandmother, also named Susan. During the night the little girl dreamed her grandmother had died. She was awakened from her dream by her cousin Kenneth with the sad news that her grandmother had indeed died during the night.

There had always been a close relationship between her and her father, so when her father was taken to the hospital with a heart attack in 1967 she was naturally concerned. After a while the doctors allowed him to return to his home life, and by the time her little boy was a year old in March of 1968 her father seemed completely well and there was no thought of further illness on the family's mind. Two days after they had all been together for the first birthday celebration of her little boy she awoke in the middle of the night with an overpowering anxiety about her father's well-being. She became convinced that her father would leave them soon. The next morning she telephoned her sister and started to discuss her concern for her father. At that moment her father interrupted her call by asking her sister to get her mother immediately. He died on the way to the hospital that very afternoon.

Susan's father had had a very close friend by the name of Joe F., with whom he had shared a great love of college football games. Joe F. had passed on a short time before. A little later, Susan and her husband attended one of the games of the University of South Carolina, in the fall of 1968. On the way to their seats Susan looked up toward the rear section of the arena and quickly turned her head back to her husband. She was so upset at what she saw that it took her a moment to calm down and take her seat. There, not more than eight feet away from her, stood her late father just as he had looked in life. Moreover, she heard him speak to her clearly and in his usual tone of voice. Her husband had not noticed anything and she decided not to tell him about it. As she slowly turned her head back to where they had come from she noticed her father again. This time Joe F., his lifelong friend, was with him. The two dead men were walking down the walkway in front of the seats and she had a good opportunity to see them clearly. They seemed as much alive then as they had ever been when she knew them both in the flesh.

Susan D. has an aunt by the name of Mrs. Fred V. They had frequently discussed the possibility of life after death and psychic phenomena in general, especially after the death of the aunt's husband, which had come rather unexpectedly. It was then that the two women realized that they had shared a similar extraordinary experience. Mrs. Fred V. had also gone to a football game at the University of South Carolina, but her visit was a week later, for a different game than Susan's had been. Since the two women had not met for some time there had been no opportunity to discuss Susan's original psychic experience at the football game with her aunt. Nevertheless, Mrs. V. told her niece that something quite extraordinary had happened to her at that particular football game. She too had seen the two dead men watch the game as if they were still very much in the flesh. To Mrs. V. this was a signal that her own husband was to join them, for the three had been very close friends in life. As it happened, she was right. He passed on soon afterward.

Susan D. has heard the voice of her father since then on

several occasions, although she hasn't seen him again. It appears that her father intercedes frequently when Susan is about to lose her temper in some matter or take a wrong step. On such occasions she hears his voice telling her to take it easy.

Tennessee

The Ghost of the Henpecked Husband

Mike L. lives in Tennessee, where his family has been in residence for several generations. Ever since he can remember, he has had psychic ability. At the time when a favorite uncle was in the hospital, he was awakened in the middle of the night to see his uncle standing by his bed. "Goodbye, Michael," the uncle said, and then the image faded away. At that instant, Mike knew that his uncle had passed away, so he went back to sleep. The following morning, his mother awoke him to tell him that his uncle had passed away during the night.

In April, he and his wife moved to a residential section in one of the large cities of Tennessee. They bought a house from a lady well in her seventies who had the reputation of being somewhat cranky. She was not too well liked in the neighborhood.

Shortly after they had settled down in the house, they noticed footsteps in the rafters over their bedroom. Regardless of the hour, these footsteps would come across the ceiling from one side of the room to the other. Whenever they checked, there was no one there who could have caused the footsteps.

While they were still puzzled about the matter, though not shocked, and since they had had psychic presences in other houses, something still more remarkable occurred. There were two floor lamps in the living room, on opposite sides of the room. One night, Mr. L. awoke and noticed one of the floor lamps lit. Since he clearly remembered having turned it off on going to bed, he was puzzled, but got out of bed and switched it off again. As if to complement this incident, the other floor lamp came on by itself a few nights later, even though it had been turned off by hand a short time before.

This was the beginning of an entire series of lights being turned on in various parts of the house, seemingly by unseen hands. Since it was their practice not to leave any lights on except for a small night light in their daughter's room, there was no way in which this could be explained by negligence or on rational grounds. The house has a basement, including a small space below the wooden front porch. As a result of this hollow space, if anyone were walking on the porch, the steps would reverberate that much more audibly. The L.'s frequently heard someone come up the porch, approach the door, and stop there. Whenever they looked out, they saw no one about. Not much later, they were awakened by the noise of a large number of dishes crashing to the floor of the kitchen, at least so they thought. When they checked, everything was in order; no dish had been disturbed.

They were still wondering about this when they caught the movement of something—or someone—out of the corner of their eye in the living room. When they looked closer, there was no one there. Then the dresser in the bedroom *seemed* to be moving across the floor, or so it sounded. By the time they got to the room, nothing had been changed.

One night, just after retiring, Mr. L. was shocked by a great deal of noise in the basement. It sounded as if someone were wrecking his shop. He jumped out of bed, grabbed a gun, opened the basement door, and turned on the light. There was an audible scurrying sound, as if someone were moving about, followed by silence.

Immediately Mr. L. thought he had a burglar, but realized he would be unable to go downstairs undetected. Under the circumstances, he called for his wife to telephone the police while he stood at the head of the stairs guarding the basement exit. As soon as he heard the police arrive, he locked the only door to the basement and joined them on the outside of the house. Together they investigated, only to find no one about, no evidence of foul play. Even more inexplicable, nothing in the shop had been touched. About that time, Mr. L. noticed a tendency of the basement door to unlock itself seemingly of its own volition, even though it was Mr. L.'s custom to lock it both at night and when leaving the house. During the daytime, Mrs. L. frequently heard footsteps overhead when she was in the basement, even though she was fully aware of the fact that there was no one in the house but her.

By now, Mr. and Mrs. L. realized that someone was trying to get their attention. They became aware of an unseen presence staring at them in the dining room, or bothering Mrs. L. in one of the other rooms of the house. Finally, Mike L. remembered that a Rosicrucian friend had given them a so-called Hermetic Cross when they had encountered ghostly troubles in another house. He brought the cross to the dining room and nailed it to the wall. This seemed to relieve the pressure somewhat, until they found a calendar hung in front of the cross, as if to downgrade its power.

Mr. L. made some further inquiries in the neighborhood to find out who the unseen intruder might be. Eventually he managed to piece the story together. The woman from whom they had bought the house had been a widow of about nine years when they had met her. The husband had been extremely unhappy in the house; he was not permitted to smoke, for instance, and had to hide his cigarettes in a neighbor's basement. Nothing he did in his own house met with his wife's approval, it appeared, and he died a very unhappy man. Could it not be that his restless spirit, once freed from the shackles of the body, finally enjoyed his unobstructed power to roam the house and do whatever he pleased? Or perhaps he could now even enjoy the vicarious thrill of frightening the later owners, and for the first time in his long life, become the stronger party in the house.

Texas

The Bryce
Avenue Murders

ot all ghosts have selfish motives, so to speak, in reasserting
their previous ownership of a home: some even help later occupants, although the limits of a ghost's rationality are very narrow.
For one thing, if a ghost personality is aware of later inhabitants of
a house and wants to communicate with them—not in order to get
them out but to warn them—such a ghost is still unable to realize
that the warning may be entirely unnecessary because time has
passed, and the present reality no longer corresponds to the reality he or she knew when his or her own tragedy occurred.

Still, there is the strange case of Rose S., now a resident of
New York State, but at one time living in Fort Worth, Texas. Miss
S. is a secretary by profession, and during the middle 1960s
worked for a well-known social leader. That summer, Miss S.
moved into an old house in Fort Worth, renting a room at one end
of the house. At the time, she wanted to be near her fiancé, an
army pilot who was stationed not far away.

The old house she chanced upon was located on Bryce Avenue, in one of the older sections of Fort Worth. The owner was
renting out a furnished room because the house had become too
large for her. Her husband, an attorney, had passed away, and
their children were all grown and living away from home.

The house seemed pleasant enough, and the room large and
suitable, so Miss S. was indeed happy to have found it. Moreover,
her landlady did not restrict her to the rented room, but allowed
her to use the kitchen and in fact have the freedom of the house,
especially as there were no other tenants. The landlady seemed a
pleasant enough woman in her middle or late sixties at the time,
and except for an occasional habit of talking to herself, there was

nothing particularly unusual about her. Miss S. looked forward to a pleasant, if uneventful stay at the house on Bryce Avenue.

Not long after moving in, it happened that the landlady went off to visit a daughter in Houston, leaving the house entirely to Miss S. That night, Rose S. decided to read and then retire early. As soon as she switched off the lights to go to sleep, she began to hear footsteps walking around the house. At the same time, the light in the bathroom, which she had intended to leave on all night, started to grow dimmer and brighter alternately, which puzzled her. Frightened because she thought she had to face an intruder, Miss S. got up to investigate, but found not a living soul anywhere in the house. She then decided that the whole thing was simply her imagination acting up because she had been left alone in the house for the first time, and went to bed. The days passed and the incident was forgotten.

A few weeks later, the landlady was again off for Houston, but this time Miss S.'s fiancé was visiting her. It was evening, and the couple was spending the time after dinner relaxing. Miss S.'s fiance, the pilot, had fallen asleep. Suddenly, in the quiet of the night, Miss S. heard someone whistle loudly and clearly from the next room. It was a marching song, which vaguely reminded her of the well-known melody the Colonel Bogey March. Neither TV nor radio were playing at the time, and there was no one about. When she realized that the source of the whistling was uncanny, she decided not to tell her fiancé, not wishing to upset him.

Time went on, and another periodical trip by her landlady left Miss S. alone again in the house. This time she was in the TV den, trying to read and write. It was a warm night, and the air conditioner was on.

As she was sitting there, Miss S. gradually got the feeling that she was not alone. She had the distinct impression that someone was watching her, and then there came the faint whining voice of a woman above the sound of the air conditioner. The voice kept talking, and though Miss S. tried to ignore it, she had to listen. Whether by voice or telepathy, she received the impression that she was not to stay in the house, and that the voice was warning her to move out immediately. After another restless night with very little sleep, Miss S. decided she could take the phenomena no longer.

As soon as the landlady returned, she informed her that she

was leaving, and moved in with friends temporarily. Eventually, her experiences at the house on Bryce Avenue aroused her curiosity and she made some quiet inquiries. It was then that she discovered the reasons for the haunting. On the very corner where the house stood, a woman and a girl had been murdered by a man while waiting for a bus. As if that were not enough to upset her, something happened to her fiancé from that moment on. Following the incident with the whistling ghost, of which her fiancé knew nothing, his behavior toward her changed drastically. It was as if he was not quite himself any more, but under the influence of another personality. Shortly afterwards, Miss S. and her pilot broke off their engagement.

The Case of the Tyler Poltergeists

I am frequently asked to comment on Poltergeists, or noisy ghosts, a term conjuring up the image of violent physical activity beyond the pale of ordinary understanding. Poltergeists have generally been considered the work of youngsters in a house—youngsters below the age of puberty, when their physical energies have not yet been channeled either sexually or occupationally and are therefore free to play pranks on others in the household. The majority of parapsychologists consider Poltergeists the unconscious expression of such repressed feelings, attention-getters on the part of young people, and do not connect them to supernormal beings such as spirit entities or any other form of outside influence. I, however, have investigated dozens of cases involving Poltergeists where physical objects have been moved or moved seemingly by their own volition and found that another explanation might be the true one. In each case, to be sure, there were young people in the household, or sometimes mentally handicapped adults, whom, I discovered, have the same kind of suppressed kinetic energy capable of being tapped by outside forces to perform the physical phenomena as the unused energy of youngsters. I also discovered that in each and every case with which I came in contact personally there had been some form of unfinished business in the house or on the grounds on which the house stood. Sometimes this involved a previous building on the same spot. At other times it involved the same building in which the activities took place. But in each instance there was some form of psychic entity present, and it is my conviction that the entity from beyond the physical world was responsible for the happenings, using, of course, the physical energy in the young people or in the adult. Thus, to me, Poltergeists are the physical activities of ghosts directed solely by outside entities no longer in the flesh. This link between the physical energies of living persons and the usually demented minds of dead persons produces the physical phenomena known as Poltergeist activities, which can be very destructive, sometimes threatening, sometimes baffling to those who do not understand the underlying causes.

The purpose of these physical activities is always to get the attention of living persons or perhaps to annoy them for personal reasons. The mentality behind this phenomenon is somewhere between the psychotic and the infantile, but at all times far from emotionally and mentally normal. But it can still be dealt with on the same basis as I deal with ordinary hauntings. That is to say, the cause of the activities must be understood before a cure for them can be found. Making contact with the troubled entity in the nonphysical world is, of course, the best way. When that is not possible, a shielding device has to be created for the living to protect them from the unwanted Poltergeist activities. In a well-publicized case in Seaford, Long Island, a young boy in the household was held responsible for the movement of objects in plain daylight. Even so astute an investigator as Dr. Karlis Osis of the American Society of Psychical Research, who was then working for Parapsychology Foundation of New York City, could not discern the link between the boy's unconscious thought and the unseen, but very real, psychic entities beyond the world of the flesh. In his report he intimates that the activities were due to the unconscious desires of the youngster to be noticed and to get the sort of attention his unconscious self craved. I was not involved in the Seaford case personally, although I was familiar with it, having discussed the matter with Mr. Herman, the boy's father. I did not enter the case because certain aspects of it suggested publicity-seeking on the part of the family, and at any rate others in my field had already entered the case. I saw no reason to crowd the scene, but I did go into the background of the house with the help of medium Ethel Johnson Meyers independently of the investigation conducted by Dr. Osis. For what it may be worth at this late date, my sitting with Mrs. Meyers disclosed that an Indian burial ground had existed on the very site of the Seaford house and that the disturbances were due to the fact that the house had been erected on the spot. They had not occurred earlier because no physical medium lived in the house. When the young man reached the age of puberty, or nearly so, his energies were available to those wishing to manifest, and it was then that the well-publicized movement of objects occurred.

Similarly, not too long ago a case attracted public attention in the city of Rosenheim, Bavaria. A young lady working for an attorney in that city was somehow able to move solid objects by her very presence. A long list of paranormal phenomena was recorded by reputable witnesses, including the attorney himself. Eventually Dr. Hans Bender of the University of Freiburg entered the case and after investigation pronounced it a classical Poltergeist situation. He too did not link the activity with any outside entity that might have been present on the premises from either this house or a previous one standing on the spot. It seems to me that at the time great haste was taken to make sure that a physical or temporal solution could be put forward, making it unnecessary to link the phenomena with any kind of spirit activity.

But perhaps the most famous of all Poltergeist cases, the classical American case, is the so-called Bell Witch of Tennessee. This case goes back to the 1820s and even so illustrious a witness as Andrew Jackson figures in the proceedings. Much has been written and published about the Bell Witch of Tennessee. Suffice it to say here that it involved the hatred of a certain woman for a farmer named John Bell. This relationship resulted in a postmortem campaign of hatred and destructiveness ultimately costing the lives of two people.

In the Bell Witch case of Tennessee the entire range of physical phenomena usually associated with Poltergeist activities was observed. Included were such astounding happenings as the appearance or disappearance of solid objects into and out of thin air; strange smells and fires of unknown origin; slow, deliberate movement of objects in plain sight without a seeming physical source; and voices being heard out of the air when no one present was speaking. Anyone studying the proceedings of this case would notice that the phenomena were clearly the work of a demented individual. Even though a certain degree of cunning and cleverness is necessary to produce them, the reasoning, or rather the lack of reasoning, clearly indicates a disturbed mind. All Poltergeist activities must therefore be related to the psychotic, or at the very least, schizophrenic, state of mind of the one causing them.

As yet we do not clearly understand the relationship between insanity and free energies capable of performing acts seemingly in contradiction of physical laws, but there seems to be a very close relationship between these two aspects of the human personality. When insanity exists certain energies become free and are capable of roaming at will at times and of performing feats in contradiction to physical laws. When the state of insanity in the mind under discussion is reduced to normalcy these powers cease abruptly.

I have, on occasion, reported cases of hauntings and ghostly activities bordering upon or including some Poltergeist activities. Generally we speak of them as physical phenomena. A case in point is the haunted house belonging to Mr. and Mrs. John Smythe of Rye, New York. The phenomena in this house included such physical activities as doors opening by themselves, footsteps, the sound of chains rattling, ashtrays flying off the table by themselves, and, most frightening of all, a carving knife taking off by itself on a Sunday morning in full view of two sane adults and flinging itself at their feet, not to hurt them but to call attention to an existing unseen entity in the house. These are, of course, the kind of activities present in Poltergeist cases, but they are merely a fringe activity underlining the need for communication. They are not the entire case, nor are they as disorganized and wanton as the true Poltergeist cases. In the case of Rye, New York, the physical activities followed longtime mental activities such as apparitions and impressions of a presence. The physical phenomena were primarily used here to make the message more urgent. Not so with the true Poltergeist case, where there is no possibility of mental communication simply because the causing person is incapable of actual thinking. In such a case all energies are channeled toward destructive physical activity and there is neither the will nor the ability to give mental impressions to those capable of receiving them, since the prime mover of these activities is so filled with hatred and the desire to manifest in the physical world that he or she will not bother with so rational an activity as a thought message.

It is therefore difficult to cope with cases of this kind since there is no access to reasoning, as there is in true ghost cases when a trance medium can frequently make contact with the disturbed and disturbing entity in the house and slowly but surely, bring it back to the realm of reason. With the true Poltergeist case nothing of the sort can be established and other means to solve it have to be found. It is therefore quite natural that anyone who becomes the victim of such activities and is not familiar with them or with what causes them will be in a state of panic, even to the point of wanting to abandon his property and run for his life.

On September 1, 1968, I was contacted by a gentleman by the name of L. H. Beaird. He wrote to me from Tyler, Texas, requesting that I help him understand some of the extraordinary happenings that had made his life hell on earth during the three-year period between 1965 and 1968. Through his daughter, who was married in Austin, he learned of my work with ghosts and finally concluded that only someone as familiar with the subject as I could shed light on the mysterious happenings in his home. He had purchased their home in 1964, but after three years of living with a Poltergeist and fighting a losing battle for survival he decided that his sanity and survival were more important, and in 1968 he sold it again, losing everything he had put into it. The move, however, was a fortuitous one, for the new home turned out to be quiet and peaceful. Once Mr. Beaird got his bearings again and learned to relax once more, he decided to investigate what had occurred during the previous three years and find some sort of answer to this extraordinary problem.

I had never heard of Tyler before and decided to look it up on the map. It turned out to be a city known as the "rose capital" because of the large number of horticultural activities in the area. Tyler is connected with Dallas and Houston by a local airline and lies about halfway between Dallas and Shreveport, Louisiana. The people of Tyler whom I got to know a little after my visit later on are not concerned with such things as the occult. In fact, anyone trying to lecture on the subject would do so in empty halls.

Howard Beaird works in a nearby hospital and also runs a rubber-stamp shop in which he has the company of his wife and more orders than he can possibly fill. Their son, Andy, was enrolled in barber school at the time of my visit and presumably is now cutting people's hair to everyone's satisfaction somewhere in Texas. The big local hotel is called the Blackstone and it is about the same as other big hotels in small towns. Everything is very quiet in Tyler, and you can really sleep at night. There is a spirit of not wanting to change things pervading the town, and I have the distinct impression that cases such as the Poltergeist case were not exactly welcome subjects for discussion over a drink at the local bar.

It must be held to Mr. Beaird's credit that despite the indications of small-town life, he felt compelled to make inquiries into the extraordinary happenings in his life, to look into them without fear and with great compassion for those involved—his wife and son. Others in his position might have buried the matter and tried to forget it. This is particularly important since Mr. Beaird is reasonably prosperous, does business with his neighbors, and has no intention of leaving Tyler. To ask me for an investigation was tantamount to stirring things up, but Beaird took this calculated risk because he could not live with the knowledge of what he had observed without knowing what caused it.

At the time of our correspondence in September 1968 the phenomena had already ended, as abruptly as they had come. This too is typical of genuine Poltergeist activities, since they depend solely on the available free energies of living people. As will be seen in the course of my investigation, that energy became no longer available when the principals were removed from the house. There are other factors involved, of course. It is not as simple as plugging in on a power line, but in essence Poltergeist activities depend not only on the desire of the disturbing entity to manifest but also on the physical condition of the unconscious part of those whom they wish to use as power supplies.

The house the Beairds had to leave under pressure from their Poltergeists is on Elizabeth Street. It is a one-story ranch-type dwelling, pleasant enough to look at and about fourteen or fifteen years old at the time. The new owners are not particularly keen on the history of their house, and it is for that reason that I am keeping confidential the actual location, but the house has not been altered in any way since it has been sold to Mr. M. and his family. One enters the house through a porch that is located somewhat above the road. There is a garage and a steep driveway to the right of the porch. Once one is inside the house one is in the living room with a den to the left and a dining area to the right. Beyond the living room are the kitchen and a rather long room leading directly to a breakfast room. On the extreme left are two bedrooms. To the right of the house behind the garage is the workshop, which, in the period when Mr. Beaird owned the house, was used as such. There is also a concrete slab separating the shop from the garage proper, and the garage contains a ladder leading up to the attic.

Howard Beaird, sixty-five years of age, is a pleasant man with a soft Texas accent, polite, firm, and obliging in his manner. He was overjoyed when I expressed an interest in his case and promised to cooperate in every way. In order to get a better understanding of the extraordinary happenings at Tyler I asked that he dictate in his own words the story of those three years in the house that had come to be years of unrelenting terror. The principals in this true account besides Howard Beaird are his wife, Johnnie, whom he has always called John; a daughter named Amy who lives in another city and was in no way involved in the strange experiences at Tyler; and a son, Andy, now nineteen, who shared all of the unspeakable horror of the experiences between 1965 and the early part of 1968 with his parents. Most of the others mentioned in his account have been dead for several years. A few are still alive, and there are some names in this account Mr. Beaird has never heard of. Here then is his own account of what occurred in the little house on Elizabeth Street in Tyler, Texas:

"My story begins late in 1962, which marked the end of nearly thirty-nine years of employment with the same company. During the last twenty years of that time John worked in the same office with me; in fact her desk was only a few feet from mine. We were both retired during September 1962.

"John had always been an excellent employee, but devoted much more time to her work than the company required for any one person. She would never take a vacation, and was rarely away from her job for more than an occasional half-day at a time, mainly, I think, because she would trust no one with her work. I cannot say when her mind began to show signs of being disturbed, although as I think back on it today, she had acted a little strangely for several years prior to the time of our retirement. This, however, did not affect her work in any way; in fact she was even more precise in it than ever, and I suppose I just could not bring myself to admit that there was anything wrong with her mind. At any rate, during the next twelve months she began to act more abnormally than ever, especially when at home, until finally it was necessary that she enter a mental institution. Although the doctors there were reluctant to release her, they did not seem to be having any success in whatever treatment they were giving her, so I asked for her release after about three months. Being of very modest means I naturally had to obtain employment as soon as possible, but after working about three months in another city I felt that it was most urgent that I move my family from Grand Saline, Texas, to some other place, believing that the mere change of environment would play a big part in helping John to get well. So about the middle of 1964 we moved to Tyler, Texas, a place where John had always said she would like to live. We bought a house, and after about a month I obtained employment which, in addition to a sideline business I had begun a few years before, gave us a satisfactory, if not affluent, living. For almost a year John did seem to be better; she would go places with Andy and me, to the Little League baseball games in which Andy played, to the movies occasionally, sometimes to bowling alleys and a miniature golf course, but all of a sudden she stopped.

"She had not actually kept house since we made the move and had not cooked a single meal for Andy or me. About this time she started walking to a drugstore in a nearby shopping center for breakfast, and then in the late afternoon just before I would get home she would walk to a restaurant a few blocks away for the evening meal, usually by herself. A little later she began calling a taxi nearly every morning to go to a different place for breakfast: once to a downtown hotel; once way out on the other side of town to a roadside restaurant on the Mineola Highway, and to many other places within the course of a few weeks. Always in the evenings though she would go to the restaurant near our home. She would come home usually just after I arrived, and would change clothes and stay in her room from then on. She would get up very early in the morning, about five o'clock, something *she had never done* during our entire married life. For the past few years she insisted that people were spying on her, and finally, when I did not agree with her, she accused me of being at the head of this group set out to torment her, and even said that I had television cameras set up in the house to spy on her.

"John smoked almost incessantly, every kind of cigarette made, but later began to smoke little cigars the size of a cigarette, and still later started on the big regular ones that men smoke. Once she bought a small can of snuff. She had never used snuff before. This was a little while after she had begun to lay cigarettes down just anywhere, although there were plenty of ashtrays throughout the house. She also began putting lighted cigarettes on table tops, the arms of a divan, or even on the bed, and if Andy or I had not been there to put them out, no doubt the house would have eventually been burned down. She did burn holes in several sheets and in the mattress on her bed. When that happened I told her that she simply could not smoke any more. She did not protest. Andy and I searched the house and found cigarettes and matches everywhere. John had hidden them everywhere, inside a little table radio by removing the back, inside a flashlight where the batteries are supposed to be, in those little shoe pockets she had hanging in her closet, in a little opening at the end of the bathtub where a trap door in the closet exposes the pipes for repairs, under the mattress, inside pillow covers, and even in the dog house outdoors. We gathered up cigarettes, matches, and cigarette lighters every day when I got home and there is no telling how many we finally found and destroyed. Of course she would get more every day at the shopping center, and once we even found one of those little automatic rollers that a person can use to make his own cigarettes.

"Exactly what part John played in the frightening events that took place at our house I cannot say. I am convinced though, as is Amy, that there was some connection. The three years from late 1962 to the summer of 1965 preceded the most awesome, fantastic chain of events that the human mind can imagine. In fact, as these unbelievable episodes began to unfold before us I was beginning to doubt my own sanity. Andy, who was 13 at the time this began, shared with me every one of the horrible experiences, which started in midsummer of 1965 and lasted without interruption until near the end of 1966, when we were 'told' that they were over with, only to find that during the next fifteen months we were in for even worse things. If Andy had not been with me to substantiate these awful experiences I would have indeed considered myself hopelessly insane.

"The frightening events began to take place near the middle of 1965, about the time John quit going places with Andy and me. When at home she would stay in her bedroom and close the door and leave it closed after she went to bed. Andy and I slept in the same bed in another room.

"During our first year at this house we were not bothered by the usual summertime insects, so I did not bother to repair the screens needing fixing at that time. However, during July 1965, Andy and I would go to bed, and as soon as we turned out the light we were plagued by hordes of June bugs of all sizes, which would hit us on our heads and faces, some glancing off on the floor, others landing on the bed, and some missing us entirely and smashing themselves against the metal window blinds. Night after night we fought these bugs in the dark, grabbing those that landed on the bed and throwing them against the blinds as hard as we could.

"Then we discovered that at least half of the bugs that hit us were *already dead*, in fact had been dead so long that they were crisp and would crumble between our fingers when we picked them up! I would get up and turn on the lights, and the raids would cease immediately; we could see no sign of them in the air —only those hundreds that littered the floor and bed. The instant I turned off the light, though, the air would be filled with bugs again, just as if someone were standing there ready to throw handfuls at us *as soon as it was dark*. One night I got up and swept and vacuumed the entire room, moved every piece of furniture away from the walls, dusted the backs of the dresser, chest and tables, and vacuumed the floor again. When I was through I could swear that there was not a living creature in that room other than Andy and me. I got some rags and stuffed them in the cracks beneath the closet door and the one leading from the room into the hall. The windows were closed. The room was *absolutely clean*. Andy was in bed, awake. I turned off the light. At that exact instant hundreds of bugs hit us!

"About this time John began to act more strangely than ever, doing things she would not dream of doing under ordinary circumstances. For example, I might look in my closet to get a shirt or a pair of trousers, and there would not be any there. I do not know what prompted me to do it, but I would go to John's closet, and there would be my clothes hanging alongside some of hers.

"At this time I had a rubber-stamp shop in a room behind the garage, which was a part of the house, and I worked out there every night. There was no direct connection from the house. One had to go out the kitchen door into the garage and then through another door into the shop. On many occasions I would hear the kitchen door being opened, and would rush to the shop door to see who it was. No matter how hard I tried, though, I could never get there fast enough to see *anybody*—only my clothes, suits, shirts, and so on, on hangers *just as they landed in the middle of the garage floor.*

"It was during the hottest part of summer while we had the air-conditioners running that other strange things took place for which we assumed John was responsible. Andy or I would suddenly find the bathroom wall heater lighted and the flames running out the top, with the door closed. The room would be hot enough to burst into flames. John insisted that she had not lit the heater—that one of *us* had. After this had happened several times, I removed the handle that turns on the gas. A short time later, while I was out in the shop, Andy came running out and called me in. There was a bunch of paper towels stuffed into the heater where the burners are and they were on fire, some of them on the floor, burning. I then decided to turn off all the pilot lights in the house. This was on the weekend before Labor Day, and I did not know how I could possibly go to work on Tuesday following the holiday and leave John at home alone, since Andy would be in school. I had talked with the doctor until I could determine what I would eventually be able to do with her, but the psychiatric wards were already running over, and he did not want to admit her as a patient. I decided to tell John that if she did 'any of those things' again I would have to put her in jail. Monday night she started waving a pistol around, so I called the police station and told them the predicament I was in. They said they would keep her until things could be settled and told me to bring her on down. She went without protest. When my lawyer returned he made appointments for her to be examined by two psychiatrists, after which I thought there would be no further question about the need for commitment, and she stayed at home that week. However, on the Monday following Labor Day she called her sister-in-law Mack in Daingerfield, Texas, about a hundred miles from Tyler, and asked if she could visit her at once. I was at work and knew nothing of this until Mack got to Tyler and asked if it would be all right for John to go with her. I objected, but my lawyer advised me that I should let her go, as she could be brought back for the commitment hearing, so they left that day for Daingerfield.

"A few days later John's lawyer had her examined by a psy-

chiatrist again, and he finally said that she might benefit somewhat from getting a job, although she would have to undergo
psychiatric treatment at various times in the future. It would be
almost impossible to have her committed involuntarily, so we
decided to just let things stand as they were. For the record,
John's attorney insisted that I be examined by the same doctors
who had examined her. The reports on me were favorable.

"Shortly after John had gone off to stay with Mack, Andy and
I were lying in bed with the lights off, talking about the terrible
things we had gone through. *Suddenly I heard a voice calling my
name*, a high-pitched, falsetto voice that seemed to be coming
from out in space. The voice said it was John, and although it
sounded nothing at all like her, I am convinced it was, since she
talked about several things that only she and I knew of. One was
about some disagreeable words she had had with one of my sisters
at the time of my father's death in 1950. She said that although my
other sister had insulted her, she was good, and that she had
forgiven her. Andy did not hear any part of this conversation.
Apparently John, or the voice, could talk to either of us without
the other listening to the voice. I even suspected that Andy was
doing the talking, and I held my fingers to his lips while listening
to the voice. I knew then it could not have been coming from his
lips.

"One night while I was lying in bed and Andy was in the
bathroom I heard his voice say 'goodbye,' just before he came to
bed, and he told me he had been talking with his mother. During
the following weeks we heard six other voices *from right out of
nowhere*, all from people *who had been dead for some time*. I knew
all but one of them while they were living. Two of them had always
been friendly toward me, and both were old enough to be my
mother. Andy also knew these two women and one of the men,
named George Swinney. This latter person was killed in an accident some time *after* he visited us 'by voice.' The other two women
were mothers of friends of mine and both had died some time
before we moved to Tyler. One was Mrs. Snow and the other was
Mrs. Elliott, and theirs were the next two voices we heard after
John had left, and they came to us about the time the visits by
Henry Anglin started. He was the only one of the lot who gave us
trouble to start with; in fact I am convinced that he is the one

responsible for the bug raids and other awful things that happened to us.

"One of the work benches in my shop was against the wall dividing the shop and the kitchen, and at the bottom of the wall was an opening with a grill over it to handle the return air from the central heating system. For some reason the grill on the shop side had been removed, and by stooping down near the floor under the bench I could see much of what was going on in the kitchen. I worked in the shop every night, and when these 'ghosts' first began visiting us they would call my name, the voices seeming to come from the opening into the kitchen. I would stoop down and answer. At that time I would carry on lengthy conversations with all of them. Mrs. Snow and Mrs. Elliot were very friendly and seemed to want to give me all kinds of good advice. Henry Anglin was just the opposite. He was extremely mean and demanded that I do all sorts of things I would not do. When I refused, he would be very nasty. Once he got a can of insect spray we kept on the kitchen cabinet top and held it down at the opening to my shop. He would start spraying through the hole. He used a whole can of spray and in that little room I nearly suffocated. One cannot imagine what a feeling it is *to see a can of insect spray suspended in midair with apparently nothing holding it and to have it sprayed right in one's face!* When I went inside I could see the dents made by the edge of the can where he had banged it against the wall.

"About the middle of September 1965 the nightly bug raids began to taper off. We thought that we were going to get a few nights' sleep without fear. However, when we went to bed we would feel something moving on an arm or in our hair—after we had turned off the lights. We jumped up and found one or several slugs somewhere on us or on the bed. They are the ugliest, slimiest wormlike creatures that can be imagined, big at the head and tapering to a point toward their rear end. They have whiskers on each side of the head, and although they have eyes, they are not supposed to see very well, according to Andy, who, strangely enough, was studying them at school at that time. The large ones are as big as a Vienna sausage, about three inches long, and leave a silvery-looking trail wherever they crawl. When the first few of these creatures appeared Andy thought they had clung to his shoes while he was playing in the yard and had gotten into the house that way. However, night after night the number of slugs increased, and we went through the same torture as with the bugs, only much worse. One cannot imagine how awful it is to wake up in the middle of the night and find oneself surrounded by a horde of slimy, ugly worms! Andy said that salt would dissolve the slugs. So we sprinkled salt all around the baseboard, around the bed legs, but still the slugs came *as soon as the lights were out.* A few nights later we were again bombarded with bugs, not June bugs this time, but the wood louse, the little bug about the size of a blackeyed pea. They have lots of tiny legs, will roll up into a round ball when touched, and are generally called pill bugs. I knew they could not fly, yet there they came, *hitting us just as if they were shot out of a gun,* at the exact moment we turned out the lights! Mixed in with these were some bugs I had never seen anywhere before, like a doodle bug but brown in color. I knew doodle bugs couldn't fly, and these things no more had wings than I did. Yet there they came, shooting through the air, and, just as the June bugs had done, they started out one or two at a time, until finally dozens began hitting us at once the moment the lights were out. I also found little pieces of clear material which looked like pieces of broken glass. I finally discovered that these pieces were making the loud noise against the blinds; some of them landed on the bed along with the peculiar bugs. I then washed off a piece about the size of a pea and tasted it; it was pure rock salt! I had not the slightest idea where it came from, as we certainly had had no use for any here. As baffling as the idea of bugs flying without wings was, it was no more so than rock salt sailing through the air with apparently nothing to propel it. There was absolutely no human being in the house except Andy and me.

"A day or two after John had left, I cleaned up her room thoroughly, moved every piece of furniture, swept, vacuumed, dusted, and made up the bed, putting on a spread that came nearly to the floor. A few days after the second series of bug raids, Andy called me into John's room. He raised up the spread, and there under the bed was a conglomeration of objects, among which was a ten-pound sack of rock salt, most of which had been poured in a pile on the carpet under the bed. There was an old hair net mixed with it, some burned matches, an unwrapped cake of 'hotel' soap, and on top of the pile was a note, printed the way a six-year-old child would do it, 'Evil spirit go away.'

"In the next few days we began looking through things in John's room and found lots of notes written in longhand, most of which were like those of a child just learning to write, although a few words were unmistakably John's handwriting. They were mainly of people's names, a date that might be the birthdate, and then another date some time in the future, some up past 1977. There were many names contained in the notes. One name was of a man I am sure John could not have known. He was Henry Anglin, a pitifully ignorant old man who used to farm just west of Grand Saline. Like all farmers in the adjoining territory back in 1918, he would come to town each Saturday to buy groceries and other supplies for the following week. When I was about fourteen years old I worked in a department store that also handled groceries. My job was to keep track of the farmers' stacks of groceries so that when they were ready to leave in the evening I could show them where their purchases were and help load their wagons. Henry Anglin was among the people I regularly waited on. He seemed old to me then and that was about fifty years ago. I have no doubt that he has long since died. I cannot imagine how his name entered John's mind. There were also some typewritten sheets in John's room that contained the same items as the notes we had found. One mentioned a certain 'Tink' Byford. There was a date that was probably his birthdate, then a date in 1964. We had moved to Tyler in July of 1964, and it was several months after that when I read in the paper that 'Tink' Byford had been killed in an auto accident while returning to Grand Saline from Dallas. Another name was 'Bill' Robertson, a friend of both of us. There was an early date, then 'Hosp. 1965, death 1967.' There were many other names, some now dead, but most still living, *always with two dates!* One day when I got home from work Andy and I found in the living room between the divan and table a new bar of soap that had been crumbled up and scattered over a two- or three-foot area. Andy found a potato masher in John's room with soap on it, so we assumed it was used in the living room where the soap was scattered. We did not clean it up right away. That night, after we went to bed, several pieces of soap about the size of a quarter hit our blinds like bullets, although the door to the living room was closed and the den and hallway are between the living room and our bedroom.

"I had had to wash some clothes that night, and it was after dark when I hung them on the line. While I was doing that, Andy came to the door and advised me that bugs and slugs were *flying* all over the house. I told him I thought I had heard something thud against the dog house near the clothesline. He checked and picked up a little leather wallet about the size of a billfold, which we had seen earlier in John's room, filled with loose tobacco. I told him to put it into the garbage can at the end of the house. The can had a lid on it. When I got through, it was time to take a bath and go to bed. While I was in the tub and Andy in the den, I heard something that sounded like a shotgun just outside the bathroom window. I called Andy to run out and see what he could find; he had heard the noise too. Just beneath the window he picked up the *same leather purse* he had put into the garbage can *an hour earlier!* It had hit the house flat, I suppose, near the bathroom window, to cause such a loud noise.

"During the preceding days we had found several other notes, all written or printed in the same peculiar way, as a little child might write. I had no idea what they meant, if anything, but some examples are:

Johnnie Beaird

1913 Murder
Bill Robertson—1967
The dog—leave 1965
Die 1972

Joe Bailey—1972
Reid Lesser—1966
Tink Byford—1964

Amy Beaird
The End

"In a little notebook we found:

Allie L. Lewis [This woman worked for the same company we did, and probably still does].
Luther Anderson [He owns a truck line that hauls salt].
   Die 1980
Jeraldine Fail [This woman used to be a good friend of John's].
   Die 1977
Louise Beaird [This is my sister, who would be 118 years of age in 2018].
   Die 2018

"One day we found an old wooden box where John had kept her canceled checks. She had burned something in it, as the ashes were still in the box. The only thing left was one half of a calling card saying, 'burn spirit burn.' On just a scratch of paper were the words 'Johnnie Beaird—Death 1991.'

"There were many more. Note the peculiar use of capital letters. All of these notes were printed:

JoHN is goIN to Die	Be NIce IN FROnt OF OLD FOOL- ish MacK	There IS A Hertz in Mt PleaSant SnEak AWAY From There [I checked, and there is not a Hertz in Mt. Pleasant].	I pOisOned little FOOLS white kittEn ShALL i poisOn The Jap Cat [Andy did have a white kitten that had died for some reason, and at this time still had a Siamese cat].

"On a Canton bank blank check was written in the 'pay to' line: Johnnie B. Walker $1,000,000; in the 'for' line: Bill is NUTTY, and on the 'signature' line: ha ha.

"The ghastly events continued through October and into November, when they seemed to be letting up a little. One day early in the month when I got home from work Andy took me into John's room. Lined up under the edge of her bed but behind the spread were some pictures in little frames of various kinds. There was one of Amy, of John and Andy, of me, of Thelma Lowrie, who had been John's best friend and who had died in 1951, and several others. I don't know what significance they were supposed to have, but I left them right there. I assumed that John had been to the house that day. Bugs, dead and alive, continued to bombard us every night; even the slugs started flying through the air, smashing against the blinds and walls, making an awful mess wherever they hit.

"I decided to clean up both bedrooms as soon as I could, and to start taking up the carpets. While I was doing that Andy found a note in John's room saying: 'Bugs will end for ThursDay Dec. 29.' I think the 23rd was the day I cleaned up our room, and the bugs were worse than ever that night, so we decided that maybe it was meant that the 23rd would be the last night. The next night, strangely enough, was pretty quiet.

"On the 24th I took up the carpet in John's room. While doing that I was hit by hundreds of bugs, slugs, and even some of the *nails I pulled out of the floor simply flew through the air and hit against the blinds.* Finally I was able to completely clean the room, paint the walls and woodwork, put up curtains, and the room looked very nice when I was finished.

"On November 26 I cleaned the house thoroughly, and no unusual activity took place that night. On the 27th bugs were everywhere. Just before dark I was taking a bath, and when I was through, standing up in the tub, I saw something hit the screen but could not tell what it was. I called Andy from the den and told him to go out to see what it was. It turned out to be one of John's rubber gloves I had put out beside the garbage can to be hauled off.

"On Thanksgiving day I took all of our outside locks and had Andy take them to a locksmith in town the next morning to have them changed and get new keys, as I was convinced that John had been somehow coming from Daingerfield and using her keys to get in. I put the locks in place on Saturday. On Wednesday, December 1, 1965, somebody (I supposed it was John) punched a hole in the back screen door near the hook and unhooked the door. If it was John, though, her key would not fit.

"December 4 was the worst. It was Saturday, and we went to bed about 10:30. Something that sounded exactly like fingers drummed lightly on the bed. Although we were under the covers we could feel *whatever it was tugging at the sheets,* actually trying to jerk the covers off us! We would turn on the light and the tugging would stop. There were no bugs that night, but when the lights were off both Andy and I could feel something on our arms that seemed like small flying bugs bouncing up and down, sort of like gnats might do. We would slap at them, but there was absolutely nothing there. We would turn the lights on and see nothing.

We sprayed the air everywhere with insect spray but it did no good. It felt exactly like someone lightly grabbing the hair on your arms with the thumb and forefinger, not actually pulling very hard at first, but later jerking the hair hard enough to hurt.

"While we were lying in bed with the light on, my shoes, weighing possibly two pounds each, *flew right over our heads* and landed on the other side of the bed. Andy's house shoes got up from the floor and flung themselves against the blinds. My clothes, which were hanging in the closet *with the door closed*, got out of there somehow *without the door being opened and landed* across the room. Finally we turned off the lights and heard a strange sound we could not identify. It was under the bed, and sounded like bed rollers being turned rapidly with the fingers; but the bed was not even on rollers! Suddenly something hit the blind like a bullet. We turned on the light and found that the handle from the gas jet *under the bed had unscrewed itself, and both the bolt and the handle had flung themselves against the blind.* Then the bed started moving away from the wall. We would roll it back again only to have it do the same thing over and over. That was about all we could stand, and as it was 2 A.M. Sunday, I told Andy to put on his clothes. We went to a motel to spend the rest of the night.

"As we were walking down the driveway, after closing and locking the door, *a handkerchief, still folded, hit me on the back of the neck.* Just as we got in the car another handkerchief I had left on the bedside table hit me on the back after I had closed the car doors.

"We were so weary that we were asleep almost by the time we were in bed at the motel, and nothing happened to us while we were there. We came home about 9:30 the next morning. Some of John's clothes were in my closet, and most of mine were in hers. All sorts of weird notes were flying all about the house. I cleaned the house, and just as I was through, *a big cigar hit the back of my neck from out of nowhere.* I put it in the kitchen waste basket. Andy wanted some soup, so I started to a Cabell grocery store a few blocks away. Just as I left the house Andy saw the cigar jump up out of the waste basket and land on the floor. He put it back in the basket. When he came to the door to tell me about it I was getting into the car parked at the foot of the driveway, and when I turned toward him *I saw the cigar come sailing over his head and land at the side of the car,* about sixty feet from the house. When I came back and stepped in the door from the garage to the kitchen *I saw a clean shirt of mine come flying from the den* and land near the back door of the kitchen.

"By this time I had decided that it did absolutely no good to change the locks on the doors, although John had not broken in, if, indeed, this was John. Apparently whoever it was did not *need* a door, nor did he need to break in. Andy and I were standing in the kitchen watching things fly through the air, when all of a sudden his cap, which had been resting on the refrigerator, hit me in the back of the head. A roll of paper towels flew through the air; a can of soup on the cabinet top jumped off onto the floor several times after Andy picked it up and put it back.

"All of a sudden we heard a click. The toaster had been turned on, and the click meant it had turned itself off. *There was a piece of soap in it, melted!* A note nearby read 'clean toaster.' I felt something like a slight brush on my shoulder and heard Andy shout, 'Look out!' He saw the faint *outline of a hand that looked like his mother's* vanish near my head.

"Later, while in the den, I began to ask questions aloud, such as: 'John, tell me where we stayed last night.' A few seconds later a note came floating down in front of us, reading: 'Motel on T. B. Road. Couldn't get in.' 'Got to go, you've ruined me.' We did spend the night before at a motel on the road to the Tuberculosis Hospital where I work. I then said aloud, trying to sound funny in a totally unfunny situation: 'With all that power, why don't you just drop $5,000 on us?' Almost immediately a check with nothing but $5,000 written on the face dropped from out of nowhere. I said, 'John, why don't you appear here before us right this minute?' In about five seconds a note came down saying, 'Can't come ToDay haPPy YuLeTide.' I then asked, 'Are we going to be able to sleep tonight?' This answer came down to us: 'CaN't maKE aNyTHing haPPen tONighT you BROKE MY POWER Call HOUsTon.'

"Previously she told me to call Houston police and ask them about a witch who had solved the murder of a man named Gonzales. I felt like a fool, but I did call the Houston police department. I told them they could think I was drunk, crazy, or anything they wished to, but I just wanted a yes or no answer, and asked if they had any record of a witch ever helping the Houston police solve a murder of a man named Gonzales. The man I talked to did not appear surprised and simply asked me to wait a moment, and a few seconds later said that he could find no record of any such event.

"John had also given us directions for breaking her power. It was to 'break an egg, mix with a little water and a dash of salt and then throw it out in the back yard.'

"I have never been superstitious before, and this sounded awfully silly to me, but I think I would have done absolutely anything I was told if it meant a chance to put an end to these uncanny events, so I told Andy to go ahead and follow the directions. That night we had a few bugs and a note came floating down reading, 'power will end at 10 o'clock give or take an hour.'

"For several days we received what seemed like hundreds of *notes from right out of nowhere, simply materializing in midair, some folding themselves as they came toward us.* Some time after he had seen the hand vanish near my head, Andy was sitting in the den facing the outside windows. For a few fleeting seconds he saw the outline of John in front of the windows. Her back was to him as she looked out the windows, and Andy heard a faint 'good-bye' just as the figure melted in the air.

"We heard other voices after talking with John. All seemed very strained, especially the female speakers, and they would often say that they had a 'mist' in their throat and could not continue talking to me, although they could always talk to Andy and he would hear them. I have dozens of notes that fell down to us from somewhere above, and most of them are from the same two people who stayed with us for the longest period of time. One of these was Mrs. Elliot, who had been dead for three or four years when all this began to happen. The other was from a Mr. Gree, of whom I had never heard, but who seemed eager to help Andy and me with advice, especially concerning the care of Andy's cats and dogs. We were 'visited' by a great variety of 'people,' some long since dead, some still living, most of whom we know, or knew, but also some well-known public figures whose names were often in the news. I dated the notes from then on, but at times so many descended on us at once that I did not try to record the exact order in which we received them.

"It was Henry Anglin who tormented us from the very begin-

ning, and who caused us to move out of the house. One night
Anglin came to our room after we had gone to bed and his voice
asked if he could cook himself an egg. We heard nothing else from
him that night, but the next morning when I went to the kitchen to
prepare breakfast, there in a teflon-lined skillet on the stove
burner which was turned down low was an egg burned to a crisp!

"Another night Anglin came to our room and insisted that I
call Houston. This was about the time he was beginning to be so
terribly mean. I told him that I had already made one silly call to
the Houston police, and that I had no intention of doing it again.
He countered that I had not questioned them enough, and for me
to phone them again. I refused, and he tormented us relentlessly.
Finally he said he would leave us alone if we would drive around
the loop, which was a distance of a little over twenty miles around
the city of Tyler. Andy and I put on our clothes and did just that.
We drove completely around the town, and sure enough, when we
got home we were able to sleep the rest of the night without
further trouble.

"A few nights after this, both Mrs. Elliott and Mrs. Snow told
me verbally, while I was working in my shop, that they had taken
Henry Anglin 'back to his grave,' and had driven a stake, prepared
by Mr. Gree, through Anglin's heart. They promised that he would
not bother us again.

"About this time we received notes allegedly from people who
were still living, and also some from persons other than those
previously mentioned who had been dead for several years.
Among those still living were Mrs. W. H. Jarvis, and Odell Young,
who lives in Grand Saline at this time. I also had one note from
Mr. W. H. Quinn, who had been dead for several years. He used to
be a railroad agent in Grand Saline. For a number of years I had
occasion to have him sign numerous shipping papers, so I had
become familiar with his handwriting. The note I got from him
was written in the same backhand fashion. I believe that this note
was written by him:

Dear Howard and Andy,
I pay tribute to you. You have put up with a lot from old man
Anglin. It is all over now. Friday I am going to my grave to join my
wife, whom I love. I am going to Marion's house to see him once

*more. He is my favorite child. I have always liked you, John and the
boy and hope someday you will be together again.*

                                                        Hiram Quinn

*P.S. I enjoyed hearing about John going with Marion to get new
teeth.*

"The P.S. about his son's false teeth refers to the time about
thirty years ago when John and I went to see Marion just after he
had received his first set of dentures. At that time we lived just
across the street from Marion and his wife and were friendly with
them.

"We also got notes allegedly from Marilyn Monroe, Dorothy
Kilgallen, and former governor Jim Allred, who sympathized with
us for what Henry Anglin was doing to us and about John's condition. Mrs. Snow and Mrs. Elliot had previously told us that Anglin
had caused many deaths, some by auto accident, and some by
switching a person's pills as they said he had done in the case of
Dorothy Kilgallen. The note we received with her name also said
that was the cause of her death. I am not certain, but I believe they
also said Anglin caused Marilyn Monroe's death.

"None of the people still living, except John, ever spoke to
me; they just dropped their notes from the air. Mrs. Jarvis actually
spoke to Andy, though, and had him tell me to answer aloud each
of the questions she put in her note to me. Mr. Quinn's note was
stuck in the grate between the kitchen and my shop.

"For the first few weeks in January 1966 only Mrs. Elliott and
Mr. Jack Gree 'visited' us. She and I had lots of conversations, but
she gradually got so she could barely talk to me, although Andy
could still hear her. The notes were written either on some note
paper Andy kept in the kitchen or on some Canton, Texas, bank
deposit slips in John's room. If I was working in the shop she
would stick the notes in the grill and bang on the wall to attract
my attention, and then I would stoop down under the work bench
and retrieve the note. Mr. Gree, who told us we had never heard of
him, had a very low, deep, gruff voice. Most of his communications to me were in the form of notes, but he and Andy carried on
lengthy conversations nearly every day. He also used the grill
'post office' for depositing his notes, then banged on the wall to let
me know they were there.

"At times, when Andy and I were in the car, Mrs. Elliott or

Mr. Gree would be with us. They would ride along for a while and then suddenly say they were going to Canada, Russia, Minnesota, or some other far-off place, saying it took only two or three minutes for them to travel those distances, and then we might not hear anything else from them until the next day or night. Early in January 1966 Andy came out to my shop and said Mr. Gree wanted to know if it was okay for him to use the telephone, and of course I told him it was. I did not know what control I would have had over the situation anyway. That first time he said it was something personal and asked Andy if he would mind leaving the room. *I could hear the phone being dialed,* and stooped down near the floor so I could look through the grilled opening, but of course I could not see anyone there and could not quite see the phone itself. After that he used the phone many times, while I was working and while Andy was studying at the kitchen table in full view of the telephone. *It was really spooky to see the receiver stand up on end by itself, and then after a while put itself back down where it belonged,* but always upside down. Some nights he would dial many times after we had gone to bed, and we could hear the sound plainly in our bedroom. The next morning I would find the receiver on the phone upside down. One night while Andy was taking a bath Mr. Gree called somebody *and I heard him say* in a low, deep voice, 'I'm weird . . . I'm unusual.' I thought to myself, 'You can say that again.' He repeated it several times and then all I could hear would be a series of low grunts, from which I could not make out any real words. One evening while we were in the car coming home from the post office I asked Andy whom he supposed Mr. Gree called on the phone. Without a moment's hesitation Mrs. Elliott, who we did not know was with us, spoke up and said he was calling her. We did not ask her where she was when she received the call!

"Both Mr. Gree and Mrs. Elliott certainly had Andy's welfare in mind. Practically every day for the whole month of January there was a note from one of them stuck in the screen door. It appeared to be Mrs. Elliott's job to help get John home and to take care of Andy. She said if she could do that she would probably go back to her grave early.

"After John had left home I felt sorry for Andy. He was lonely being at home alone so much of the time. He indicated a desire for a cat, and a little later for a dog. At the insistence and complete direction of Mrs. Elliott I spent quite a sum of money for such pets. Mr. Gree then took over completely the direction for our taking care of these dogs and cats.

"On January 29, 1966, while I was writing a letter, there was a pounding on the kitchen wall, indicating that there was a note in our 'post office.' It was from Mrs. Elliott. 'I love that beagle. Sorry the dogs have been sick. I feel responsible. Andy worries. He loves them so much. If something does happen I only hope it isn't the beagle. The beagle will be a better companion. Andy would give up one if you asked him to. Not that he wants to. But he would understand. He loves dogs. He understands. El. Reply to this note. Reply to every line I wrote.'

"The other dog she referred to was a brown dachshund, which did not look very healthy when we bought it. It never did gain any weight and after we had given away the black dachshund the brown one continued to get worse. During the next few days and nights some of the most unbelievable things happened in connection with this brown dachshund. I would be working in my shop and suddenly hear a slight noise on the roof of the house. It would be utterly impossible for the dog to jump up there from the ground, and there was nothing else around for him to get on in order to jump up on the house. Yet *there he was clear up on the peak, walking from one end to the other!* We would get a ladder and finally coax him down into the eave, where we could get hold of him and put him on the ground. This happened time after time. We finally decided to leave him up there and go on to bed. The next night Mrs. Elliott told us she knew about the dog. We asked her how it was possible and said we would like to see how the dog got up there. She said we could not see it—that it was just a case of 'now he's down here, now he's up there.' She said that even if we were watching him, he would just simply vanish from his spot on the ground and at the same instant be on the roof. Later that night Mrs. Elliott called Andy and me and said the dog was trying to commit suicide and for us to go to the back door and look in the flower bed on the south side of the back steps. Sure enough we looked, and the ground had been freshly dug and looked as if it had been loosely put back in place. We could see the dirt moving, and I told Andy to go and get the shovel from the garage. Mrs. Elliott said it was not in the garage, but for us to wait just a few seconds and we would find it out in the front yard under the tree, where it would be when it got back from 'Heaven.' Andy did go and found the shovel just where she said it would be and brought it to me. I dug down beside where the dirt was moving and pulled the dog out by the tail. He was barely breathing and looked very pitiful, but after a few seconds was able to feebly walk a little. Mrs. Elliott told us that we had better put it out of its misery that night. I told her I did not have anything to put it to sleep with, but she finally told me to just go ahead and kill it, using a hammer, a brick, or anything that would put it to death. It was a sickening experience, but I did kill the dog with a brick, as I was certain that it was in pain and would be better off dead. *We buried the dog where it had apparently dug its own grave!* I cannot say that the dog actually dug this hole, crawled into it, and covered itself up with dirt, as I find it hard to see how it could possibly have dragged the dirt in on top of it—I have only Mrs. Elliott's word for that. I am merely stating what she told us, although I did find the dog in the hole, covered with loose dirt, and barely breathing when I pulled it out.

"While John was away in Daingerfield, I had bought a little plastic toilet bowl cleaner on which a disposable pad is used. The handle had come apart the first time I tried to use it. It cost only a few cents, and ordinarily I would have just bought another and forgotten about it. However, I decided to write the manufacturer, and some time later I received a letter from them, advising me that they were sending me another handle. Eventually I received a notice that there was a package at the post office. I would have had to drive about ten miles from the place where I work to the post office and back during the noon hour to pick it up, and since it was of no importance I intended to just wait until Saturday to call for the package. That evening, though, when I went to my shop to start work there was a package on my work bench. The shop had been locked all day and was still locked when I started to work. I asked Andy if he knew anything about it and he assured me that he did not even know about the package being in the post office. At that moment Mrs. Elliott spoke up and admitted she had gotten it out of the post office and brought it home to me!

"Not long after John had gone to Daingerfield another mystifying thing happened. In one of the kitchen drawers where we kept some silverware in one of those little compartments made for that purpose, there was a space five or six inches behind that section clear across the drawer. In there I kept a few tools such as a screwdriver, pliers, tack hammer, where they would be conveniently available when I needed them. I had not had occasion to look in there for some time, and when I finally did I noticed a pistol. It was a .22 cal. and looked very real, and only when I picked it up did I discover it was just a blank pistol. I asked Andy where it came from, but he knew nothing whatever about it. Mrs. Elliott spoke and said *she* had brought it from Daingerfield. She told us that John had ordered it from some magazine ad and had paid $12 for it. She said it was awfully hard for her to bring it to our house and that it had taken her several hours to do so. She did not say why she did it but intimated that she just wanted us to know about it. Later, when we were moving away from that house, the pistol was gone, and I have not seen it since.

"For many years I had owned a .25 cal. Colt automatic pistol. I always kept it in good condition but it had not been fired in thirty years at the time we moved to Tyler. John's mother also had had a pistol exactly like mine except for the handles, as I bought a pair of white, carved bone handles for mine. When she died we brought that pistol to our house, although we never had occasion to shoot it either. We still had them both when we moved to Tyler. With so many mysterious events taking place, I decided to keep a pistol out in my shop, so I brought the one that had belonged to John's mother and left it on top of my work bench. It stayed there for several weeks. One night it was missing. My shop was always locked and I had the only key. I had wrapped my own gun in a polyethylene bag after cleaning it thoroughly, and put it in a little compartment between the two drawers in a chest in my room. One of the drawers had to be removed completely to get the gun, and even then one had to look closely to find it. I had told no one about the hiding place. When the gun in my shop suddenly disappeared I decided to get mine that I had hidden in the chest. However, when I looked in the hiding place my pistol was not there, *but in its place was the one that had been in the shop!* I did not take it to my shop then, but some time later when I did decide to, that gun too was gone, and we have seen neither of them since that time.

"Occasionally during all this time I would write to John, saying that I wished she would come home so that we might be able to get her well and be happy together again. She never replied to any of my letters, although she wrote Andy a note now and then when he would write her first. I talked to her on the phone a short while later. I do not remember whether I called her on the phone or whether she was the one who called, but she finally said she would be home on a given date in February 1967, and that Mack would bring her. When she got to Tyler she called me at work. She had taken a room in a private home for a few days before coming back to our house. Andy and I talked her into coming home that night, though, and during the remainder of 1967 things seemed to be more normal for us than they had been in many years.

"During March 1967 I moved my shop to a building downtown. I was getting too crowded in the little room I had been using at the house, and when I got things all set up at the new location I thought that it would be good for John to run the shop during the day, or at least part of each day, which she agreed to do. Things went along very well throughout the rest of the year. Our daughter, Amy, came for a few days' visit at Christmastime. A little while before this, though, John had begun to throw cigarettes all over the house again, and there were burned places everywhere. John, of course, insisted that she had *not* thrown them there.

"Some time in late 1967 Mrs. Elliott reappeared and began giving us more advice about how to handle John. By this time I believe Andy was about to go to pieces. One of the officials of the school Andy attended called me and asked why Andy had not been to school. Mrs. Elliott had said for him not to go to school any more, that he could take a correspondence course and get his high school diploma that way. I tried to convince him to return to school.

"I received all sorts of notes from Mrs. Elliott, telling me that Andy was becoming a nervous wreck, and that if I tried to make him go back to school she would take him with her. Andy also told me he would rather go with *her* than to return to school. Finally I asked her why she did not get away from us and never return. The last note I received from her read as follows:

Howard,
You might wish I wouldn't come back but I did. You can do whatever you want to with John. I won't ask Jr. if he wants to come with me, though he might kill himself. Taking John away will only make

*him worry more. You don't care. THERE IS ONE THING YOU
CARE ABOUT AND THAT IS YOU. I wish you would leave Jr.
alone. He can get a course to finish school and get a diploma and
leave you. If you cause any trouble I'll take him or he'll kill himself.
I could help him go to California but that wouldn't be good he be
better off dead, which he probably will be. There's not going to be a
world in 15 years so he doesn't care. He just wants to have some
enjoyment. You are real silly. John's going to get violent. That's the
silliest thing I ever heard. Now you are really going to hurt things
when you send John away. All I asked was 1 week. You don't want
John well you just want rid of her, so you cause trouble and get her
mad. John doesn't cost you all that money you selfish fool. I can't
make John love you but I could get her to clean house and if you
had any sense (which you don't) you would leave her at Trumark.
Now when you send her away and start giving Jr. trouble you are
going to be sorrier than you have been or will ever be. I don't know
Jr. is good at music and would be excellent and be able to make 3
times your money. Maybe he will be better off gone. You silly old
selfish idiot.*

*You can holler and anything else but it will be of no avail.
When you see the nut doctor, tell him about me, maybe they'll put
you away.*

"During the last part of March and early February the most
ghastly things yet began to happen at the house. Henry Anglin
came back. I could not hear him, but Andy said he talked very
little and what few words he did speak were barely understand-
able. Andy could hear his evil laughter. He began by putting an
egg under the mattress about where my head would be. We would
not have known at the time, of course, but he would tell Andy to
have me look in certain places. There was an egg, broken, in one
of my house shoes, one in a pocket of my robe, one in the shade of
the ceiling light, one broken in the corner of the room where it
was running down the wall, and one broken against the chest of
drawers. There was even one inside my pillow case. Andy said
that Anglin would just give a sort of insane-sounding laugh each
time we would find another egg. We cleaned up the mess, and that
was the end of the egg episode.

"A few days later when I got home from work, Andy called me
into our room and there *in the middle of the bed was our dresser.* It

was not very heavy, and I was able to lift it down by myself. The next day the chest of drawers was on the bed. This was very heavy, and it took both Andy and me to set it on the floor again. The following day, when I got home, Andy was not there. I noticed that the door to the room he and I shared was closed. That was not unusual, though, as we often kept it closed during the day. However, when I started to open it, *it simply came off the hinges in my hands.* I could see that the pins had been removed from the hinges, so I just leaned the door against the wall. The next day I found the closet door wrenched from the opening, bringing most of the door facing with it. These were hollow doors and both of them had holes knocked in them about the size of a fist. The next night, about nine o'clock, while I was working at the shop, Andy telephoned me and said *the refrigerator was in our room.* He had heard a noise while he and John were watching television, and got up to see what it was. To reach the bedroom the refrigerator had had to go through the length of the breakfast room, the den, and a hallway before reaching our room. I knew we could not move it back that night so I told Andy to just leave it alone and we would decide what to do the next day. However, a little later he called and said the washing machine, which was located in the kitchen, had been pulled away from the wall and the faucets behind it were leaking and water was running all over the floor.

"I told him to cut off the hydrants, which he did. I then called the police and asked them to meet me at the house. When we got there the holes in the two doors in the bedroom had *increased to about fifteen or twenty* and some of them were through both sides of the doors and big enough to put one's head through.

"Pretty soon, the house was swarming with policemen and detectives. That is when I decided to tell them as briefly as I could what we had been going through. Some of them, I am certain, thought the whole thing was a hoax, and came right out and said they thought I was being hoodwinked by John, who had enlisted Andy's help. That was absolutely ridiculous, though, as practically all of the strange happenings *occurred when Andy and I were together, and while John was staying with Mack about a hundred miles away.* One of the chief detectives talked a long time with John, and later told me that she talked sensibly, but that he was amazed *at her lack of concern about the strange things* that had happened. I too had noticed that she was wholly indifferent to the entire 'show.'

"About the middle of February 1968 things got so bad that I made John give me her key to the shop, and told her that I was going to have to do one of three things. I was going to try and have her committed to a state hospital as I was not financially able to have her take psychiatric treatments, or she could take them and pay for them herself, or I was going to get a divorce. A divorce at my age I thought was ridiculous, but I felt as if I could not stand to go on as things were. Andy was going to move with me as soon as I found a suitable place. John did not seem perturbed one way or the other, and probably did not believe I would really do any of those things. However, on February 24, I did move out of the house, and had my attorney begin divorce proceedings, since he again stated that he did not think I would have a chance in trying to have her committed. I think that when the papers were served on John it was the first time she actually realized what was happening. I got an apartment only a few blocks from my shop. I told Andy to call me every night to let me know how things were at home. I met him at a nearby shopping center each Saturday and gave him enough money to buy food for himself and John during the following week.

"For several weeks we went on this way. One night Andy called me and said that *the dining table was up in the attic*. The only opening to the attic was a rectangular hole in the garage ceiling about 16 by 24 inches, through which *it was absolutely impossible for the table to go*. The next night the table was back in the house again. This happened several times. Other things also 'went' to the attic, such as a small table, an ottoman, and a kidney-shaped end table. Finally, the dining table came down and Andy found it in the garage, and after considerable work was able to get it inside the house where it belonged.

"Eventually, John was beginning to believe that the strange things we had been talking about were really happening. Previously she had just made fun of us whenever we would mention them. Several weeks after I had left, Andy was sitting in the den, playing his guitar, when the lights went out. At first he thought that a bulb had burned out, but when he looked at the switch he could see that it had *been turned off*. This happened several times. Once when John was going through the den the light went out and she too saw that the switch had been turned; Andy was not any-where near it, and there was nobody else who could have done it.

"It was well into the second month after I left home. I had just finished work in the shop. The telephone rang. It was John and she sounded hysterical. She said she was very sick and begged me to come home. I got there a few minutes later, and she could hardly talk. She continued to beg me to come home, but I told her I could never spend another night in that house. Finally I got her calmed down enough to talk seriously. I finally told her that I would come back, but that first we would have to find another place to live. I demanded that she never smoke again. Finally, on April 15, 1968, we moved out of the house of horrors, and I have not been there since.

"John has not smoked since that time. It has now been over three months since we left the house, and John does the normal things about the house except cook. She is again at my rubber-stamp shop and seems to enjoy it."

In retrospect, as I read over these words, I realized how diffi-cult it must have been for Mr. Beaird to report on his experiences, especially to a stranger. What had appeared completely impossi-ble to him would, of course, have been even more unbelievable to someone who was not present when it happened, and he doubted his own sanity at times, which was not surprising.

Having met Howard Beaird, I am sure that he is completely sane, in fact, so sane he could not even be called neurotic. Had I not heard of parallel cases before, perhaps I too would have won-dered about it. None of the phenomena reported by Mr. Beaird are, however, impossible in the light of parapsychological re-search. We are dealing here with forces that seem to be in contra-diction of ordinary or orthodox physical laws, but the more we learn of the nature of matter and the structure of the atom, the more it seems likely that poltergeist activities connect with phys-ics in such a way as to make seeming dematerialization and re-materialization of solid objects possible practically without time loss. But the case was a question of studying not so much the techniques involved in the phenomena as the reasons behind them and those causing them.

I informed Mr. Beaird that I was eager to enter the case, especially as I wanted to make sure that the Poltergeist activities had really ceased once and for all and would never recur at his new location. In cases of this kind there is always the possibility that the phenomena are attached to one or the other person in the household rather than to a location. Moving to another house seems to have stopped the activities, but as there had been pauses before that culminated in renewed and even stronger physical activities, I wanted to be sure that this would not be the case in this new location. I explained that I would have to interview all those concerned, even the police detectives who had come to the house on that fateful night. Mr. Beaird assured me that he would make all the necessary arrangements, and, after discussing my plans with his wife and son, they too agreed to talk to me. Mack, the sister-in-law who had been hostess to Mrs. Beaird while most of the phenomena took place at the house, was unable to meet me in Tyler, but I was assured that Mrs. Beaird had never left her care during all that time. For a while Howard Beaird had thought that his wife had returned without his knowledge and done some of the things about the house that had startled him. This, of course, turned out to be a false impression. At no time did Mrs. Beaird leave her sister-in-law's house in Daingerfield, seventy-five miles away. Whether or not her astral self visited the home is another matter and would be subject to my investigation and verification as far as possible.

Mr. Beaird also went back to his former home to talk to the present owners. Somewhat suspicious of him for no apparent reason, they were willing to see me if I came to Tyler. Mr. M. works for a local bakery and returns home at 5:30 P.M., and since his wife would not entertain strange visitors in the absence of her husband, my visit would have to be at such an hour as was convenient to the M.'s. Perhaps the somewhat battered condition of the house when the M.'s had bought it from Mr. Beaird might be the reason for their reluctance to discuss my visit. At any rate it was agreed that I could call briefly on them and talk to them about the matter at hand.

Howard Beaird's daughter, who is now Mrs. Howard Wilson, lives in Austin, Texas. She has had some interest in the occult and mind development and had suggested that someone from the Silva Mind Center in Laredo should come up to Tyler to investigate the case. That was prior to my entering the situation, however, and now Mrs. Wilson wanted very much to come up to Tyler herself and be present during my investigation. Unfortunately it turned out later that she was unable to keep the date due to prior commitments.

Thorough man that he is, Howard Beaird also talked to Detective Weaver at the police station to make sure I could see him and question him about his own investigation of the house. I was assured of the welcome mat at the police station, so I decided to set the time when I could go down to Tyler and look for myself into what appeared to be one of the most unusual cases of psychic phenomena.

On February 5, 1969, I arrived at the Tyler airport. It was 5:42 in the afternoon and Howard Beaird was there to welcome me. We had made exact plans beforehand so he whisked me away to the Blackstone Hotel, allowed me to check in quickly, then went with me to see Detective Weaver at the police station.

As we passed through town I had the opportunity to observe what Tyler, Texas, was all about. Clean shops, quiet streets, a few tree-lined avenues, small houses, many of them very old—well, old in terms of the United States—and people quietly going about their business seem to be characteristic of this small town. We passed by Howard Beaird's neat, tidy shop, the company name Trumark written plainly on the window pane. As in many small towns, the telephone wires were all above ground, strung in a lazy haphazard fashion from street to street. The police station turned out to be a modern concrete building set back a little from the street. Detective Weaver readily agreed to talk to me. Howard Beaird left us for the moment in a fine sense of propriety just in case the detective wanted to say something not destined for his ears. As it turned out, there wasn't anything he could not have said in front of him. Was there anything in the detective's opinion indicating participation by either the boy or Mrs. Beaird in the strange phenomena? The detective shrugged. There was nothing he could pinpoint along those lines. He then went to the files and extricated a manila envelope inscribed "pictures and letter, reference mysterious call at —— Elizabeth, February 19, 1968, 11:00 P.M., case number 67273. Officer B. Rosenstein and officer M. Garrett." Inside the envelope there were two pictures, photographs taken at the time by a police photographer named George Bain. One picture was of the door, clearly showing the extreme violence with which a hole had been punched into it. The entire rim of the hole was splintered as if extremely strong methods had been employed to punch this hole through the door.

The other picture showed a heavy chest of drawers of dark wood sitting squarely upon a bed. Quite clearly the description given to me by Howard Beaird had been correct. What exactly did the two police officers find when they arrived at the house on Elizabeth Street? The house was in disorder, the detective explained, and furniture in places where it wasn't supposed to be. On the whole he bore out the description of events given by Howard Beaird.

Somehow he made me understand that the police did not accept the supernatural origin of the phenomena even though they could not come up with anything better in the way of a solution. Almost reluctantly, the officer wondered whether perhaps Andy wasn't in some way responsible for the phenomena, although he did not say so in direct words. I decided to discuss the practical theories concerning Poltergeists with him and found him amazingly interested. "Would you like to have the photographs?" the detective asked and handed me the folder. Surprised by his generosity, I took the folder and I still have it in my files. It isn't very often that a researcher such as I is given the original folder from the files of a police department. But then the mystery on Elizabeth Street is no longer an active situation—or is it?

After we had thanked Detective Weaver for his courtesies we decided to pay a visit to the house itself. After a moment of hesitation, the officer suggested that he come along since it might make things easier for us. How right he was. When we arrived at the house on Elizabeth Street and cautiously approached the entrance, with me staying behind at first, there was something less than a cordial reception awaiting us. Mr. M. was fully aware of my purpose, of course, so that we were hardly surprising him with all this.

After a moment of low-key discussion at the door between Howard Beaird and Detective Weaver on one hand and Mr. M. on the other, I was permitted to enter the house and look around for myself. The M. family had come to see me, if not to greet me, and looked at me with curious eyes. I explained politely and briefly that I wanted to take some photographs for the record and I was permitted to do so. I took black-and-white pictures with a high-sensitivity film in various areas of the house, especially the kitchen area where it connects with the garage and the living room, both places where many of the phenomena have been reported in Mr. Beaird's testimony.

On developing these under laboratory conditions, we found there was nothing unusual except perhaps certain bright light formations in the kitchen area where there should be none since no reflective surfaces existed. Then I returned to the living room to talk briefly with Mr. M. and his family.

Was there anything unusual about the house that he had noticed since he had moved in? Almost too fast he replied, "Nothing whatsoever. Everything was just fine." When Mr. M. explained how splendid things were with the house he shot an anxious look at his wife, and I had the distinct impression they were trying to be as pleasant and superficial as possible and to get rid of me as fast as they could. Did they have any interest in occult phenomena such as ghosts? I finally asked. Mr. M. shook his head. Their religion did not allow them such considerations, he explained somewhat sternly. Then I knew the time had come to make my departure.

I made inquiries with real estate people in the area and discovered a few things about the house neither Mr. Beaird nor Mr. M. had told me. The house was thirteen years old and had been built by a certain Terry Graham. There had been two tenants before the Beairds. Prior to 1835 the area had been Indian territory and was used as a cow pasture by the Cherokee Indians.

I also discovered that Mrs. M. had complained to the authorities about footsteps in the house when there was no one walking, of doors opening by themselves, and the uncanny feeling of being watched by someone she could not see. That was shortly after the M.'s had moved into the house. The M.'s also have young children. It is conceivable that the entities who caused such problems to the Beaird family might have been able to manifest through them also. Be that as it may, the matter was not followed up. Perhaps their religious upbringing and beliefs did not permit them to discuss such matters and they preferred to ignore them, or perhaps the activities died of their own volition. At any rate, it seemed pretty certain to me that the Poltergeist activities did not entirely cease with the removal of the Beairds from the house. But did these activities continue in the new house the Beairds had chosen for their own? That was a far more important question.

I asked Howard Beaird to send me a report of further activities if and when they occurred at the new house. On February 23 he communicated with me by letter. I had asked him to send me samples of John's and Andy's handwriting so that I could compare them with the notes he had let me have for further study. In order to arrive at a satisfactory explanation of the phenomena it was, of course, necessary to consider all ordinary sources for them. Amongst the explanations one would have to take into account was the possibility of either conscious or unconscious fraud, that is to say, the writing of the notes by either John or Andy and their somehow manipulating them so that they would seem to appear out of nowhere in front of Mr. Beaird. For that purpose I needed examples of the two handwritings to compare them with some of the handwritings on the notes.

There were a number of noises in the new home that could be attributed to natural causes. But there were two separate incidents that, in the opinion of Howard Beaird, could not be so explained. Shortly before I arrived in Tyler a minor incident occurred that makes Howard wonder whether the entities from beyond the veil are still with him in the new house. One evening he had peeled two hard-boiled eggs in order to have them for lunch the following day. He had placed them in the refrigerator on a paper towel. The following morning he discovered that both eggs were frozen solid even though they were still on the lower shelf of the refrigerator. This could only have been accomplished if they had spent considerable time in the freezer compartment during the night. Questioning his wife and son as to whether they had put the eggs in the freezer, he discovered that neither of them had done so. He decided to test the occurrence by repeating the process. He found that the two new eggs he had placed in the refrigerator that night were still only chilled but not frozen the next day. What had made the first pair of eggs as hard as stone he is unable to understand, but he is satisfied that the occurrence may be of nonpsychic origin.

Then there was the matter of a clock playing a certain tune as part of its alarm clock device. For no apparent reason this clock went off several times, even though no one had been near it. Even though it had not been wound for a long time and had only a twenty-four-hour movement, it played this tune several times from deep inside a chest of drawers. Eventually the clock was removed, and in retrospect Mr. Beaird does not think that a supernatural situation could have been responsible for it. But the two separate incidents did frighten the Beairds somewhat. They were afraid that the change of address had not been sufficient to free them from the influences of the past. As it turned out, the move was successful and the separation complete.

I had to work with two kinds of evidence. There was, first of all, the massive evidence of mysterious notes that had fallen out of the sky and that showed handwriting of various kinds. Perhaps I could make something out of that by comparing them with the handwritings of living people. Then there was the question of talking personally and in depth with the main participants, the Beairds, and, finally, to see what others who knew them had to say about them. Howard Beaird's daughter, Amy, thought that the real victim of what she thought "a circus of horrors" was her brother, Andy. "If you had known Andy when he was small, up to the time mother began to show real signs of her illness, it would be impossible for you to recognize him as the same person now. He was typically, for a little boy, simply brimming over with mischievous humor. He would do anything to make people laugh and would run simply hooting with joy through the house when he had done something devilish." That was not the Andy I met when I came to Tyler. The boy I talked to was quiet, withdrawn, painfully shy, and showed definite signs of being disturbed.

The following morning I went to see the Beairds at their new home. The home itself is pleasant and small and stands in a quiet, tree-lined street. As prearranged, Mr. Beaird left me alone with each of the two other members of his family so that I could speak to them in complete confidence. Andy, a lanky boy, seemed ill at ease at first when we sat down. In order to gain his confidence, I talked about songs and the records popular at the time, since I had seen a number of record albums in his room. Somehow this helped open him up; he spoke more freely after that. Now sixteen, he was studying at a local barber college. When I wondered how a young man, in this day and age, would choose this somewhat unusual profession, he assured me that the money was good in this line of work and that he really liked it. He felt he could put his heart and soul into it. After some discussion of the future as far as Andy was concerned, I brought the conversation around to the matter at hand.

"When these peculiar events took place you and your father lived alone in the other house. Did you ever see anyone?" "Well, I had seen a vision of my mother this one time. It looked like her but nobody was there really . . . kind of like a shadow, or a form." "Have you seen the notes?" "Yes." "Did you ever actually see anyone writing them?" "No." "Did you ever hear any voices?" "Yeh. I talked to them." "How did they sound?" "Well, the women that were here all sounded alike . . . real high voices. The men were dead, you know . . . the spirits, or whatever you want to call them. They had real deep voices. They were hard to understand." "Did they talk to you in the room?" "From out of nowhere. No matter where I might be." "You didn't see them anywhere?" "Never saw them." "Was your father with you at the time you heard the voices or were you alone?" "He was with me at times and not at others." "These voices . . . are they mostly in the daytime or are they at night?" "At night . . . mostly at night, or afternoon, when I'd get home from school." "Did it start right after you moved in?" "No . . . it was two or three months after." "Did you see the insects?" "Oh yes." "Where did they come from?" "It seemed like just out of the ceiling." "Could they have come in any other way?" "They couldn't have come in . . . not that many." "Whose voices did you hear?" "First of all my mother's." "The time she was away at Daingerfield?" "Yes." "What did the voice sound like?" "The same high voice. It sounded a little like her." "What did she say?" "She started to talk about my grandfather's funeral and about someone being mean to her."

Clearly the boy was not at his best. Whether it was my presence and the pressure the questioning was putting on him or whether he genuinely did not remember, he was somewhat uncertain about a lot of the things his father had told me about. But he was quite sure that he had heard his mother's voice at a time when she was away at Daingerfield. He was equally sure that none of the insects could have gotten into the house by ordinary means and that the notes came down, somehow of their own volition, from the ceiling. I did not wish to frighten him and thanked him for his testimony, short though it was. I then asked that John join me in the front room so we could talk quietly. Mrs. Beaird seemed quite at ease with me and belied the rather turbulent history I knew she had had. Evidently the stay at her sister-in-law's house and the prior psychiatric treatment had done some good. Her behavior was not at all unusual; in fact, it was deceptively normal. Having seen one of her earlier photographs I realized that she had aged tremendously. Of course I realized that her husband would have discussed many of the things with her so that she would have gained secondhand knowledge of the phenomena. Nevertheless, I felt it important to probe into them because sometimes a person thinks she is covering up while, in fact, she is giving evidence.

"Now we are going to discuss the other house," I said pleasantly. "Do you remember some of the events that happened in the other house?" "Well, I wasn't there when they took place. They told me about it . . . and actually, you will learn more from my son than from me because I don't know anything." "You were away all that time?" "Yes." "Before you went, did anything unusual happen?" "Nothing." "After you came back did anything happen?" "Well, I don't know . . . I don't remember anything." "Before you bought the house, did you have any unusual experience involving extrasensory perception at any time?" "Never. I know nothing whatever about it." "You were living somewhere else for a while." "I was with my sister-in-law." "How would you describe that period of your life? Was it an unhappy one? A confusing one? What would you say that period was?" "I have never been unhappy. I have never been confused." "Why did you go?" "I felt I needed to for personal reasons." "During that time did you have contact with your husband and son? Did you telephone or did you come back from time to time?" "I did not come back, but I had some letters from them and I believe that I talked some." "Did your husband ever tell you some of the things that had happened in your absence?" "Yes. He told me." "What did you make of it?" "I didn't understand it. If I had seen it, I'd have gotten to the bottom of it somehow." "The people who are mentioned in some of these notes, are you familiar with them? Were there any of them that you had a personal difficulty with or grudge against?" "None whatever. They were friends." "Now, you are familiar with this lady, Mrs. Elliott, who has, apparently, sent some notes." "Oh yes. She was a very good friend of mine. Of course, she is much older. She had a daughter my age and we were very good friends." "Did you have any difficulties?" "I have no difficulties," she replied and her eyes filled with tears. "No? You had at the time you left here." "Not real difficulties. For several reasons, I needed a change. I didn't intend to stay so long. She was living alone and she worked during the day. And we sort of got into a most enjoyable relationship whereby I took care of certain household chores while she was gone." "What made you stay so long?" "I just really can't tell you what it was." "You still have no answer to the puzzle as to what happened?" "None. I have no idea." "Do you remember having any treatments?" "I'm just getting old. That is the difficulty."

It was clear that her mind had blocked out all memory of the unpleasant occurrences in her life. As often happens with people who have undergone psychiatric treatment, there remains a void afterward, even if electric shock therapy has not been used. Partially this is, of course, due to the treatment, but sometimes it is self-induced by the patient deliberately in order to avoid discussing the unpleasant. Mrs. Beaird had returned to her husband and son to resume life and try to make the best of it. To go back over the past would have served no purpose from her point of view. This was not a matter of refusing to discuss these things with me. She quite consciously did not remember them and no amount of probing would have helped, except perhaps in-depth hypnosis, and I was not prepared to undertake this with a former mental patient. Clearly then I could not get any additional material from the principal. I decided to reexamine the evidence and talk again with the one man who seemed, after all, the most reliable witness in the entire case, Mr. Beaird himself.

In particular, I wanted to reexamine his own personal observations of certain phenomena, for it is one thing to make a report alone, quietly, filled with the memory of what one has experienced, and another to report on phenomena while being interrogated by a knowledgeable, experienced investigator. Quite possibly some new aspects might be unearthed in this fashion. At the very least it would solidify some of the incredible things that had happened in the Beaird household.

On the morning of February 6, 1969, I met with Howard Beaird at my hotel and we sat down, quietly, to go over the fantastic events of the past three years. In order to arrive at some sort of conclusion, which I wanted very much to do, I had to be sure that Mr. Beaird's powers of observation had been completely reliable. In going over some of his statements once again I wasn't trying to be repetitive but rather to observe his reaction to my questions and to better determine in my own mind whether or not he had observed correctly. In retrospect I can only say that Howard Beaird was completely unshaken and repeated, in essence, exactly what he had reported to me earlier. I feel that he has been telling the truth all along, neither embellishing it nor diminishing it. Our conversation started on a calm emotional note, which was now much more possible than at the time he first made his report to me, when he was still under the influence of recent events. Things had been quiet at the house and seemed to continue to remain quiet, so he was able to gather his thoughts more clearly and speak of the past without the emotional involvement that would have made it somewhat more difficult for me to judge his veracity.

"Now we had better start at the beginning. I am interested in discussing whatever *you yourself* observed. Your wife was still in the house when the first thing happened?" "Yes." "Were those *real* bugs?" "Yes." "When you turned the light on?" "You could see thousands of bugs on the floor." "How did you get rid of them?" "We had a vacuum cleaner." "Did they come from the direction of the windows or the door?" "The door." "Now, after the bugs, what was the next thing that you personally observed?" "I heard my wife's voice. After my son and I had gone to bed we were lying there talking about these things that had happened. That was after she had left Tyler." "Did it sound like her voice?" "No. It didn't sound like her voice to me but it was *her*." "Well, how did you know it was her?" "She told me it was and was talking about my sister having insulted her. Nobody else knew that except my wife and I." "Where did the voice seem to come from? Was it in the room?" "Yes." "What happened after that?" "Several nights after that, she appeared to Andy. I heard him talking in the bathroom. He talked for two or three minutes, and then I heard him say, well, good-bye." "Didn't it make you feel peculiar? His mother was obviously not there and he was talking to her?" "Well, I had already had my encounter with her." "Did you call your wife in Daingerfield?" "No." "Why not?" "Well, she wouldn't have believed me. I had thought about writing her sister-in-law and telling her that you've got to keep my wife in Daingerfield. I don't want her here. Yet, I thought, that's a foolish thing to do, because all she'll say is, *she wasn't here*. She wasn't in person. Her body

wasn't here." "After the voice, what came next?" "Well, it was
shortly after that we started hearing these other voices." "Did you
hear those voices?" "All of them, yes. All four." "Did they sound
alike or did they sound different?" "The men had deep rough
voices, but I could tell them apart. And the ladies were all subtle
voices and I couldn't tell them apart, except when they told me."
"Did you ever hear two voices at the same time?" "I don't believe
so. However, Mrs. Snow and Mrs. Elliott were there at the same
time. That is, they *said* they were. That was when Henry Anglin
was giving us so much trouble and they had to carry him back to
his grave." "Let's talk about anything that you have actually seen
move." "I saw these notes that were folded. Sometimes as many
as ten or fifteen notes a day." "From an enclosed room?" "Well,
the doors weren't closed between the rooms, but I'd be sitting at
the table eating something, and all of a sudden I'd see one fall. I'd
look up toward the ceiling and there'd be one up there." "Most of
these notes were signed 'Mrs. Elliott'?" "Yes. Later she signed
them. At first, Elie and then El. Now after my wife came back from
Daingerfield she, too, would send me notes through Andy. I was
working in my shop and Andy would bring me a note written with
numbers, in code. 1 was A, 2 was B, and so forth. I hated to take
the time to decipher those things, but I would sit down and find
out what they said. In one note she asked me if I didn't 'lose' some
weight?" "Did your wife ever write you a note in longhand or in
block letters?" "No." "Was there any similarity in the writing of
your wife's note and those that later came down from the ceiling?" "I can't say, but Mrs. Elliott had been after me to lose
weight. I thought it was peculiar—that my wife came from Daingerfield and asked about my losing weight also." "Mrs. Elliott
was a contemporary of your wife?" "She died in 1963. About a
year before we moved here." "Were those two women very close
in life?" "Not particularly. They were neighbors." "What about
Mrs. Snow?" "She was peculiar." "What objects did you see
move in person?" "I saw a heavy pair of shoes lift themselves off
the floor and fly right over my bed and land on the opposite side of
the bed." "Did they land fast or did they land slowly?" "It was just
as if I'd picked them up and thrown them. Andy's house shoes
came the same way. I've watched the cat being lifted up about a
foot from where he was sitting and just be suspended for several
seconds and it didn't fall on the floor. I saw a can of insect spray

that was sitting on the cabinet come over and suspend itself right over that opening, and spray into that little room, and I was nearly suffocated. I had to open the doors or the insect spray would have got me." "You weren't holding the can?" "No." "I am particularly interested in anything where you were *actually* present when movement occurred, or voices were heard." "I've seen my clothes fly through the air as I was coming home." "Did these things occur whether your wife was physically in the house or not?" "Yes." "Did anything ever happen while neither your son nor your wife was at home but you were alone?" "I believe so." "Your wife had some personal shock in 1951, I believe, when her best friend died suddenly. Do you feel her mental state changed as a result?" "Very gradually, yes. She was very happy, though, when she found out she was going to have another child, because she thought this would make up for the loss of her friend. She was just crazy about him." "Now, when was the first time you noticed there was something wrong with her mentally?" "In 1960 my wife took over her daughter's room. She stopped up all the windows with newspapers scotch-taped against the wall and hung a blanket in each window of the bedroom." "Why did she do that?" "She felt someone was spying on her. At the office, she took the telephone apart, and adding machines and typewriters, looking for microphones to see who was spying on her." "But the phenomena themselves did not start until you moved into this house?" "That's right."

I thanked Mr. Beaird for his honest testimony, for he had not claimed anything beyond or different from his original report to me. I took the voluminous handwritten notes and the letters pertaining to the case and went back to New York to study them. This would take some time since I planned to compare the handwriting by both Mrs. Beaird and Andy. I didn't, for a moment, think that the notes had been written consciously by either one of them and simply thrown at Mr. Beaird in the ordinary way. Quite obviously Mr. Beaird was no fool, and any such clumsy attempt at fake phenomena would not have gone unnoticed, but there are other possibilities that could account for the presense of either Mrs. Beaird's or Andy's handwriting in the notes, if indeed there was that similarity.

There were already, clearly visible to me, certain parallels between this case and the Bell Witch case of Tennessee. Ven-

geance was being wrought on Howard Beaird by some entity or
entities for alleged wrongs, in this case his failure to execute minor orders given him. But there were other elements differing
greatly from the classic case. In the Bell Witch situation there was
not present, in the household, anyone who could be classed as
psychotic. In Tyler we have two individuals capable of supplying
unused psychic energies. One definitely psychotic, the other on
the borderline, or at least psychoneurotic.

I then decided to examine the notes written in this peculiar
style longhand, almost always in block letters but upper-case letters in the middle of words where they do not belong. It became
immediately clear to me that this was a crude way of disguising
handwriting and was not used for any other reason. It is of course
a fact that no one can effectively disguise handwriting to fool the
expert; an expert graphologist can always trace the peculiarities
of a person's handwriting back to the original writer, provided
samples are available to compare the two handwritings letter by
letter, word for word. Some of the notes were downright infantile.
For instance, on December 6, 1965, a note read "My power is
decreasing. I'm going back to Mack. I must hurry. I would like to
come home but I don't guess I will. I love you. Please give me a
Yule gift. I can't restore my power. I am allowed only three a year.
Phone police." What the cryptic remark "I am allowed only three
a year" is supposed to mean is not explained.

Sometimes Howard Beaird played right into the hands of the
unknown writer. The Sunday morning after he and Andy had
spent the night at a motel because of the goings-on in the house,
he received the notice of a package at the post office. He knew that
he couldn't get it except by noon on a week day, so he asked aloud,
"Is this notice about anything important, as I don't want to come
in from the hospital if it doesn't amount to anything?" A few
seconds later a note fluttered down from the ceiling reading only
"something." That of course was not a satisfactory answer such as
an adult or reasonable person would give. It sounded more like a
petulant child having a game. On December 6, 1965, a note materialized equally mysteriously, reading, "I don't want to admit to
Mack that I'm nutty." Another note dated December 6, 1965,
simply read, "Howard got jilted." Another note read "My powers
were restored by the Houston witch. Call the police and ask about
her." There doesn't seem to be any great difference between the

notes signed by Henry Anglin or by Mrs. Elliott or not signed at all by someone intimating that they were the work of Mrs. Beaird. The letters and the formation of the words are similar. A note dated December 8, 1965, read: "Dear Howard, I love you. I have been wrong. I want to come home but I don't want stupid Mack to know I am unusual. I am really two people. If things end I won't remember nothin'. I can be in three places at once. I love you and Junior. Please dear."

The note signed "Dorothy Kilgallen," mentioned previously and received by Howard Beaird December 22, 1965, reads, "Dear Mr. Beaird: Mrs. Elliott told me about what all has happened to your family and what Henry Anglin is responsible for. It is very tragic. He is the reason I am dead because he changed my pills. Good night and good luck." Having been personally acquainted with the late Hearst columnist Dorothy Kilgallen, I am quite certain that she would not have expressed herself in this manner, dead or alive.

A note signed Pont Thornton, dated December 23, 1965, reads, "Dear Howard P.S. an Andy: I no yu well. I no yu good. I don't drinck much do yu haf had hardships. Anglin is a mean man. I am smarter than Henry Lee. I am a distant kin of Abe Lincoln and Lewis Armstrong and Sam Davis Junior and Jon F. Kenede." Not only was the note atrociously misspelled but it lists several quite improbable relationships. When writing as Mrs. Elliott the personality is much more concise and logical than when the writer is supposed to be Henry Anglin or Mrs. Beaird. But despite the difference in style the letters are very similar. Of course since the notes came down for almost three years it is to be expected that there are some differences in both style and appearance between them.

On September 17, 1967, Howard Beaird observed, "About 9 or 10 P.M. Andy heard Mrs. Elliott call. She told him he could talk to her and that mother could not hear so he did and apparently mother knew nothing of it. Just as I was getting ready for bed I heard Mrs. Elliott calling me. The sound seemed to come toward the kitchen and as Andy and Johnny were watching TV in her bedroom I went to the kitchen. Mrs. Elliott called me several more times and the sound then seemed to be coming from my room. She said that Johnny couldn't hear me so I tried to talk to her but Andy said she told him she never could hear me. Anyway before going to bed I found a very small piece of paper folded so small on the floor in the hall and also a South Side Bank deposit slip folded near it. The small note said 'Be very generous. Say hi to me. Mrs. Snow.' The larger note said, 'Don't be stingy Sam be a generous Joe. George Swiney.' After I had gone to bed I heard Mrs. Elliott calling me several times but could never make her hear me answer. Just as I was about to go to sleep, Andy came in and said Mrs. Elliott told him she had left me a note on the floor. Just as I got up to look for it a note dropped in the chair next to my bed. I took it to the kitchen to get my glasses and it said, 'Howard, I hope there won't be any slugs. Try to be generous, you have a lot of money. There's so much you could get you, John and Andy.' " This was followed by a list of objects, clothing primarily, which he could get for his family on her suggestion. Howard Beaird tried to talk to Mrs. Elliott to ask her where all that alleged money was but he could never get an answer to that.

On September 29, 1967, Howard Beaird noticed that Mrs. Elliott came to visit him around 7:30 P.M. He can't understand how she can make him hear her when she calls him by name and then make it impossible for him to hear the rest of the conversation, which has to be relayed through Andy. On the other hand, if he speaks loudly enough she can hear him. That night Mrs. Elliott informed him that a Mr. Quinn had been by earlier. A little later Mr. Quinn himself came back and Howard Beaird actually heard him call, but he could hear nothing else, and again Andy had to be the interpreter. Andy said that Mr. Quinn sounded like a robot talking, and that, of course, made sense to Mr. Beaird, since he knew that Quinn, who had lost his voice due to cancer prior to his death, used an instrument held to his throat to enable him to talk. The late Mr. Quinn apparently wanted to know how some of the people back in Grand Saline were, including Mrs. Drake, Mr. and Mrs. Watkins, and the McMullens. This information, of course, could not have been known to Andy, who had been much too young at the time the Beairds knew these people in the town where they formerly lived.

Mrs. Elliott also explained the reason she and the other spirits were able to be with Mr. Beaird that evening was that they had been given time off for the holidays—because of Halloween, although that was a little early for All Hallow's Eve. Mr. Beaird thought it peculiar that spirits get furloughs from whatever place they are in.

On September 30, 1967, Beaird had heard nothing at all from Mrs. Elliott during the day. Andy had been out pretty late that night and Mr. Beaird was asleep when he came in. Sometime after, Andy woke him and said that Mrs. Elliott had left him a note. They found it on his bed. It read, "Howard, think about what I said. Are you going to do it Monday. Elliott." Just below it was a note reading, "John wants a vacuum cleaner and a purse. Junior wants a coat for school and some banjo strings. Hiram." Now the remarkable thing about this note is that the first part was definitely in the handwriting of Mrs. Beaird, while the second part was a crude note put together with a lot of capital letters where they did not belong and generally disorganized. Hiram Quinn, the alleged writer, was a very sick man for some time prior to his passing. When Howard Beaird confronted the alleged Mrs. Elliott with the fact that her note was written in the handwriting of his wife, she shrugged it off by explaining that she could write like anybody she wished.

On October 2, 1967, Mr. Beaird noted, "About 7:30 P.M. Mrs. Snow called my name. I was in the kitchen and the voice seemed to come from the back part of the house where Andy and John were. The voice sounded exactly like Mrs. Elliott's and although I could hear it plainly enough and answered aloud immediately I could hear nothing else and Andy had to tell me what she had said. She just wanted to tell me about my stamp business and how John had been. She could barely hear me and told Andy to turn off the attic fan and for me to go into my room and close the door so she could hear. She couldn't explain how I could hear her call my name and then hear nothing more and said it was some kind of 'law.' "

The notes signed by Mrs. Elliott from that period onward frequently looked as if they had been written by Mrs. Beaird. The handwriting is unquestionably hers. That is to say, it looks like hers. Howard Beaird does not doubt that the notes were genuinely materialized in a psychic sense. On October 23 he had dozed off to sleep several times and on one occasion was awakened by the rustling of papers on the floor beside his bed. He was alone in the room at the time. He turned the light on and found a sort of pornographic magazine folded up on the floor. Andy came in at this point and explained that Mrs. Elliott had told him she had found this magazine in Mrs. Beaird's room. She said that Mrs. Beaird had gotten it at the beauty shop and the piece of paper was torn from it. On the note was printed "Somebody loves you," signed underneath, El.

On November 12, 1967, a Sunday, Howard Beaird heard Mrs. Elliott talk to him. She advised him that he should go to Mrs. Beaird's room and look for some nudist pictures and also some hand-drawn pictures of naked men and women. Mr. Beaird found all these things but his wife denied any knowledge of them. The following night was particularly remarkable in the kind of phenomena experienced by Howard Beaird. "Mrs. Elliott came by before I left for the shop and told me to look for some more lewd pictures. I found some and destroyed them. Mrs. Elliott told me to be sure and tear them up in front of John and maybe she would quit drawing them, and also quit buying the nudist magazine pictures. Later that night, about 9:15, Mrs. Elliott called me on the telephone. *That's the first time I ever talked to a ghost on the telephone.* I could understand what she said on the phone, yet I could never hear anything except her calling my name when I was at home. Of course all she said on the phone was to come home. I then talked to Andy and he said she wanted me to come home right then and get some more drawings and nudist magazines from John's hiding places. I did go home and got the pictures and went back to the shop after I had destroyed them."

Some of the notes showed the underlying conflict, imagined or real, between the young boy and his father that was of much concern to the "guardian angel," Mrs. Elliott. On January 11, 1968, a note read, "Howard, I need to write you notes. Junior has had to worry so much. Why do you mind him coming with me? He would be happy. It would be right for him not to worry. I agree he must get an education but at seventeen he could get a course and then to college. In the meantime I will help John and him. He could play music and he would be great at seventeen. He would also like to take care of the house. John would get so much better. You would be better financially and Junior could get better. This is the only thing I will allow or I will take him with me if he wants to. . . . He said he would tell me to go and wouldn't go but that wouldn't change him from wanting to. You had better pay attention cause he wants to come. I have all the divine right to take

him. El." This threat by the spirit of Mrs. Elliott to take the young
boy with her into the spirit world did not sit lightly with his father,
of course. Analyzed on its face value, it has the ring of a threat a
petulant youngster would make against his parents if he didn't get
his way. If Mrs. Elliott was the spirit of a mature and rational
person then this kind of threat didn't seem, to me, to be in character with the personality of the alleged Mrs. Elliott.

The following night, January 12, 1968, the communicator
wrote, "Howard, I have the divine right. I will prove it by taking
Junior and I take him tonight. You don't love him at all. You don't
care about anyone." Mrs. Elliott had not taken Andy by January
15, but she let Howard know that she might do so anyway any
time now. In fact, her notes sounded more and more like a spokes-
man for Andy if he wanted to complain about life at home but
didn't have the courage to say so consciously and openly. On
January 18, Mrs. Elliott decided she wasn't going to take the boy
after all. She had promised several times before that she would
not come back any longer and that her appearance was the last
one. But she always broke this pledge.

By now any orthodox psychologist or even parapsychologist
would assume that the young man was materially involved not
only in the composition of the notes but in actually writing them. I
don't like to jump to conclusions needlessly, especially not when a
prejudice concerning the method of communication would
clearly be involved in assuming that the young man did the actual
writing. But I decided to continue examining each and every word
and to see whether the letters or the words themselves gave me
any clue as to what human hand had actually written them, if any.
It appeared clear to me by now that some if not all of the notes
purporting to be the work of Mrs. Elliott were in the hand of Mrs.
Beaird. But it was not a very good copy of her handwriting.
Rather did it seem to me that someone had attempted to write in
Mrs. Beaird's hand who wasn't actually Mrs. Beaird. As for the
other notes—those signed by Henry Anglin, Hiram Quinn, and
those unsigned but seemingly the work of Mrs. Beaird herself—
they had certain common denominators. I had asked Mr. Beaird
to supply me with adequate examples of the handwriting of both
Andy and Mrs. Beaird: handwritten notes not connected in any
way with the psychic phenomena at the house. I then studied
these examples and compared them with the notes that allegedly

came from nowhere or that materialized by falling from the ceiling in front of a very astonished Mr. Beaird.

I singled out the following letters as being characteristic of the writer, whoever he or she may be. The capital T, the lower-case e, lower-case p, g, y, r, and capital B, C, L, and the figure 9. All of these appeared in a number of notes. They also appear in the sample of Andy's handwriting, in this case a list of songs he liked and was apparently going to learn on his guitar. There is no doubt in my mind that the letters in the psychic notes and the letters on Andy's song list are identical—*they were written by the same hand.* By that I do not mean to say that Andy necessarily wrote the notes. I do say, however, that the hand used to create the psychic notes is the same hand used consciously by Andy Beaird when writing notes of his own. I am less sure, but suspect, that even the notes seemingly in the handwriting of his mother are also done in the same fashion and also traceable to Andy Beaird.

On December 7, 1965, one of the few drawings in the stack of notes appeared. It showed a man in a barber chair and read, among other annotations, "Aren't the barbers sweet, ha ha." It should be remembered that Andy's great ambition in life was to be a barber. In fact, when I met and interviewed him he was going to barber school.

What then is the meaning of all this? Let us not jump to conclusions and say Andy Beaird wrote the notes somehow unobserved, smuggled them into Mr. Beaird's room somehow unnoticed, and made them fall from the ceiling seemingly of their own volition, somehow without Mr. Beaird noticing this. In a number of reported instances this is a possibility, but in the majority of cases it simply couldn't have happened in this manner, not unless Howard Beaird was not a rational individual and was, in fact, telling me lies. I have no doubt that Mr. Beaird is telling me the truth and that he is a keen and rational observer. Consequently the burden of truth for the validity of the phenomena does not rest on his gift of observation, but on the possibility of producing such paranormal occurrences despite their seeming improbability yet reconciling this with the ominous fact that they show strong indications of being Andy Beaird's handwriting.

We must recognize the tension existing for many years in the Beaird household, the unhappy condition in which young Andy found himself as he grew up, and the fact that for a number of years he was an introspected and suppressed human being unable to relate properly to the outside world and forced to find stimulation where he could. Under such conditions certain forces within a young person can be exteriorized and become almost independent of the person himself. Since these forces are part of the unconscious and therefore not subject to the logical controls of the conscious mind, they are, in fact, childish and frequently irrational. They are easily angered and easily appeased and, in general, behave in an infantile fashion. By the same token these split-off parts of personality are capable of performing physical feats, moving objects, materializing things out of nowhere, and, in general, contravening the ordinary laws of science. This we know already because cases of Poltergeists have occurred with reasonable frequency in many parts of the world. In the case of the Beaird family, however, we have two other circumstances that must be taken into account. The first is the presence in the house of not one but two emotionally unstable individuals. Mrs. Beaird's increasing divorce from reality, leading to a state of schizophrenia, must have freed some powerful forces within her. Her seemingly unconscious preoccupation with some aspects of sex indicates a degree of frustration on her part yet an inability to do anything about it at the conscious level. We have long recognized that the power supply used to perform psychic phenomena is the same power inherent in the life force or the sexual drive, and when this force is not used in the ordinary way it can be diverted to the supernormal expression, which in this case took the form of Poltergeist phenomena. We have, therefore, in the Beaird case, a tremendous reservoir of untapped psychic energy subject to very little conscious control on the part of the two individuals in whose bodies these energies were stored and developed.

Were the entities purporting to use these facilities to express themselves beyond the grave actually the people who had once lived and died in the community? Were they, in fact, who they claimed to be, or were they simply being reenacted unconsciously perhaps by the split-off part of the personalities of both Andy and Mrs. Beaird? Since Howard Beaird has examined the signature of one of those entities, at least, and found it to be closely similar, if not identical, with the signature of the person while alive, and since, in that particular case, access to the signature was not possible to either Andy or Mrs. Beaird, I'm inclined to believe that

actual nonphysical entities were, in fact, using the untapped energies of these two unfortunate individuals to express themselves in
the physical world. Additional evidence, I think, would be the fact
that in several cases the names and certain details concerning the
personalities of several individuals whom Howard Beaird knew in
their former residence in Grand Saline were not known or accessible to either his wife or the young man. I am not fully satisfied
that there could not have been some form of collusion between
Andy and these so-called spirit entities in creating the phenomena, but if there was such collusion it was on the unconscious
level. It is my view that Andy's unexpressed frustrations and
desires were picked up by some of these discarnate entities and
mingled with their own desire to continue involving themselves in
earth conditions and thus became the driving force in making the
manifestations possible.

What about the fact that Andy Beaird's handwriting appears
in the majority of the notes? If Andy did not write these notes
physically himself, could they have been produced in some other
manner? There is no doubt in my mind that in at least a large
percentage of the notes Andy could not have written them physically and dropped them in front of his father without Mr. Beaird
noticing it. Yet, these very same notes also bear unmistakable
signs that they are the work of Andy Beaird's hand. Therefore the
only plausible solution is to assume that a spiritual part of Andy's
body was used to create the notes in the same way in which
seemingly solid objects have, at times, been materialized and de-
materialized. This is known as a "physical" phenomenon and it is
not entirely restricted to Poltergeist cases but has, on occasion,
been observed with solid objects that were moved from one place
to another, or that appeared at a place seemingly out of nowhere,
or disappeared from a place without leaving any trace. The phenomenon is not unique nor particularly new. What is unique, or
nearly so in the case of the Beaird family of Tyler, Texas, is the fact
that here the obvious is not the most likely explanation. I do not
think Andy Beaird wrote those notes consciously. I do believe that
his writing ability was used by the entities expressing themselves
through him. I believe that Andy was telling the truth when he
said he was surprised by the appearance of the notes and at no
time did he have knowledge of their contents except when one of
the other spirit entities informed him about them. The same ap-

plies, of course, to Mrs. Beaird. In the phenomenon known as automatic writing, the hand of a living person, normally a fully rational and conscious individual, is used to express the views, memories, and frequently the style of writing of a dead individual. The notes that fluttered down from the ceiling at the Beaird home are not of the same kind. Here the paper had first to be taken from one place and impressed with pencil writing in the hand of another person before the note itself could be materialized in plain view of witnesses. This is far more complex than merely impressing the muscular apparatus of a human being to write certain words in a certain way.

Why, then, did the phenomena cease when the Beairds moved from one house to another if the entities expressing themselves through Andy and Mrs. Beaird had not found satisfaction? There was no need for them simply to leave off just because the Beairds moved from one house to the other. There must have been something in the atmosphere of the first house that in combination with the untapped psychic energies of Andy and Mrs. Beaird provided a fertile ground for the phenomena.

Apparently some disturbances have continued in the former Beaird home, while none have been reported by them in their new house. The current owners of the old Beaird home, however, refused to discuss such matters as psychic phenomena in the house. They are fully convinced that their fundamentalist religion will allow them to take care of these occurrences. To them psychic phenomena are all the work of the devil.

And so the devil in Tyler, Texas, may yet erupt once again to engulf a family, if not an entire community, with the strange and frightening goings-on that for three years have plagued the Beaird family to the point of emotional and physical exhaustion. The Beairds themselves are out of danger. Andy has grown up and his untapped powers will unquestionably be used in more constructive channels as the years go by. Mrs. Beaird has assumed her rightful position in her husband's house and has closed the door on her unhappy past. Howard Beaird, the main victim of all the terrible goings-on between 1965 and 1968, is satisfied that they are nothing but memories now. He has no desire to bring them back. His sole interest in my publishing an account of these incredible happenings was to inform the public and to help those who might have had similar experiences.

Virginia

Evelyn

No part of America resembles the estates and great houses of England, Scotland, and Ireland more than Virginia, where so much of America's history was made. Foremost among manor houses is the magnificent estate of Westover on the James River. Built originally in 1730 by William Byrd II, the man who founded Richmond, it stands amid an 11,000-acre working farm. The formal gardens surrounding the house are open to the public, but the house itself is not. A magnificent eighteenth-century ceiling in the entrance hall matches the paneling of the walls. Throughout the manor house there is evidence of grandeur. This is not the home of a country squire but of a statesman of great wealth. When William Byrd was killed during the Revolutionary War, the widow sold the original furniture in 1813. Eventually the house passed into the hands of Mrs. Bruce Crane Fisher. Her grandfather had bought the house in 1921 and became the eleventh owner since the plantation had been in existence. Mrs. Fisher has furnished the house in recent years with authentic eighteenth-century English and European furniture to restore it as closely as possible to the original appearance.

The Georgian house stands amid tall old trees and consists of a central portion and two wings. The central portion has three stories of elegant brickwork and two tall chimneys. The two wings were originally not connected to the center portion of the house, but the right wing had to be restored in 1900 since it had been damaged by fire from a shelling during the Civil War. At that time the two wings were also connected to the house and are now accessible directly from the main portion. The main entrance faces the James River and has the original wrought-iron entrance gate with stone eagles surmounting the gateposts. Thus, with minimal additions and restorations, the house today presents pretty much the same picture it did when it was first built in 1730.

Colonel Byrd took his beautiful daughter Evelyn (pronounced *Ee*velyn in Virginia) to London for the coronation of King George I. That was in 1717 when the great men of the colonies, when they could afford it, would come to the mother country when the occasion arose. Evelyn, at the time, was eighteen years old and her father decided to leave her in England to be educated. Soon he received disquieting news from his confidants at the London court. It appeared that Evelyn had been seen with a certain Charles Mordaunt and that the two young people were hopelessly in love with each other. Normally this would be a matter for rejoicing, but not so in this case. Charles was an ardent Roman Catholic and the grandson of the Earl of Petersborough. Colonel Byrd, on the other hand, was politically and personally a staunch Protestant, and the idea of his daughter marrying into the enemy camp, so to speak, was totally unacceptable to him. Immediately he ordered her to return to Westover and Evelyn had no choice but to obey. As soon as she arrived at the family plantation she went into isolation. She refused to see any other suitors her father sent her or to consider, or even discuss, the possibility of marriage.

This went on for some time, and Evelyn quite literally "pined away." Some weeks before her death, however, she had a very emotional discussion with her best friend, Anne Harrison. The two girls were walking up a hill when Evelyn, feeling faint, knew that her days were numbered. She turned to her friend and promised her that she would return after her death. Mrs. Harrison did not take this very seriously, but she knew that Evelyn was not well and her death did not come as a shock.

The following spring, after Westover had somehow returned to a degree of normalcy and the tragic events of the previous year were not so strongly in evidence, Mrs. Harrison was walking in the garden sadly remembering what had transpired the year before. Suddenly she saw her old friend standing beside her in a dazzling white gown. The vision then drifted forward two steps, waved its hand at her, and smiled. An instant later it had vanished. At the time of her untimely death Evelyn Byrd had been twenty-nine years of age, but in the apparition she seemed much younger and lovelier than she had appeared toward the end of her life.

The specter has reappeared from time to time to a number of people, both those who live in the area and those who are guests at Westover. A lady who lives nearby who has been there for nearly three decades saw her in the mid-1960s. She had been coming out of the front door one summer and was walking down the path when she looked back toward the house and saw a woman come out behind her. At first she thought it was a friend and stopped at the gate to wait for her. When the woman came closer, however, she didn't recognize her. There was something very strange about the woman; there seemed to be a glow all about her person, her black hair, and the white dress. When the woman had arrived close to her she stopped and seemed to sink into the ground.

On December 11, 1929, some guests from Washington were staying at Westover, and on the evening of their arrival the conversation turned to ghosts. The house was then owned by Mr. and Mrs. Richard H. Crane, who explained that they themselves had not seen the ghost during their tenancy. One of the house guests retired to the room assigned to her on the side of the house overlooking the great gates from which one has a fine view into the formal gardens. Sometime that night she awoke and went to the window. There was no apparent reason for her behavior. It was quite dark outside and very quiet. As she glanced out the window she saw the figure of Evelyn Byrd. She described the apparition to her hosts as filmy, nebulous, and cloudy, so transparent no features could be distinguished, only a gauzy texture of a woman's form. The figure seemed to be floating a little above the lawn and almost on the level of the window itself. As she looked at it almost transfixed, the apparition acknowledged her by raising her hand and motioning to her to go back into the room and away from the window. The gesture seemed so imperative that the house guest obeyed it.

When I requested permission to investigate the house I was politely denied access. Perhaps the present owners are afraid that I might induce the lovely Evelyn to leave Westover for a better life in paradise, and that would never do, for Westover is, after all, the nearest thing to paradise on earth, at least to an eighteenth-century lass whose lover has gone away. Had I had the opportunity to come into contact with her through some reputable medium perhaps I might have reunited the two in a land and under conditions where her stern father, Colonel Byrd, could no longer keep them apart.